Planning for Higher Education

This book focuses on some of the last decade's more significant writing about developments in higher education planning, organizing the wide-ranging commentaries and studies to show the administrator, the faculty member and the informed layman what the current status of higher education appears to be.

Allan Pfnister has taught at the Universities of Chicago, Michigan, and Wittenberg, and has been a dean and Acting President at Wittenberg University. At present, he is Professor of Higher Education at the University of Denver.

Allan O. Pfnister

Planning for Higher Education

Background & Application

Westview Press
Boulder, Colorado

Copyright 1976 by Westview Press, Inc.

Published 1976 in the United States of America by

Westview Press, Inc.
1898 Flatiron Court
Boulder, Colorado 80301
Frederick A. Praeger, Publisher and Editorial Director

Library of Congress Cataloging in Publication Data

Pfnister, Allan O.
  Planning for higher education.

  (Westview special studies in higher education)
  Includes bibliographical references.
1. Education, Higher. 2. Educational planning.
I. Title.
LB2322.P46   378.1'07   76-5906
ISBN 0-89158-035-2

Printed and bound in the United States of America.

Contents

Preface

When Henry Dunster reopened the nearly bankrupt Puritan boarding school on the banks of the Charles in 1640—almost all of John Harvard's legacy had been dissipated by Dunster's predecessor—he undoubtedly thought of how different and yet how similar this modest foundation was in comparison to his own alma mater, Magdalene College of the University of Cambridge, already nearly 100 years old. He could hardly have predicted the changes that would take place in Harvard College even during the 14 years of his own administration, and he surely could not have anticipated the nature of the complex system that America would have developed 340 years after the opening of the first collegiate school in 1638. (Harvard was founded in 1636, opened in 1638, closed in 1639, and reopened in 1640.) From its beginnings at Cambridge, Massachusetts, in the 1630s, to the present day, American higher education has been in a continuing state of change. Some periods have brought greater and more rapid change than others. There are those who see in the last quarter of the twentieth century prospects for changes nearly as momentous as those from 1870 to 1910, when colleges became universities and American higher education began to take its place among the educational systems of the world.

In the 1970s the demands on American higher education have increased, and new voices are adding the call for greater accountability: What are you accomplishing? And why? The pressures upon those directly involved in American higher educational institutions have become formidable. As one byproduct of the new conditions, administrators, especially, are being forced into more systematic approaches to planning; it has become obvious that the "adhocracy" of the past is no longer acceptable. And as the problems and the opinions regarding their solutions have multiplied, so have the written commentaries. The literature in higher education has become voluminous, and it is difficult for the planner to gain any perspective on what is transpiring among American colleges and universities. If it is difficult for the college administrator engaged in planning to gain perspective, it is more difficult for the faculty member, immersed in the work of his own discipline, and almost impossible for the layman who wants to become better informed, to find their ways through the mass of material appearing in print.

This volume was written to bring together some of the more significant writing about developments in higher education during the past decade, to organize the wide range of commentaries and studies, and to show the administrator, the faculty member, and the informed layman what the current status of American higher education appears to one observer to be. The book is more than a compilation of information; it is a commentary as well. The emphasis, however, is upon describing trends in the development of higher education. In working with individual institutions and groups of institutions in their long-range planning, the author has become convinced that as much as anything institutional planners need perspective. The "how-to" books have their place, but the proposed solutions seldom fit with the promised precision the conditions of the institutions facing the problems. If, however, those concerned about the future development of American colleges and universities are able to develop a perspective on how problems have developed, what factors seem to be involved in the changes taking place, and what has been the experience of others in trying to cope with the problems, they are, I am convinced, in a better position to apply with appropriate modifications the suggestions made by others.

The basic outline of this volume was developed in the course of my preparing a series of monographs on trends in higher education for the Commission on the Future of the Lutheran Educational Conference of North America. The six monographs were distributed in the spring of 1975, and then combined into a single volume for use at the summer 1975 workshop of the Council for the Advancement of Small Colleges and during the summer by the colleges of the groups affiliated with the Lutheran Educational Conference of North America and by the colleges of the United Methodist Church. I am particularly indebted to the Lutheran Educational Conference of North America for commissioning me to develop the first set of monographs. Much of the basic material from the monographs is incorporated in this volume, although the material has been completely reorganized and rewritten. My colleague Dr. James Davis, Associate Professor of Higher Education at the University of Denver, suggested the introductions to each of the chapters.

The book focuses on five problems that seem in the mid-1970s to be particularly pressing. It begins with a review of the shifting college enrollments, a topic which has provoked some study and much speculation. While most writers find a leveling off of enrollments in the late 1970s, observers differ widely about prospects for the 1980s and 1990s. Next, attention is directed to the discussions of the contemporary college student. The revolts of the 1960s commanded the front pages of the nation's dailies, but to many observers the apparent quiet of the mid-1970s is baffling; is it really that quiet, or are we just preparing for the next outburst? Third, we find governance in a state of crisis. New pressures are being brought to bear on administration and faculty. New types of organizational structures are being tried and others are being proposed. Tenure is openly debated, and collective bargaining seems to have become a permanent part of the college and university scene. Next, curriculum seems to be undergoing significant change, and there is much writing about reforms in the instructional program. Yet, how different are these "innovations" of the 1970s from many of the "experiments" of earlier decades? What forms will the curriculum take in the 1980s? Last, a topic that has emerged with special force in the mid-1970s is addressed: How do we finance the enterprise? Are there new forms for fiscal policy? Are there new sources of income, new economies that can be applied in times of financial stringency?

These are the five topics discussed. The pages that follow bring to bear on each of the topics what some of the best informed minds have to say about the conditions and about the possible directions that might be taken in the years to come. Other topics might have been included, but these are the five that to this observer present some of the most critical challenges to administrators, faculty, and involved laymen. Each of the topics is introduced with a scene from the life of a new dean, a form of introduction suggested, as I have already noted, by Dr. James Davis. The incidents, with some poetic license, are drawn from the experiences of the writer and his colleagues. The events are typical, all too typical, of the situations the college administrator faces in the mid-1970s. The visit with the dean is followed by a review of the situation as it appears in the general literature, studies, and research reports. Each section concludes with some advice to the dean for his own planning. Thus the volume provides the background for planning, together with suggested applications.

—*Allan O. Pfnister*
Denver, Colorado
November 1975

Chapter 1

A Question of Numbers

I was the first to emerge from the conference room. I walked with more than usual haste down the hall toward the nearest exit. What had promised to be a brief meeting had extended well into the afternoon, and the room had become close and oppressive. A few deep breaths of the crisp autumn air began to restore me. I had been on the job barely three months, and I felt as though I were slowly drowning, not just from the lack of oxygen in all those meetings, but from the overwhelming flood of problems. The president had been as candid as anyone could have been during the interviews last spring, but when I accepted the appointment as Dean of the Arts and Sciences College, I never dreamed there would be so many problems—problems that just didn't seem to have any solutions.

I walked across the Green and dropped into a bench partly shaded from the late afternoon sun by one of the few remaining elms on the campus. The president had called together the vice-presidents and the deans of all the schools to get the latest count on enrollments and to find out, as he put it, "just how grim the year was going to be." The registrar gave the overall report, and then each of the deans reported, school by school. The Law School was holding steady, though the number of applicants from which the selection was made was down slightly. The Business School seemed to be doing more than holding its own. The School of Education was down. Finally, we came to Arts and Sciences. I felt every eye turned on me, although I was probably being overly sensitive about it all. Yes, we were down, but was that so bad? As a matter of fact, it was bad. It was a disaster. We were off 400 students, and as any idiot sitting around that table could quickly calculate, at our outrageous, but necessary, tuition charge, we were talking about a "loss" of over a million dollars.

But I had been here only three months. Why should they look at me as if it were my personal fault? What could I do about it now? Yes, but what about next year? What kind of report could I give then? In the eyes of the group around that table, I would be responsible. And would I have to say, "I'm sorry to report that we seem to be down in Arts and Sciences again this year"?

The sky was blue and the sun reached around the tree and felt warm. Fall had always been a happy time. I looked forward to the beginning of a new school year, a fresh start, and all the students coming back to the campus. I didn't even mind the last-minute scurry for new sections of popular classes—and finding ways to staff them. Only, during the past few years, there had been little of that kind of pressure here—and this year the registration lines were uncomfortably short. Okay, I said to myself, so what can I do besides feel sorry for myself? The question is: How many students are out there, and how do we get our fair share? What is our fair share? Surely, we don't have to be resigned to enrollment declines every year. Yes, there are a lot of other colleges competing with us. But can't we be better than the rest? Or can't we at least be different? Maybe we need to come up with some new programs that will be so attractive that students will be standing in line again to enter this university.

Well, better check into the office before going home. Old Main was on the other side of the Green. I climbed the stairs to my office in a building that had been created just before the turn of the century. My secretary greeted me at the door, "Dean Neumann, the president called while you were out."

"He did? Did he say what he wanted?"

"I don't think he wanted anything. He just wanted to tell you that he hoped you weren't too discouraged at the meeting today. You left before he had a chance to talk with you."

"Discouraged?" I said, "Why should I feel discouraged?"

"The president said to tell you not to let the enrollment situation get you down, and then he added, 'but tell him not to let it happen next year.' "

What do we say to Dean Neumann, and the hundreds of deans like him whose institutions will be scrambling for students in the years ahead? What will it be like for Dean Neumann next year, and the year after, and on into the 1980s? What will be the scope and nature of higher education in the next quarter century and how

2

should college administrators go about planning for their institutions within the context of postsecondary education in the latter part of the twentieth century? What changes should the dean be prepared to see, and how should he respond to them?

Too Few Students and Too Many Places?

If he reviews the writing of the middle and late 1970s, the dean will soon learn that there is general agreement that, to the extent higher institutions are dependent on the conventional categories of college-going persons, enrollments are leveling off in the 1970s and are likely to show an actual decrease in the 1980s. But, beyond this generalization, there are wide variations of opinion about when, in what degree, and how the overall enrollment conditions will be reflected among the different groups of institutions. And among those who are making projections, there are fairly substantial differences in the numbers of students they are estimating will be in attendance in the 1980s and 1990s.

In its 1971 assessment of American higher education, the Carnegie Commission stated that the three decades before the year 2000 will be a time of substantial innovation and change, comparable in significance to the period following the Civil War, "when many of the leading colleges were transformed into universities," and the period since the end of World War II, which was characterized not only by rapid enrollment increases and a steady increase in the share of public institutions in total enrollment, but also by the emergence of state systems of public higher education and the rapid growth of the community college.[1] Among the changes the commission anticipates in the 1980s and 1990s are: (1) a movement toward a more "free-flowing pattern of participation spread over a broader span of years," (2) the combining of work experience with a more extended collegiate attendance, (3) the giving of more attention to career goals, (4) broader development of open universities and external degree systems, and (5) the introduction of other approaches to flexibility. The final report of the commission refers to the same possibilities, but it characterizes the 1970s as a time during which higher education has moved "from golden age to time of troubles."[2]

3

The revisions in enrollment projections made by the Carnegie Commission are illustrative of the shifts in judgment that have been taking place generally among those engaged in estimating future enrollments in American higher education. Revisions in the 1971 report were made when the final report of the commission was issued in 1973; but even as the final report was being published, the parent body, the Carnegie Foundation for the Advancement of Teaching, acknowledged that in a period of rapid social change there could be no "final" report as such and established a Council on Policy Studies in Higher Education.[3] Although the council is directly related to the Carnegie Foundation as an administrative arm and has been characterized as something other than a direct successor to the Carnegie Commission on Higher Education, the council has been issuing commission-like reports. One of the first council reports dealt with enrollment projections, and it referred to "dramatic, even traumatic" changes in the condition of higher education and to the "decline of the old and the birth of a new vision of the future for higher education."[4]

In 1971 the Carnegie Commission predicted a total enrollment of 13,015,000 for 1980, a slight decrease to 12,654,000 in 1990, and a significant increase to 16,559,000 in the year 2000.[5] Two years later, in 1973, the commission issued a new set of projections, 12 percent lower than the previous set—11,336,000 in 1980, a decrease to 10,555,000 in 1990, and an increase to 13,209,000 in 2000.[6] The council has provided a further reduced set of projections in 1975— 11,513,000 in 1980, a slight increase in 1990 to 11,818,000, then another modest increase to 12,794,000 in 2000.[7] While the council's estimates for 1980 and 1990 are larger than the 1973 commission projections, the estimate for the year 2000 is some 400,000 less than that of 1973. Indeed, assuming an enrollment rate constant from 1973, the council notes that in 2000 the enrollments could be below 10,000,000.[8] Projecting enrollments is clearly more of an art than a science!

Reviews of enrollment trends call attention to two basic developments during the late 1960s and early 1970s that will have long-term consequences for higher education in the United States. First, there has been a striking change in birth rates. In 1972 the birth rate in the United States appeared to have reached the lowest in the century, 15.6 live births per 1,000 population. Moreover, the actual *number* of live births in 1972 was the lowest in 27 years. In

1945, with a smaller population base and a higher birth rate, the number of live births recorded was 2,858,000, and the following year the number increased to 3,411,000. By way of comparison, in 1972 the number of live births recorded was 3,256,000, more than in 1945 but less than in 1946. This decline in birth rates in the United States began in 1958 when the rate dropped below the 25 per 1,000 that had been reached in 1952 and sustained through 1957. More recent data show a continuing decline. By the end of 1973 it was reported that American women were having only 1.9 children each, insufficient to replace the present population.[9] The Bureau of the Census has provided a new series of population estimates, Series F, which is based on a fertility rate of 1.8. The conclusion is inevitable: there are fewer young people in the population, and the proportion will be decreasing in the years to come.

Second, there is an apparent shift in attitude in the population toward college-going. The Carnegie Commission observes that there has been a shift away from formal programs in higher education to a wide range of other kinds of postsecondary learning. The National Commission on the Financing of Postsecondary Education reports the same phenomenon and calls attention to the growth of the "noncollegiate" sector of education. The latter commission, on the basis of a review of recent studies, comments that data indicate "that the college-going rate has risen slowly during the past two decades and may decline somewhat during the next two decades."[10] There may already be a hint of the decline in college-going in recent reports of the Bureau of the Census. Some 53.1 percent of the high school graduates in 1971 attended college that same year, but in 1972 the estimate was 48.8 percent, lower than at any point in recent years. And the proportion of 18- through 24-year-old persons enrolled in college was lower in 1972 than in 1971.[11] Data for 1973 indicate also that the percentage of 18- and 19-year-olds entering college has continued to decline since 1971.[12]

These two factors, declining birth rates and the decreasing proportion of the traditional age group enrolling in college, will obviously not in themselves account for all of the changes that will take place in higher education in the next three decades. The value society places on advanced education, the availability of financial resources, the perceived needs of society—these and other factors will also influence the directions colleges and universities will take. The Carnegie Council singles out four factors that are presumed to

5

have had an impact on enrollments: the abolition of the draft, the increased costs of college-going, the changes in the job market for college graduates, and the liberalizing of college regulations to permit the interruption of the college career, "stopping in" and "stopping out."[13]

In the light of so many variables that can influence college attendance it is difficult to predict how the general trends will affect groups of institutions, much less individual institutions. In applying the general trends to institutional types, the Carnegie Council offers six different sets of possibilities,[14] refers to an "intricate series of possibilities," and notes that there is no "agreed-upon map of the future." We are sobered by knowledge that earlier the Carnegie Commission, within two years (1971 to 1973), had revised its projections significantly. And, as John K. Folger points out, the Carnegie Commission's projections were "very carefully done, utilizing the best available projection methods."[15] We wonder how some recent state-wide studies that have attempted to establish 5- to 10-year projections for individual institutions will stand up. Ronald Thompson has made projections for public and private colleges and universities state-by-state.[16]

In spite of all of the difficulties, it is incumbent upon persons such as Dean Neumann to develop long-range plans for their institutions' futures. There is really no alternative to systematic, rational planning, and while growing like Topsy was an option for some institutions in the 1960s, "adhocracy" will not work in the 1970s and '80s. Dean Neumann and his associates will need to do some planning, however tentative and subject to frequent revision.

As numerous reports and articles have documented, higher education in the United States has experienced an almost continuous growth pattern since its establishment with the founding of Harvard in 1636. Planning among higher educational institutions, such as it was, had long been based on the assumption that continuing growth is inevitable. In the early 1970s, however, an increasing number of voices began to question the standard assumptions. Even the earlier Carnegie report, whose enrollment projections were subsequently reduced, as we have noted, raised a strong caution against assuming continuous growth.

6

Higher education in the United States comprised a continuous rapid growth segment of the nation for more than three centuries. During that time, it has experienced steady enrollment increases at a rate faster than the expansion of American society generally. Over the past century, in particular, enrollments in higher education have doubled regularly every 14 to 15 years. But never again.[17]

Some writers have suggested that a decrease in enrollments is by no means a wholly negative matter. Indeed, the Carnegie Council finds there are those who view the decrease in enrollments as wholly beneficial; but as the council observes, "these predictions are seldom made by those most directly and immediately affected."[18] The annual meeting of the American Council on Education in 1970 focused on the theme, "Higher Education for Everybody?"[19] While the major addresses seemed to reply to the question in the affirmative, the bases for the responses were far from consensual. In exploring the feasibility of further expansion of the higher educational enterprise, several of the contributors pointed up the kinds of issues that arise out of a policy of universal access. James L. Miller, Jr., observed that the year 1970 marked the end of a 25-year period in American higher education "during which the outstanding characteristic has been unprecedented growth."[20] As a result of the growth, the relationships of higher education to society were fundamentally altered. But an era ends as we observe a "reduction in the rate of enrollment growth, leveling-off of federal financial support . . . [and] the search for better ways of sensing and meeting students' educational needs"; these new developments "pose unfamiliar challenges to administrators whose earlier experiences had prepared them instead to cope with challenges of growth."[21] Martin Trow, speaking at the same convention, referred to the new forces operating both internally and externally on the university and predicted "very marked discontinuities in the development of these institutions" with the result that new forms and structures are almost inevitable, and the particular forms and structures become more and more problematic.[22]

An early report on enrollments for the fall of 1974 found a mixed picture.[23] There were increases among some sectors, but as the writer of the report notes, the increases were "far from universal." From a survey of 800 private colleges and universities undertaken by the Association of American Colleges, it was found that approximately half of the institutions experienced increases, 25 percent remained the same, and 25 percent decreased in enrollment. The American Association of State Colleges and Universities earlier reported on 241 state institutions and found 43 percent expected enrollments to increase, 30 percent expected to remain the same, and 27 percent predicted decreased enrollments. The same issue of the *Chronicle of Higher Education* in which the report appeared carried a story of how one private women's college had increased the freshman class by 170 percent.[24]

When the National Center for Educational Statistics released preliminary figures on the fall 1974 enrollments, it was found that there had actually been more of an increase in enrollment between 1973 and 1974 than between 1972 and 1973.[25] In the fall of 1974 enrollment in American higher educational institutions had passed the 10 million mark with a total of 10,231,878. This was more than half a million above 1973 and an increase of 5.5 percent. (Between 1972 and 1973 the increase was only 396,510, approximately 4.3 percent over 1972.) Public institutions increased their enrollment by 6.3 percent and private institutions by 3.0 percent. Public two-year institutions reported an increase of 17.3 percent. These increases occurred when the estimated number of high school graduates increased only by 1.7 percent between 1972-73 and 1973-74. The major factor in the 1974 increase appeared to be the presence of a larger number of women on the campuses; more than 60 percent of the additional students were women.

The academic year 1975-76 began with predictions that enrollments would increase again, 4 percent over 1974-75—not as large a percentage increase as for the previous year, but still the largest enrollment America's colleges and universities had ever experienced.[26] The National Center for Educational Statistics predicted a total enrollment of 10,619,000, an increase of 395,000 over the last year's total. It was estimated also that about two-thirds of the additional students would be enrolled on a part-time basis.

For some institutions, these continuing increases in enrollments, at a time when some observers were expecting decreases, may suggest that the enrollment crisis is over. What should be noted, however, is that the rate of increase is apparently slowing down and that the increases have in large part been due to more women and part-timers enrolling. The latter means that the full-time-equivalent enrollment is not increasing greatly, and the former means only that one segment of the population is catching up with the enrollment pattern. The long-range predictions are not influenced greatly by the modest increases in enrollments in the late 1970s.

How Large Is the Potential Pool from Which College Enrollments Are Traditionally Drawn?

For his planning, Dean Neumann needs some basic data about what is happening to the sources from which college students have typically come. By convention we have been accustomed to think of persons within the ages of 18 to 21 years or 18 to 24 years as the "college age" group, and most projections of enrollment refer to or work with ratios employing one or the other of these age groups. This is not to say that all persons enrolled in colleges fall within these age ranges, but it is to recognize that *in the past* the majority of college students have been from 18 to 21 years or 18 to 24 years of age. In most currently used projections it is assumed that even with shifts in the pattern of college-going these ranges will continue to be useful in predicting enrollments for planning purposes. John Folger suggests that more elaborate cohort methods of projection "have not proved demonstrably better than the ratio methods for long-run projections," and he is prepared to use the ratio method, at least as a beginning point.[27] But how useful will the age ranges of 18 to 21 and 18 to 24 be in applying the ratio method in the future? Is a broader age range more appropriate for the 1980s and 1990s?

Based upon data collected for 1971, it appears that 58.4 percent of the students enrolled in higher educational institutions were between 18 and 21 years of age and that 76.8 percent fell within the range of 18 to 24. Only 3.5 percent were less than 18 years of age, and 19.7 percent were 25 or older. Thus, while the ranges of 18 to 21 or 18 to 24 do not include all students, the latter presently does include over three-quarters of those currently enrolled in degree-credit courses. And when one is considering the entering student, it is still reasonably accurate to use 18 years as the most common age of entrance.[28]

There is, however, some indication in data for recent years that the average age of persons attending college is increasing. For example, by comparing the report for 1971 with the same data for 1968 (see table 1), we find that 63.6 percent of the college students four years earlier were in the range of 18 to 21 years of age, while the range of 18 to 24 years included 78.7 percent.[29] In a report issued late in 1974 there seems to be further evidence of the increase in average age. In 1947 persons 25 to 34 years old constituted about 18 percent of the *resident* (as distinct from the *totals* shown above) students; in the fall of 1973 they constituted 22 percent of the resident enrollment.[30]

Table 1

Comparison of Age Distributions of College Students, 1968 and 1971

Age Ranges of College Students	Proportion of Enrolled Students Within Each Age Range	
	1968	1971
16 and 17 years	4.1	3.5
18 and 19 years	36.8	33.7
20 and 21 years	26.8	24.7
22 to 24 years	15.1	18.4
25 to 29 years	11.6	13.2
30 to 34 years	5.5	6.5
Total	99.9	100.0

Source: U.S. Department of Health, Education, and Welfare, National Center for Educational Statistics, *Digest of Educational Statistics, 1970* (Washington, D.C.: Government Printing Office, 1970), p. 73, and in the 1972 edition, p. 81.

The shift, largely in the recent past, to a more diverse student body in terms of age lends substance to Todd Furniss's more sweeping statement that

> higher education in the United States must make a long overdue effort to redefine "the college student." Today's working definition is based on an out-of-date stereotype—the full-time undergraduate resident in a four year college. . . . [We need to] look at our students as they actually are: some young, some older, some highly skilled, some wedded to nontraditional cultures, some

10

intellectually far beyond introductory college work. Recognition of their real characteristics will call for the establishment of a variety of untraditional programs and, in turn, a reversal of the recent trend of institutions that house them to become more alike.[31]

Thus, while the majority of college-attenders are under the age of 25, the fact that the 25-and-older group is increasing numerically and proportionally suggests that the ratios employing 18 to 21 or 18 to 24 will be less serviceable in the future.

Let us, however, for the present analysis, consider that the basic source of students is the age range from 18 to 24. Data presently available enable us to make fairly firm predictions about the size of this group in the decades ahead.

In the final report of the Carnegie Commission, *Priorities for Action,* data from reports of the U.S. Bureau of the Census are combined in a single basic table showing birth rate and number of live births from 1910 through 1972. Also included are projections developed by the bureau for 1972-73 through 1992-93. In 1972 the bureau developed two new sets of projections, Series E and Series F. These were developed on the basis of the striking change in birth rates in 1972, which revealed that the earlier projections, Series C and D, were already in error. The assumptions in C and D were that fertility rates would be 2.8 and 2.5 average number of births per women, respectively. In 1972 these rates appeared unrealistic, and E and F were developed on the assumptions of fertility rates of 2.1 and 1.8, respectively.[32]

What becomes apparent from an examination of the data compiled by the Bureau of the Census is that by 1979-80 there will be fewer persons 18 years old than in 1974 and that at no time after 1980 and through the rest of the century will there be as many persons 18 years old as there are in 1974. This generalization is based upon the following line of reasoning. Those who are 18 years old in 1974 were born in 1956. We note that in 1956 the number of live births was 4,218,000. From 1956 until 1962, the number of live births increased beyond that number, with some little variation, each year. Beginning in 1962, however, the number decreased almost every year, and the lowest number was recorded in 1972. Information on

11

trends beyond 1972 indicates a continuing decrease in live births through 1974. Assuming the same mortality rate, we can expect based on these data that the number of 18 year olds will increase each year until 1980, when those born in 1962, the year in which the number of live births began to decrease, become 18. Thereafter, the number of 18 year olds will decrease, and based on data now available, the number will decrease through 1992, when those born in 1974 reach 18. If, going beyond 1992, we use either Series E or Series F of the projections developed by the Bureau of the Census, it is clear that through the rest of the century the number of persons 18 years old will never reach the level of 1979. On the basis of the experience of the last few years, the Series E or Series F projections appear to be more realistic than the earlier projections given in Series D.

Another analysis by the Bureau of the Census uses the data on births to project the numbers of persons who will be in age ranges appropriate to high school and college attendance through 1985.[33] From table 2, based on the bureau's analysis, it is clear that the number of persons of high school age (14-17 years old) has been increasing regularly, except for some decrease in 1950, from 1920 to the present date and will continue to increase until the mid-1970s, when the decrease shown in the data on birth rate begins to have an effect on the population group. The same trends are apparent, coming at somewhat later dates, for the persons of college age (18-21 years old and 22-25 years old) in the early 1980s.

The same conclusions are evident in an examination of the projections of the number of high school graduates presented in a 1973 edition of *Projections of Educational Statistics*.[34] The projections reveal that the number of high school graduates continues to increase after 1973-74 until 1976-77, reaching a total of 3,199,000. The number decreases slightly in 1977-78 and continues to decrease through the period for which the projections are made, to 2,835,000 in 1982-83. Indeed, in 1982-83 the number of graduates is approximately what it was in 1968-69.

Thus, by whatever method of analysis one might employ, it becomes abundantly clear that the pool from which American colleges and universities have traditionally drawn the major portion of their enrollments will decidedly diminish in the 1980s. These projections can be taken as well-established possibilities, since the basis for each projection is the number of persons in each age group currently known to exist.

Table 2

Persons 14 to 25 Years Old in 1920 to 1972 and Projections to 1985 (In Thousands)

Year	14-17 years old	18-21 years old	22-25 years old
1985 (projection)	14,252	15,026	16,774
1984	14,001	15,608	16,899
1980	15,516	16,819	16,652
1976	16,734	16,574	15,361
1975	16,826	16,318	15,039
1974	16,817	15,964	14,754
1973	16,645	15,632	14,464
1972 (estimate)	16,429	15,203	14,234
1971	16,157	14,902	13,367
1970	15,844	14,613	12,631
1960	11,162	9,440	8,711
1950	8,473	8,998	9,607
1940	9,720	9,754	9,166
1930	9,341	9,027	8,523
1920	7,736	7,344	7,597

Source: U.S. Department of Commerce, Bureau of the Census, *Characteristics of American Youth: 1972.* Current Population Reports, Series P-23, no. 44, March, 1973 (Washington, D.C.: Government Printing Office, 1973) p. 7.

In the early 1990s we enter the realm of speculation, because we must make estimates about fertility rates and about numbers of persons yet unborn. We have suggested that the Bureau of the Census has provided a reasonably "realistic" series of guesses in its Series F projections (1.8 average births per woman). An analysis by Richard Berendzen uses the Series C (2.8 average births per woman) and the Series E (2.1 average births per woman) projections to estimate possible college enrollments beyond 1990.[35] The Series C projections would allow a distinct rise in the number of persons 18 to 24 years after 1990. However, the statisticians of the Bureau of the

Census have suggested the need to consider lower estimates such as might be reflected in the Series E and F fertility rates, and Berendzen observes that by 1973 the birth rate had already fallen below the population replacement rate of 2.1.

We would also note, with Berendzen, that while the college-age group comprised in the late 1960s and early 1970s an abnormally large portion of the U.S. population, by 2000, under almost any circumstances, youth will be a distinct minority. Berendzen suggests, "Thus it would appear that insofar as a youth culture arises from the presence of large numbers of young people, the dominance of youth is ended for the rest of this century." In the 1980s the dominant group will be the pre-middle-agers, those in their late twenties and mid-thirties. Yet, for the next several decades, the "dominant cohort ... will be composed of the same individuals—the youth of the late 1960s grown older."[36]

Who Will Go to College?

Projecting changes in the pool from which college students have been drawn traditionally is relatively straightforward. We know the number of live births through most of 1974, and we can be reasonably sure, barring some catastrophe, how many persons of 18 and above there will be each year for the next two decades. When we begin to estimate how many persons from the pool will actually enroll, we enter a more complex arena. Until 1972 the proportion of college-age youth actually entering college had, with some little fluctuation, grown at a fairly steady rate. But in 1972, and apparently in 1973 as well, the proportion declined. Is this a temporary decline, or is it indicative of a changed attitude on the part of college-age youth toward college-going?

The consistent increase over the past century in the ratio between the number of persons enrolled in colleges and the number of persons aged 18 to 21 or 18 to 24 is well documented. Drawing from publications of the Bureau of the Census, the Carnegie Commission has provided summaries based both on the 18- to 21-year-old and the 18- to 24-year-old groups. From 1870 to 1970 the ratio has increased from 1.7 per hundred to 47.6 per hundred in relation to the 18- to 21-year group and from 1.1 to 31.7 in relation to the 18- to 24-year group. The commission in 1971 projected an increase in the

14

ratio to 59.2 in 1980, to 67.4 in 1990, and to 72.6 in 2000 for the 18- to 21-year group, and to 39.5 in 1980, to 45 in 1990, and to 49.4 in 2000 for the 18- to 24-year group.[37] These ratios, together with earlier population projections, led in 1971 to the commission's projections of enrollments of 13,015,000 in 1980, 12,654,000 in 1990, and 16,559,000 in the year 2000. However, by 1973 the commission was prepared to revise the estimates downward—by 12 percent for 1980 and over 20 percent by 2000—based on a slight downward adjustment of high school graduation and college entrance rates, an assumption that the proportion of bachelor's recipients that would continue into postbaccalaureate work would remain at the 1969 level, and the use of the Census Bureau's Series E projections.[38] The Carnegie Council suggests a further downward revision for the year 2000 and accepts the Census Bureau F projections as "reasonably reliable."[39] Both the commission and the council assume, on somewhat different bases, a continuing increase in the enrollment ratio (based on current distributions of students in various age groups and projected in the light of a complex set of assumptions detailed in the reports).

The National Commission on the Financing of Postsecondary Education, reporting at the close of 1973, compared three sets of projections, those of the Office of Education, the Carnegie Commission (revised figures), and the Bureau of the Census. Of the three sets, the projections of the Carnegie Commission, even when revised downward, continue to be the most optimistic.[40] The comparison developed by the National Commission is shown in table 3.

While in each set of projections there is an assumption that the ratio of college attenders to the number of persons 18 to 21 or 18 to 24 will increase, even that assumption is under question. It seems clear, at least, that the ratio cannot increase in the next few decades as rapidly as it did between 1960 and 1970, when the ratio for the 18- to 21-year group grew from 33.8 per hundred to 47.6 per hundred (an increase of 13.8 percentage points), although under the Carnegie Commission assumptions it should increase 11.6 percentage points (47.6 to 59.2) from 1970 to 1980. A number of recent reports of the Bureau of the Census suggest there is already a slowing down, if not a reversal, in the ratio. One report shows that while there has been only a slight decline between 1968 to 1971 (from 54.8 to 53.1) in the proportion of persons entering college in the year of their high school graduation, the change between 1971 and 1972 was striking, from 53.1 percent to 48.8 percent. There has been a decline for both males and females, but the decline has been especially sharp for males, down from 62.3 percent in 1968 to 57.4 percent in 1971 and 52.4 percent in 1972.[41] Another report shows that, whereas the percentage of persons 18 and 19 years old actually enrolled in college increased from 28.8 to 39 from 1963 to 1969, there was a slight decrease in 1970, some recovery in 1971, and another and larger drop in 1972, from 38 percent in 1971 to 34.7 in 1972.[42] The Bureau of the Census has also reported that for high school seniors in October 1973 the proportion definitely planning to attend college was less than for high school seniors studied in the fall of 1972.[43]

Table 3

Enrollment Projections for the Collegiate Sector, Degree and Nondegree Credit, Fall 1970 to 1990 (Individuals)

Year	Office of Education[1]	Carnegie Commission[2]	Census Series E-2[3]
1970	8,581,000	8,499,000	—
1975	9,802,000	—	9,147,000
1980	10,517,000	11,446,000	10,284,000
1985	—	—	10,207,000
1990	—	10,555,000	10,397,000

Source: National Commission on the Financing of Postsecondary Education, *Financing Postsecondary Education* (Washington, D.C.: Government Printing Office, 1973), p. 23.

[1]U.S. Office of Education, National Center for Educational Statistics, 1973.

[2]Carnegie Commission Projection II, *Priorities for Action: Final Report of the Carnegie Commission,* 1973.

[3]U.S. Bureau of the Census, "Population Estimates and Projections: Projections of School and College Enrollment, 1971-2000" (January 1972), mid-range estimate.

That there is some relation between the level of family income and the changing pattern of college enrollments is shown in a study

16

issued by the Bureau of the Census in April 1975 and based on data collected through October 1973.[44] Overall, among families with dependent members 18 to 24 years old and reporting on income, the highest rate of attendance was reached in 1969. At that time 42 percent of families with dependent members 18 to 24 years old reported one or more persons enrolled full-time in college. There has been a steady decline through 1973, when the percentage of families with one or more persons in full-time attendance dropped to just over 32 percent, a decline of almost 7 percentage points. Among the family units, the sharpest decline was for those with incomes from $10,000 to $14,999 (constant 1973 dollars). In 1969 just over 45 percent of families in this category reported one or more persons 18 to 24 years old enrolled full-time in college; in 1973 the proportion had fallen to just over 36 percent, a decline of 9 percentage points. Least affected were the low income families. Those with incomes under $3,000 changed from 16.4 percent with dependents in college to 12.7 percent, a drop of 3.7 percentage points. Those with income of $5,000 to $7,499 changed from 22.5 percent to 18 percent, a decline of 4.5 percentage points. However, the rate of attendance from families with higher incomes also declined, though to a lesser degree than among middle income families. Among those with incomes of $15,000 and above, the decline was from 58.5 percent to 53.7 percent, a reduction of 4.8 percentage points. Income for all families with dependents 18 to 24 years old averaged $11,898 in 1973, while the income for families with dependent children enrolled in college averaged $14,679.

The census data probably reflect the effect of both increased costs and changes in value placed on college-going. Lower income families may still view the college degree as a means of moving up in status, while middle and upper income persons may view college attendance as a less significant factor in relation to status. Richard Freeman and J. Herbert Hollomon of the Center for Policy Alternatives, Massachusetts Institute of Technology, have analyzed the changing job market for college graduates and point out that— at the outset of the 1970s for the first time in recent history—new bachelor's degree graduates began to face difficulty in securing jobs. They view the new situation as "a far-reaching, unprecedented development of sizable dimensions" and show that the rate of return (in subsequent earnings) on investment in college attendance has fallen significantly.[45] They are of the opinion that the decline in economic opportunity for college graduates is a distinctive factor in the decline in proportion of young men choosing to enroll in college.[46] This is particularly the case for white males; the enrollment among black males has increased. The economic factor may have a much greater depressing effect on college enrollments than the demographic factor of fewer persons of college age in the general population.[47]

Stephen Dresch carries the analysis of the economic factors further and proposes that enrollments will to a greater degree than recognized be related to the capacity of the economy to absorb college-educated people and the changes in the overall supply of highly educated labor resulting from the rapid growth of the higher educational enterprise in the late 1950s and 1960s.[48] As the educated proportion in the active adult population increases and moves beyond an equilibrium of supply and demand, the relative wages for educated persons fall, and the proportion of persons seeking higher education falls. Thus, if the wages "appear sufficiently high for educated persons, then increasing proportions . . . will attempt to be educated. When this no longer appears true, the proportion of young people attempting college education will decrease."[49] Instead of some increase in college enrollments as projected by the Carnegie Commission, Dresch sees an overall contraction of 33 percent between 1970 and 2000.

Still another factor in estimating changes in the proportion of college-age youth who will ultimately enroll is the relation between financial ability and scholastic ability. In 1968, Humphrey Doermann, Director of Admissions of Harvard College from 1961 through 1966, published a study in which he sought to establish a correlation between SAT verbal scores and family income and then to predict from among the total high school graduates how many could be included in a particular cohort based on academic ability and financial level. Institutions could then estimate the pool from which their particular group of entering students might be drawn. Using data from Educational Testing Service and the College Entrance Examination Board, he developed some estimates of the proportion of high school graduates within each of the several levels of the SAT verbal scores. Then, employing census data, he estimated the proportion of families within each of several income levels. His next step was to relate in tabular form these two sets of data in order to indicate the proportion of individuals who would

18

fall within a certain range of SAT scores and whose families were located within a certain income level.

In order to update Doermann's tables, one would have to review current ranges of SAT scores, since the ones on which he based his table grew out of studies made in 1960. Subsequently the average scores have dropped somewhat, although there was some indication of a reversal upward in 1974.[50] The family income information would also have to be revised in the light of inflationary trends, but offsetting increases in family income are increases in costs. In the fall of 1974 the College Scholarship Service sharply reduced its estimates of how much parents could be expected to contribute to their children's college education. For example, a family with adjusted income of $20,000 and two children was expected to contribute $5,470 in 1974-75, but only $3,990 in 1975-76.[51] This latter figure is less than Doermann estimated for the same income when he developed his tables in the 1960s.

If the fluctuations in SAT scores have just about evened out, and if increases in family income have been balanced by increases in costs—and increased costs may even have outstripped increased income—the distributions according to income used by Doermann in the 1960s may be useful enough in 1974-75 if one notes "expected contribution" rather than income alone. That is to say, it is probably appropriate to use the "expected contribution" in Doermann's table as a way of locating the potential pool of students in terms of academic ability and financial ability in 1974-75. Thus, referring to Doermann's study, we may say, for example, that in 1974-75 there are 22,000 to 34,000 young men, graduates of high schools, who have SAT verbal average scores of 600 and above and whose families could contribute approximately $4,000 to college expenses.[52] Doubling the figure gives the total graduates, men and women, falling within a particular group.

Doermann provides two sets of figures for each group defined by SAT scores and family ability to pay. For example, for men with SAT scores of 600 and above and whose families can provide at least $4,000 for college expenses, there are 22,000 to 34,000 shown. The smaller figure is derived using a correlation coefficient of 0.4—for which Doermann musters a fair amount of evidence—and the larger figure is based on a correlation of 0.7 between income and SAT score—which Doermann considers entirely too high.[53] In each cell, the numbers shown indicate the estimate of the *total male high school graduates who meet or exceed the conditions specified.* For coeducational schools, the numbers should be doubled.

In using tables such as Doermann has developed, we must employ some caution, even as Doermann himself warns. The correlations, while based on some empirical evidence, are by no means firmly established. Yet, these estimates should provide a good beginning point for any institution's enrollment planning, for planning should begin with some realistic estimates of the actual pool of students available that meet the institution's conditions. It is sobering to note that out of nearly 3.2 million high school graduates in 1974-75, at most there are some 70,000 who have SAT verbal scores above 600 and whose families can provide over $4,000 toward college expenses. Probably only 35,000 will apply for and enter college. Clearly, high ability (measured by SAT scores) cash-paying students are in short supply. And how many institutions might be competing for such students? If a thousand institutions divided them up equally, each institution would get only 35 students, hardly a solid base for building one's reputation as a highly selective institution. There clearly are going to be few highly selective institutions.

For a college locating its potential entering class among high school graduates of 600 average verbal SAT whose parents can be expected to contribute at least $4,000 to college expenses, not only must it be noted that there are probably only 45,000 to 70,000 such men and women available in 1974-75, but it must be recognized that students in this category have traditionally been college attenders and for any given institution to increase its share of the pool will be difficult. William Turnbull notes that by 1960 some 80 percent of students in the top quarter of their high school class were going to college in contrast to 19 percent of those in the lower quarter;[54] and Patricia Cross points out that in the 1970s very few additional college students can be expected from among high school graduates "who are high in both academic aptitude and socioeconomic status."[55] The conclusion is that colleges seeking students with high academic ability and high family income and who are not now drawing heavily from that group will face fierce competition in breaking into the circle. The pool simply is not going to increase in the years to come.

20

Thus, for postsecondary institutions responding to the more traditional clientele, the pool of available students is leveling off and will decrease numerically in the 1980s. If the proportion of 18 and 19 year olds entering college during the year of their high school graduation continues to decline, as it appeared to be doing in 1972, 1973, and 1974, the pool will decrease dramatically, and enrollments in such institutions cannot but decrease. On the other hand, if such institutions are prepared and able to admit students of lower SAT scores and of lower socioeconomic status (and greater financial need), the pool of available students will at least remain fairly stable. What if such colleges look increasingly to the less traditional sources? Will their situations be different? We explore the implications of turning to the "new student" and the "nontraditional student" in the next section.

Transcending the Trends: The New Student?

Howard Bowen of the Claremont Schools, among others, disagrees with the predictions of declining enrollments for American higher educational institutions. At the spring 1974 meeting of the Association of Governing Boards he argued that most of the assumptions regarding future enrollments are based on unduly narrow views of enrollment potentialities. Instead of using the more traditional structures as a basis, he called for considering enrollments in terms of "diversified education with low fees and liberal student aid, offered at convenient times and places and catering to many different classes and backgrounds."[56] He also pointed to the increase in numbers of persons beyond the typical college age as a factor in potentially larger enrollments in the future. And he suggested that training needs could expand if more professional health services were provided for the population, if early childhood education were expanded, and if greater provisions were made for art museums, symphonies, operas, and theaters. He condemned as fallacious the assumption "that the number of jobs that require college training are relatively few . . . that the jobs available for college-educated people should be congruent with their educational background, [and] that the economy needs many people to do menial tasks and that these people should not be over educated."[57] In opposition he argued that education is not simply designed to prepare people for specific and limited occupations, but that rather "it is intended to produce people of vision and

21

sensitivity who will be motivated to direct technology into humanly constructed channels."

President Bowen is pointing to new markets and to a broader constituency than higher education has heretofore served. How and to what extent the bulk of higher institutions will approach and develop new "markets" remains to be seen. The "noncollegiate sector," the "other postsecondary schools" and "other learning opportunities" to which the National Commission on the Financing of Postsecondary Education refers, already serve nearly two million persons.[58] Will noncollegiate agencies be doing what Bowen calls upon the collegiate structure to undertake?

Whether they are motivated by the desire to maintain enrollments or to serve a constituency hitherto unserved or only partially served, at least some American higher educational institutions are beginning to respond to the urging of study commissions and an increasing number of writers that more attention be given to other clienteles. These potential sources of new students appear to fall into two categories: (1) those persons within the traditional age ranges (18 to 21 or 18 to 24) who for reasons of scores on aptitude tests or class standing have not previously been considered admissable, and (2) those persons classified as older adults, whether capable of attending full-time or part-time, on-campus or off-campus. Patricia Cross has provided as comprehensive an overview as any person on the first group, and the Commission on Non-Traditional Study has pleaded the case of the older adult.[59]

The Carnegie Commission in its final report called for more of an open-access system of education in the United States and for programs adjusted to students from a wider variety of backgrounds:

> We have suggested special admissions provisions for dis- advantaged students where their ability and the special assis- tance of the college will make possible their meeting, in full, the academic standards of the college within a reasonable period of time, and certainly by graduation. . . . Colleges should also make provision for the cultural interests of more of the members of their increasingly varied student populations.[60]

The commission also asked for adequate financing of student costs where students and families cannot meet the demands from available resources, and in an earlier report called for continued efforts to increase the number of minority and low income students.[61] While reference could be made to other reports and writings echoing the same concerns, the point is clearly enough stated by the Carnegie Commission that the less able (so defined by performance on standard aptitude tests), minorities, and those of lower income constitute a potential source of new students.

Low Achievers

Patricia Cross refers to the academically low-achieving segment of the college-age population as the "New Students." Drawing from four major studies, she provides a highly useful profile of this group as a potential addition to the college-going ranks. The evidence is clear that when low levels of academic ability, aptitude, and achievement are combined with low socioeconomic status, the chances of a person entering college are vastly lowered. For example, only 9 percent of the males in the lowest quarter on both ability and socioeconomic status in the 1961 TALENT sample entered college, while 90 percent in the upper quarter on both characteristics enrolled in college in the fall following high school graduation.[62] It is equally clear, as has already been noted, that very few additional college students can be expected in the 1970s and beyond from among the high ability and high income students— most of them already enroll; the increase, if any, will be from the low ability, low income group.

What happens when the New Student is admitted to college? One of the first and obvious consequences is that if the New Student is from the low income segment, whatever the ability level, significantly larger amounts of student aid will be required. Some smaller and private colleges, with student aid budgets already strained, will be unable to fund increased enrollments from this segment. In *Beyond the Open Door* Cross does not examine the financial-aid issue, but goes on to deal with the other aspect, the consequences of admitting students of lesser ability, as ability is measured by traditional aptitude tests.

How are potential college students who do meet conventional admissions requirements to be characterized? Cross offers the following profile:

23

Most of the New Students . . . are Caucasians whose fathers work at blue-collar jobs. A substantial number, however, are members of minority ethnic groups. Most of the parents have never attended college, and the expectation of college is new to the family. The New Students themselves have not been especially successful at their high school studies. Whereas traditional college students (upper third) have made A's and B's in high school, New Students have made mostly C's. Traditional students are attracted primarily to four-year colleges and universities, whereas New Students plan to enter public community colleges or vocational schools.

Fundamentally, these New Students to higher education are swept into college by the rising educational aspirations of the citizenry. For the majority, the motivation for college does not arise from anticipation of interest in learning the things they will be learning in college but from the recognition that education is the way to a better job and a better life than that of their parents.[63]

She notes further that while the majority of the New Students come from financially and educationally impoverished homes, more than a quarter come from families in which fathers have attended college; these persons have not done well in school and the sense of failure for them is as intense as for their financially disadvantaged peers. And in analyzing the low achievers in terms of the Atkinson-Feather fear-of-failure theory, Cross points up the need for more than the typical remedial or compensatory programs:

For those students who do apply and are accepted, the college should be prepared to allocate adequate resources to provide the necessary instructional and counseling support while the fear-of-failure pattern is replaced with a more positive self-confident approach to learning.[64]

Those colleges admitting such students will have to be prepared to provide "a new perception of the learning process."

The New Students are not as interested in the strictly academic pursuits as is the case for the more traditional college-going person. And "this lack of interest, accompanied as it is by a lack of practice and familiarity with academic subject matter, is most assuredly a

24

handicap to New Students in school."[65] Moreover, the New Students, according to Cross, are more uncomfortable in the traditional academic setting than are the students for whom the present academic environment is designed.[66] New Students are more pragmatic in their vocational aspirations.[67] In short, the college that admits the New Student and that honestly does so with the intent that the New Student have at least a fighting chance for success, is faced with a challenge to reexamine all aspects of its educational environment. Admitting such students to the more traditional programs is almost to guarantee exceedingly high attrition—as has been the experience for many institutions that have not been prepared to take new approaches that go beyond remedial programs.

While membership in a minority group is frequently accomplished by low income, low socioeconomic status, and low test scores and thus places many from ethnic minorities among the New Students, the problems of ethnic minorities are even more complex.

> For the next several decades, higher education will be held accountable for devising the methods that can assist in eradicating the educational disadvantages of minority youth born in a majority culture.[68]

That some progress is being made is revealed in statistics compiled by the Department of Health, Education, and Welfare and released in late 1974. The data are for 1972 and indicate the highest enrollments of ethnic minorities to date. In 29 states the proportion of undergraduates from minority groups approached or exceeded the proportion of those minorities in the state's resident population.[69] Other reports suggest, however, that the trend toward increased enrollments of minorities may have peaked in 1972. And speakers at a fall 1974 meeting of the National Scholarship Service and Fund for Negro Services suggested the future involvement of minorities may be in jeopardy.[70]

Older Adults

What of another potential source of new students, the older adults? A *Chronicle of Higher Education* story on the report of the

25

Commission on Non-Traditional Study highlighted the commission's recommendation that there be a substantial broadening of opportunities in "basic, continuing, and recurrent education" for adults 18 to 60 years old with the headline, "Colleges Are Not Meeting Needs of Adults, Panel on Non-Traditional Study Finds."[71] As the review assessed the report, the major theme was that "colleges should shift their emphasis from degree-granting to providing service to learners—'clarifying the need to counter . . . a degree-earning obsession.'" When queried as to what they would like to study, some 78 percent of the adults in a commission-sponsored study of over 2,000 representative persons indicated vocational subjects, and 43 percent of the sample ranked such study as "first choice." Almost 63 percent wanted to study something related to hobbies and recreation, and over 13 percent ranked this first. General education, the more traditional academic studies, ranked third among "first choices," with 12.6 percent so ranking it; less than half of the total sample (47.9 percent) indicated that they were interested in these more traditional areas.[72]

The Commission on Non-Traditional Study was created in 1971 and issued its final report in 1973. Noting the increased emphasis in interdisciplinary opportunities, the growing acceptance of interrupted study, the need for altered patterns of residence, and the increased concern for closer articulation between early and higher education, the commission found many signs that more flexibility is being introduced into existing programs.[73] Nonetheless, the commission came out forcibly for the development of more adult-oriented programs:

> The Commission strongly urges college and university policy-makers and administrators to cooperate in—and, if necessary, provide the leadership for—coordinated planning among all educational institutions for . . . adult education. The Commission also urges them to accept adult education as integral to the work of their institutions rather than offering it only if it pays for itself or helps support other activities.[74]

The commission study of over 2,000 representative persons, referred to earlier, revealed that nearly 31 percent had in the 12 months up to the time of the study received some kind of instruction (evening classes, extensive courses, correspondence courses, on-the-job training, private lessons, independent study, television courses, or

26

"anything like that"). Roughly half of the sample could be characterized as "would-be learners" in that, while not having engaged in a learning activity of the type just listed, they indicated a desire to undertake further study. The commission infers that the adult "learners" and "would-be learners" constitute in the general population a potential of 79.8 million people who report an interest in more education; the actual "learners" represent 32.1 million engaged in some form of education.[75]

Such evidence would seem to bolster Howard Bowen's optimism for continued growth in the higher educational enterprise.[76] Note, however, that less than half of the commission sample indicated interest in the more traditional subject matters of the academy, and the commission itself throughout the report calls for new approaches to education for adults. Most of the commission's "learners" were enrolled in other than traditional programs and in other than traditional colleges and universities. Still, continuing-education campus-associated activities apparently enroll almost as many persons as "regular" programs. In 1967-68 it was estimated that colleges and universities enrolled 5,643,958 persons in noncredit activities; the "regular" enrollment in the fall of 1967 was just under 7,000,000.[77]

In a more detailed analysis of the study of the adult "learner" and "would-be learner" undertaken by the Commission on Non-Traditional Study, Carp, Peterson, and Roelfs show rather conclusively that adults are not interested in learning for its own sake and that they demand the kind of knowledge that can be immediately applied.[78] Some 82 percent of the commission's sample included persons of age 25 or above. Among the "would-be learners" only 13 percent placed general education, including "basic education," first among choices for additional education. Vocational subjects ranked first for 43 percent of the group. Among the "learners" only 16 percent were enrolled in college level or graduate level courses, and only 8 percent were taking courses in four-year colleges and universities or graduate schools. The largest group, 17 percent, were studying at home. The next largest group, 13 percent, were studying at the place of employment. Only 11 percent of the "would-be learners" indicated four-year colleges and universities or graduate schools as a preferred place of learning. And only 17 percent of the "would-be learners" indicated a desire for college degrees. Some 73 percent apparently would be satisfied with no formal credit or with some kind of certificate.

The data from the commission study strongly suggest that the traditional degree-credit programs are going to attract only a small proportion of the potential adult market. While special degree programs for adults have been underway for some 20 years, hardly more than a dozen established programs have had any measure of experience.[79] Another survey undertaken on behalf of the commission found that among 1,185 representative higher institutions only 5 percent admitted most adults into special part-time programs, and the "overwhelming majority of colleges and universities expect their adult students to enroll in regular programs along with younger students."[80] A study completed in mid-1974 by the American Council on Education reported that part-time students are a "majority group that suffers massive and pervasive economic discrimination at the hands of educators and policy-makers." Among other observations made, the report notes that colleges tend to consider part-time students "less serious than full-time students." Even more significant, I think, is the observation that university officials were of the opinion that "failure to pursue and complete a degree program is largely frivolous and wasteful of academic resources."[81]

One turns from these reports on the New Students and "would-be learners" among adults with mixed reactions. The commissions and their interpreters point to a vast new clientele. Institutional response seems enthusiastic, *until* we recognize the vast changes in attitudes and programming that will be required if colleges are indeed going to tap these new sources. Are American colleges and universities going to respond in such terms? One can well wonder.

The Twenty-Ninth National Conference on Higher Education, sponsored by the American Association for Higher Education, had as its theme, "Lifelong Learners—A New Clientele for Higher Education." Dyckman Vermilye, the editor of the conference report, sets the task succinctly when he notes that the speakers at the conference set forth a new role for American higher education and several suggested that colleges and universities are prepared to make necessary changes. They can "pass from the dog days into a new era," asserts Vermilye, but to restore flagging faith and flagging markets, these institutions will have to become inviting and useful to many persons formerly screened out or ignored: older learners, part-time learners, off-campus learners. These active adults have little time or inclination to adjust to the upper-middle-class youth ghetto we know as the modern university.[82]

Are American colleges and universities going to respond in such terms? One wonders.

Other Sources

In early spring 1975, the *Chronicle of Higher Education* called attention to efforts of institutions in the United States to attract students from abroad. It was noted that some 30,000 more students in U.S. institutions were from abroad in 1974-75 than was the case five years before and that the number of foreign students in the United States had doubled over a ten-year period of time. One university official estimated that at least 50 American institutions were actively involved in recruiting students abroad and that another 100 were considering doing the same. The largest contingent of foreign students was from the Far East. Increased interest was being shown in Venezuela and the Middle East.[83]

The Institute for International Education has over the years provided the most comprehensive summary of foreign students studying in colleges in the United States. In 1974, the last year for which total data are available, just over 151,000 foreign students were enrolled in American colleges and universities. Approximately 53 percent of these students were classified as undergraduates. Over 53,000 were from the Far East, and the next largest contingent was from Latin America, some 30,276. Europe provided 15,539; within Europe the largest group was from the United Kingdom.[84]

Considerable interest was aroused in 1973 by what at the time seemed to be a bona fide proposal to airlift some 20,000 German students to the United States. The proposal was made by Christian Schwartz-Schilling, a leader of the Christian Democratic Union. Noting that there were spaces available in American institutions and that 40,000 to 50,000 qualified German students were unable to find places in German universities, he urged that the West German government pay students' expenses, including air fare, to study in the United States, just as if they were studying in their home states.[85] Some branded the efforts of Mr. Schwartz-Schilling as wholly political—he was seeking reelection—and a way of discrediting the educational planning of the party in power. Since 1960 the number of persons qualifying for university admission in Germany has increased by 300 percent. With ever increasing crowding of facilities, the states began to impose a *numerus clausus,* restricting enrollment in certain studies. In 1973 the Zentralstelle für die Vergabe von Studienplätze was created to oversee admissions in the most crowded fields in all of the nation's universities. But in spite of the pressures in Germany, as of late 1975 Mr. Schwartz-Schilling's plan was effectively "dead."

In Great Britain the enrollment during the decade of 1962-63 to 1972-73 has nearly doubled, but in the last two years British universities have begun to accommodate to a "steady state" in enrollments, or even to a decrease.[86] In November 1974 the Department for Education and Science in Britain announced a new planning figure of 640,000 students in universities, colleges, and polytechnics by 1981. This is to be compared with an unofficial projection of 825,000 made in 1970 and 750,000 indicated in a government White Paper in 1972.[87] The current experience in Britain with enrollments in higher education, while within a different structure, is not unlike that in the United States.

Planning in Canada seems to be fairly close to the target. The number of full-time students in courses comparable to the baccalaureate sequence in the United States nearly quadrupled in the fifteen years between 1951-52 and 1967-68. In 1967-68 it was anticipated that undergraduate and graduate enrollments would reach 539,000 by 1975-76.[88] A report issued in December 1974 shows an estimated enrollment of 513,690 in 1974-75 and a projected enrollment for 1975-76 of 530,670.[89]

If overseas students are to be a source of additional enrollments in American colleges and universities, their origins will not likely be Canada or Western Europe. Latin America and the Middle East will probably increasingly export students, and the Far East will continue to provide a substantial number. But not all institutions can or should try to serve overseas students. Smaller institutions will probably not have the resources, either in needed courses or in language assistance, to provide attractive places for overseas students.

A Note on Private Higher Education

What are the prospects for the next few decades for private institutions, and in particular for the subgroup of private undergraduate and church-related institutions? Documentation of the decline in the proportion of total enrollment going to private colleges and universities is provided in a number of references. Figures from the annual reports of the Department of Health, Education, and Welfare will vary for given years depending on whether total resident and extension enrollment, degree-credit enrollment, or some variation is used. Ronald Thompson's review of public and private enrollment uses the fall resident and extension enrollment and is as useful as any such summary.[90] From his data it is clear that private higher educational institutions since 1950, with a brief resurgence in 1951, have enrolled a steadily declining proportion of the total collegiate enrollment. In 1972, according to Thompson's tabulation, private institutions enrolled only 23.5 percent of the total collegiate enrollment for that year. While enrollments have increased numerically from 1950 to 1970, the rate of increase has been much slower than for public institutions. And there have even been years in which the private colleges as a group have shown numerical decreases—from 1967 to 1968, from 1969 to 1970, and from 1971 to 1972.

In another publication showing projections for 1970-1987, Thompson indicates a continuing decline in the proportion of students enrolling in private colleges. Using as a base the trends of 1950 to 1969, he predicts that private colleges will have only 18.7 percent of the total enrollment in 1987, and numerically barely 6,000 more than were enrolled in 1972. Using another set of trends, those of 1960-1969, he credits private higher education with only 14.2 percent of the enrollment in 1987, and numerically some 300,000 *less* than in 1972.[91]

While more refined breakdowns are not regularly available in the data reported by the Department of Health, Education, and Welfare, the annual *Digest of Educational Statistics* has reported

31

enrollments for Protestant colleges for three different years, 1965, 1967, and 1970:[92]

1970	478,604
1967	482,211
1965	454,637

It is clear that the Protestant colleges as a group enroll but a small portion of the total enrollment in higher education in the United States. What is of concern, however, is what appears to be a decrease in enrollments in these colleges between 1967 and 1970.

Between 1972 and 1973 private higher education as a whole increased by 40,978 students, a growth of 1.9 percent. Private four-year colleges other than university colleges increased from 1,351,256 to 1,386,953, a gain of 35,697 and a somewhat better 2.6 percent increase. All of higher education combined, however, registered an increase of 4.3 percent. Particularly telling for the four-year private colleges was a virtually stable (decrease of 62 students) entering class.[93]

Between 1973 and 1974 private higher education registered a gain of 67,211 students, or an increase of slightly over 3 percent, somewhat better than in 1972 to 1973. Private four-year colleges other than university colleges increased from 1,386,953 to 1,430,883, a gain of 43,930, or approximately 3.2 percent. First-time students increased by 2.7 percent in these four years. All of higher education combined increased by 5.5 percent between 1973 and 1974. Private higher education continued to decline in proportion to the total, however, in that private institutions enrolled 23.4 percent of the total in 1972 and only 22.3 percent in 1974.[94]

Where Do We Go from Here?

What advice can we give Dean Neumann and the hundreds of deans like him whose institutions will be facing such uncertain enrollment prospects in the years to come?

Dean Neumann can spend his afternoons sitting under the elm tree trying to find a solution that will bring dramatic relief to his institution, or he can run off to the golf course and spend increasing hours of his time with his head firmly down, ostrich style, in a sand trap. Or, he can decide to spend a lot of time in those conference rooms with his colleagues, facing together the crucial policy issues that present themselves each day. Obviously, we opt for the third choice. The other two approaches will probably result in Dean Neumann's institution being listed among those closed or merged or absorbed as the future reports on changes in higher education are issued.

It will be important for Dean Neumann's institution to develop a planning model that enables operation in a situation that is beginning, as far as enrollments are concerned, to approach a "steady state." While some may argue whether the term "steady state" is appropriate, few will debate the proposition that we are not going to experience the same kind of growth pattern that characterized the late 1950s and the decade of the 1960s. The facts are in, and the number within the traditional college-going cohort (18 to 21 or 18 to 24) is leveling off and will decline in the 1980s and probably in the 1990s. The dean can count on some modest growth in the 1970s, followed by serious declines in the 1980s—unless he can change the composition of the student body in significant ways. It is unlikely that his admissions office will be able to attract a larger percentage of the college-going age group, and it is highly unlikely that his institution will be able to become more highly selective.

Depending upon the nature of his institution, four-year or two-year, public or private, it may, through a realignment of goals, attempt to attract a different clientele. There are those who look to the less academically prepared, at least less academically prepared under past criteria, and there are those who look to the older segment of the population and to the continuing education market as sources for increased enrollment. In either case, there is little doubt that there exists a larger population to be served. But this larger population cannot be served without some significant reorientation of goals and procedures. Dean Neumann's institution, if it does move to reach a new clientele, must take into consideration the changes that will have to be made in structure and curriculum and methodology.

Whatever directions Dean Neumann's planning may take, the data in the preceding pages should at least provide some basic points of departure for a review of policies for the coming decades.

Colleges must examine more realistically their enrollment projections, must develop new strategies to reach students who would be interested in, able to profit from, and able to pay for the kind of education they are providing. The new circumstances for colleges cannot be ignored. It is impossible to indicate how each institution should respond, because the response will be conditioned by the institution's own history, present clientele, flexibility for change, and the political realities it faces. At the very least, each institution needs to develop a series of plans that take into account the reality of a "steady state" of enrollment, if not a declining state. Each institution needs to consider the implications of changing its pattern of enrollment in terms of ability level and socioeconomic status. The implications for a faculty that may be accustomed to dealing with higher ability students and is now faced with the necessity of working with lower ability students cannot be ignored. Indeed, it may become necessary to examine the whole question of ability in a different light. The demands to provide stronger and more effective teaching will become greater. The need for orienting faculty to the new circumstances and the new students will increase. Institutions will do well to focus on serving better and retaining the students who are already enrolled there.

The emphasis upon recognizing the possibilities and demands of working within a "steady state" is not a counsel of despair. I prefer to call it a tough-minded realism. There are no automatic and no easy solutions to the enrollment problems. The sooner Dean Neumann and his institution look upon the present with a tough-minded realism, the sooner they can begin to formulate optional approaches that will deal with the situation as it is, not as they wish it were.

Notes

[1]Carnegie Commission on Higher Education, *New Students and New Places* (New York: McGraw-Hill Book Co., 1971), p. 39.
[2]Carnegie Commission on Higher Education, *Priorities for Action: Final Report of the Carnegie Commission on Higher Education* (New York: McGraw-Hill Book Co., 1973), pp. 3-4.
[3]"New Carnegie Council, Under Kerr, To Study Higher Education Issues," *Chronicle of Higher Education,* 8 (January 21, 1974), pp. 1, 6.
[4]Carnegie Foundation for the Advancement of Teaching, *More Than Survival: Prospects for Higher Education in a Period of Uncertainty* (San Francisco: Jossey-Bass, 1975), p. ix.

[5]Based on computations first reported in *New Students and New Places* and summarized in Carnegie Commission on *Priorities for Action,* p. 100.

[6]Carnegie Commission on Higher Education on *Priorities for Action,* p. 100.

[7]Carnegie Foundation for the Advancement of Teaching, *More Than Survival,* p. 45.

[8]*Ibid.,* p. 43.

[9]"Those Missing Babies," *Time,* 104 (September 16, 1974), p. 55.

[10]National Commission on the Financing of Postsecondary Education, *Financing Postsecondary Education in the United States* (Washington, D.C.: U.S. Government Printing Office, 1973), p. 24.

[11]U.S. Department of Commerce, Bureau of the Census, *College Plans of High School Seniors, October 1972,* Current Population Reports: Population Characteristics, Series P-20, no. 252, August 1973 (Washington, D.C.: Government Printing Office, 1973), p. 4. Also, U.S. Department of Commerce, Bureau of the Census, *Social and Economic Characteristics of Students, October 1972,* Current Population Reports: Population Characteristics, Series P-20, no. 260, February 1974 (Washington, D.C.: Government Printing Office, 1974), p. 3.

[12]"25- to 34-Year-Old Students on Increase in Nation's Colleges," *Chronicle of Higher Education,* IX (December 2, 1974), p. 6.

[13]Carnegie Foundation for the Advancement of Teaching, *More Than Survival,* p. 31.

[14]*Ibid.,* pp. 52ff.

[15]John K. Folger, "On Enrollment Projections: Clearing up the Crystal Ball," *Journal of Higher Education,* 9 (June 1974), p. 407.

[16]As an example, see Kenneth E. Anderson and George B. Smith, *A Study of Enrollment Trends in Higher Education in Kansas* (Topeka, Kansas: State Education Commission, February 1973) and Ronald B. Thompson, *Projections of Enrollments, Public and Private Colleges and Universities, 1970-1987* (Washington, D.C.: American Association of Collegiate Registrars and Admissions Officers, 1970.)

[17]Carnegie Commission, *New Students and New Places,* p. 1.

[18]Carnegie Foundation for the Advancement of Teaching, *More Than Survival,* p. 9.

[19]See W. Todd Furniss, ed., *Higher Education for Everybody?* (Washington, D.C.: American Council on Education, 1971), p. xv.

[20]James L. Miller, Jr., "Who Needs Higher Education?" in Furniss, *Higher Education for Everybody?,* p. 94.

[21]*Ibid.,* p. 95.

[22]Martin Trow, "Admissions and the Crisis in American Higher Education," in Furniss, *Higher Education for Everybody?,* pp. 28, 29.

[23]Jack Magarrell, "Enrollments: Up, Down, and Hovering," *Chronicle of Higher Education,* 9 (October 15, 1974), pp. 1, 2.

[24] Jack Magarrell, "Turnabout at Hood," *Chronicle of Higher Education,* 9, (October 15, 1974), p. 3.

[25]"Half Million More Students," *Chronicle of Higher Education,* 9 (December 16, 1974), p. 2. See also "Fact-File," where full report on enrollments for 1972, 1973, and 1974 are given, in same issue, p. 8.

[26]Jack Magarrell, "Fall Enrollment May Set Record," *Chronicle of Higher Education,* 10 (August 18, 1975), pp. 1, 7.

[27]Folger, "On Enrollment Projections," p. 467.

[28]U.S. Department of Health, Education, and Welfare, National Center for Educational Statistics, *Digest of Educational Statistics, 1972* (Washington, D.C.: Government Printing Office, 1973), p. 81.

[29]U.S. Department of Health, Education, and Welfare, National Center for Educational Statistics, *Digest of Educational Statistics, 1970* (Washington, D.C.: Government Printing Office, 1970), p. 73.

[30]See "25- to 34-Year-Old Students On Increase in Nation's Colleges," p. 6.

[31]Furniss, *Higher Education for Everybody?,* p. xv.

[32]See U.S. Department of Commerce, Bureau of the Census, *Projections of the Population of the United States, by Age and Sex: 1972-2020,* Current Population Reports, Series P-25, no. 493, December 1972 (Washington, D.C.: Government Printing Office, 1972.)

[33]See U.S. Department of Commerce, Bureau of the Census, *Characteristics of American Youth: 1972,* Current Population Reports, Series P-23, no. 44, March 1973 (Washington, D.C.: Government Printing Office, 1973).

[34]U.S. Department of Health, Education, and Welfare, National Center for Educational Statistics, *Projections of Educational Statistics to 1982-83* (Washington, D.C.: Government Printing Office, 1973), p. 45.

[35]See Richard Berendzen, "Population Changes in Higher Education," *Educational Record,* 55 (Spring, 1974), pp. 116-118.

[36]*Ibid.,* p. 117, 118.

[37]Carnegie Commission on Higher Education, *New Students and New Places,* pp. 127, 128.

[38]Carnegie Commission on Higher Education, *Priorities for Action,* p. 100.

[39]See Carnegie Foundation for the Advancement of Teaching, *More Than Survival,* pp. 45ff.

[40]National Commission on the Financing of Postsecondary Education, *Financing Postsecondary Education,* pp. 23-24.

[41]U.S. Department of Commerce, Bureau of the Census, *College Plans of High School Seniors,* p. 4.

[42]U.S. Department of Commerce, Bureau of the Census, *Social and Economic Characteristics of Students,* p. 3.

[43]"Fewer Seniors College-Bound," *Chronicle of Higher Education,* 9 (November 18, 1974), p. 5.

[44]U.S. Department of Commerce, Bureau of the Census, *Characteristics of American Youth: 1974,* Current Population Reports: Series P-23, no. 51, April 1975 (Washington, D.C.: Government Printing Office, 1975), p. 13. For a brief report on implications for higher education, see "Enrollment Slowdown," *Chronicle of Higher Education,* 10 (May 19, 1975), p. 6.

[45]Richard Freeman and J. Herbert Hollomon, "The Declining Value of College Going," *Change,* 7 (September, 1975), pp. 24-25.

[46]*Ibid.,* p. 26.

[47]*Ibid.,* p. 29.

[48]See Stephen P. Dresch, "The Crisis of the Scholarly Enterprise," in *Planning the Future of the Undergraduate College,* ed. Donald G. Trites (San Francisco: Jossey-Bass, 1975), pp. 65ff.

[49]*Ibid.,* p. 72.

[50]"This Year's Freshmen: Decline in SAT Scores Halted, Says College Board," *Chronicle of Higher Education,* 8 (September 16, 1974), p. 3.

[51]Malcolm G. Scully, "How Much Can Parents Pay," *Chronicle of Higher Education,* 9, (September 23, 1974), p. 2.

[52]See Humphrey Doermann, *Crosscurrents in College Admissions* (New York: Teachers College Press, Columbia University, 1968), pp. 19-31.

[53]Doermann, *Crosscurrents in College Admissions,* pp. 29-30.

[54]William K. Turnbull, "Dimensions of Quality in Higher Education," in Furniss, *Higher Education for Everybody?,* pp. 126-127.

[55]K. Patricia Cross, *Beyond the Open Door* (San Francisco: Jossey-Bass, 1972), p. 8.

[56]Quoted in Malcolm G. Scully, "Higher Education's Expansion Outlook Held Almost Unlimited," *Chronicle of Higher Education,* 8 (May 13, 1974), p. 4.

[57]*Ibid.*

[58]National Commission on the Financing of Postsecondary Education, *Financing Postsecondary Education,* pp. 18-20.

[59]See especially Cross, *Beyond the Open Door,* and the Commission on Non-Traditional Study, *Diversity by Design* (San Francisco: Jossey-Bass, 1973).

[60]Carnegie Commission, *Priorities for Action,* p. 37.

[61]See Carnegie Commission, *New Students and New Places,* pp. 25-31.

[62]Cross, *Beyond the Open Door,* pp. 8, 9, 10.

[63]*Ibid.,* p. 15.

[64]*Ibid.,* p. 25.

[65]*Ibid.,* p. 68.

[66]*Ibid.,* p. 83.

[67]*Ibid.,* p. 98.

[68]*Ibid.,* p. 130.

[69]Karen J. Winkler, "Minority Enrollments: They Rose in '72 Government Data Show," *Chronicle of Higher Education,* 9 (November 11, 1974), p. 1.

[70]"Minorities on the Campus: Their Involvement 'In Serious Jeopardy'?" *Chronicle of Higher Education,* 9 (October 29, 1974), p. 3.

[71]Robert L. Jacobson, "Colleges Are Not Meeting Needs for Adults, Panel on Non-Traditional Study Finds," *Chronicle of Higher Education,* 7 (February 5, 1973), pp. 1, 7.

[72]*Ibid.,* p. 7.

[73]Commission on Non-Traditional Study, *Diversity by Design* (San Francisco: Jossey-Bass, 1973), p. xvii.

[74]*Ibid.,* p. 24.

[75]*Ibid.,* p. 16.

[76]See Scully, "Higher Education's Expansion Outlook Held Almost Unlimited," p. 4.

[77]See U.S. Department of Health, Education, and Welfare, National Center for Educational Statistics, *Noncredit Activities in Institutions of Higher Education, Registrations 1967-68* (Washington, D.C. Government Printing Office, 1972).

[78]Abraham Carp, Richard Peterson, and Pamela Roelfs, "Adult Learning Interests and Experiences," in *Planning Non-Traditional Programs,* ed. K. Patricia Cross et al. (San Francisco: Jossey-Bass, 1974), pp. 11-52.

[79]See Roy Troutt, *Special Degree Programs for Adults,* ACT Special Report 4 (Iowa City: The American College Testing Program, 1971).

[80]Janet Ruyle and Lucy Ann Geiselman, "Non-Traditional Opportunities and Programs," in Cross et al., *Planning Non-Traditional Programs,* p. 56.

[81]Jack Magarrell, "Part-Timers: Students Massively Discriminated Against," *Chronicle of Higher Education,* 8 (July 8, 1974), p. 12.

[82]Dyckman W. Vermilye, ed., *Lifelong Learners—A New Clientele for Higher Education* (San Francisco: Jossey-Bass, 1974), p. ix.

[83]Philip W. Semas, "Foreign Students: More Coming," *Chronicle of Higher Education,* 10 (March 24, 1975), pp. 1, 8.

[84]See Institute of International Education, *Open Doors 1974: Report on International Exchange* (New York: Institute of International Educational Exchange, 1975).

[85]Philip W. Semas, "Where Are All Those Germans?" *Chronicle of Higher Education,* (February 24, 1975), p. 3.

[86]See "The Universities in a Steady State: The Prospect from Cambridge," *Minerva,* 13 (Summer 1975), pp. 270ff.

[87]See Brian MacArthur, "In Britain: Fewer Students," *Chronicle of Higher Education,* 9 (October 15, 1974) p. 3, and his "Student Cut-Back of 110,000 'Still Maintains Robbins Ideal,' " *the Times Higher Education Supplement,* no. 163 (November 29, 1974), pp. 1, 24.

[88]Barbara Burn, *Higher Education in Nine Countries* (New York: McGraw-Hill Book Co., 1971), p. 95.

[89]"Canadian College Statistics: Enrollments," *Chronicle of Higher Education.* 9 (December 23, 1974), p. 9.

[90]See Ronald B. Thompson, "Changing Enrollment Trends in Higher Education," *North Central Association Quarterly,* 47 (Spring 1973), pp. 343-351.

[91]Ronald B. Thompson, *Projections of Enrollment, Public and Private Colleges and Universities, 1970-1987,* (Washington, D.C.: American Association of Collegiate Registrars and Admissions Officers, 1970), p. 5.

[92]See U.S. Department of Health, Education, and Welfare, Office of Education, *Digest of Educational Statistics, 1966* (Washington, D.C.: Government Printing Office, 1966), p. 63. Also later editions, *Digest of Educational Statistics, 1967,* p. 66, and *Digest of Educational Statistics, 1971,* p. 66.

[93]Reported in the *Chronicle of Higher Education,* 9 (December 16, 1974), p. 8, and based on data from the Department of Health, Education, and Welfare, National Center for Educational Statistics.

[94]*Ibid.*

Chapter 2

Students in the Seventies: A New Breed?

My desk was completely covered by the accumulation of paper; I just had to clear some of this away. It was already 5:00 p.m., so I phoned home to say that I would be staying at the office into the evening. Then I decided to walk over to the freshman dorm and get a quick bite to eat before tackling the paperwork.

The tennis courts were busy, some soccer players were doing wind sprints on the practice field, and the rugby team—I didn't even know we had one—was running some intricate lateral pass exercise. I passed a group of students wandering back to the dorm and overheard bits and pieces of what seemed to be a gripe session about the lab they had just left.

*I'd been thinking a lot about our students lately. It was becoming clear to me that we were going to have to do more to serve the students who **did** come to the university. If we could retain more of those who came as freshmen, maybe we wouldn't have to spend so much time trying to dream up new gimmicks for recruitment, and if those who were here were satisfied, they might just spread the word that this is a good place to be.*

The noise nearly knocked me over as I opened the door to the cafeteria. One of the reasons given for appointing me to this job was that I was young and energetic and could "relate to the students," but suddenly I felt quite out of place. Wearing a suit and tie made me conspicuous, but even as I kept telling myself that they really weren't staring at me, I had the almost irresistible urge to go out to my car and drive over to the Holiday Inn. I put a few things—no wonder they complained about the food—on my tray and walked over to a table that had a free chair.

"Hi! I'm Dean Neumann, the Arts and Sciences dean. Mind if I join you?"

41

I tried to sound nonchalant. There was a painful silence, but finally one friendly-looking fellow peered at me over the top of his wire-rimmed glasses, shrugged, and said, "Sure, go ahead."

It was quite a collection, to say the least. Next to the one who finally issued the invitation was a big bruiser with a bushy beard and a fuzzy head of hair all strung out like an afro, only it was sandy-colored. He seemed unusually composed and thoughtful, almost meditative. Next to him was a striking girl with long black hair and arching eyebrows. And beside me sat this tiny little girl—she looked altogether too young for college—with huge round glasses that kept slipping down her nose. All I could hear was the sound of chewing, and it was clear that I was going to have to work at getting any conversation out of them.

"How's it going with you? What's it like, going to college here?"

I could see their eyes shooting around the table at each other. There was more painful silence, and then the little girl next to me started choking. My "host" came to my rescue again.

"Not bad, I mean, not bad for me. But, I'm different. I just want to get out."

"What's different about that?" said the girl with the long black hair.

"Okay. What I mean is, I'm just here to learn what I have to learn to get a good job—accounting, taxes, marketing. And I can get what I need, so this place suits me."

"How about some of the rest of you?" I tried again.

"I'm going into drama," the dark-haired girl said, "if I ever get through all these stupid requirements." Silence again.

"What do you want from college? What do you want to take with you when you leave?" I was sounding all too formal.

"I want to take with me a transcript that will get me a job where I can make a bundle and make it fast."

"Oh, come on, Jerry." They all jumped on him.

*"Not me." It was the "afro." "I couldn't care less about the bundle bit. It's the **kind** of job that counts. I could work in a school, or a clinic, or even a restaurant. Something with people. But it's the setting that counts. It will have to be someplace where I can be me and live the way I want to live. Maybe it'll only be part-time. I don't need that much money to keep going. But I do need time, time for meditation, time to enjoy each day as it comes."*

"Right, that's the way it is with me. That's why I'm into drama. I have to do something that has some meaning, something that's going to make people think."

"So, how is the university helping you get ready for that?" I knew I was breaking in, but I wanted to know what they thought about the university.

"Well, to be honest, not too well. The drama department is great, if I could ever get to it. I just don't know if I'm going to last the two years of requirements."

"I don't mind the requirements," the "afro" chimed in. "I like just exploring around. Half of it's a waste of time, but I'm trying to sort stuff out, and for me that's okay. It all depends on the prof."

They all nodded in agreement to that last remark.

"And how about you?" I turned to the little girl beside me. "You haven't said much."

She was sitting cross-legged on her chair. She looked up at me over the top of the oversized glasses and let fly, "I think the world is a pretty shitty place, and I'm going to do something about it."

They all snickered a little and watched to see how I would respond.

"Good, a reformer!" I tried to sound enthusiastic.

"No, don't get me wrong. I'm not the kind to carry a sign or lead a demonstration. I just do what I have to do in my own way."

"Like what?"

"Like tutor kids down in the project every afternoon, like work for the wilderness club and do stuff for Nader. I mean, I just don't see how people can say all they want to do is make a bundle; my God, with all that's going on. . . ."

She started off into a long speech that apparently they had all heard before, but they listened politely as her glasses bounced up and down on her nose. We talked some more, and after a while I noticed that it was quieter and that the cafeteria was almost empty. I thanked them and headed back to the piled-up desk.

A motley crew, indeed. And each one so different. How could we ever hope to please them all? But at least they weren't trying to tear the place down as their predecessors in the sixties had done. They seemed different from those students, but how? More interested in careers? Well, yes and no. More self-centered? Not really. Apolitical? Again, yes and no. About the only thing I was sure of was that I was going to have more conversations with the students on our own campus.

The Mid-Seventies—A New Time?

It seems almost inevitable that any discussion of contemporary (mid-1970s) American college students begins with a reference to the 1960s; we speak of today's student in terms of how much he or she is similar or dissimilar to the student of the 1960s; the student activism of that decade has become the point of reference for discussions of the pre- and post-1960s.

Calvin Lee has observed that the 1960s began with a conviction "in the immediate betterment of man" and concluded, for the college students at any rate, with a sense of distress at "the complexity of life around them."[1] He continues in summary:

> The Sixties brought to the American colleges commitment, involvement, relevance, and pot. It brought participatory democracy, student evaluation of professors, student involvement in the decision-making process, the end of academic credit for R.O.T.C.
>
> The Sixties brought mass take-overs of classroom buildings, administrative offices, and computer centers, fires in libraries, clashes with police, confrontation with the National Guard. It produced a backlash of state legislators, members of Congress, the courts, the general public, parents, alumni, and academic administrators. The richness of the Sixties brought the idealism, style, graciousness, and dedication of JFK. It also brought cynicism and disgust with war, the draft, the System, and a greater awareness of the anomie of human existence in modern society. The Sixties brought a larger and more talented student body than ever before. It also brought students who questioned the values on which the academic community was built, its structure and basic rationale for continuing.[2]

The halls of ivy have never been wholly isolated from society, romantic notions to the contrary notwithstanding, but to observers and participants alike the sixties were somehow different from anything in the past.

The early months of the decade witnessed the first sit-in on February 1, 1960, and students were soon involved in the civil rights movement. In 1964 three civil rights workers were murdered in Mississippi. The Berkeley student revolt began in September 1964, and protests moved from concerns over civil rights to include reactions to the war in Viet Nam. Protestors marched on the Pentagon, an Oakland draft-induction center was surrounded by 10,000 protestors, and Oberlin College students kept a Navy

44

recruiter trapped in his car for hours. Five buildings at Columbia University were occupied in the late spring of 1968. The Institute for Defense Analysis was blockaded at Princeton in the fall, and in April 1969 the Administration Building at Harvard was occupied. In the fall of 1968 San Francisco State College was closed down because of tension over black studies. Then Kent State and Jackson State broke into the headlines in May 1970. And finally it became quiet again.

In the foreword of the Carnegie Commission report dealing with the events at Kent State, Clark Kerr, chairman of the commission, observed:

> Campus turmoil is almost certainly not solely a thing of the past. But the climax of dissent, disruption, and tragedy in all American history to date occurred in May 1970. That month saw the involvement of students and institutions in protests in greater number than ever before in history. The variety of protest activities—both violent and non-violent—seemed to exhaust the entire known repertoire of forms of dissent.[3]

Another Carnegie report, *Dissent and Disruption,* indicated that nearly one-quarter of the institutions in the United States had experienced incidents of violence or disruptive protests during 1968-69.[4] That particular volume went on to say that "the campuses have, in recent years, been in the greatest turmoil in all their history of over three centuries."[5] The commission volume calls attention to the number of official reports on dissent and disruption issued during 1969 and 1970, the most widely read being the Report of the President's Commission on Campus Unrest, 1970, the so-called Scranton Report.[6]

In contrast to the literature of the 1960s, the writings in the seventies report that students have switched from activism to privatism and are now apparently working for change, if at all, inside the system.[7] The students of the mid-1970s combine "an intense sense of their private worlds with a most practical view of the prospects before them."[8] A researcher who has conducted surveys of American youth since 1967 finds in 1973 that campus rebellion has become moribund, that criticism of the universities has decreased, and that college students appear to have developed greater acceptance of the requirements of law and order.[9]

45

Do we indeed have a "new breed" of student in the mid-1970s? What is in the offing for the second half of the 1970s? What factors should Dean Neumann take into account in his planning? What do his students want and need?

What "Really" Happened in the 1960s?

In a presentation to the American Council on Education in the fall of 1969, Kenneth Keniston, a Yale research psychologist and noted student-watcher, proposed a three-way classification of college students, based on the way in which groups of students related to what Keniston called the "two revolutions."[10] The first revolution is the continuation of the liberal egalitarian revolution that began in France and the United States, in particular, at the turn of the eighteenth century and calls for the inclusion of all persons as full members of society and with full legal rights and equal esteem. The second revolution, or the new revolution, is that of the postindustrial society of the twentieth century, in which those who have achieved status in the existing system, who have full citizenship and full legal rights, are seeking to find meaning and quality of life and new goals relevant to the twentieth and twenty-first centuries.

It is in the contrast between the two revolutions, contends Keniston, that one finds a possible framework for an analysis of the tensions of the sixties on the campus. In relation to the two revolutions, one may refer to three broad categories of students— the "excluded," the "tenaciously in" (in another Keniston essay these are the "dislocated"), and the "solidly in" (in another essay these are the "change-identified").[11] The "excluded" are those still seeking to realize the results of the first revolution. They are the blacks and other minority groups who have been excluded in the sense that they are still struggling to attain the basic rights of the first revolution. The "tenaciously in" consist of the silent majority of college students, those who have secured the basic rights, have had a taste of affluence, but do not yet feel secure in their status. Their dominant motivation is vocational and "is not to challenge the system, but to enter it without much questioning the price of admission."[12] Such dissatisfaction as they express is largely a matter of immediate and personal issues. They are also "dislocated" in the process of social change, because they identify with the world as it is and do not particularly want it to change. The "solidly in" are those who take for granted the benefits and privileges of an affluent society; they are largely from families of college graduates who are now professionals, executives, teachers, and the like. Looking for new meaning to life, they are in the forefront of the second revolution. From within this third category of students are drawn the "activists" and the "hippies."

There are problems with any classification system, and Keniston himself warns that students, as is true of other persons, do not fit into neat categories. Nonetheless, these categories are useful in sorting out some of the events of the 1960s. It seems clear now that at the time almost all of the attention of the educators and the general public was directed to the activities of the "solidly in" group and in particular to the "activists" and the "hippies." It was almost as if there were no other students around. In fact, and in retrospect, the "activists" and "hippies" constituted a minority of the students, but it was the minority that made news and it was the minority with which writers, including academicians, were primarily concerned. But the story of the 1960s is the story of all three groups.

The Excluded

In many respects, the pattern of social protest which dominated the decade was begun by the "excluded." As the "Report of the President's Commission on Campus Unrest" notes:

> The Berkeley revolt did not explode in a vacuum. It was preceded by a chain of developments during the late 1950's and early 1960's which helped to revive campus activism. . . . After four black students from North Carolina Agricultural and Technical College staged an historic sit-in at a segregated lunch counter in Greensboro, North Carolina, in February 1960, the spread of sit-ins and other civil rights activities aroused the conscience of the nation and encouraged many students to express their support for civil rights through nonviolent direct action.[13]

Many of the techniques used by campus activists were learned through participation in the early days of the civil rights movement. As the 1960s wore on, however, the concerns of the blacks and the aims of the activists grew apart. The bond that enabled blacks and whites to work together for integration rapidly dissolved after the death of Martin Luther King. As blacks became more militant, they became more determined to fight their fight alone and were more preoccupied with their own black identity. The President's Commission calls attention to this shift:

> The summer of 1964 was the last in which black and white students, liberals and radicals, worked together in a spirit of cooperation and nonviolence. But urban riots in Harlem, in Rochester, and in Watts divided many white liberals and moderates from those white and black militants who considered the riots legitimate rebellion. In 1965, Stokely Carmichael helped establish an all-black political party in Lowndes County, Alabama.[14]

Subsequently, Carmichael led in the blacks' taking over of the Student Nonviolent Coordinating Committee and expelled whites from the organization. And in the summer of 1966 Huey Newton and Bobby Seale founded the Black Panther party. The cry of "Black Power" was heard for the first time.

With the focus being placed on the separateness of black concerns, there was no longer any place for a coalition of blacks and white activists, much to the amazement and disappointment of many of the activists. It was becoming clear that the goals of blacks and white activists were quite different. The blacks were fighting the battle of the excluded: they wanted to participate in society. They had little time for criticism of the larger society; their immediate concerns were too pressing. As Stokely Carmichael put it in an article entitled "What We Want":

> We should begin with the basic fact that black Americans have two problems: they are poor and they are black. All other problems arise from this two-sided reality: lack of education, the so-called apathy of black men. Any program to end racism must address itself to that double reality.[15]

White activists, many from a far more privileged position, were criticizing the foundations of the society itself. It is not surprising that they were not able to understand how blacks felt, nor that the blacks could not understand how the white activists felt. In the end, each went separate ways, and the parallel incidents at Kent State and Jackson State seemed to mark the end of both movements.

The Tenaciously In

Little was written specifically about this group during the 1960s. In a sense, everyone knew that there were large numbers of students who not only dissociated themselves from the protests but also deeply opposed them. But few were paying any attention to this largely silent majority. Most of the studies seem to agree that the students involved in active dissent represented a minority of the student body. John Horn and Paul Knott judged that, based on most estimates, no more than 15 percent of the students were involved in demonstrations.[16] James Trent referred to some of his own studies and concluded that "a very few select students and a very few select colleges and universities" were involved, at least up to 1966. He went on to summarize other studies, noting that at Berkeley no more than 3 percent of the student body were committed enough to the Free Speech Movement to risk arrest and that an American College Survey report on sophomores in 1965 found that less than 3 percent of the students could be classified as activists.[17] Richard Peterson's first study found only 9 percent of the students were involved in protest movements, and in his second study he noted that the proportions of activists within the student bodies had not changed.[18]

In 1969 the Greenwich College Research Center, Inc., published *The College Scene: Students Tell It Like It Is*. Based upon numerous personal interviews at more than a hundred college campuses, the volume summarizes responses to a "College Poll" administered during the sixties up to and through the year 1967. The "College Poll" reflects that at least some of the students of the late 1960s were growing skeptical of the value of a college education. It is reported that college students did not expect college education to have the immediate or long-term value that parents may have expected, and "the cross section of student opinion reflects a growing disbelief that a college education leads either to fulfillment or satisfaction."[19] Even then there was a growing segment of career-oriented students. It is noted that "the average student goes his or her way to and from class and to and from meals with little thought of a rumble, or a riot, and probably little interest in direct action of any kind to effectuate change in the college administration."[20] The poll found that most students had never taken part in a demonstration of any kind, let alone a riot. Most of the students were reported to be against violence of any kind in bringing about changes in the university.

What one gains from a review of *The College Scene* is a picture of the majority of students on campus concerned that some changes take place in organization and curriculum, but surprisingly satisfied with most of what they find, out of sympathy with the dissenters, and more inclined to allow things to continue as they were than to become directly involved in effecting radical changes.

One finds a similar view in Harold Hodgkinson's data in *Institutions in Transition.* His description of students is based upon questionnaire responses from 1,230 presidents of institutions of higher education in 1968-69. In the view of the presidents the students do not appear to be suggesting radical changes. Some 20 percent of the presidents indicated an increase in the percentage of students completing their degree requirements. And the percentage of freshmen going on to complete degree requirements had gone up in half of the institutions. Almost three-quarters of those reporting indicated that the percentage of the graduating class planning on further education had gone up. There was some indication that students had become more involved in establishing and enforcing regulations and in controlling academic and institution-wide policies; well over half of the presidents reported more student participation or involvement in these areas.[21]

During 1969-70 the Carnegie Commission on High Education sponsored a survey of academic opinion involving 70,000 undergraduates, 30,000 graduate students, and 60,000 faculty members.[22] Two-thirds of the undergraduate students responded that they were "satisfied" or "very satisfied" with college, and 77 percent of the graduate students signified satisfaction with their programs. Yet, while generally satisfied overall with college, faculty relations, relations with other students, and the quality of classroom instruction, some 90 percent of the undergraduates indicated that course work should be "more relevant to contemporary life and problems." Undergraduates disagreed with faculty in that more than half of them indicated they favored "making all courses elective, abolishing grades, and giving faculty members and students complete control of the universities. Most faculty members opposed those ideas."[23]

Some 20 percent of the undergraduates indicated that students should be able to vote on faculty appointments, course content, and degree requirements, but only 5 percent of the faculty agreed and only 15 percent of the faculty agreed that students should be consulted on such matters. The majority of undergraduates (62 percent), graduate students (72 percent), and faculty (79 percent) agreed that "students who disrupt the functioning of a college should be expelled or suspended," but only 21 percent of the undergraduates agreed that "student demonstrations have no place on a college campus."

It seems evident that there were large numbers of students in the 1960s who fit the "tenaciously in" label, who had little interest in protests and were quite happy with their college experience. Their main concern seems to have been getting on with their education, making the curriculum more "relevant," and getting their institutions to be more responsive to their immediate educational needs.

The Solidly In: The Activists

By far the greatest attention in the literature relating to the 1960s has been devoted to the activists. The events of the sixties and early seventies generated not only a series of official reports but a multitude of books and articles analyzing the activists at the time and offering suggestions regarding the causes and cures of disruption. A doctoral study by Robert Karsten, completed in August 1972, reviewed over 90 volumes that specifically analyzed the causes of campus disturbance and referred in addition to a score or more volumes that were addressed to the broader social and political issues of the period.[24] The last volumes reviewed in that study had been published in late 1971 or early 1972, and there have been many more published since.

Harold A. Korn, in the preface to *Student Activism and Protest,* observes that the 1960s were a time of national turmoil and crisis, a period of outbursts of mass discontent that challenged the legitimacy of the authority of social institutions and established leadership; many social scientists "became psychological newsmen, analyzing the day's events that same evening and preparing their reports for publication the next day." Scores of "scholarly" pieces were hastily turned out to interpret what was happening and why, but "none of us, even now, have had sufficient time away from the battle lines to take stock of the numerous change in events. We all suffer from the lack of perspective that the passage of time provides—the guide that permits the analyst to gaze backward and to see clearly and in perspective the key events and turning points that mark the given era."[25]

Robert Karsten's study, as it sought to identify the various interpretations of the meanings of the campus unrest, found no less than eight different categories of explanation. Karsten referred to the categories as: (1) holistic—the university reflected the problems of society in general; (2) failures in higher education—the enterprise had itself fallen short of expectations; (3) psychological—these were personal problems and personal responses to a period of conflict and tension; (4) technological society—persons were revolting against a dehumanizing technology; (5) call to agenda—persons were calling society to face the explicit and implicit ideals of society; (6) counter culture—American society was experiencing the birth of a counter culture; (7) political—the protests were essentially expressions of political activity; (8) conspiracy—certain leaders were behind the rash of outbursts and were pursuing their own private goals. But he concluded that the distinctions are never finely drawn:

> The classification does not show a systematic tendency among the interpretations of campus disturbance to favor one interpretive group over the others. To be sure, the theories on psychological causes and on failures within higher education are the most frequently represented in the literature, and contain the greatest variation. However, authoritative sources have been included among the witnesses to each of the other theories, and, in the light of this, it is difficult to argue that the weight of scholarly opinion can be taken to suggest that one set of causes or meanings was more likely to have been concretely operative than another.

It seems more likely, in the light of the relatively uniform distribution of the interpretations among the eight interpretive groups, and in the presence of the multiple relationships among them, that the literature on campus disturbance must be taken to suggest that the causes and meanings of the protest movement were many, and interrelated. Indeed, we are perhaps permitted to think of the classification as a kind of table for a multivariant analysis, or a matrix of inter-related propositions which must, in common with all matrices, be looked at whole in order to make sense. That is to say, the theories do not allow us to think of the causes and meanings of campus disturbance in terms of single variables, but only in terms of their relationships.

Some of the most important authorities on campus disturbances say the phenomenon was complex in its causality. For example, John Searle said that the student revolts were caused by many things and that they were, if anything, "over-determined." The Presidential Commission on the Causes and Prevention of Violence reported: "The problem of campus unrest is more than a campus problem. Its roots lie deep in the larger society. There is no single cause, no single solution."[26]

One of the more frequently quoted set of explanations for the student unrest points up, as does Karsten, the complexity of the matter. Professor S. L. Halleck of the University of Wisconsin presented to the meeting of the American Association for Higher Education in 1968 what he termed "Twelve Hypotheses of Student Unrest."[27] Emphasizing that hypotheses were at best only partial explanations, he divided his 12 into "favorable," "unfavorable," and "neutral." The "unfavorable" suggested that there was something wrong with the students, the "favorable" suggested the problems lay with man-made circumstances, and the "neutral" grew out of changes in a highly complex society. Many of the same categories developed by Karsten are paralleled in Halleck's analysis, though Karsten's covers a wider range of possibilities.

Another analysis emphasizing the great complexity of interaction among the factors that appear to have been involved in the student unrest is Donald R. Brown's.[28] Brown proposed that there were some 13 factors associated with the "greater visibility and activity" of the students. Referring to the characteristics of the 1960s, he stated that: (1) the increase in the number of students on campus contributed both to the pressures within the campus and to visibility off-campus; (2) while college attendance appeared to be required in an increasingly technological and affluent society, the work in college was seen as having little pragmatic relevance; (3) the broader range of students enrolled in higher institutions set new challenges to the colleges as socializing agencies; (4) once admitted, students were under considerable competitive stress for admission and survival; (5) the news media contributed to the spread of dissent by being overly zealous in reporting events associated with disruption; (6) students had grown in sophistication regarding their individual rights and become more irritated at the insensitivity of faculties and administrators; (7) students were better prepared for college in the 1960s than were their predecessors, and they demanded more; (8) in their idealism, students rebelled at the contradictions of a society in which affluence and freedom existed side by side with poverty, ignorance, and discrimination; (9) students accepted and themselves emphasized their sense of self-determination and responsibility, in their search for self-identity; (10) youth is inherently lonely in its search for self-definition and clarity; (11) the student generation had developed a phobia over the increasingly technological mechanization of society "as personified in the IBM card, which threatens the less stouthearted with an overwhelming crisis of depersonalization"; (12) with increased emphasis on the intellectual development in colleges, students developed unrealistically high expectations of the curriculum, faculty, and their peers; (13) while physical maturation was developing more rapidly, psychological, social, and economic maturity in the young was being delayed.[29] Some of Brown's observations appear dated, but at the time this was a helpful analysis.

What kinds of students were involved in the protests? There is still some disagreement on the matter. Most of the earlier written reports contended that the students most actively involved were generally among the elite of the student body. Edward F. Sampson refers to "a select group of protest-prone intelligent persons who share egalitarian familial backgrounds."[30] Kenneth Keniston, after reviewing a number of studies of those involved in protest, generalized that "student protestors appear to be generally outstanding students: the higher the student's grade point average and the more outstanding his academic achievement, the more likely he is to become involved in any particular political demonstration.

Similarly, student activists come from families with liberal political values."[31] Julian Foster, Richard Flacks, and Leonard Baird each drew similar conclusions, although Baird noted that activists did not necessarily have higher grades. Alexander Astin's study seemed to demonstrate that the single most important predictive value in determining who might be among the activists was "no formal religious affiliation."[32]

While scores of comments of the sort noted above could be cited, some subsequent analyses have questioned these generalizations. John Horn and Paul Knott did not find clear evidence one way or the other; to them it is not clear whether the activist was more intelligent than the nonactivist, but "the results clearly indicate that activists were capable students in the fields in which they chose to major."[33]

More recently, Larry Kerpelman has observed that many of the researchers in the sixties had concluded that the activists were "close to being psychological noblemen." He argues that from his own review of the literature he found severe flaws in "the supposedly solid evidential base that served as the basis for that view." After pointing out some of the problems in the student-activist research, he goes on to report on his own study, a "carefully selected questionnaire battery administered to 229 students at three leading institutions of higher education in the United States in the late 60's," and he notes that the most striking finding in this intelligence and personality test "was that there were no measures on which any of the six activism-ideology subgroups differed from the others."[34] He did find some measures by which various groups of activists were clearly different from various groups of nonactivists—there were some personality differences in that activists seem to value leadership more, to be more sociable, and more ascendant and assertive, and to be less needful of social support—but he found no differences with regard to "intelligence, emotional stability, or responsibility and restraint." He concludes his article:

> To be sure, left activists have sought positive changes in American society—an end to war as a way of resolving conflicts and an end to secret research on American campuses, to cite a couple of examples. But in an effusion of positive halo effect, social science and education researchers have rushed to place positive value as well on the psychological qualities of the

55

student activist. The result has been a picture of those students that has been clouded by questionable methods and questionable conclusions. That picture is only now beginning to clear.[35]

Richard Peterson and John Biloursky take note of other studies that call into question the generalization that the activists were the "brighter" students.[36] They do observe, however, that campus activism seems clearly to have been associated with some general and overall quality of the student body. While not all "bright" youths were involved, those campuses where the overall average in intellectual ability was high were more likely to have been involved in dissent.[37] Peterson's earlier report noted that the incidence of activism was higher in the more select colleges and universities. His subsequent report, dealing with 1967-68, seemed to suggest the same conclusion, although the only correlations that had any significance were those related to war issues, i.e., those campuses in which war issues provided the basis for disruption or protest seemed to be "higher quality" institutions.[38]

The student activism of the 1960s resulted from a multiplicity of causes. To the extent to which the conditions which caused the protests are repeatable, the protests could occur in the 1980s or 1990s. At least we have learned (or should have learned) that we cannot take the student population for granted, and we should certainly be less ready to say in 1976 what Clark Kerr said in 1959: "I can just see . . . that they are not going to press many grievances . . . they are going to do their jobs, they are going to be easy to handle. There aren't going to be riots. There aren't going to be revolutions. There aren't going to be many strikes."[39] We should be more aware of forces operating on the campus and less inclined to make such predictions in the future.

The Solidly In: The Hippies

Much less has been written about the other group within the "solidly in," the "hippies." For want of a better term, we use this label to describe those students whose protest was against the total culture and whose response was to drop out of the mainstream of society in order to explore alternate life styles. There have always been hippies, of course, such as the Paris bohemian expatriates of the 1920s and Dean Moriarty in Jack Kerouac's story in the 1950s of the beat generation, *On the Road*. These were in some ways the spiritual forerunners of the hippies of the 1960s. Keniston makes a clear distinction between the activists and the hippies:

> In contrast to the politically optimistic, active, and socially concerned protester, the culturally alienated student is far too pessimistic and too firmly opposed to "the System" to wish to demonstrate his disapproval in any organized public way. His demonstrations of dissent are private: Through non-conformity of behavior, ideology, and dress, through personal experimentation and, above all, through efforts to intensify his own subjective experience, he shows his distaste and disinterest in politics and society.[40]

The activist is the kind of person who tries to change the world around him, but the hippie is convinced that it is impossible to change the world in any meaningful way, and the only option he sees is that of "dropping out."

The hippies and other alienated youth are important for what they began, a wide-sweeping change in values and attitudes that grew more and more diffuse as the 1960s wore on and became a cultural transformation that was eventually co-opted by much of the larger society. What was at first shocking—a change of dress and hair style, a challenge to the Protestant work ethic, and a search for new understandings of self and personal relationships—gradually became more palatable to larger and larger numbers, including many beyond the student age group. The hippies were important not so much for what they did as for what they started; like the Beatles, they set something in motion. What started as a fringe movement of a few offbeats was soon being labeled the "counter culture."

There was disagreement about how widespread the influence of the counter culture really was. Theodore Roszak compared the counter culture to an invasion of the festivities of the gods by drunken and incensed centaurs, and called it "a culture so radically disaffiliated from the mainstream assumptions of our society that it scarcely looks to many as a culture at all, but takes on the alarming appearance of a barbaric intrusion."[41] Roszak saw the counter culture as a rebellion against the technocracy, a culture in which all matters are reduced to so-called "objective" and "scientific" judgments.

Charles Reich, another interpreter of the counter culture, was even more optimistic about the growth of a cultural revolution. He saw in the movement the development of a totally new way of looking at life which he termed Consciousness III, and he looked forward to a new springtime in which the counter culture would permeate and transform the existing society.[42] From the vantage point of the mid-1970s it seems safe enough to say that America never "greened" in the way Reich predicted. Commenting critically on Reich's "rebirth of people in a sterile land," Fred Hechinger, former education editor of the *New York Times,* wrote:

> In retrospect, it is evident that professor Reich's euphoric account was actually written not at the beginning but at the tail end of a mini-revolution that would not survive the dawn of the new decade. But at the time, the utopian delusion was so widespread that Reich may be forgiven for his misreading of a phenomenon that seemed to him and to so many others a historic tide rather than a political flash flood that has since receded.[43]

Some would suggest, however, that while the counter culture did not bring about the "greening," it did in subtle ways influence subsequent culture, as we have already noted.

The Students of the Seventies

It all seemed to end as abruptly as it began. Writing about the involvement of large numbers of students all over the country in May 1970 in response to the Kent State events, Peterson and Biloursky concluded that "American mass student political movements, as phenomena involving continuing participation and collective actions by many more than the heretofore highly committed activists, are unable to sustain themselves in the absence of new or continuing issues or provocations."[44] They found that the May protests had begun to fade by mid-month, and the relative calm of the campuses the following fall astonished almost all observers. Peterson and Biloursky suggest some of the reasons for the lack of sustained action: students became involved in their own personal priorities; some were cynical and pessimistic over the possibility of bringing about any significant changes; some saw that the campus climate was in fact changing positively; and some responded favorably to national and international events. The following year, 1971, was calm, as if a new era had begun.

How are the students of the 1970s being characterized in the current literature? Many writers are pointing to the great variation among students and suggesting that it is difficult, if not impossible, to capture this variety in any single characterization. David Gottlieb and Benjamin Hodgkins argue that any assumption of a homogeneous student population is highly questionable, and that the assumption should rather be that the "very heterogeneity of American society results in college student bodies with diverse origins and values within most institutions of higher learning."[45]

When Harold Hodgkinson characterizes the students of the seventies, he calls attention to one of the most significant changes in the collective student body: the increase in numbers. He goes on, however, to say that

> the American student body has become more diverse in background, more transient, less willing to play higher education's games to get the gold stars that degrees represent, more politically aware and politically powerful, less easily led around by the nose, more aware of the world outside the campus, more willing to take direct action on issues they deem important to their self-interest, less willing to police their fellow students, and less loyal to abstract institutions.[46]

The new students are also more sophisticated, represent a broader range in background, and are generally of higher ability than their predecessors. It is interesting that, even as writers contend students are so diverse that it is impossible to characterize them in any simple way, these same writers make their own generalizations about "the student generation." Yet, the theme of diversity runs through most of the commentaries.

The Popular and Educational Press

The popular news magazines in the annual assessments of the college student they have been undertaking, particularly since the sixties, began in 1971 to write about significant changes in the nation's universities. In October 1971 *U.S. News and World Report*

59

headlined a report, "Turn From Campus Violence," and went on with a lengthy subhead: "There's a significant change at the nation's universities. Relative quiet reigns after years of turmoil. Discontent? Yes—but many students are turning to peaceful means of changing 'the system.' " The article then described a "new breed" of student that is taking over the campus. The new breed continues to question traditional politics, sexual morals, and capitalism, and to hold meetings; but "no longer . . . do students see America's broad problem as simple afflictions to be solved by a curse, a march or a bombing. And increasingly," the report said, "educators find young people are looking 'within the system' for practical solutions to those problems."[47]

Eight months later the same magazine again described the "New Mood of College Students." This time the long subhead read: "Violence is ebbing and interest in learning is rising at the nation's universities. Staff members of *U.S. News and World Report* find many new trends in campus life today." The lead paragraph referred to a "high tide of change" that is "rolling across American college campuses, sweeping away many old issues and leaving students in a fresh mood." The new direction was away from confrontation and violence toward "some kind of working arrangement with the world outside college walls." Interest in studies was up; students were working harder and were even to be found in the library on Saturday night and Sunday afternoon. One administrator referred to "a high academic work ethic." According to the university and college presidents interviewed by the magazine staff, the college student in 1972-73 was less radical, more interested in getting an education and a job, more involved in off-campus politics, and was becoming more interested in social life and religion.[48]

In February 1974 the report was that "college militants by the thousands are moving student crusades from the streets into the political arena—buttonholing legislators, ringing doorbells and flooding the mails on issues ranging from food costs to conservation."[49]

A similar series of descriptions issued forth from *Newsweek*. In November 1972 the magazine referred to "A Separate Peace." But while the education editor of the magazine reported the relative quiet on the campuses, he did not take it all at face value:

To say that campuses are quiet is not news, for the campuses have been more or less quiet for some two years. More important, though, it is not even accurate. For if the 50's meant obedience, and unquestioning acceptance of the status quo and the simple pleasure of being in college, the 70's are not at all the same. The placid surface conceals tension—and an uneasiness that in some hard-to-pin-down way gnaws at students, administrators and faculty alike.[50]

He went on to try to describe the underlying tension, suggesting that college students might be a lot less idealistic than many thought, that, having won certain concessions related to their own interest, they were now actually little concerned about other developments. With the racial issue less in the limelight, students were attending to it less. Because they were not threatened by the draft, they protested the war less. Because jobs were increasingly difficult to get, they were more worried about the job market.

In March 1974 *Newsweek* provided a "Campus Snapshot." Students, the writer observed, seem "to be a study in opposites, combining an intense sense of their private and interior worlds with a most practical view of the prospects before them." It was suggested that students had not lost their idealism, but that they had become much more realistic about the world they face, a world in which jobs are increasingly scarce; the college was reflecting student reaction in the increased competition for admission into professional fields. The theme throughout the report was that students in 1974 could be characterized by the terms "privatism" and "realism."[51]

Fortune magazine in March 1973 reported on a survey of six universities, three community colleges, and five high schools, in which interviews were conducted with 200 students and more than 100 educators. The theme of the report was that the youth revolution of the sixties has come and gone. The reporters referred to a "new normalcy"; they contended that we were not seeing in 1973 simply a return to the calmness of the fifties, but that we were experiencing the birth of a new kind of tolerance—"if any single word sums up the viewpoint of students in 1973, it is tolerance." The story goes on to say that in view of the relative rareness of tolerance, particularly among the young, "the blossoming of tolerance on campus is a phenomenon worth pausing over." The students were described as being "more aware" and "better informed" in comparison with the students of the fifties, and the tolerance as arising, in part, from "a new awareness that nobody—young or old—has all the answers." Such tolerance is a sign of realism rather than of apathy.

The report in *Fortune* suggested that one reason many of the parts of the traditional system were being accepted was that students had won concessions in a number of areas, including sitting on all types of academic and disciplinary bodies. A majority of the students, the report noted, seemed to have specific career goals, and the general mood was one of seriousness.[52]

Echoing many of the observations in other reports, the November 1973 *Chronicle of Higher Education* carried the headline, "Student Demands for 'Practical' Education Are Forcing Major Changes in Curricula."[53] While the article was directed to a discussion of some of the curricular changes underway, it called attention to what appeared to be a growing preference of students for "practical education that can be put to use immediately" and a demand for "short career-occupational education, a credential, and a job." A subsequent article in the same periodical pointed up the impact of the "new practicality" on the humanities.[54] According to the reporter, students were "abandoning theoretical, abstract, and purely academic fields for those that relate directly to jobs." Enrollments were shown to be down in English, history, and the foreign languages, and some faculties were turning to attempts to develop "applied humanities," to the application of the skills of people in the humanities to interdisciplinary problems wherein the contemporary issues were to be dealt with from a humanistic viewpoint.

But how is this apparently overwhelming practical orientation of students to be squared with what some others see as a new emphasis on religion? Larry Van Dyne reports on a new reformation, a new spiritualism, a new mysticism: "Call it what you will . . . a new cultural phenomenon is evident among youth."[55] He refers to the campus best sellers—Castaneda's writings about the Mexican Indian mystic Don Juan, and volumes such as *The I Ching, The Exorcist, Chariots of the Gods*—the regular appearance on campus of the Hare Krishnas and the mobs following Guru Maharaj Ji, the interest in astrology, and in transcendental meditation. The list goes on.

According to Van Dyne, Paul Goodman in 1969 saw evidence of and referred to the rise of a new religious sensibility, a New Reformation. Theodore Roszak refers to "a strange, new radicalism abroad which refuses to respect the conventions of secular thought and value, which insists on making the visionary powers a central point of political reference." Andrew Kopkind calls it the "New Mysticism," an outgrowth of the failure of the revolution of the sixties and a response to the pressures of the current scene. David Riesman is quoted as saying that the upper-middle-class young are looking "for something transcendent."

In June 1973 *Change* magazine reported interviews with four students at Princeton, who were asked to talk among themselves and with the reporters about "their sense of themselves as students, as people preparing for lives in a complex and difficult world."[56] Phrases and sentences such as the following emerged:

"I want to be involved—I want to find out about myself."

"It's hard to walk by and not put on a red armband if everybody's doing it, and if this is the cause to be protesting. But it doesn't help anything."

"I believe we are here in some sense to prepare for making a contribution. And that contribution should have something to do with furthering the stability and happiness and the comfort of life on earth in a broad sense."

But there was also concern for jobs, what they might mean, whether they would be boring, or fulfilling, or creative. The conclusion of one of the *Change* editors was that the conversation "at the very least" belied "the charge that students today are self-satisfied and crass, that the idealism that brought the campuses of the sixties to such vibrant life is merely a relic of history."

Virtually the entire issue of *Change* in October 1974 was given over to essays written for the magazine by students.[57] One of the contributors described the new student activists and noted that in some two dozen states there were statewide student political organizations "working to guarantee that administrators and politicians hear a student voice."[58] Undergraduate student governments in 18 states had committed "vast amounts of time and money to a Ralph Nader inspired project, the Public Interest Research Group." The author contended that through these and other activities "hundreds of thousands of college students" had become involved in a new political activism that reflected the idealism and energy of the sixties, but "tempered by the sophisticated and pragmatic politics of the seventies." As if to reinforce this view, a report in an October 1974 issue of the *Chronicle of Higher Education* took note of the efforts of student lobbies in a number of states and in Washington:

> The student lobbies that have appeared in Washington and several state capitals in the last four years are now concentrating much of their energy on trying to hold tuition down, push financial aid up, and secure economic benefits for their constituents.[59]

The lobbies followed conventional tactics, and they apparently are having their share of successes.

Popular assessment of the student in the 1970s suggests a degree of quiet and calmness on the campus, but it is a quiet that is different from that of the 1950s. Students are supposedly as committed to change as ever, but they seem prepared to work within the system. At the same time that they are characterized as being more concerned about their own personal interests, they are also seen to be more realistic about the way in which the world and the university can be reformed. It is also suggested that some of the activism has been co-opted, and that many of the things that were sought in the 1960s have been realized on the college campus; at least the campus is much more open than it was to variations in life style and objectives.

But there are differences of opinion regarding the quiet state at the universities. Byron Evans, vice-president for student affairs at Rensselaer Polytechnic Institute, warned against falling into complacency: "Higher education has not returned to the past, nor is it possible."[60] He contended that the "present lull" should not be misunderstood; the revolution has "recessed," but we should "harbor no illusion that it is ended." And we should, according to Evans, begin preparing for the next wave of activism.

Time magazine reported in June 1974 on conflict at Ohio University: "Tranquility has returned to most U.S. campuses, but Ohio University at Athens stands out as a troubled exception. In the past month alone, the campus has been rocked by a strike of student workers, two successive nights of rioting, and demands that President Claude R. Sowle resign." And the president had submitted his resignation with the statement that he could "no longer ask myself or my family to serve the university under such insane conditions."[61]

In 1975, demonstrations on college campuses were again in the news. They had never really stopped after 1970, but in the interim they had been of largely local concern, and the news media gave little attention to such outbursts. In 1975, the demonstrations focused on economic and academic issues. In February, the students at Iowa State University asked for a boycott of the political science courses at the university, because a popular teacher was not being rehired for the coming year; but there was no noticeable decline in the enrollments in political science in the spring term. The proposal to phase out the school of forestry and the primate research center brought out 600 Duke University students in protest in early March. And a student filed suit against the University of Bridgeport, in which she charged that the courses did not match the descriptions in the college catalogue and that "she didn't learn anything."[62] In April, almost 3,000 students voted to strike at Brown University over budget cutbacks.[63] In May, Brown was again in the news, as black and Latin American students occupied University Hall for over 38 hours and secured pledges that the university would try to increase the number of blacks and Latin Americans enrolled at Brown by 25 percent over the next three years.[64] At about the same time, 100 students staged a brief sit-in at the Massachusetts Institute of Technology in protest of the institute's agreement to train engineers for Iran. At Brandeis a group of students picketed a classroom building in support of minority programs, and at the State University of New York at Buffalo, 10 students were arrested when 100 persons were evicted from a campus building as they were protesting administrative action on the use of certain student funds.[65]

There were also reports in April of protests at Princeton, Rutgers, and the Universities of Maryland, Massachusetts, Minnesota, and Pennsylvania—each focused, for the most part, on economic considerations. The students were protesting higher tuition, higher rates for room and board, threats to jobs of faculty members and students, lowered student aid, and reduced student services.[66] Police broke up a three-hour sit-in at Santa Barbara in May.[67] In a review of the spring's events, the *Chronicle of Higher Education* noted that there had been more campus demonstrations in 1974-75 than at any time since 1971. There was, however, little of the violence that accompanied protests in the 1960s. Many of the more militant protests involved minority-group students, as rising tuitions and decreasing student aid affected these students most severely. Some observers, administrators as well as student leaders, suggested that protests might be again part of the college scene in the next few years.[68]

In the meantime, a federal court jury decided that the nine students who were wounded and the parents of four who were killed at Kent State University in 1970 were not entitled to damages from state officials and the former members of the Ohio National Guard.[69] On campus the Kent State students seemed more interested in classes, grades, and jobs, and until the spring of 1975 had been without a student government for three years. At Jackson State College, where 2 students were killed and 12 others wounded 11 days after the incident at Kent State, the students had held memorial services every year since 1970, but in 1975 no formal plans were made to commemorate the event.[70]

Long-Range Studies

In addition to the reports from the popular and educational press, at least two long-range (longitudinal) studies provide some insight into the students of the seventies. I refer to studies conducted since 1965 and 1967 by the Daniel Yankelovich opinion research firm and the study of American college freshmen begun in 1966 by Alexander Astin. Yankelovich's first study was begun in 1965 and published by the Institute of Life Insurance. In the fall of 1967 the Yankelovich organization undertook a nationwide survey of college students for *Fortune* magazine, exploring student values with regard to love, marriage, religion, work, saving, success, drugs, technology, authority, and career choice, and in 1969 the *Fortune* survey was updated at the request of CBS News. In 1970 the organization was commissioned by John D. Rockefeller III to undertake a new study, and in 1971 the J.D.R. 3rd Fund requested a further study. Most recently, in 1973 the organization conducted a similar study for five private foundations, including the J.D.R. 3rd Fund and the Carnegie Corporation. The latter study involved interviews with 3,522 persons in a national sampling of both college and noncollege youth.[71]

In reporting the results of the 1969 study, the Yankelovich researchers noted that the so-called generation gap represented a half-truth. It was observed that, while college students held views different from those of their parents, "their values conflicted even more sharply with the values of other young people in their own generation who were *not* attending college." The study concluded that the gap within the generation was greater than the gap between generations and that there was indeed a "strong bond of shared core values between parents and their college-age children."[72] In contrast, Lewis Feuer in 1969 had just issued a lengthy and heavily documented volume that argued that one of the primary sources for the student movements, such as those in the 1960s in the United States and in Europe, was "generational consciousness."[73]

The 1970 Yankelovich study focused upon the conflict between college youth and the so-called Establishment and revealed "a surprisingly large core of common concerns shared by the business executives and college students."[74] However, the study also pointed up "an awesome collection of obstacles, both practical and psychological, that stood in the way of productive Youth/Establishment collaboration."[75] The report showed a sharp increase in college-student mistrust, alienation, and despair.

In 1971 a change in mood appeared. The 1971 Yankelovich study included hour-long personal interviews with more than 1,200 college students in 53 colleges and universities throughout the country, and it appeared that significant changes had taken place on the campus. The study suggested that there was a beginning of a separation between radical political values and life-style values in 1971; that is, whereas radical political and radical life-style values were found together in the mid-1960s, in 1971 the changing cultural values became even more pronounced while the political values appeared to be moving toward a more tolerant mood. Students in 1971 appeared to be less critical of the major institutional forms, the political parties, business, universities, the union, and the like. There appeared to be even further separation between political and life-style values in 1973.

The 1971 study also noted a move away from the mood of personal despair and depression. It suggests that "the best single phrase describing the current student mood is, *confused but not despairing.*"[76] While being less despairing about their own personal lives, however, students were no more optimistic about society in general. To the contrary, more of them were of the opinion that American society was sick than was the case in the previous years. Although they were not very optimistic about social change, by 1973 they seemed even more prepared to accept or at least work within the established political lines; in 1971 some 57 percent identified with the Republican or Democratic party, while in 1973 some 73 percent identified themselves with one of the two major parties.[78]

The 1971 report referred to changing moral codes and "surprising contrast" in what students viewed as morally right or wrong. For example, it pointed out that a plurality of students considered it more immoral to collect welfare when one was capable of working than to pay one's way through college by selling dope. And pilfering was considered more immoral than destroying private property, selling dope, interchanging partners among couples, and general disregard of the law.[78] By 1973 the percentage of college students who disapproved of casual premarital sex had dropped from 34 percent to 22 percent and disapproval of homosexual relations had dropped from 42 percent to 25 percent.

In the 1969 study there was considerable evidence that the campus was becoming highly politicized, and although a small proportion of the students were characterized as out-and-out revolutionaries (3 percent), a large proportion, approximately 40 percent of the students, shared the criticisms made by the revolutionaries. In 1971 some 55 percent of the students said that campus radicalism was leveling off or declining, whereas only 33 percent so declared in 1970. In 1973 an even smaller proportion saw campus rebellion as a significant factor, and an increasing number of students indicated that it was morally wrong to use violence even in a good cause.

68

Since 1966 the Cooperative Institutional Research Program, under the direction of Alexander Astin, has been surveying the entering freshmen in a large sample of American higher educational institutions. From 1966 to 1970 his sample included approximately 15 percent of the colleges and universities in the United States. From 1971 the program invited all institutions with entering freshman classes and that completed the HEGIS forms for the U.S. Office of Education to participate. Although items and wording have changed somewhat since the study was begun, it is still possible to compare the freshmen of 1966 with those of 1973 and 1974 on a number of items.[79]

If one compares the profile of freshmen entering college in 1966 with that for the groups entering in 1973 and 1974, one finds some striking differences even in this brief span of time. More freshmen appeared to be undecided about probable career occupation in the 1970s than in 1966. Earlier, less than 5 percent reported themselves undecided, while by 1973 just over 11 percent were undecided, and by 1974 the proportion had gone beyond 12 percent. This growth in the proportion of students undecided about future career was occurring, oddly enough, at a time that students were supposed to be more vocationally oriented! Among the choices of probable professions, secondary teaching was high in 1966. In 1973 less than 5 percent of the students listed this as a possible career choice, and by 1974 only 2 percent selected it. Business was high on the list of choices in 1966, but by 1973 it was the career most often checked; even with a slight decline in the percentage of freshmen checking it in 1974, business was still the occupation most often checked as probable career choice. Medicine and law were more frequently designated in the 1970s than in 1966. During this period there was a significant increase in the proportion of students indicating "other" as a probable career choice; does this mean that the more traditional fields listed were proving less attractive? Or, perhaps, that fewer jobs were available in these fields? Over one-quarter of the students indicated "other" in 1974.

In 1973 a larger proportion of students reported "none" under religious preference than was the case in 1966; by 1974, over 10 percent of the entering freshmen indicated no particular religious preference, and in the western part of the country this response was made by over 14 percent of the students. On the other hand, when asked to check objectives considered essential or very important, over two-thirds of the entering freshmen included "to develop a philosophy of life"; almost as large a proportion checked this as an essential or very important goal in 1974. The statement was not included as an option in 1966. And, as Larry Van Dyne reported in 1973, there seems to be a wide-spread interest in spiritualism and mysticism.[80] Perhaps when youth report no religious preference they are indicating that they have no preference for any of the more established and traditional religious groups. The next most important goal in 1973 was to "help others in difficulty"; nearly two-thirds of the entering students rated this as an essential or very important goal. A higher proportion rated this goal as essential or very important in 1966. The third most often checked essential or very important goal in 1973 was to "be an authority in my field." A slightly higher proportion indicated this to be an important goal in 1966. A considerably higher proportion of students in 1973 checked to "be well-off financially" as an essential or very important goal in 1973, but in 1974 this goal was checked as essential or very important by 45.8 percent as compared with over 55 percent in 1973.

Continuities with the 1960s?

What may we conclude about the students of the 1970s? How different are they from the students in the 1960s? Did an entirely new student suddenly emerge, or did the student culture, or more accurately, the student cultures of the 1960s help to shape the new students? How do Kenneth Keniston's categories of students apply in the 1970s?

The *"excluded"* are somewhat more included. Although the number of blacks enrolled in higher educational institutions does not yet approach the number equal to the proportion of black Americans aged 18 to 21, enrollments of black students have increased much faster than the total college enrollment. The Bureau of the Census has estimated that black enrollment has increased 56 percent between 1970 and the 1974-75 academic year, for an increase of nearly 250 percent since 1964. While about 12 out of every 100 Americans aged 18 to 21 are black, however, only 9 out of every 100 college students are black—up from 5 in 100 in 1964.[81]

Important changes have taken place in higher education and in society generally. Perhaps most important are the sweeping changes

70

that have occurred in public accommodations and employment opportunities. Although there are still important areas where blacks are denied equal access within the society, the focus of the black excluded is now on consolidating past gains. Black students in particular seem to be focusing on career preparation. If, as Stokely Carmichael has noted, the problem is that of being black and poor, the emphasis today seems to be on the problem of being poor.

But the ranks of the excluded are being filled with other minority groups, including America's only majority-minority: women. The protest over exclusion has been carried over into the women's movement, but today much of the fight of the excluded is carried on not by sit-ins and marches but through federal executive orders, equal rights legislation, and affirmative action. And while the proportion of white males attending higher educational institutions is declining, the proportion of women has been increasing. Reports on enrollments for the fall of 1974 show that the number of women enrolling increased by 7.7 percent over 1973, while the enrollment of men increased by only 3.8 percent. It was noted:

> The accelerating growth [in enrollments] can be attributed largely to the presence of more women on the campuses. Among both full-time and part-time students in almost every kind of institution, the number of women has grown faster than that of their male classmates.[82]

Another group of the excluded is becoming more included!

Two other groups of formerly excluded persons are also making inroads in higher education, the less academically oriented and the older student. (To include these two groups among the "excluded" is admittedly going beyond the meaning of the term as used by Keniston.) In an address at the 1973 meeting of the American Association for Higher Education, Patricia Cross pointed out that although higher education was never designed to educate the masses, most high school students can now enter college; over 75 percent of those in the upper half of the high school graduating class do enroll.[83] She draws the conclusion that "a group of young people whom we used to dismiss as 'not college material' are now walking through the open doors of colleges," and these students "constitute a growing proportion of the college population."[84] These new students bring with them new problems; as they increase in numbers, colleges will have to develop new kinds of programs to accommodate them. Remedial programs have not been particularly successful in the past, and Cross calls for restructuring the college curriculum on a "problem-oriented" base with clear differentiation in goals among colleges.[85]

In many respects the older student is psychologically more like the "tenaciously in," but by virtue of being left out of and even discouraged from higher education, the older student has also been excluded from an area of life and has lacked status. Now, however, this student is also appearing with increasing frequency in the college classrooms—and brings another set of problems. Engin Holmstrom reports on a special aspect of the annual survey of entering freshmen conducted by the American Council on Education, the experience of the "older" freshman. Using data from the 1967 entering class and a follow-up on the group in 1971, Holmstrom found that older students (20 years or older as entering freshmen) made lower grade-point averages (except in two-year colleges), included more who planned to get no more than a baccalaureate, and included fewer who attained a baccalaureate in four years than did the 18-year-old entering freshmen. The older students came in large proportions from socioeconomically disadvantaged backgrounds and tended to enroll in public rather than private institutions and in smaller or less selective institutions. Yet those older students who enrolled in highly selective institutions were more likely to complete the baccalaureate than were those older students enrolled in other types of institutions.[86] It was also noted that

> older students were somewhat different from average-age students in their attitudes and life goals, but some of the differences were not consistent and varied by type of institution in which . . . [they] were initially enrolled. Generally, more of the older . . . students agreed that the major benefit of a college education is monetary. Further, older students were more favorable to open admissions. . . .[87]

In the AEC survey for 1967 only 4.9 percent of the entering students were aged 20 or above, but more than half of these were older than 21 years.

The report of the Carnegie Commission on alternative channels to life, work, and service calls for "more opportunities in colleges for part-time and for adult students," but raises the question of whether older adults will mix well with youth:

> They [older students] may be handicapped by less inclination toward theory and by less retentive memories, but they will often bring greater motivation and more judgment based upon experience. The GI's after World War II were excellent students and raised the level of academic effort of all students. They were, however, only a few years older than other students.[88]

Strictly speaking, if one uses the age of 21 as marking "adulthood"— even though the Twenty-sixth Amendment brought the lowering of the age of majority in many states—as the Carnegie Commission points out, about 42 percent of all students on college and university campuses are adults.[89] And by 1972 some 19.7 percent of the students were 25 years or older.[90] Yet, *for the traditional on-campus, full-time program,* even with the increases in the age range of students, the majority of the students are still in the late teens and early twenties. As institutions, colleges and universities are probably moving toward a "new kind of student," but they are doing so slowly—and at the undergraduate level, at least, the pattern of instruction is geared to what faculty think is appropriate to the younger adult.

It is when we look to the special evening programs, the adult education sector, and the so-called nontraditional and broader "postsecondary" programs that we are likely to find more evidence of the presence of the new kind of student, insofar as "older" identifies the new student. The Current Population Survey of May 1969 revealed that among persons 35 years old and over and among those 17 to 34 years of age not enrolled in "regular" school full-time, some 13.2 million (or 11 percent of 119.7 million "eligible" adults) had participated in some kind of schooling the year before. The Commission on Non-Traditional Study found in 1972 that an estimated 32.1 million persons 18 to 60 years of age (or 30.9 percent of 104 million "eligible" adults) had received instruction during the previous year in "evening classes, extension courses, on-the-job training, private lessons, independent study, T.V. courses. . . ."[91]

Several presentations during the Twenty-ninth National Conference on Higher Education in March 1974, dealt with the growth of interest among persons in the "older" sector and with "recurrent education" as the term is being used in Europe. James R. Goss, director of the Center for Educational Research and Innovation, OECD, documented the growth of part-time training and evening classes in Europe. He noted that, while much effort is being expended in "upper secondary education," more of the effort is in industry and in the "educational leave of absence."[92] James O'Toole of the University of Southern California outlined the need for developing opportunities for the disadvantaged, elderly, blue-collar workers, and middle-class men and women. He pointed out that "increasing numbers of people are demanding greater choice in the *form* of education." They are requesting "self-mastery courses, and flexible time schedules, and on-the-job and in-the-field training." They also want "a greater range of curricular content . . . greater flexibility from their jobs . . . freedom to drop out of school and into work, out of work and into school."[93]

The *"tenaciously in"* seem to have carried the day. By far the largest group in the 1960s, their ranks have swelled, so that in the middle of the 1970s the preoccupation with occupations seems to dominate the student body. The current pressure on this group is not so much that which comes from rapid cultural and social change, but from economic change. As *Time* magazine notes, "The overriding influence on student attitudes today is the economy. *Time* reporters recently visited two dozen campuses and found that the greatest worry among students is that there will be no jobs for them after graduation."[94] Coming out of the 1960s, students developed the expectation that their careers would provide them with greater self-expression and self-fulfillment as well as high salaries, but, says *Time,* "that is a significant departure from what young people sought in the 1950s and substantially narrows their job options."

The job market for college graduates is a recurring subject for discussion in the literature of the mid-1970s. While, as John Folger points out, we have a bad record in predicting shortages and surpluses of educated personnel in America, the current confused market has prompted more than the average number of commentaries.[95] Headlines such as that over Jack Magarrell's story in the *Chronicle of Higher Education,* "College Graduates Seen Exceeding Demand by 10 Percent Between 1980 and 1985," have become commonplace.[96] References to particular academic disciplines are calculated to be even more sobering, as, for example, "Academic Job Outlook Bleak for Ph.D.'s in English."[97] Magarrell's report on the excess of college graduates notes that, on the basis of data from the Bureau of Labor Statistics, between 1972 and 1980 some 8.8 million graduates will be competing for 8.7 million job openings, and between 1980 and 1985 there will be 6.5 million graduates competing for 5.8 million openings.

Those who were once a silent majority are now a vocal majority: they want an education that is brief and to the point and that has the clear guarantee of a job after graduation. And the job market is working against them.

The *"solidly in" activists* apparently have retreated. Even the demonstrations of 1975 seem to be of a different sort than those of the 1960s. Much of the evidence points to the conclusion that student activism is dead—or if it is not dead, it has "gone straight"—and there seems to be a strong apolitical strain on the campus. *Time* magazine observes:

> For the most part, students seem unwilling to involve themselves directly in the U.S. political process. A recent survey showed that half of the students polled at the University of Missouri are not even registered to vote. At the University of Kansas, campus Democrats concluded after a poll that large numbers of students did not know that State Attorney General Vern Miller was a candidate for Governor, even though he had gained much notoriety for his flamboyant drug arrests of Kansas students.[98]

Fred Hechinger saw the election of 1972—when fewer than half of the newly enfranchised youth voted, in comparison to 71 percent of the eligible voters over 45—as an indication of the fading concern of the activists. The activists had accomplished some few reforms, hardly a revolution, and in the main, Hechinger said, the young are back at work and play, competing for grades and for jobs.[99]

The characterization is not completely fair. Some students are involved, but in ways that are very different from the 1960s. They are developing housing and food co-ops, they are running day-care centers, they are working for Ralph Nader's public interest groups, or they are quietly working for their own party candidates. If small numbers are involved, that should not be so surprising; as we have noted, most of the studies of activism in the sixties showed that small numbers of students were involved then. Since political involvements in the 1960s often took the form of radical protests, the importance and scope of political activism in that decade seems in retrospect to have been given a prominence and significance far beyond its actual scope. Student political involvement today is of a different kind, but it remains today, as it was in the 1960s, an important concern of a small group of students. The difference lies not so much in the numbers of students involved, but in the form of expression.

What the *hippies* began took on the characteristics of a counter culture that was in time co-opted by the youth culture and eventually by many within the larger culture to which the movement supposedly ran "counter." It is difficult to know exactly the extent of influence of the counter culture, but it does seem that the changes in values reflected in recent reports and surveys of students are at least in part the final working out of a cultural change initiated by the hippies. Students today have brought out of the 1960s an intense concern for personal development, self-fulfillment, intensification of experience, and personal freedom. The music to which students listen and the paperbacks they read reinforce and carry forward a value system first promulgated by the counter culture. The radical tone and style of the counter culture has been softened, but the essential outlook—an inward search for self-fulfillment—is much in evidence.

76

A number of the changes promoted and effected in the sixties in curriculum and structure have extended into the 1970s. Some of the reforms, including "pass-fail" as a substitute for regular grading, seem to be falling out of favor, and some of the more unstructured "experimental courses" are not as popular as they were, but in other respects there are some significant and continuing differences. An article in *U.S. News and World Report* notes that college students are being treated more as adults, that faculty members are more committed to teaching, that there is more experimentation, but experimentation within the context of maintaining academic standards. The article points to changes in calendar, adoption of interim programs, provision of more flexible ways of meeting requirements, reduction of requirements, and more direct involvement of students in governance as examples of reforms originating in the 1960s. With reference to the last item it is noted that students have "a much larger voice than ever before in running America's universities and colleges, and in establishing the pattern of their own education."[100]

Stephen Weissman has found that, while students have stopped seizing buildings and breaking windows, they have in no sense retreated from social concerns and commitments. During his year as a political science research associate at Stanford he interviewed many students, faculty members, and administrators and concluded that at least at Stanford there is a "high level of critical social and political consciousness, although its manifestations are less dramatic, disruptive of academic routines, and all-pervasive than they were in the days of mass mobilization." The active minority is not, he contends, disillusioned, but is better organized, less "millenarian," and more strategy-oriented. Weissman sees no return to the 1950s. He comments on the increase of student-conceived courses and more openness within the university to variations in thought.[101]

Maintaining Perspective

What, finally, shall we conclude? What advice can we give to Dean Neumann? Clearly, his task in the 1970s, as it was in the 1960s, is to work with a mixed batch. The diverse student body is likely to become even more disparate as the term "college student" comes to embrace persons with wider variations in background, interests, and abilities and as various minorities, women, and older adults increase in numbers on the campus. The dean will probably have to deal with fewer organized student protests, although the possibilities of demonstrations of some sort, with the attendant confrontations, cannot be dismissed. He will continue to need to effectively explain and defend the college to a concerned constituency. There will be pockets of politically concerned and potentially active students who think of themselves as excluded, and he may find himself spending more time trying to devise new programs for them as well as for the "new students," programs that meet their particular needs. Much of his attention will be focused on working out within the college the concerns of the students who seek some kind of synthesis between life-style, career, and the academic program.

If we have learned anything from the decade of the 1960s, it is that we cannot take students for granted. The dean will need to find ways to include more students in his review of programs and in his planning for changes. He will do well to keep in touch with the latest articles and surveys that describe students generally, but more important, he will need to find ways of keeping in touch with the students at his own institution. He will need the assistance of many of the offices and staff persons on campus, but he will not be able to escape more dinners in the cafeteria with random groups of students if he wants more direct encounters with student views and concerns.

Notes

[1]Calvin Lee, *The Campus Scene, 1900-1970: Changing Styles in Undergraduate Life* (New York: David McKay Co., 1970), p. 109.
[2]*Ibid.,* pp. 108, 109.
[3]Richard E. Peterson and John A. Biloursky, *May 1970: The Campus Aftermath of Cambodia and Kent State* (Berkeley: The Carnegie Commission on Higher Education, 1971), p. xi.
[4]Carnegie Commission on Higher Education, *Dissent and Disruption: Proposals for Consideration by the Campus* (New York: McGraw-Hill Book Co., 1971), p. 29.
[5]*Ibid.,* p. 103.
[6]The President's Commission on Campus Unrest, *Campus Unrest: The Report of the President's Commission on Campus Unrest* (Washington, D.C.: Government Printing Office, 1970).
[7]"Switch for Student Activities—Working Inside 'the System' ", *U.S. News and World Report,* 76 (February 4, 1974), p. 68.

[8]Kermet Lanser, "Campus Snapshot," *Newsweek,* March 11, 1974, p. 32.

[9]Jack Magarrell, " 'Startling Shifts' Found in Youths' Views of Work, Morals," *Chronicle of Higher Education,* 8 (May 28, 1974), p. 3. Quotes from study by Daniel Yankelovich.

[10]See Kenneth Keniston, *Youth and Dissent: The Rise of a New Opposition* (New York: Harcourt Brace Jovanovich, 1971), pp. 318ff. The article, "What's Bugging the Students?" earlier appeared in the *Educational Record,* 51 (Spring 1970), pp. 116-29; references here are to the reprint in *Youth and Dissent.*

[11]Keniston subsequently presented a lecture (entitled "The Fire Outside") under the sponsorship of the Department of Higher Education of the National Council of Churches of Christ in the U.S.A., one of the Campbell Lectures for 1970, in which he elaborated on the themes of his address before the American Council on Education and used different terms for his last two categories of students.

[12]Keniston, *Youth and Dissent,* p. 329.

[13]The President's Commission on Campus Unrest, *Campus Unrest,* p. 21.

[14]*Ibid.,* pp. 32-33.

[15]Stokely Carmichael, "What We Want," in *The New Student Left: An Anthology,* ed. Michael Cohen and Dennis Hale (Boston: Beacon Press, 1966), p. 110.

[16]John Horn and Paul Knott, "Activist Youth of the 1960's: Summary and Prognosis," *Science,* 171 (March 12, 1971), p. 978.

[17]James W. Trent, "Revolution, Reformation, and Reevaluation," in *Student Activism and Protest,* ed. Harold A. Korn and Edward E. Sampson (San Francisco: Jossey-Bass, 1970), p. 29.

[18]Richard E. Peterson, *The Scope of Organized Student Protest in 1967-68* (Princeton, N.J.: Educational Testing Service, 1968), and *The Scope of Organized Student Protest in 1964-65* (Princeton, N.J.: Educational Testing Service, 1966).

[19]James A. Foley and Robert K. Foley, *The College Scene: Students Tell It Like It Is* (New York: Cowles Book Co., 1969), p. 6.

[20]*Ibid.,* pp. 49-50.

[21]Harold Hodgkinson, *Institutions in Transition* (New York: McGraw-Hill Book Co., 1971), passim.

[22]See Carnegie Commission on Higher Education, *Reform on Campus: Changing Students, Changing Academic Programs* (New York: McGraw-Hill Book Co., 1972); Carnegie Commission on Higher Education, *The Purposes and the Performance of Higher Education in the United States* (New York: McGraw-Hill Book Co., 1973); and Philip W. Semas, "Students 'Satisfied' with Education, Most of Them and Teachers Agree," *Chronicle of Higher Education,* 5 (January 18, 1971), pp. 1-2.

[23]Semas, "Students 'Satisfied' with Education," p. 1.

[24]Robert E. Karsten, "A Classification of Interpretations of the Causes and Meanings of Campus Disturbance," (Ph.D. dissertation, University of Denver, 1972).

[25]Korn and Sampson, *Student Activism and Protest,* p. ix.

[26]Karsten, "A Classification of Interpretations of the Causes and Meanings of Campus Disturbance," pp. 436-437.

[27]S. L. Halleck, "Twelve Hypotheses of Student Unrest," in *Stress and Campus Response: Current Issues in Higher Education, 1968,* ed. G. Kerry Smith, (San Francisco: Jossey-Bass, 1968), pp. 115-133.

[28]Donald R. Brown, "Student Activism and Developmental Stress," in Korn and Sampson, *Student Activism and Protest,* pp. 89-116.

[29]*Ibid.,* pp. 92-94.

[30]Edward E. Sampson, "Student Activism in a Decade of Protest," in Korn and Sampson, *Student Activism and Protest,* p. 4.

[31]Kenneth Keniston, "Sources of Student Dissent," in Korn and Sampson, *Student Activism and Protest,* p. 169.

[32]The studies are reported in Julian Foster and Durward Long, eds., *Protest! Student Activism in America* (New York: William Morrow and Co., 1970).

[33]Horn and Knott, "Activist Youth of the 1960's," pp. 977-985.

[34]Larry C. Kerpelman, "The Radical Activists: Natural Elite?" *Chronicle of Higher Education,* 7 (March 26, 1973), p. 16.

[35]*Ibid.* For a full treatment of Kerpelman's findings, see Larry C. Kerpelman, *Activists and Nonactivists: A Psychological Study of American College Students* (New York: Behavioral Publications, 1972).

[36]Peterson and Biloursky, *May 1970,* pp. 50-51.

[37]*Ibid.,* p. 52.

[38]See Peterson, "The Scope of Organized Student Protest in 1967-68," and "The Scope of Organized Student Protest in 1964-65."

[39]Quoted in Calvin Lee, *The Campus Scene,* p. 108.

[40]Kenneth Keniston, *Young Radicals: Notes on Committed Youth* (New York: Harcourt, Brace and World, 1968), pp. 301-302.

[41]Theodore Roszak, *The Making of a Counter Culture* (Garden City, N.Y.: Doubleday and Co., 1969), p. 42.

[42]Charles Reich, *The Greening of America* (New York: Random House, 1969).

[43]Fred Hechinger, "Students of the Sixties: Salvaging the Youth Movement," *Change,* 5 (June, 1973), p. 30.

[44]Peterson and Biloursky, *May 1970,* p. 80.

[45]David Gottlieb and Benjamin Hodgkins, "College Student Subcultures," in *The College Student and His Culture: An Analysis,* ed. Kaoru Yamamoto (Boston: Houghton Mifflin Co., 1968), p. 238.

[46] Harold L. Hodgkinson, *Institutions in Transition,* pp. 14-15.

[47] "Turn from Campus Violence," *U.S. News and World Report,* 71 (October 25, 1971), pp. 40-43.

[48] "New Mood of College Students," *U.S. News and World Report,* 72 (June 19, 1972), pp. 28-36.

[49] "Switch for Student Activists—Working Inside 'The System' ", p. 68.

[50] Jerrold K. Footlick, "On Campus: A Separate Peace," *Newsweek,* November 6, 1972, p. 108.

[51] Kermet Lanser, "Campus Snapshot," p. 32.

[52] Edward Faltermayer, "Youth After 'The Revolution,' " *Fortune,* 87 (March, 1973), pp. 145-158.

[53] Beverly T. Watkins, "Student Demands for 'Practical' Education Are Forcing Major Changes in Curricula," *Chronicle of Higher Education,* 8 (November 26, 1973), p. 2.

[54] Malcolm G. Scully, "Student Focus on Practicality Hits Humanities," *Chronicle of Higher Education,* 8 (February 4, 1974), pp. 1, 3.

[55] Larry Van Dyne, "5 Analyze New Religious Element in Youth Movements," *Chronicle of Higher Education,* 8 (December 3, 1973), p. 6.

[56] "What Really Matters?" *Change,* 5 (June, 1973), p. 38.

[57] "Student Voices, 1974, on Work, Love, Politics," *Change,* 6 (October, 1974), pp. 13ff.

[58] Al Senia, "The New Student Activists," *Change,* 6 (October, 1974), p. 29.

[59] Larry Van Dyne, "Student Lobbyists Shift Emphasis," *Chronicle of Higher Education,* 9 (October 15, 1974), pp. 1, 4.

[60] Byron F. Evans, "Today's Quiet Campus: Is It Just a Lull in the Revolution?" *Current,* 151 (May 1973), p. 46.

[61] "Troubles at Ohio U.," *Time,* (June 3, 1974), p. 46.

[62] Reported in the *Chronicle of Higher Education,* 10 (March 10, 1975), p. 2, under headings "Protest at Iowa State over Publish-or-Perish," "Proposed Cuts at Duke Spark Student Protest," and "Student Sues University; Says She Learned Nothing."

[63] "Brown Students Strike over Budget Issues," *Chronicles of Higher Education,* 10, (April 21, 1975), p. 2.

[64] "Sit-ins, At Brown, Minority Students Win Most Demands," *Chronicle of Higher Education,* 10 (May 5, 1975), p. 2.

[65] "At M.I.T., Students Protest Agreement to Train Engineers for Iran," *Chronicle of Higher Education,* 10 (May 5, 1975), p. 2. See also stories about Brandeis and Buffalo on same page.

[66] Jack Magarrell, "Students Fight Retrenchment: Tuition Hikes, Faculty Cuts, Service Curtailments Hit," *Chronicle of Higher Education,* 10 (April 28, 1975), pp. 1, 4.

[67]"25 Protesters Arrested at Santa Barbara," *Chronicle of Higher Education,* 10 (May 12, 1975), p. 2.

[68]"Student Protest, 1975: Stress on Economic Issues," *Chronicle of Higher Education,* 10 (June 9, 1975), p. 3.

[69]"Kent State Verdict: Plaintiffs Denied Damages in 1970 Shootings," *Chronicle of Higher Education,* 10 (September 2, 1975), p. 2.

[70]"Jackson State: Is the Memory Dimming," *Chronicle of Higher Education,* 10 (May 12, 1975), p. 1.

[71]See Daniel Yankelovich, Inc., *The Changing Values on Campus: Political and Personal Attitudes of Today's College Students,* A Survey for the JDR 3rd Fund (New York: Washington Square Press, 1972); Magarrell, " 'Startling Shifts' Found in Youths' Views of Work, Morals"; and Daniel Yankelovich, "Counterculture vs. Conservatism," the *Denver Post,* February 18, 1973, p. 37.

[72]Yankelovich, *The Changing Values on Campus,* p. 5.

[73]Lewis S. Feuer, *The Conflict of Generations* (New York: Basic Books, 1969).

[74]Yankelovich, *The Changing Values on Campus,* p. 6.

[75]*Ibid.,* p. 6.

[76]*Ibid.,* p. 8.

[77]Magarrell, " 'Startling Shifts' Found in Youths' Views of Work, Morals."

[78]The *Chronicle of Higher Education* in the fall of 1975 noted that a large number of institutions had in recent years abandoned honor codes. Cheating has increased in the highly competitive atmosphere of most colleges, and students simply will not report on fellow students. See Malcolm G. Scully, "Are Honor Systems Doomed?" *Chronicle of Higher Education,* 10 (September 2, 1975), p. 14.

[79]See Alexander Astin et al., *Supplementary Norms for Freshmen Entering College in 1966,* American Council on Education Research Reports, vol. 2, no. 3 (Washington, D.C.: American Council on Education, 1967), and *The American Freshman: National Norms for Fall, 1973,* Cooperative Institutional Research Program of the University of California at Los Angeles (Los Angeles: Graduate School of Education, University of California, Los Angeles, 1974); and Alan E. Bayer et al., *Four Years After Entry,* American Council on Education Research Reports, vol. 8, no. 1 (Washington, D.C.: American Council on Education, 1973). For recent profiles see "A Profile of This Year's Freshmen," *Chronicle of Higher Education,* 4 (January 5, 1970), p. 2, and "This Year's College Freshmen," *Chronicle of Higher Education,* 9 (January 20, 1975), p. 8.

[80]See Larry Van Dyne, "5 Analyze New Religious Elements in Youth Movement."

[81]Jack Magarrell, "Black Enrollment Rising Again," *Chronicle of Higher Education,* 10 (March 17, 1975), pp. 1, 3.

[82]"Half Million More Students: Women Dominate Fall Enrollment Increase," *Chronicle of Higher Education,* 9 (December 16, 1974), p. 2.

[83]But it should be noted that in 1972 only about one-half of the high school graduates entered college the same year they were graduated. See U.S. Department of Commerce, Bureau of the Census, *College Plans of High School Seniors, October 1972,* Current Population Reports: Population Characteristics, Series P-20, no. 252, August 1973 (Washington, D.C.: Government Printing Office, 1973), p. 4.

[84]K. Patricia Cross, "New Students in a New World," *The Future in the Making: Current Issues in Higher Education, 1973* ed. Dyckman W. Vermilye (San Francisco: Jossey-Bass, 1974), p. 89.

[85]While Cross scores the earlier attempts at remedial work for the less adequately prepared, it should be noted that in 1975 more and more colleges were returning to remedial English courses. Even the selective University of California at Berkeley reported that in the fall of 1974 some 45 percent of the entering freshman class required remedial work in English. See Malcolm G. Scully, " 'Bonehead English' with Thousands of Youth Unable to Write Properly, Colleges and High Schools Step Up Remedial Efforts," *Chronicle of Higher Education,* 10 (March 17, 1975), p. 3.

[86]Engin I. Holmstrom, *"Older" Freshmen: Do They Differ from "Typical" Undergraduates?,* American Council on Education Research Reports, vol. 8, no. 7 (Washington, D.C.: American Council on Education, 1973), passim.

[87]*Ibid.,* p. 13.

[88]Carnegie Commission on Higher Education, *Toward a Learning Society: Alternative Channels to Life, Work, and Service* (McGraw-Hill Book Co., 1973), pp. 5-6.

[89]*Ibid.,* p. 24.

[90]See U.S. Department of Health, Education, and Welfare, National Center for Educational Statistics, *Digest of Educational Statistics, 1972* (Washington, D.C.: Government Printing Office, 1972), p. 81.

[91]Carnegie Commission on Higher Education, *Toward a Learning Society,* p. 27.

[92]James R. Gass, "Learning in An Open Society: A European Viewpoint," paper presented at Twenty-ninth National Conference on Higher Education, sponsored by the American Association for Higher Education, Chicago, March 12, 1974.

[93]James O'Toole, "Education, Work and the Quality of Life," paper presented at Twenty-ninth National Conference on Higher Education, sponsored by the American Association for Higher Education, Chicago, March 11, 1974.

[94]"Now, the Self-Centered Generation," *Time,* September 23, 1974 p. 84.

[95]See John K. Folger, "The Job Market for College Graduates," *Journal of Higher Education,* 43 (March 1972), pp. 203-223.

[96]Jack Magarrell, "College Graduates Seen Exceeding Demand by 10 Percent Between 1980 and 1985," *Chronicle of Higher Education,* 8 (June 24, 1974), p. 7.

[97]Malcolm G. Scully, "Academic Job Outlook Bleak for Ph.D.'s in English," *Chronicle of Higher Education,* 8 (June 24, 1972), p. 7.

[98]"Now, the Self-Centered Generation," p. 85.

[99]Hechinger, "Students of the Sixties: Salvaging the Youth Movement," p. 32.

[100]"A Report Card on All Those Campus Reforms of the 60s," *U.S. News and World Report,* (May 6, 1974), pp. 29-40.

[101]Stephen Weissman, "No Retreat from Commitment," *The Nation,* 216 (June 18, 1973), pp. 781-785.

Governance of the University:
Systems Under Attack

"What a meeting! But I guess I shouldn't have expected anything different from a committee of senior professors. Still, as a group of rational people—supposedly the most rational our society can produce—they can be awfully irrational at times." I was sounding off to my assistant dean as we walked over to the Union for coffee.

"You're right, of course. They seem to insist on being rational about everyone else's affairs, but not their own."

We found a booth in a relatively quiet corner where we could talk more freely. He continued, "I guess their self-interest is at stake, and when that's threatened, they're going to respond with their emotions, not their heads."

"True. But what are we supposed to do, just keep going along with a status quo operation that makes everyone feel nice and secure all the time? If we never make any new proposals, no one will be threatened."

Dean Starker had soon become a valuable part of my office, a rich inheritance from my predecessor. Bright and aggressive, he was not afraid to step on a few toes. He was also a good listener, and I found myself using him increasingly as a sounding board for my latest dilemma. I continued, "Two things have become clearer to me in the last few weeks. One, we need some changes in the educational program, and the changes will probably be major ones. We've got to do something about the declining enrollments, and we have to do more for our present students. And I think I know **what** *changes to make. In the second place, whatever the changes, they won't come through that faculty Curriculum Committee, at least as it is presently constituted. I can't get them to see the whole picture; they just won't take the larger view of things."*

"So the problem is, can we come up with a committee that **will** *see things that way?"*

"Yes, but the problem may go deeper than that. It's not just a matter of who's on what committee. I've been reviewing the whole structure of the university and of our college. I think we're going to have to develop some radically new structures for making decisions. Now, everything goes through the same little group. No matter what committee meeting you go to, those same people, plus a few others, are there."

"Niemann, Crabtree, and Dunkelwald, otherwise known as the 'Academic Mafia.' "

"May I quote you?"

"You wouldn't dare."

"Okay, but you see my point?"

"And agree."

"So, what do we do?"

"For one thing, we've got to get more students on the committees. The Student Senate has a point of view that we should get into the discussion, and it won't do for us to keep reporting what the students are saying. They have to say it; and the faculty have to hear it."

"Right, we've got to get the students involved; after all, a large part of the reason we're here is because of them." I was getting more animated as the coffee worked into my system. "But, they aren't the only group. Everywhere everyone is screaming about accountability. Okay, let's take that seriously for a moment. Who are we supposed to be accountable to? To the students? To their parents? To the public? And who is the public? Employers, the government, Joe Citizen?"

"I expect the trustees fit in at some point, don't they?"

"Yes, somehow. But I have a feeling that our bright ideas won't be any more welcomed by the trustees than by the Curriculum Committee. I mean, can you see the president of Midwest Can Company even understanding what we mean by experience-based learning?"

"He might surprise you. At least, he would know what you mean by having better preparation for careers."

"Maybe, but I've been to a few board meetings. It's like I'd imagine the John Birch Society at prayer."

"Turn them loose on the Academic Mafia." Dean Starker had a twinkle in his eye. Deep down he enjoyed a bit of conflict; that was one of his strong points. As for me, I would prefer to have things peaceful. It was painful for me to referee controversies, but more and more I was seeing that controversy and progress have an unusually high correlation.

"So, why don't you bring together the Birchers and the Mafia and the students in one room and let them shoot it out?"

"A hazardous move, of course; but compared to some of your hare-brained proposals, Dean Starker, not a bad idea. We'll hold it in the *psych lab in that room with the one-way windows—and you can sit on the other side and observe."*

The Organization in Crisis

Few topics dealing with the status of higher education in the mid-1970s have elicited such broad-ranging discussion as that of governance. The disruption in the operations of colleges and universities in the United States in the 1960s projected governance to the forefront of educational discussions. In 1970, the President's Commission on Campus Unrest referred to patterns of governance as the focal point for the question of "who shall have the power to make organizational and educational decisions" and contended that governance was becoming "one of the most hotly disputed topics on American campuses today."[1] The report and recommendations of the Carnegie Commission on Higher Education on the subject of college governance begins with the statement: "The governance of higher education in the United States is currently more subject to challenge than it has been in most earlier historical periods." The report goes on to observe that governance

> has been subject, particularly over the past decade, to a number of internal and external attacks and collisions. This development reflects the pressures of conflict and change now affecting academic life, because both conflict and change make the processes of decision-making more important to those who participate in, or are substantially affected by, higher education. Central issues have been raised. Basic principles are at stake.[2]

The development of collective bargaining in the academy and the continuing debates over the nature and appropriateness of tenure have kept the discussions lively and, if anything, have made the whole situation more complex.

The discussion is not limited to the United States. In Canada, for example, the concern over the governance of postsecondary institutions also emerged with special force in the 1960s and continues to full debate in the 1970s. Reginald Edwards points to the increased presence of the federal government in higher education in

Canada following World War II and to such events in the sixties as the negotiations of Quebec for federal funds, the establishment of a Standing Committee of Ministers of Education, which in 1967 became the Inter-provincial Council of Ministers of Education, and the Technical and Vocational Training Assistance Act (1960) as signs of ferment in Canada. He observes also that virtually every province initiated an inquiry into education generally, or higher education specifically, between 1950 and 1968.[3] A publication addressed to the future of postsecondary education in Ontario calls attention to the emergence of "the student power movement as a potent factor in the educational affairs of the province" and notes the growing conflict over tenure and collective bargaining in Canada.[4] Murray Ross refers to developments in Canada as "the most profound in university government in Canada in the past half century."[5] In Germany, France, and England, too, as well as in other countries, attitudes and policies concerning governance of higher education are being reassessed and revised.

But to some observers, the situation in the United States has reached crisis proportions. Writing in the *Journal of Higher Education,* George Allan states without reservation that "we suffer a crisis in governance at our institutions of higher education."[6] In the next issue of the same journal, E.D. Duryea, writing about reform in university government, contends, "American higher education in the year 1971 clearly has entered a period of significant transition, not without parallel to a situation of a century ago."[7] Some months later, again in the same journal, Stanley Ikenberry states:

> Colleges and universities, as institutions, are in a period of stress—a great climacteric it has been called—which may well extend into the foreseeable future. In the face of the several serious challenges that have confronted and continued to trouble nearly all of higher education, it is not at all surprising that there has been incessant demands for increased institutional accountability, for stronger corporate controls, for greater power and authority of the office of the president, and for curbs on faculty autonomy.[8]

A former department chairman, looking back upon his experience writes in another journal, "My stint as department chairman convinced me our present system of academic governance is unworkable."[9]

T. R. McConnell, writing on "Faculty Government," calls attention to the "internal struggle for participation and power among students, faculty, administration, and trustees" and refers to an observation of McGeorge Bundy that "the distribution of authority and responsibility among the various members of the university is now in question as it has not been for generations."[10] Clark Kerr writes that the system of governance in American colleges and universities "is now in a crisis as never before."[11] Howard R. Bowen suggests that the universities may be at about the same stage as were industrial relations during the 1930s, a time marked by "a bitter and passionate struggle for power," but that "relationships in the universities are vastly more complex than those in industry."[12] Paul Dressel, William Faricy, and their colleagues refer to the challenges from both external and internal sources that are making governance on the campus more political in nature and "Concerns about who holds the power, how to get a piece of it, or how to influence those who hold it become the center of attention," they note. "The resolution of this complex of internal and external issues and pressures is not yet in sight."[13]

The Nature of the Crisis

Vacuum in Leadership

If there is a crisis in governance—and many other voices echo the sentiments expressed above—just how is this crisis to be described? What seem to be the fundamental issues? The literature reflects a broad spectrum of opinion in response to this question. The crisis, according to some, lies in so broadening the basis of decision-making that needed decisions can no longer be made. Scott Edwards, for one, finds academic governance based upon the "democratic-pluralist model" breaking down at the point at which decisions have to be made; he finds the organizations filled with indecision and lack of direction. Murray Ross is convinced that some moves in Canada which are broadening the base of university decision-making will destroy the nature of the university itself. George Allan sums up the issue as that of persons within the university being unable to agree with competence to exercise authority: "we cannot decide who ought to decide."

89

Duryea perceives the essential problem in governance as one of a "vacuum in central leadership" and suggests that the situation has developed because as universities have grown in size and complexity the form of governance has changed very little from that characteristic of an earlier and much simpler set of circumstances.[14] Two conflicting points of view have grown up concurrently within the university: (1) governance is viewed as a process of managing an institution, for which the primary authority is derived from the governing board, and (2) governance is viewed as essentially a function of the internal constituency, the professors and students. These two points of view have led, according to Duryea, to the development of two bureaucracies: (1) the faculty bureaucracy with the structure of departments, schools, faculty senates, and committees, and (2) the administrative structure that calls for a hierarchy of functions and officers. Duryea says the solution to the problem is "not only coordinating the two bureaucracies but combining them into joint consideration of matters of mutual interest."[15]

Clark Kerr appears to agree, and he calls for a different kind of leadership for the contemporary college and university.[16] He traces the development of leadership within the American higher educational institution from the period in which the pattern was a combination of president and lay board (until about 1860), through the emergence of the "presidential giants" (until the 1920s), to the third stage in which the faculty gained substantial power and authority (through the period of World War II), and into the fourth stage (the post-War stage) in which the function of leadership was primarily to manage the growth of the enterprise. The new period, the fifth stage, begins with the late 1960s and calls for leadership that is prepared to manage change and conflict.

In the new period, says Kerr, certain forces are pressing in from outside the institution: (1) the demographic shift in which higher institutions are experiencing a slowing down of growth, (2) the changing labor market for college graduates, (3) the increase in public power and control for higher education, (4) the increasing tendency on the part of students to demand specific changes and developments, (5) the new electronic technology that is changing forms and modes of communication, (6) the expansion of variety and types of postsecondary educational opportunities, and (7) a reemphasis upon individual and humanistic values. Other pressures are coming from within: (1) students asking for more influence over more parts of the university, (2) the greater fluctuation in student choice of specialization and less flexibility on the part of faculty, (3) the greater interest on the part of faculty in collective bargaining, (4) the greater divergence among faculty regarding academic matters, (5) the pressure from women and ethnic minorities for more places in the faculty ranks, (6) the general aging of the faculty, (7) more evidence of counter-cultural life styles among both students and faculty, (8) the greater opposition to the general culture from the academics, and (9) the narrowing income differential between the more and less highly educated.[17] These combined pressures lead to basic conflicts over power and principle and to increased demands upon administrators. Administrators will now be cast more frequently into the role of political leaders, "such as a mayor or governor, using persuasion and working with others to move in progressive ways to keep conflict within reasonable bounds." The administrator in the new period will need to focus on the "selection of goals, the procurement and assignment of means, the achievement of consent for new approaches, and the interpretation of the new order to interested publics."[18] The administrator will be a manager of both change and conflict.

Conflicting Structures

In a series of essays on *The Embattled University*, Stephen R. Graubard also calls attention to the "erosion of authority" and observes that not only have the students become more political, but the faculty as well have developed a political stance.[19] Presidents and deans are hard put to respond to the conflicting pressures, and at the same time there has been "a massive loss of public confidence in America's higher educational system."[20] He predicts that out of the tensions will develop new types of institutional arrangements.

In a similar vein, but placing the situation in the broader context of the relationship between parties of interest within the university, George Allan sees the crisis as arising out of the tension between authoritarianism and democracy, both essential characteristics of the university.[21] The challenge, as he sees it, is to keep the two principles operative, to keep the "two forms of decision-making so that each can complement the others." An organization which is excessively authoritarian or excessively democratic suffers either from its arrogance or its ignorance. It is not a matter of developing a means of working between the two extremes, but rather of devising "an interplay between these extremes themselves."[22] Allan proposes some structures which he believes will make possible this interplay.

Kenneth Mortimer is less sanguine about the possibility of developing such an interplay, because he sees serious problems in making clear distinctions between joint participation (which may be referred to as "democratic") and separate jurisdiction (a form of "authoritarianism"). Over 300 institutions are in the process of experimenting with various types of campus governance bodies composed of students, faculty, and administrators. To establish structures for joint participation, these institutions face the critical matters of determining representation, the appropriate structures to be developed, and the relationship between campus-wide structures and existing structures. He argues that "those who yearn for peace in colleges and universities will find it a relative condition. Institutions of higher education will have to learn to live with more or less permanent conflicts and seek to make them serve the organization rather than destroy it."[23]

Broader Accountability

The issues are not limited to the way in which the university functions as an organization in relationship to its own needs and purposes. As T. R. McConnell points out, universities are finding themselves being called upon to respond in more ways to the wide public: "Perhaps as never before, institutions, administrators, faculty members, and even students find themselves accountable to a wide range of both internal and external agencies. Institutions and faculties, much to their concern and distress, have discovered that their autonomy is by no means absolute, but that in fact it is often highly vulnerable."[24]

If the university is being increasingly held accountable, is it accountable in the same way in which a business enterprise is accountable to a board of directors or to the public-at-large? Earl Bolton and Fredric Genck refer to the university as a management enterprise, and from the point of view of management consultants, they make a number of recommendations to improve the efficiency of the organization.[25] This is only one of many articles that might be noted which discuss the university in terms of more efficient management procedures. Without entering the debate as to whether the college and university should be viewed as another kind of managed enterprise, one may refer to the observation of Stanley Ikenberry in which, while recognizing many similarities between academic institutions and other complex organizations, he points up some critical differences. He calls for "new patterns of accommodation that preserve the special qualities of academic organizations, including the academic freedom and professorial flexibility essential to effective faculty performance, but that also strengthen the central institutional leadership capacity and accountability."[26] He notes that colleges and universities do not or are unable to define goals with a great precision, that they are inherently decentralized organizations, and that they are composed principally of professional personnel.

It is with regard to the third characteristic that the issue of accountability becomes sharpened. Professionals are oriented to their own voluntary associations and are accustomed to exercising their own form of self-control. On the other hand, complex organizations are more bureaucratically structured and call for following procedures and establishing institutional goals. The issue of accountability is joined in the requirement that institutions "strike a better balance between the requirements for professional autonomy and academic freedom on the one hand and the necessity for greater institutional accountability and effectiveness on the other."[27]

A Complex Problem

How does one summarize the views regarding the issues facing the contemporary university in the realm of governance? Ikenberry lists the major themes that emerged when a group of 15 scholars met to discuss the restructuring of university organization and governance. There were certain recurring themes: (1) a decline in individual and institutional autonomy, (2) increased procedural regularization, (3) more candid recognition and management of conflict, (4) greater decentralization, (5) an emerging challenge to professional values, and (6) the apparent demise of the academic mystique. The decline in autonomy is reflected in broader participation and involvement in decision-making by persons

93

within the academic community as well as without. Procedural regularization refers to the move to establish campus-wide and community-wide councils and assemblies and the development of more specific regulations for the conduct of activities within the university. Several of the papers in the conference pointed up the factor of conflict and the need to recognize and manage it. Decentralization was noted as a way of dealing with some of the conflicts within the institutions, namely by developing ways for better representation of the factions within the university. The professional characteristic of the faculty is being challenged, and the seeming rationality of the academic community is being questioned as the public becomes more and more aware of the conflicts and problems within the university.[28]

The Carnegie Commission report on *Governance of Higher Education* lists six priority problems. These are: (1) adequate provision for institutional independence, (2) the role of the board of trustees and of the president, (3) collective bargaining by faculty members, (4) rules and practices governing tenure, (5) student influence on the campus, and (6) the handling of emergencies.[29]

There seems to be general agreement that colleges and universities are facing a governance crisis. We use the word "governance" as a broad term to distinguish it from the concerns which seem to be emerging in administration, because administration in its narrower definition relates only to implementation of established policy. The crisis in governance is much broader and goes to the heart of the matter of who will decide what and under what circumstances. It is likely that new structures for making policy will evolve in the years ahead. The patterns that emerge will be different types of institutions, but as I see it, all institutions will have to answer two fundamental questions: Who shall be involved in making policy? How shall they be involved? We now examine in more detail the constituent groups that will be involved in working out the new governance patterns.

Participation of the Public

With increased emphasis upon accountability for private as well as tax-supported institutions, various segments of the public will demand and secure more opportunity to debate the goals and policies of colleges and universities. In particular, two kinds of groups will be more involved: (1) board of control and (2) state authorities through legislative committees, boards, and other agencies. In California, the State University governing board has on occasion entered directly into the internal operations of the university system and has been criticized for so doing by faculty and administration. Some presidents in other circumstances seem to take pride in being able to report that they keep the board concentrating on approving budgets and building plans and keep them relatively ignorant of the internal operations of the institution. In the meantime, both faculties and students are seeking more direct access to the board of control, both to engage members of the board in discussion and debate and to achieve membership on the board. Of course legislatures have always exercised a measure of control, direct or indirect, on public institutions, but for both the private and public sectors, the emergence of governing or coordinating boards in more and more states has had an impact on the day-to-day decisions of these institutions. While statewide governing boards have restricted their efforts to the public sector, coordinating boards, still in the majority, have in some states effectively incorporated private institutions into statewide planning.

Boards of Control

An executive of an international public relations firm, John F. Budd, Jr., thinks that college boards in the 1970s have very little power, that for decades they have "betrayed their trust by neglecting to live up to their powers and responsibilities."[30] On the other hand, in an article written some years earlier, M. M. Chambers asserts that

> the university is appropriately governed, in the eyes of the law, by a body of men and women chosen as representatives of the general public. This body—the governing board, constituting a single artificial person—legally is the university.[31]

Chambers' statement may be contrasted not only with Budd's allegation, but also with this observation by Steven V. Roberts in a discussion of the battle at UCLA in 1969 over the status of Angela Davis:

More important, the issue calls into question the basic relationship between the regents and the university. Who is boss? Twenty-four men, most of them appointed by the Governor, who have little expertise in the field? Or the faculties and the administration of the university's nine campuses?[32]

And thus the issue is joined. What is the role of the board of control in the contemporary university? What should it be?

Early in its history, American higher education became committed to a system of lay government, a system in which the major decisions were to be made by boards of nonresident governors who were not teachers. With regard to this structure, Richard Hofstadter observes:

> The essence of lay government is that the trustees, not the faculties, are, in law, the college or university, and that legally they can hire and fire faculty members and make almost all the decisions governing the institution.[33]

He contends, however, that the appearance of the lay board has hampered the organization, initiative, and self-confidence of the American college professoriate and has in general lowered the status of the professor in the wider community.

The American system of lay government was not planned by the founders of the colonial colleges, but rather it grew out of the conditions of religious and social life in the new world. The first two colonial colleges, Harvard and William and Mary, attempted at the beginning to follow the governmental patterns of the English colleges, which placed control in the hands of the faculty. The problem was that when the colleges were established in the New World there was no established body of scholars, and it was difficult, if not impossible, to commit a college to a group of men yet unknown and unchosen and to give to this group the full powers of management and resources. Thus, both of these new colleges developed dual boards; at Harvard, the Board of Overseers and the Corporation; at William and Mary, the Board of Visitors and the President and Masters. By the early nineteenth century the Harvard Corporation had become essentially a lay group, and at William and Mary the President and Masters apparently never developed any great power. In the creation of the third and fourth colonial colleges the governing power was clearly placed in a lay board. The first charter of Yale (1701) gave the trustees the authority to "erect, form, direct, order, establish, improve and at all times and in all suitable ways for the future to encourage" the new school. Princeton (1746) began under a charter which granted all powers of government to the trustees.

In the early years, indeed well toward the end of the nineteenth century, the boards of control appear to have exercised significant power in directing the course of American colleges and universities. But with the emergence of the academic freedom debates at the end of the nineteenth century and during the early years of the twentieth century, new forces were brought to play which increased the autonomy of the faculty. Some observers would suggest that from that time until the latter part of the 1960s, with the rise of dissent and revolt, boards of control had become relatively ineffective and powerless. This is an overgeneralization, and there are certainly exceptions, but the broad conclusion can probably be documented.

One of the first more or less systematic studies of boards of control was that produced by Hubert T. Beck. Beck observed that board members hardly represented the general population. Because they came almost entirely from the wealthy and more conservative elements within the general population, he questioned whether these men and women could understand sufficiently the nature of the problems facing American colleges and universities.[34] Later, Christopher Jencks and David Riesman observed:

> We did not think colleges were primarily shaped by the boards that formally control them, since they were much more alike than their boards. Still less do we believe that the character of colleges depends on who appoints and regulates the board. Colleges are shaped by many interest groups. A few exercise their influence through representation on the board, but most do not.[35]

Differing with the conclusion of Jencks and Riesman, Rodney T. Hartnett, in a later study of boards of directors undertaken under the auspices of the Educational Testing Service, states:

> Those who would argue that the trustee holds no authority or influence need only to examine some of the trustee attitudes

regarding academic freedom against the backdrop of trustee faculty conflicts. In the fall of 1968, for example, the regents of the University of California voted to withhold regular college credit for a series of speeches by Eldridge Cleaver.[36]

Hartnett was responsible for a questionnaire study of boards of control in connection with the revision of Morton Rauh's book on college trustees. In collaboration with Rauh, he developed an eight-page questionnaire which was mailed to trustees of over 500 colleges and universities. Responses were received from more than 5,000 board members. On the basis of the trustees' responses Hartnett concluded that it would be naive to refer to "the college trustee" as if there were one such type of person. Indeed, he found a good bit of diversity between and among the trustees serving on boards of different types of institutions. Nevertheless, Hartnett did generalize to the extent that he identified a modal or typical trustee, described as "white, male, in his late 50's, well educated and financially very successful." Moreover, the current trusteeship was likely to be the board member's first and he was serving on only one board. Trustees were also found to be somewhat cautious and conservative on matters of academic freedom, particularly trustees of institutions in the South and the Rocky Mountain regions. Oddly enough, while trustees who were business executives were *most* likely to favor "running the college like a business," those boards with the largest proportion of business executives were found to be *least* likely to espouse a "business orientation" for the institution.[37]

In general, trustees were found to prefer a modified "top-down" form of institutional government, one in which the president is clearly in charge, and often they preferred to exclude members of the faculty from those decisions having to do with the academic program of the institution. These decisions they wanted the administration to make, while they themselves were prepared to act directly in the selection of the president, in matters of finance and the physical plant, and in "external affairs." Trustees were also found to be more conservative than faculty in political party affiliation and ideology and in attitudes about higher education. The amount of time spent in trustee matters varied greatly, both within institutions and across institutions of different types. For the total sample, the median number of hours per month spent on trustee business was slightly more than five, with attendance at full board meetings and committee meetings comprising more than half of all the time expended. Trustees were found not to have read, or even to have heard of, the more relevant books and journals in higher education.[38]

The January 1967 issue of *Fortune* magazine provided an abbreviated case study of the role of the board of trustees at two institutions, the University of Pittsburgh and the University of Rochester. The opening paragraph is worth quoting:

> For U.S. business executives of a generation or so ago, election to a university trusteeship was as commonplace—and often about as meaningful—as the award of a good conduct medal for a G.I. Though the charters of private universities invest the lay trustees with supreme legal authority and final responsibility, the post was regarded for the most part as honorific. But that was yesterday's university and yesterday's trustee. Today the world of higher education is seething with expansion, change, and challenge. . . . All this has substantially changed the role of the trustee. His job is no longer merely to conserve funds; he must think up imaginative new ways to finance projects of monumental magnitude. And where he once discretely kept hands off the curricula and everything else that had to do with the learning process, he now must at least acquaint himself with the educational, research, and auxiliary service programs, not only because he has to determine their financial feasibility, but because he has to interpret the goals and needs of the university to the community, to the surrounding business interests, and to the government.[39]

The article describes the relationships of the boards of trustees to the two institutions. Both institutions were seeking improved academic quality. Both in a sense achieved their goals. But the University of Pittsburgh became virtually bankrupt and had to ask for state assistance. The University of Rochester developed an investment policy that in 1967 gave it an endowment with a market value of $268,680,000, sixth highest among American colleges and universities.

In the case of the University of Pittsburgh, the board of trustees left the management of the enterprise almost entirely to President Litchfield. Problems arose from misunderstandings regarding the contributions the trustees themselves would make to the funding of

99

the institution. Also, Litchfield operated on an ever-growing annual deficit. On the other hand, the University of Rochester trustees had developed a long tradition of financial management, and while they gave considerable freedom to President Wallis, they were informed and involved in the financial development of the institution.

In an essay in one of the publications of the Carnegie Commission on Higher Education, James A. Perkins writes about the conflicting responsibilities of governing boards. He points out that the original role of the board, particularly in the United States, was that of an agent of its creator, the church or the state; it was the agency of the organization that brought the institution into existence. Subsequently, the board was asked to serve as a "bridge" between society and the university: as the university became more and more involved in research and service, the board began to represent the university's interest to society as well as society's interest to the university. But now the board is being asked to serve as an agent of the university community. The board "has assumed more and more the function as a court of last resort for the university's various internal constituencies," and it is also being asked "to transform the university into an active instrument for achieving social justice in society."[40]

Perkins refers to the internal tensions within an institution in which the board must assert its decision-making rights based upon legal authority and the university's internal assembly must assert its decision-making rights based upon representation of internal university constituencies: "The two voices will have to be merged into a new and larger notion of public and private interest. . . . The task for the board may now have to become a link between the university assembly and the external coordinating body, a task which will require patient statesmanship to succeed."[41]

There are those who would consider Perkins's statement too moderate. At the annual meeting of the Association of Governing Boards in 1974, there seemed to be "widespread agreement that trustees should assume a bigger role in handling such issues as faculty workloads, tenure, and even the content of the curriculum."[42] One speaker at the conference called for much more involvement in curriculum and faculty workloads. He called for the trustees to become more accountable for what is happening within the institutions and stated, "The very essence of the university is

wrapped up in two phrases: 'What is taught' and 'how it is taught.' "
He went on to say that trustees themselves must either exact
accountability of the institution or see to it that someone else does
and reports back to the trustees.

John Budd, who was earlier quoted as accusing the trustees of
"neglecting to live up to their powers and responsibilities,"
suggested the system should be "either abandoned outright or
drastically revived and restructured."[43] If the trustees are to begin to
make an important contribution to higher education, they must,
according to Budd,

> abandon their traditional secrecy; open their meetings to the
> public and to students; give the public, on their own initiative,
> an annual and candid accounting of their university; seek out
> platforms and opportunities to talk about higher education; use
> the machinery of communication they apply so swiftly in their
> own businesses to the problems of communications in higher
> education.[44]

In much the same vein, if somewhat more moderately, Harold
Martin, president of Union College, has emphasized the importance
of an active role on the part of trustees:

> By the average college and university faculty body, trustees are
> most admired for generous passivity. In their view, the academic
> business of the college or university is their business. In fact,
> however, the business, even the academic business, of a college
> or university is faculty business only in a narrow sense. It is
> fundamentally public business, whether the college or university
> is private or public; and because it is public business, the
> management of it must clearly link responsibility with public
> accountability.[45]

Martin calls for trustees with an "informed perspective," and
emphasizes the need for administration to take more initiative in
providing the trustees with the kind of input that will assist them to
be better informed on campus developments. T. R. McConnell
writes that, if trustees are to exercise their powers effectively, boards
will have to be reconstituted to provide for a much greater diversity
in membership. He contends that membership should no longer be
confined "to those who represent wealth, position, or political

power, but should be extended to those who represent a wide range of economic and political interests and a diverse pattern of ethnic and cultural backgrounds." He suggests that boards should include a substantial proportion of faculty. He finds, however, relatively little actual change in the composition of governing boards in recent years.[46]

Henry Mason entitles his review of the literature about governing boards, "The Reality of Limited Power vs. The Myth of Unlimited Sovereignty." He finds that while the board is "supreme" and "sovereign" in a legal sense, it "interferes only sporadically and superficially with a university's decision-making."[47] The key function, as Mason sees it, is that the board represents the "outside public." The board reminds the university of its place in society, shields the university from dysfunctional public pressures, and sometimes points out that extremes in academic freedom cannot be tolerated. He also, with McConnell, argues for some faculty membership on boards.

Examining further the data collected for his 1968 survey of boards of trustees, Rodney Hartnett later found fairly high correlations between the views of trustees and faculty. He observed "that on a campus where the trustees have liberal views regarding academic freedom, the faculty members tend to perceive the institution as being a 'free' place."[48] To Hartnett, this and other positive correlations between views of trustees and perceptions of faculty suggest that the trustees do influence the climate of the college. The problem is, of course, one of determining which came first, i.e., do trustees set the climate, or does the climate condition the kinds of trustees selected? A study by Junus Davis and Steve Batchelor found both presidents and trustees agreeing that the president of the institution is the key figure in decision-making.[49] It might be inferred, accordingly, that if the trustees influence the climate of the institution, they, in turn, are greatly influenced by the president as a decision-maker.

As revealed by the studies that have been undertaken involving board members—and there are but a few comprehensive studies—we have only a limited understanding of how effective boards function or even of what constitutes an effective board. Yet we have calls for reconstituting the board, having the board more effectively take up its proper power, or even doing away with the lay board.

102

There is little question that the board has legal responsibility for the college or university it maintains; but the specific role played by boards is far from clear, or, perhaps more accurately, the role varies greatly with type of institution, time, and circumstances. And perhaps that is the strength of the lay board: it can vary its role with type of institution, time, and circumstances. As collective bargaining becomes more a part of the collegiate scene, however, it will be interesting to see what new role the board may be called upon to play. Among public institutions, the board may be bypassed in favor of executive or legislative offices. Among private institutions, the board will almost inevitably be the locus of final appeal.

State Coordinating Boards and Federal Legislation

The extent to which the board of control, as a representative of the public, has been and will become more directly involved in the internal activity of the university is still a matter of debate, although some critics of the past performance of the board are asking that it have a much greater involvement in deciding internal policies and that new structures be developed to effect such involvement. But the board of control is not the only means by which public interest has been or can be represented in policy formation and internal operations. The statewide higher education coordinating body, whatever its official title, may be emerging in the 1970s as a significant agency of public concern. Lyman Glenny wrote in the mid-1960s that prior to 1945 the main characteristic of higher education in most states was a "lack of system and rationality in organization."[50] Colleges and universities, public and private, were largely independent of each other, even within a state. After World War II, however, the "happy anarchy" began to change to new forms of cooperation and coordination "with institutional independence only within certain new parameters." The move to coordination did not come out of foresight and planning by educators, but arose rather "from demands of legislators and governmental agencies for more efficient use of public monies." In further characterizing the development, Glenny writes that legislators

> wanted to eliminate wasteful duplication of programs resulting from competition among state institutions, to facilitate realistic and scientific budget requests, and to establish the rationale for developing new institutions and campuses. In attempting to

103

protect the integrity of their own institutions, educators until recently generally have opposed coordination, particularly through new state commissions with legal power.[51]

Whether they opposed the development or not, educators in the mid-1970s are faced with the reality of increased statewide coordination. In 1965 Glenny could write about the "classic condition of autonomy" in ten states. Ten years later, there were only three states with no statewide agency—Delaware, Nebraska, and Vermont—and one of the three, Nebraska, had a voluntary association.

Robert Berdahl's study, published in 1971, constituted up to that date the most comprehensive review of these developments. In introducing his survey, Berdahl pointed up the significance of state involvement in higher education, even if, as then appeared to be the case, the federal government would be taking an increasingly important role in setting directions for American higher education. He wrote:

> Increased Federal aid notwithstanding, state governments will continue to be the major source of funds for all public institutions of higher education . . . [and] it is likely that state support for private as well as public higher education will increase in some states. . . . Even if Federal aid to higher education grows by a large percentage, it does not necessarily mean a proportionate decrease in state influence. . . . If Federal block grants are given to the states, the latter will have even wider influence over higher education than they presently exercise. . . . Even if the state role in financing higher education were to diminish markedly, all institutions—public and private—would still have to function in a context of state law and state sovereignty.[52]

The development of the so-called "1202 commissions," to which reference will be made later, would seem to make Berdahl's final statement above almost prophetic.

The catalogue of state agencies compiled by Berdahl, accurate up to early 1970, shows 27 coordinating boards, 14 of which were given regulating powers, and 19 consolidated statewide governing boards. Four states reported no boards; one, Indiana, has since established a statewide coordinating agency. The oldest governing board is that of Nevada, the Board of Regents, established in 1864. The oldest coordinating board is New York's Board of Regents, established in 1784. Of the 27 coordinating boards, 18 had been established during or since 1960. Only 5 of the governing boards had been established during or since 1960; some 13 were in existence by 1945 or before.[53]

A later review of developments on the statewide scene is that by Larry Van Dyne. Writing in late 1974, Van Dyne noted the rapid development of the coordinating board; in 1954 there were only 4 coordinating boards, while in 1974 there were 27.[54] There had been some shifts, however, since Berdahl's study. Berdahl classified both New Hampshire and Oregon as having "governing" boards; both are listed by Van Dyne as having "coordinating" boards. And Wisconsin, Pennsylvania, and North Carolina, with "coordinating" boards according to Berdahl's list, were now identified as having "governing" boards. Indiana in Berdahl's list had a voluntary committee, but was shown as having a coordinating board in 1974. We thus have a net increase of one governing board and no change in number of coordinating boards since 1969–70.

The distinction between the governing and coordinating board is that the former is the legal governing and regulating agency for the institutions under its control, while in the latter various levels of review and moral and political suasion are employed. Governing boards relate almost exclusively, if not entirely, to the public institutions under their direction. Coordinating boards can and do relate to private institutions in various ways. A study completed in the fall of 1969 observed that in 14 states the official state planning agency was charged "with some responsibility for private institutions in overall planning for higher education," and in 3 of the states the law stipulated that private institutions *must* be included.[55] Some 15 additional state agencies indicated some degree of recognition of private institutions in their planning activities. (The planning agencies to which the study refers were not in all cases the state coordinating boards.)

Berdahl wrote that except for scattered programs and certain state scholarship plans—in 1974 there were almost 40 state scholarship or aid programs in effect—few state actions have been directly relevant to private higher education.[56] The emergence of several state reports—Illinois, Missouri, New York, Texas—dealing exclusively with the role of private higher education suggests, however, that more of a concern for public-private relations is developing. California and Washington State studies also devoted chapters to private higher education. One of the first, if not the first, of such reports examined state-by-state the programs relevant to private institutions.[57] One of the authors of that report, in a subsequent paper prepared for a Legislative Work Conference of the Southern Regional Education Board, noted some of the reasons for involving private higher educational institutions in statewide planning. He concluded:

> Of all of the arguments advanced, I think the most telling is that certain private higher educational institutions by virtue of history, strength of programs, or even chance development, have made and continue to make significant contributions to the advancement of the purposes of higher education in the state and in the nation. They are performing a public purpose with the assistance of private benefactions. Statewide planning should take into consideration these contributions. States ought not to ignore any resources available within the confines of the state.[58]

In outlining the advantages of the coordinating board over the governing board, Lyman Glenny and his colleagues observe that the "one great paramount advantage" is that coordinating boards can act as umbrella agencies under which a variety of institutions, agencies, commissions, and councils can be related to statewide efforts. They note in particular how private institutions can participate in funding programs, state planning, and information gathering.[59]

Van Dyne's review of developments in statewide coordination calls attention to the organization of the State Higher Education Executive Officers (SHEEO) and suggests that SHEEO may be credited with a substantial role in getting Congress to recognize the importance of statewide planning and coordination in the 1972 amendments on higher education.[60] Section 1202 of the Higher Education Amendments of 1972 requires any state that wants to receive assistance under Section 1203—which authorizes grants and assistance for comprehensive statewide planning—to establish a state postsecondary commission that is broadly and equitably representative of various types of postsecondary educational institutions.

106

After a year of giving the commissions limited emphasis, the Office of Education apparently decided actively to encourage the creation of the new agencies. The U.S. Commissioner of Education wrote to all governors announcing that the Office of Education would allocate at least $1 million for statewide planning grants to be administered by the "1202 commissions."[61] The governors were to notify the commissioner by April 15, 1974, if they had decided to establish a 1202 commission. The deadline was subsequently extended to April 25, and 43 states plus the District of Columbia, American Samoa, Guam, and Puerto Rico reported having established such commissions. The states had three options in meeting the request: 15 established new agencies; 19 designated an existing agency or commission; 9 augmented an existing agency or commission to meet the requirements of the legislation.[62] By April 1975, a total of 46 states and all 5 eligible territories had established or designated state commissions to meet the requirements of Section 1202. At that time, only Colorado, North Carolina, Tennessee, and Wisconsin had not established such planning agencies.[63]

Commenting on the intent of Section 1202, John D. Phillips, associate commissioner for student assistance of the United States Office of Education, listed six concerns of Congress: (1) to encourage and support comprehensive state planning for postsecondary education through representative postsecondary state commissions; (2) to insure that representatives from various types of postsecondary education would, with representatives of the general public, work together in planning at the state level; (3) to encourage the establishment of committees or task forces that include as broad a range as possible of publics and agencies that can be related to the work of the commissions; (4) to encourage states to develop an overall framework and process to encompass an integrated plan for all postsecondary institutions, public and private, nonprofit and proprietary; (5) to encourage comprehensive, coordinated approaches to statewide planning; (6) to insure that proposals for funding under sections of the law referring to the improvement of postsecondary education are within the context of statewide planning.[64]

Through the requirement that the commissions be "broadly and equitably representative of the general public and private non-profit and proprietary institutions of postsecondary education," the legislation clearly incorporates private higher education into statewide planning. And the further comments of Phillips on his sixth point are significant:

> While it should be noted that the law empowers the state commissions only to review and not to veto such applications [for funding to improve postsecondary educational institutions], the knowledge and skills acquired by the commissions in the conduct of various statewide planning activities should be of major value to the HEW office responsible for awarding funds under this program.[65]

The commissions are thus designated as agencies to review proposal applications for federal programs. To some, this kind of intervention potentially gives the state agencies considerable power over higher education within each state, both public and private. The director of the National Center for Higher Education Management Systems, Ben Lawrence, notes a further fear expressed by some critics of the commissions, who view them as the first step in a federal effort "to standardize the organizational processes and jurisdictional arrangements by which state planning of postsecondary education takes place."[66] Is this the first step in a federal takeover of postsecondary education planning?

Whether one views the development of the 1202 commissions as a threat or a promise, it is clear that the implementation of the legislation provides more opportunity by the general public to review and influence the work of higher, or perhaps more properly, postsecondary, educational institutions.

At another level, the efforts of the federal government to encourage the employment of minorities and women is still another way in which public pressure can be brought to bear on higher education. The United States Office for Civil Rights, in requiring universities to take "affirmative action" in ending discrimination in employment practices, has had the effect of creating a new kind of academic administrator. In April 1975 some 400 affirmative action officers meeting in Austin, Texas, formed the American Association for Affirmative Action. Among the group, some were of the opinion that the new organization should serve as a political action group.[67] In June, 29 universities were warned that the federal government would withhold contracts unless the institutions came up with acceptable affirmative action plans; some $65 million in federal contracts was involved.[68] A month later several of the universities were given additional time to produce acceptable plans for hiring more women and members of minority groups. One university refused to sign such an agreement and won a temporary restraining order barring the civil rights agency from blocking the grant of $3.8 million from the National Cancer Institute.[69]

Speaking to the National Association of College and University Business Officers in July 1975, the vice-president of the American Council on Education, Stephen K. Bailey, reviewed the results of a small sampling of colleges and universities regarding responses to various types of federal social legislation. He took the position that colleges and universities were being forced to dip into their reserves to meet the rising costs of complying with federal social programs seeking to "achieve a variety of social ends only marginally related to the educational objectives of colleges and universities."[70] While recognizing that higher educational institutions had been as guilty as other segments of society in discriminating, he asked that the government be fair and follow due process in enforcing the regulations. By late summer of 1975 the conflict between federal agencies and the universities over affirmative action seemed on the way to something of a resolution. A number of the college associations were drawing up position papers on the matter, the Carnegie Council on Policy Studies in Higher Education released a series of recommendations, and the Department of Labor was holding hearings on problems encountered by colleges and universities in developing and carrying out affirmative action programs.[71] At least an uneasy peace seemed in the offing.

The Faculty

In the first universities of Europe the faculty had almost exclusive control of the affairs of the institution. Indeed, except in the University of Bologna and those following its pattern in Southern Europe, the masters were the primary elements constituting the university. The masters of Paris and Oxford set the regulations for the conduct of the academic community and determined the manner of teaching, the requirements for degrees, and the basis for entry into the guild of masters. At Paris the regent masters were the "university" and took the first steps toward forming a *universitas,* a legal corporation, about 1209. The universities usually entrusted the preparation and formulation of their statutes to a committee of masters; this was how the first statutes of Paris were formulated, and the earliest dated Oxford statute was drafted by a body of seven masters.[72] In his study of the earliest statutes of Cambridge, M. B. Hackett describes the governing body as consisting of the chancellor, the head of the corporation, and the regent masters. They, in turn, elected two of their members as rectors, to whom most of the administrative tasks were assigned; they also designated other administrative assistants. The chancellor acted on behalf of the society. The statutes described the admission of scholars, regulations concerning lectures and disputations, and machinery for safeguarding the economic and social interests of the society.[73]

While the first American foundations followed in many respects the traditions of the English universities, the establishment of the lay board, as Hofstadter has observed, effectively limited the faculty in its organization and initiative.[74] In his sketch of the historical development of the governance structure in American higher education, Walter Schenkel observes that, even in the post–Civil War period, "faculty participation in governance was unheard of. Faculty members in the early universities were hired to teach."[75] University presidents such as Gilman of Johns Hopkins and Harper of the University of Chicago made it clear that faculty participation in university governance was limited to educational concerns. University teaching emerged as a career only in the late 1800s when more advanced training for faculty led to the kind of specialization that created academic departments. The next step toward professionalization of faculty was reached with the introduction of tenure:

> Until 1906, the year the Carnegie retirement plan for professors was established, a teacher had no guarantee of a secure job. Only the introduction of tenure finally made it possible for the faculty as a group to claim the right to participate, without fear of reprisal, in some areas of governance. Limited faculty control over certain aspects of the educational program had existed in some of the early universities, but the faculty received the right of control only over the educational area in the first decade of the twentieth century.[76]

It was only with the rise of this professionalism in the first decade of the twentieth century, the conflicts over academic freedom, the emergence of the American Association of University Professors, and the increased stature of higher education itself that the critical issues of faculty involvement in institutional decision-making began to surface.

T. R. McConnell writes that the most significant period of expansion of faculty role has been since World War II:

> One of the most significant changes since World War II is the great growth of faculty power, coupled with rapid faculty professionalism. Either by formal delegation or by tacit approval, college and university faculties have attained a high degree of professional self-government.[77]

This greater involvement and the demand for even more involvement in university affairs comes at a time, oddly enough, when faculty as professionals are also becoming more identified with professional fields than with the institutions in which they hold appointments. Duryea comments on this paradox:

> The growth of specialized knowledge in terms of disciplinary and professional associations on a national and even international basis has brought with it a concomitant outward movement of faculty members. They find their professional relationships, career lines, and related values in interinstitutional rather than internal commitments. . . . Yet, in the main, faculties remain adamant about turning government over to administrators.[78]

And it would seem that it is this tension between the faculty wanting to be closely identified with their professional fields and also wanting to have an effective voice in university governance that contributes to no little degree to the crisis in governance in the 1970s.

Morris Keeton has argued that the "primary justification for faculty voice in campus governance is the fact that faculty alone have the kinds and degrees of qualification essential to the task of a college or university."[79] The faculty, he suggests, are the teachers, the researchers, and the specialists that provide the various forms of service required by the institution, and even with considerable faculty mobility, this faculty has represented the "largest element of continuity and experience with the tasks and problems of the campus." By way of contrast, the student generation is short, and turnover among top administrative officers has been fairly rapid. Keeton recognizes that there are some problems, however, in turning the operation of the institution entirely over to faculty. Educators as experts in their own respective fields tend to overestimate the significance of that expertise in issues of campus governance. Heavy involvement of faculty in governance involves heavy demands upon time and takes faculty away from tasks for which they are primarily appointed. According to Keeton's report, all of this argues for some form of shared governance as the most appropriate approach.

In pleading for more faculty involvement, Keeton rejects the idea of a "zero-sum" game, a game in which one party loses if another gains. In arguing for a "positive-sum" game, he points out that in business, for example, it is possible for the lender and the borrower both to benefit. The lender gives up certain uses of his capital and derives other benefits such as interest and possibly capital, while the borrower is able to get underway an enterprise which benefits him as well as others. In similar manner, faculty and administration need to combine their efforts.

Keeton's volume grew out of the work of the American Association for Higher Education–National Education Association task force on faculty representation and academic negotiations. Established in July 1966, the task force presented its report in 1967. The group visited 34 institutions in different parts of the country, and on the basis of the data developed some generalizations about faculty participation. The principle of "shared authority" is described as the middle zone of a continuum which ranges over administrative dominance–administrative primacy–shared authority–faculty primacy–faculty dominance. Under the concept of shared authority, "both faculty and administration exercise effective influence in decision-making."[80] The report suggested that the concept of shared authority may be implemented through various procedures, but that the most effective approach would probably be through the development of an academic senate comprised of faculty members and officials of the administration. In addition, a joint grievance committee could be established to handle disputes involving issues of personnel administration. The report stated that effective implementation calls for a careful examination of faculty and administrative roles "to help determine the allocation

112

of authority that will enhance most effectively the quality of performance of institutions of higher education."[81] The report argued that the concept of shared authority avoids the competitive model, and that through cooperation "both parties may be able to achieve their goals more fully than would be possible through antagonistic competition."[82]

The task force report carries a degree of plausibility; shared authority is probably to be preferred to the kind of open warfare suggested by writers such as Duryea, who sees "two bureaucracies" in the university. The one bureaucracy consists of the faculties who have "evolved over the past 50 years or more a hierarchy of departments, schools, and senates or executive councils, larded well with a variety of permanent and temporary committees," and claiming the right to control "the totality of the educational operation, from admission to degree requirements and graduation certification." The other bureaucracy is that of the administration, "congealed into a separate hierarchy grappling with immense problems of management related to a variety of essential yet supportive functions which maintain the university, not least of which is budget and financial management." The problem is that these two bureaucracies have moved farther and farther apart with the faculty remaining "committed to a traditional ideal of the university as an integrated community while giving constant evidence that they fail to grasp its real operational nature and managerial complications." On the other hand, the administrators find their "managerial tasks such consuming endeavors that they become absentminded about the nature of the academic enterprise which lies at the heart of the university's reason for existence." The faculty develop a "kind of academic condescension toward administrators, especially presidents and their executive staffs, which views them as servants rather than leaders of the professoriate." Duryea finds in faculty a type of schizophrenia that allows them to characterize administrators "as minions while almost in the same breath condemning them for failure to stand firmly as defenders of the academic faith in times of crisis."[83]

What *is* the situation on most campuses? Is it one in which the AAHE-NEA task force plea for shared authority is realized? Or is it more similar to the open warfare Duryea postulates? The American Council on Education published in 1968 a report by Archie R. Dykes based upon a series of personal interviews with faculty of the

College of Liberal Arts and Sciences of a large Midwestern university. Approximately 20 percent of the college's faculty, or a total of 106 persons, were involved. Dykes found that the source of much of the tension between faculty and administration grows out of the faculty conviction that any increase in administrative power and influence necessarily results in a decrease in their own power and influence. Dykes himself disagreed with this judgment and pointed out that faculty and administration are "fused, and each depends in considerable measure on the other." He writes that, "without strong central leadership, the mobilization of the collective efforts of faculty and administration toward the definition and attainment of institutional goals is impossible. And without this unvarying effort toward unification, a university falls into aimlessness, drift, disunity, and disarray. It becomes something other than a *uni*versity."[84]

What Dykes refers to as "one of the most noticeable and best documented findings" of his study was the ambivalence in faculty attitudes toward participation in decision-making. On the one hand, faculty members indicated that they should have a strong, active, and influential role in decisions. On the other hand, it was clear from the study that faculty members were very reticent to give the time that such a participatory role would require. He reported, "asserting that faculty participation is essential, they placed participation at the bottom of their professional priority list and deprecated their colleagues who do participate." Faculty members also exhibited a "nostalgia for the town meeting type of university government and failed to recognize the complexity of the modern institution,"[85] and they held "an exceedingly simplistic view of the distribution of influence and power in their own community."[86]

A study undertaken by the Center for Research and Development in Higher Education of the University of California at Berkeley also explored, among other things, faculty involvement in institutional planning at a sample of 80 colleges and universities. It was found that faculty participation in planning was "peripheral," that faculty tended to view planning as an administrative task, or were preoccupied with faculty-administrative and faculty conflicts, or were oriented to their disciplines. The conclusion of the authors is that planning is not considered by faculty as a legitimate part of the faculty role. Indeed, as one interviewee noted, "the faculty are the greatest drag on academic planning and innovation in the university."[87]

McConnell concludes that apart from some crisis, only a limited group of faculty members carry on the business for their colleagues. A relatively small number of faculty monopolize the membership of the most powerful committees. Oligarchies take over the machinery of faculty government.[88] He refers to a study of faculty-senate committee membership at the University of Minnesota, where it was found that 10 percent of the faculty had served in a period of three years on three to six different committees. At Fresno State in California, 56 persons out of 417 eligible served on three or more major senate committees. Generalizing on these and other studies, McConnell writes that the emergence of oligarchies is normal in democratic governments and that

> political analysts have divided the voting population into gladiators, spectators, and apathetics. Gladiators, a relatively small corps of "professionals" constituting something like a tenth of the population, are the political activists. . . . This small group governs without consultation except with the particular minorities or clienteles affected by their decisions. . . . The same categories apply to the academic community. Since the faculty senate or the faculty as a whole, especially in large and complex institutions, lacks the capacity to make decisions expeditiously and to act accordingly, the gladiators or oligarchs carry on the day-to-day business.[89]

Faculty are ambivalent. There is the desire to be involved, but there is also a disdain for involvement—and, after all, only 10 percent of the faculty do become involved. Henry Mason, in his review of the literature on governance, reports much the same pattern of faculty response.[90]

One of the more helpful analyses of the present state of affairs is that of Burton Clark in his article "Faculty Organization and Authority." Clark observes that one finds what seems to be the "collegial" and the "bureaucratic" in decision-making in the university. In the study of various faculties in American higher educational institutions, he and his colleagues observed

> decisions being made through informal interaction among a group of peers and through a collective action of the faculty as a whole. . . . And we have reason to characterize the faculty as a collegium. . . . We also observe on the modern campus that

information is communicated through formal channels, responsibility is fixed in formally designated positions, interaction is arranged in relations between superiors and subordinates, and decisions are based on written rules. Thus we have reason to characterize the campus as a bureaucracy.[91]

He concludes that neither the collegial nor the bureaucratic model is satisfactory to explain all that takes place on the campus. What Clark sees as a basis for a more comprehensive explanation is the development of a "professional" model. That is to say, as the faculty has become more professional and the institution as a whole reflects more of a professional orientation, the university is neither a collegium nor a simple bureaucracy. He notes how the structure and organization of the campus have changed in recent years, in the following directions:

1. The movement from a unitary to a composite or federal structure, and the emergence of the multiversity.

2. The movement from the single to multiple value systems as the faculty of a given institution becomes much more diverse.

3. The movement from nonprofessional to professional work as a faculty changes from general practitioners to those with specific knowledge and specialties.

4. The movement from the characteristics of a community where consensus rules to a bureaucracy where complex procedures govern decision-making.

These movements within the university have led to significant changes in the way in which the faculty exercises its authority. These changes are:

1. The segmentation of the faculty and the growth of representational systems.

2. The emergence of federated professionalism, a combination of professional development and the growth of bureaucratic authority. The campus has become a "holding company for professional groups rather than a single association of professionals."

3. The growth of individualism. The campus has become a place "where strong forces cause the growth of some individuals into centers of power."[92]

From all of which he comes to the conclusion that we are developing a federated structure, with the campus "more like a United Nations and less like a small town." The university becomes a "loose alliance of professional men," and to keep the many components of a campus together, "we have a superimposed coordination by the administration."[93]

Proceeding from Burton Clark's image of a federated structure, we turn to what emerges at the primary unit within which the loose alliance of professionals work, the academic department.

In his analysis of the internal governance structures in the university, Henry L. Mason concludes that the department is the "core unit" for the faculty and that its importance in the university structure can hardly be exaggerated. He observes:

> It is the one structure of the university where loyalty to the discipline is often combined with loyalty to the institution. Moreover, it is—in many institutions—the one place where meaningful participation in important decision-making is experienced by all faculty members. The department is autonomous in many crucial respects and provides shelter and protection to its faculty.[94]

In examining reported research on the department, Mason contends that the department, with all of its problems, "is likely to be the most effective and collegial unit of the university."[95]

Frederick E. Balderston refers to the department as one of the two basic units of operating in the academic organization, the other being the school or college. In institutions organized in terms of the traditional disciplines, "each department is a collectivity of faculty expertise with (in the pure case) an exclusive mandate to control what is offered to any student on the campus in that field."[96] The departments are jealous of their prerogatives and no department encroaches on the territory of another. Faculty members gain prestige not only through their individual research but by sharing the "collective reputation and visibility of the department."[97]

117

Faculty members are bound together within departments by a mutuality of concerns.

James Brann and Thomas Emmet devote an entire volume to articles and commentaries on the role of the department chairman.[98] Winston Hall and Wendell French explore the belief that the real power of the university is centered in the departments, "where all important decisions are made by the collegium, or community of scholars." They observe that the professors are of the opinion that they wield almost as much control as the control to which they are subject.[99] Paul Dressel and Donald Reichard note that the department as a unit of organization within the American higher educational enterprise is for all practical purposes a creation of the late nineteenth and early twentieth centuries; yet it has come to wield considerable power in the decision-making process in the university.[100]

Some recent studies, however, have raised questions about the efficacy of the departmental structure. Paul Dressel and his associates refer to the department as "the refuge and support of the professor" even as it is the "key unit for the academic." If there is any measure of faculty involvement in planning and decision-making, it appears to be at the departmental level. Yet, "departmental-disciplinary organization is better adapted to faculty aspirations for more courses and more majors than for an integrated liberal undergraduate education."[101] Later the authors refer to the ways in which departments and the professors in them become isolated and narrow and preoccupied with their own concerns. Departments develop their own priorities and manner of operation and

> expect the resources and the autonomy to develop their own programs; but the resources are never adequate to satisfy all departments. The choice is almost inevitably mediocrity, or worse, for all departments, or the denial of some to cultivate excellence in others. Either decision generates suspicion and dissatisfaction.[102]

The authors conclude that universities and departments within them are out of control and "must be brought under control so that their resources are allocated and used in accord with priorities set for the university by the university in cooperation with those who support it."[103]

Whenever and under whatever conditions departments have emerged as primary units within the university community, and this is the case with but few exceptions, they have become both the strongest and weakest links within that community. The strength grows out of their utility for planning and curricular development with special reference to the training of specialists. The weakness grows out of the tendency of departments to become self-centered and to accentuate the already growing fragmentation of knowledge. To meet some of the weaknesses, alternative structures are being proposed. Stanley Ikenberry, for example, has suggested that the university might be reorganized around task-oriented units. These units might be institutes or centers, but he acknowledges that it is "difficult to fashion truly distinctive alternatives, for no single office or unit within the university controls the total program."[104] Dressel takes note of the emergence of institutes, centers, and laboratories.[105]

While it is important to develop structures more effective than departments to facilitate the interaction of faculty members within the university, it has become equally important to find ways of relating the faculty to the university's other constituencies. Left to themselves, will faculties ever do anything but express their own self-interest? JB Lon Hefferlin has questioned the ability of any interest group, "whether in the tobacco industry, automobile manufacturing, the securities market, the medical profession, or colleges and universities," to exercise the kind of self-regulation that takes into account broader public interest. Even if, as some observe, institutional self-reform may be possible without external intervention, it is unlikely to occur, and as desirable as self-regulation may be, it seldom is adequate for public protection. Hefferlin goes on to say:

> No priesthood, it has been said, ever institutes its own reforms, no military service can be expected to do so, no professional association is so altrustic that it will not at some point confuse public welfare with its own; and colleges and universities tend, as do all other public trusts, toward serving the interests of their personnel—their teachers and administrators—before those of their clientele.[106]

Why then should we expect the faculties, left to themselves, to look to broader concerns? Yet, the student outbursts of the 1960s were

119

asking for the faculty to take other concerns into account, and the emergence of the term "accountability" in the 1970s signals the demands of other elements of the constituency for a part in the decision process.

New Approaches to Participation

While there have been other motivations as well, certainly both the student demands and the calls for broader accountability have encouraged the development within a number of institutions of structures for broadening the decision-making base. Most of these structures have taken the form of some type of all-institution governance pattern, an organization that includes in some acceptable proportions faculty, students, administration, and in some instances nonacademic staff.

Most of the all-institution structures have not been in operation long enough to provide any firm basis for judgment regarding their effectiveness. The July 6, 1970, issue of the *Chronicle of Higher Education* called attention to some of the problems that early appeared in the new form of government at the University of New Hampshire.[107] The New Hampshire governing body included 77 persons: 30 faculty members, 30 undergraduates, 12 administrators, and 5 graduate students. At the date of the report no clear student versus faculty splits had appeared. Some members of the New Hampshire community argued that the new structure had provided broader representation, but others contended that the organization was so unwieldy that it was not working effectively. It was reported that the overwhelming student reaction to the new senate was that of apathy. The same article reported that as many as 300 colleges and universities were at that time considering some type of student-faculty structure. Yet even as the number of experiments was growing, one researcher gathered that "faith in the idea of representation as a governance model" was declining.

Cornell University had asked a Commission on Student Involvement in Decision-Making to study ways in which students could be more effectively involved in campus decision-making, but even before the commission report was issued—and the commission was raising a number of questions about the possibility of developing a representative body—during 1968-69 the university had already

120

proceeded to the formation of a constituent assembly of nearly 400 persons drawn from every type of group on the campus.[108]

Characteristic of many all-institution governance structures is the Lehigh University Forum. Approved by the board of trustees in the spring of 1970, the new organization first met in the fall of 1970. This particular organization included 60 elected students (43 undergraduates and 17 graduate students), 60 elected faculty members, and 5 administrators (president, provost, vice-president for student affairs, and two others appointed by the president). All were given equal voting privileges. In addition, one or more trustees and/or alumni were invited to attend meetings, and the forum was to select two students and two faculty members to attend the trustees' meetings. The Forum was created to have legislative authority and to set policy on special academic programs and planning, social life and regulations, extracurricular activities and athletics, and academic environment matters such as admissions, registration, the academic calendar, residence and dining, the bookstore, buildings and grounds, the library, and the computer. The faculty as a group was to retain primary responsibility in the area of curriculum course content, instructional methods, conduct of research, employment status and tenure of faculty, academic discipline and the awarding of degrees.[109]

The ERIC compendium series on governance in 1970 included reports on some 20 institutional studies on governance. Among the institutions mentioned was Dickinson College, which rejected a faculty-student committee recommendation for a cabinet system of government and advanced instead a proposal for a system of joint faculty-student legislative and advisory committees for such areas as academic program, student affairs, admissions and financial aid, and academic standards. The University of North Carolina at Chapel Hill reported on the organization of its Consultative Forum which included representatives from all sections of the university community; the forum was to have consultative responsibilities only. Another report referred to the proposal for a 57-member Council of the Princeton University Community. Colgate's University Council, composed of faculty, students, and administrators, was also described. Other studies were noted as being underway.[110]

Another variation in structure is based upon accepting the existence of two different groups and frankly working with a dual system of organization. William F. Sturner has argued on behalf of the bicameral legislature and states that the formation of such a legislature, with one house composed of student representatives and the other consisting of faculty and administrators, could provide the "legal framework for the political solution of . . . [the] classic problem of conflicting rights and poor communication." He observes that one of the most important contributions of the division of powers would be "the clear delineation of constitutional prerogatives among the contending groups and the formal recognition, heretofore omitted, of student rights in a democratically oriented structure."[111]

Noting that faculty and students differ in the way in which they approach problems and issues, Sturner writes that the inclusion of students in faculty-administrative organizations "dilutes the strength of both groups, highlights the weaknesses of each, and does little to recognize the student as an adult in his own right."[112] And since the two groups communicate in different ways, they are usually more effective in communicating with their peers than with members of the other group. Combining the two groups in a single body has too many drawbacks and too little potential. The solution, according to Sturner, would be to divide the groups and allow each to work in its own areas of responsiblity; the two groups could then build upon their respective strengths. Each group would, however, have the right to initiate legislation for particular areas with the approval of the other group.

Kenneth Mortimer points out, however, that one of the basic problems in any bicameral approach is that of clarifying the discrete areas of responsibility for each unit, a complicated matter. Mortimer noted that in one case where separate legislative bodies were constituted, the University of Minnesota, the separate student and faculty assemblies did not meet at all during the first year of operation.[113] More generally, he commented:

> A major problem which must be confronted by the joint participation and agreements to separate jurisdictions models is that in order for them to work there must be a substantial degree of mutual respect and trust among the various constituencies. Each group must view the structures and functions of the mechanism as legitimate and the people who operate them as

trustworthy. It is increasingly apparent, however, that legitimacy and trust are scarce commodities on many campuses.[114]

He reported how campus-wide senates and councils can break down into internal political groups and how the separate groups can develop adversary relations. But he emphasized that it is difficult to draw conclusions about the effectiveness of these new approaches because of the relatively short period of time during which they have been operating. In a paper he subsequently presented at the annual meeting of the American Association of Colleges in January 1973, Mortimer reported that a recent survey of over 1,700 institutions found that 640 had or were experimenting with some type of unicameral senate. The survey also found that 40 institutions which had tried unicameral senates had dropped them after having found them unacceptable.[115]

A case study of the efforts of one institution to develop an effective all-college organization illustrates some of the difficulties, as well as the rewards, encountered in such an effort. Bardwell Smith comments on the development of the College Council at Carleton College.[116] Inaugurated in 1971, the council includes several constituencies: seven students, seven faculty members, five administrators, two alumni, and three trustees. Three policy committees were created—educational, administrative, and social—with the responsibility to recommend to the council, where authority for final approval resides. Council decisions may be challenged by any of the several constituencies; a two-thirds vote of the council overrides the challenge. Ultimate authority for the college is still with the board of trustees, but the board has delegated much of the decision-making to the local governance structure.

Smith reports on three areas of contention that emerged during the first two years of the council's operation, and a review of these areas is instructive in pointing up issues that other such agencies have faced. The first area of contention had to do with the question of identity, of definition. There emerged "genuine confusion among all parties as to what role students, faculty, administrators, trustees and others should play in determining academic policy."[117] The confusion was deep and stemmed from a serious concern about the basic nature of the academic community. Smith elaborates:

123

It should not be surprising... if instruments like college councils occasion concern about the power and authority of the faculty . . . about the rights of non-teaching professional staff (e.g., regarding tenure, sabbaticals, salary levels, prestige); about the appropriate role of administrators . . . about the meaning of trustee authority as campus affairs become immensely complex and decision-making requires intimate and continuing acquaintance with the subtleties of each situation; and about alumni relationship to institutions whose changing patterns make them seem unfamiliar, even alien, from what they once were.[118]

One specific outcome was increased concern for detailing rights and responsibilities of various groups.

The second area of contention grew out of the "recently diminished resources of higher education." Questions of how funds were to be spent quickly came to the fore:

When one combines "financial exigency" with a college council approach to decision-making, the process becomes existential. The classics scholar with only token interest heretofore in line items and planning models becomes ardently involved in discussions about what happens if one examines seriously the high cost of small classes. Students are forced to balance certain services, once taken for granted, against the possible loss of a faculty member, even that department. Faculty begin to see implications for the entire institution. . . .[119]

There is danger, Smith observes, that in such situations institutions may settle just for keeping the ship afloat.

The third area of contention had to do with accountability. The call was for "more thoughtful assessment of what is going on." After the initial skirmishes there emerged support for "more thorough evaluation of teaching, academic programs and departments, and institutional commitments."[120]

In concluding his review, Smith refers to the man-hours that "can be squandered in the process" of broadening decision-making. He writes that "a balance of costs must be struck between exhaustive discussion and delegation of responsibility."

124

The search for ways of incorporating the faculty more effectively into the decision-making process of the university as a whole continues. Attempts to develop all-university governmental units have met with mixed results, and as Bardwell Smith observes, even if successful, they demand inordinate expenditures of time and energy. It seems clear that no one pattern has emerged as more desirable than another. Such is probably inevitable in the American system where diversity in purpose and composition still seem to characterize the multiplicity of institutions that make up what is now referred to as postsecondary education. It is probably safe to say that the traditional forms—and in America tradition seems to be established on fairly short-term experience—of governance are being challenged and new combinations are being sought. In this search some institutions will discover as new and exciting prospects what other institutions have, for various reasons, some good and some not so good, discarded as old and unworkable. We do expect, however, that whatever the forms taken, governance systems will call for more participation by more members of the university constituency—faculty, students, administrators, alumni, trustees, and the larger "public." And this broadening of the decision base will be for many faculty clear evidence of the erosion of their power, an erosion they will view with considerable suspicion. At a time when jobs are scarce, the loss of power in the internal decision-making process leads to even more preoccupation with security, with the net result that more and more faculty members will be debating the basis on which tenure is awarded and will be prepared to consider in serious ways collective bargaining as the means of protecting their interests and channeling their input into the governance process.

Tenure

The slowdown in enrollment growth and the increase in fiscal pressures combined in the mid-1970s to force some serious questioning about the place of tenure in the university. Some colleges and universities instituted staff reductions, and others adopted a policy of no further growth in staff. Already threatened by some loss of power in new governance structures, faculty now found their security further endangered by staff reductions and severe limitations on tenure and promotions. In addition, reaction to the developments in colleges and universities in the late sixties and early seventies caused the general public as well as board members to ask whether there ought not to be a stronger stand taken by boards of trustees in the affairs of the university in matters of appointment, promotion, and tenure.

At the 1972 meeting of the American Association for Higher Education, Florence Moog, a professor at Washington University in St. Louis, attacked the prevailing concept of tenure. Moog said, "In a period when public confidence in universities sinks as costs rise, when students are dissatisfied and young scholars are frustrated by the shrinking job market, a system lacking effective accountability is indeed obsolete. The frequent attacks on the tenure system in recent years are a danger signal that ought to be heeded."[121] She proposed in place of the current system of tenure a series of short contracts of one to three years followed by longer contracts of perhaps as much as seven years. In such a way, she argued, it would be possible to restore some degree of accountability to academia.

Walter P. Metzger places the current debate over academic tenure within a broader historical context. He suggests that, since the emergence of the Western university, in each of its ages "some kind of tenure was established—tenure as privilege, tenure as time, tenure as judiciality."[122] In the medieval university tenure was secured by virtue of admission to the guild of the masters, and "expulsion from this body could be directly effected not by an outside agency but only by the body itself." In the developing American institutions, without the presence of a scholarly class, the relationship between the teachers and the institutions became contractual, and appointment was for a period of time, generally a short period of time. The practice was to appoint faculty for a year, "vacating their positions at the end of term, and reappointing only those among the previous incumbents who could pass a *de novo* test."[123]

At the turn of the nineteenth into the twentieth century, while technically faculty members were still appointed for one-year terms, the practice was to provide a kind of indefinite tenure. Out of the conflicts in the early 1900s came the call for the formation of a national association of professors, and in January 1915 the American Association of University Professors was established. The 1915 "General Report on Academic Freedom and Academic Tenure" is referred to as the "philosophical birth cry of the Association." Among other things, the report called for clear understandings as to the term of appointments and for a kind of due process in case of dismissals. Subsequent statements were issued in 1925, 1940, and 1958, and in 1968 the association adopted "Recommended Institutional Regulations on Academic Freedom and Tenure."[124]

In a survey taken in April 1972 it was estimated that tenure plans were in effect in all public and private universities and public four-year colleges, in 94 percent of the public colleges, and in more than two-thirds of the two-year colleges, public and private. Surveys conducted under the auspices of the Carnegie Commission and the American Council on Education suggested that just under 50 percent of the faculty members in the United States were on tenure. But since the figure on which the percentage is based included both full- and part-time faculty, it is probably the case in relation to the full-time faculty a larger percentage are on tenure.

When the American Council on Education conducted a survey to update the 1972 study, it found no overall change between 1972 and 1974. Tenure systems were found to be "nearly universal" among universities and four-year colleges and were also found in two-thirds of the two-year institutions. There was an upward shift in percentage of full-time faculty holding tenure—59 percent of the colleges with tenure systems reported half or more of the full-time faculty on tenure, compared to 43 percent so reporting in 1972. There appeared to be, however, a slight drop in the percentage of faculty formally considered for tenure who were advanced to tenure. There was also a shift of sorts toward longer probationary periods for tenure, particularly among four-year colleges and universities under public control. In procedures, a third of the institutions reported changes in review policies, and other institutions were reviewing their systems.[125]

In reviewing the ACE report, Philip Semas stated that tenure was being challenged by three emerging forces—hard times in higher education, collective bargaining, and affirmative action. Having survived the "rhetorical attacks" of the late 1960s and early 1970s, tenure now faced more formidable powers, forces which might not destroy tenure but which had already "led many colleges to review their tenure systems."[126]

The question of tenure most often arises when individuals are dismissed or released for financial exigencies. Two of the cases that came into prominence during late 1973 and early 1974 were those of Bloomfield College and Southern Illinois University. At Bloomfield the decision to reduce the budget by one-fourth led to a further decision to reduce the faculty from 72 to 54 by 1974. Among those released, 11 were tenured faculty.[127] The college had abolished the award of tenure in June 1973. At the beginning of 1974, Southern Illinois University terminated the employment of 104 faculty members, of whom 28 were tenured professors. The university referred to enrollment declines and budget cuts as a basis for the dismissals.[128] In both cases lawsuits have been brought. In the case of Bloomfield the AAUP, which had been elected the bargaining agent for the college's faculty, brought suit on behalf of the Bloomfield professors. It was reported in July 1974 that the superior court judge to whom the suit had been brought ruled in favor of the Bloomfield faculty. The position he took was that the action of the administration and trustees was primarily to bring about "the abolition of tenure at Bloomfield College, not alleviation of financial stringency." Subsequently, the college filed for bankruptcy and as of August 1974 the college was placed under court receivership.[129]

At Southern Illinois, the university filed a class-action suit against 6 representative faculty members to prevent the 104 who were dismissed from taking the university to court or making appeals through the university's internal structure. Subsequently, in June 1974, the university dropped its suit against the staff members. Then, at the end of the month, it sought to reconstitute the suit against 19 faculty members with whom it had not reached any agreement. In the meantime the university had reached settlement with 56 of the faculty and staff members, either providing new jobs or providing a cash settlement, and indicated that for an additional 29 it had no obligation, since they were on one-year contracts. But no agreement had been reached with the 19.[130]

At the same time, a federal judge in Wisconsin ruled that the Constitution provides only limited protection for tenured faculty members who are laid off because of their university's financial troubles. A preliminary injunction had been sought by 38 faculty members dismissed by the University of Wisconsin, and Judge James E. Doyle had denied the injunction while indicating that it

128

was up to the state government, not the federal courts, to determine when financial exigency required dismissal of tenured professors. He ruled that "faculty members are entitled only to an opportunity to prove that they were laid off arbitrarily or for exercising their Constitutional rights," and that the university had followed the "minimal procedures" for dismissal, furnishing each individual with a written statement of the basis for the initial decision, furnishing each person with a "reasonably adequate description of the manner in which the initial decision had been arrived at," making reasonably adequate disclosure of the data employed, and providing each individual an opportunity to respond. The 38 professors were among 88 who had been notified in May that they would be dismissed in June. The university had indicated to the 88 that they could retain their positions as tenured faculty members without duties or pay and that they would have first opportunity at any new openings. Fifty of the 88 subsequently resigned or reached settlements with the university.[131]

An Iowa district court judge ruled in August 1974 that the University of Dubuque had the right to fire a tenured professor in 1972 because of the university's financial problems. The ruling was made after a jury hearing in which the jury failed to reach a verdict. A mistrial had been declared, and the attorneys for the university asked the judge for a directed verdict. His verdict was in contrast to the decision of Judge Antell in the Bloomfield case. Spokesmen for the Iowa higher education association charged that the decision "would effectively destroy the concept of tenure."[132]

An untenured assistant professor at San Jose State University filed suit when he was denied tenure in the spring of 1974. He had been recommended by colleagues in the School of Education for tenure, but on the recommendation of the dean, the president of San Jose State decided not to grant tenure, and the professor's appointment was terminated. The professor then turned to the university grievance procedure. The hearing officer upheld the earlier decision, and the president again approved the professor's termination. In his suit the professor charged that as a faculty member he was being placed in double jeopardy, because the president had the final decision in both the promotion process and the grievance procedure.[133] A decision on behalf of the professor could have "repercussions for grievance procedures throughout the country" since the practice followed at San Jose is "a fairly common practice among colleges."[134]

In August 1975 the Ohio Supreme Court ruled that the university could change the mandatory retirement age for a faculty member, even after he had been granted tenure. Case Western Reserve University retired a professor of English and journalism at age 68, although 70 was designated as the retirement age at the time the professor was appointed. A state trial court had ruled in favor of the faculty member, but the supreme court of the state overturned the earlier decision. The significant statement in the decision of the supreme court was, "Academic tenure does not . . . vest a faculty member with the right to continued appointment."[135]

Victor G. Rosenblum, in summarizing his observations on the legal dimensions of tenure, finds what he refers to as a "paucity of definitive legal content regarding tenure," and suggests as a general principle, "once a professor has tenure, his rights *should* be well protected." He goes on to say, however, that there are differences in the approach of public and private institutions. A tenure plan under a governing board of a public institution is generally considered as a form of sublegislation having the force of law, while in a private institution any right to tenure is contractual rather than statutory. And he notes that in a public institution any dismissal contrary to the tenure plan "can generally be followed by an order to reinstate the teacher, since the discharge was, in effect, beyond the board's authority and contrary to state law," while in a private institution "courts will not decree specific performance of personal service contracts" and "a specific order of reinstatement will not ordinarily follow a conclusion that a contract has been breached through failure to observe its tenure provisions."[136]

Rosenblum suggests that in most cases the courts have been more concerned about whether or not due process has been followed than with norms or doctrines about tenure. He concludes that the courts have not yet begun to deal with tenure as such, and he argues that before further action is taken, the academic community itself must be much clearer in defining tenure, or "a judicial *in loco parentis* [will] . . . take control."[137]

As the Commission on Academic Tenure in Higher Education observes, "In the current debate about academic tenure, old arguments have been repeated, earlier arguments have been adapted to new contexts, and new arguments have emerged from concerns not central to earlier periods of crisis in the history of tenure."[138] The work of the commission was co-sponsored by the American Association of University Professors and the Association of American Colleges and covered a ten-month period in 1971-72. In its report, issued in March 1973, the commission lists the major arguments for and against tenure. In abbreviated form, the arguments against tenure are: Since academic freedom must be assured to all teachers, academic tenure is not essential to academic freedom, but what is essential is academic due process. Tenure imposes inflexible financial burdens upon institutions. It diminishes an institution's opportunity to recruit and retain younger faculty and it leads to diminished emphasis on quality undergraduate teaching. It encourages the perpetuation of established departments and specialties; diminishes accountability and fosters mediocrity; forces decisions on permanent appointments before an institution has time to assess an individual's competence; encourages controversy and litigation about nonrenewal of probationary contracts and denial of tenure; provides a cloak under which irresponsible political activity can be carried on; commits the institution but not the individual; and concentrates power in the hands of professors on permanent appointments and thus diminishes the role of students and younger faculty members in university affairs.

In support of tenure the commission gives the following arguments: Tenure is an essential of academic freedom. It creates an atmosphere favorable to academic freedom for all—the nontenured as well as the tenured. It contributes to institutional stability and spirit; assures that judgments of professional fitness will be made on professional grounds; forces decisions at definite times regarding retention; attracts men and women of ability into the teaching profession; and helps offset generally lower financial rewards of higher education in comparison to other professions by providing security.

The commission suggests that if the tenure system is compared to a contract system, tenure is considered less adequate in that the contract commits a faculty member to an institution for the period of his contract; potential nonrenewal provides incentive to good performance; contracts permit greater flexibility in institutional

131

planning; and contract arrangements are conducive to educational flexibility. On the other hand, in some areas tenure is presumably superior to the contract system. Persons under temporary contract may be influenced to support the candidacy of others in the hope of retaining their own contracts—or to oppose renewal in the hope of improving their changes. Under the contract system the role of administrative officers will increase and that of faculty decrease. Continuing exposure to uncertainties of contract renewal have a detrimental effect upon faculty morale and performance and there is no reason to expect better teaching under contract systems than under any other system. Contract arrangements do not necessarily lead to innovation; there is no evidence that the contract provisions encourage more flexibility; and there is no evidence that the contract system assures academic freedom for all through due-process procedures. [139]

Coming out strongly for tenure—"the commission sees no ground for believing that the alternatives to tenure that are now in rise or that have been proposed can deal more effectively with these problems than would a strengthened and renewed system of tenure"—the report also acknowledged that "the principle of tenure . . . will not long survive unless reform of its abuses and elimination of weaknesses are vigorously pursued."[140] Robert Jacobson estimated that as many as 100 colleges that were considering taking steps to modify or replace tenure "held back, at least temporarily, because of a strong endorsement of tenure by [this] national commission."[141]

When the report was reviewed at the annual meeting of the AAUP in May 1973, the association took exception to what appeared to be a recommendation for establishing quotas for tenured faculty (recommendation 19). The commission had recommended that each institution formulate a "faculty staffing plan," under which "an appropriate number of tenure positions . . . are available for allocation to any unit where they may be needed." In its interpretation of this recommendation, the commission made reference to the necessity of an institution facing the question "of the proper ratio of the tenured to nontenured faculty."[142] The association passed a resolution calling tenure quotas "an expedient danger to academic freedom and academic life."[143]

In a commentary on the commission report and on another collection of essays on tenure, Dabney Park, Jr., contends that both books fail to recognize that tenure, rather than guaranteeing academic freedom, "is probably the greatest single source of violations of academic freedom"; that the "marriage of tenure and collective bargaining poses serious threats to the future"; that tenure "is one of the most formidable obstacles to educational change and improvement to be found in the educational world today"; that students "receive short shrift from the tenure system"; and that the commission's suggestion of a quota system is untimely and dangerous.[144]

The American Federation of Teachers also attacked the commission report and the subsequent stand of the AAUP that "stricter standards for awarding of tenure can be developed over the years with the consequent decreases in the probability of achieving tenure." Such a stand, contended the AFT, would allow the administration to impose quotas indirectly.[145] In New Jersey, the State Board of Higher Education, adopted in 1972 a policy that required the state's four-year and two-year colleges to impose either "specific restrictions or more intensive and rigorous review procedures" in any award of tenure. The state affiliate of the National Education Association, the bargaining agent for faculty members in the state college system, filed suit in an attempt to have the policy thrown out, but the New Jersey Supreme Court upheld the policy of the Board of Higher Education.[146]

By the fall of 1974 the AAUP had begun to modify some of its earlier stands on tenure. Committee A on Academic Freedom and Tenure approved in November 1974 a revision of the 1972 "Recommended Institutional Regulations on Academic Freedom and Tenure." While holding that no tenured person should be terminated in favor of retaining a faculty member without tenure, the committee recognized that the financial situation could become so bad that the college would have to lay off professors. In situations where positions had to be terminated, the faculty should be involved at every step in the process.[147] Tenure was becoming, all protests to the contrary, a contingent kind of thing, and faculties were hardly in a position to assume confidently the security of tenure, i.e., a permanent position. Small wonder that as the last position of power seemed to dissolve, more faculty members looked to collective bargaining as one way to preserve some position of strength in the arena. There were other reasons that turned faculties to collective bargaining, but the increasing feeling of powerlessness, to which the possible loss of the tenure principle added, certainly played a part.

133

In June 1974 there were 338 campuses on which faculty members had chosen collective bargaining agents. This number represented 92 percent of the 367 institutions where elections had been held to determine whether a bargaining agent should be appointed,[148] and it constitutes 70 more institutions than were reported 18 months previously.[149] In this interim the AAUP had increased the number of institutions for which it served as bargaining agency from 13 to 29. And four-year campuses with collective bargaining had increased from 122 to 133. The most rapidly growing group in the collective bargaining camp was that of two-year institutions. These had increased from 147 to 205. In October 1972 four-year institutions constituted 45 percent of the institutions with bargaining agents, while in June 1974 they constituted 39.3 percent.

A year later, in June 1975, when the campus total had increased by 47 to a new total of 385, the percentage of institutions electing bargaining agents fell slightly. Overall, of the 426 institutions where elections had been held, just over 90 percent (the 385 noted) had decided on a bargaining agent.[150] The AAUP was agent on 35 campuses. Four-year campuses with collective bargaining had increased from 133 to 154. There were 21 new four-year campuses and 26 new two-year campuses in the 1975 listing; four-year campuses constituted 40 percent of the total.

The way in which collective bargaining has been, or seems to have been, accepted by faculty in four-year institutions is perhaps reflected in the process whereby AAUP moved from opposing collective bargaining to become a bargaining agent. In reporting on its fall 1969 meeting, AAUP's *Academe* stated that, while the association "recognizes the right of the state to pass legislation providing for collective bargaining by faculty members, it urges public agencies charged with the administration of such laws to discharge their responsibilities in a manner consistent with the principles of academic self-government and institutional autonomy." It goes on to indicate, however, that if faculties are interested in collective bargaining, they should turn to the AAUP as their representative. Officially, the AAUP appeared reluctant to accept collective bargaining.[151]

In 1972 the outgoing president of the AAUP, Sanford Kadish, argued against the principle of collective bargaining. He said that a strike "proceeds by deliberately harming the educational mission . . . in order to provoke the personal employee interest, in contradiction to the service ideal of subordinating personal interest to the advancement of the purposes of the university." He said that the collective bargaining process "tends to remit issues which faculty should themselves determine to outside agencies, such as state and federal boards, arbitrators, and union bureaucracies."[152]

At its annual meeting in May 1972, the AAUP, in apparently a different mood from its president, voted overwhelmingly, 373 to 54, to endorse a recommendation that the AAUP "pursue collective bargaining as a major additional way of realizing the Association's goals." While the vote was decisive, some of the delegates and leaders did not agree with the decision. They argued that by moving into collective bargaining the AAUP would damage its traditional activities, especially those dealing with academic freedom and tenure. One consequence of the decision was that the Association of American Colleges in July of that year in effect recommended to its 800 member colleges that they not continue to participate in the AAUP annual salary survey.[153] The recommendation had little impact on subsequent behavior of the members of the AAC.

In the meantime, the American Federation of Teachers, founded in 1916 as an affiliate of the American Federation of Labor, had from its early days enrolled some college professors among its members. It was in the 1960s, however, with the organization of the New York City teachers, that the AFT began to become a significant factor. In June 1974 the AFT accounted for 80 of the 338 organized bargaining groups. When the AFT elected a new president at that time, the organization announced that it would "allocate a larger proportion of its resources to organizing at the college, university, and post-secondary-school level," and the new president, Albert Shanker, referred to higher education as one of the major areas where the AFT would concentrate its efforts. "Higher education," he said, "is one of the great areas of organizing that is available to us"; he noted that the AFT campus membership was then some 35,000.[154] In the summer of 1975 the AFT claimed 96 campus bargaining units, and in combination with the NEA, was involved in 63 additional units.

It was also during the 1960s that the National Education Association emerged as a full-fledged teacher's union. In 1974 the

135

NEA accounted for some 195 campus bargaining units, either as the sole agent or in combination with affiliates. In July 1974 the NEA voted more than $1 million to its fund for organizing college professors and created a Special Project in Higher Education to coordinate its organizing efforts.[155] In 1975 the NEA was still the largest organization, accounting for some 220 units, either as sole agent or in combination with the AFT or AAUP.

Union leaders were predicting in the fall of 1975 that the academic year 1975–76 would witness the largest number of major faculty collective bargaining elections held thus far. The increase in union activity was predicted despite the fact that several major states, including California, Illinois, and Ohio, had failed to pass laws granting collective bargaining rights to faculty members.[156] Tax-supported institutions fall under the laws of their respective states, and by September 1975 some 23 states had faculty bargaining statutes, others had mandatory "meet and confer" laws, and still others had permissive coverage but no legislation.[157]

Private higher education became involved in collective bargaining in June 1970, when the National Labor Relations Board, in a reversal of a previous ruling, affirmed that it had jurisdiction over nonprofit colleges and universities having at least $1 million gross revenue. In the fall of 1975 the NLRB had ordered faculty bargaining elections at several smaller private institutions.[158] Regional rulings of the board in the cases of private colleges have not always been consistent. In Denver, Colorado, one ruling excluded department chairpersons as "management," and another ruling for a quite similar institution in the same city held that department chairpersons could be included in the bargaining unit and were, therefore, not "management." In April 1975 a federal appeals court upheld the NLRB's jurisdiction over private colleges. The suit had actually been brought by the board, which sought a court order forcing a Massachusetts institution, Wentworth College of Technology, to bargain with its faculty union. To force the court test, Wentworth had refused to bargain.[159]

What are the possible consequences of the development of collective bargaining among college professors? Everett Ladd and Seymour Lipset, in a volume prepared for the Carnegie Commission on Higher Education, suggest that it is still "too early to tell what degree of difference unionization will make in university life." Yet they observe that unionization will almost inevitably eliminate salary differentials for aspects other than seniority; generally speaking, collective bargaining will work against any general system of merit payment. There will also be a tendency to use seniority as a basis for reappointment and tenure. Persons employed will be expected after a "probationary" period of time to proceed into tenured positions. They will probably insist that administrative officers not have the power to review faculty peer evaluations by seeking outside judgments of the candidate's qualifications. Collective bargaining will probably also have some impact upon governance. Many aspects of the professor's activity will be determined by the negotiations between the bargaining agency and "management," and in complex state systems, "management" may be a state board or commission. While existing faculty governance groups will not necessarily be eliminated, they may have less to say about the faculty members' activities and conditions of service. Contracts already negotiated have included a wide range of concerns, all the way from appointment and tenure policies to travel funds, academic calendar, fringe benefits, and curricular matters.[160]

Ladd and Lipset suggest that collective bargaining may also have some impact upon faculty-student relations. Indeed, picking up on comments by Myron Lieberman, they suggest that there may even be the development of strong student unions that will seek to participate in bargaining between faculty and administration.[161]

In a survey conducted under the auspices of the Carnegie Commission on Higher Education, Ladd and Lipset found that 59 percent of the respondents (a total of 60,028 faculty members) said that there is a place for faculty collective bargaining on the campus, and 47 percent agreed that faculty strikes could be legitimate action. In a subsequent survey (in 1972) involving a sample of the larger group, some 43 percent agreed that the recent growth in unionization was beneficial and should be extended, and another 13 percent reported themselves to be uncertain. Some 44 percent disagreed that the extension of unionization was beneficial.[162]

In his assessment of the impact of collective bargaining on the university, William D. Boyd wrote that the evidence is already available that under conditions of collective bargaining "the system of governance will become more explicit, more uniform and more centralized." The bargaining table will attempt to clarify and define

137

matters which have been vague or variable. Boyd was not convinced that all of this will be to the good. He suggested that something of value is lost and that on most campuses the result will be the increase in board power at the expense of faculty power. "Ambiguity and a willingness to leave certain questions unraised have been important for the rise of faculty power. Explicitness and a demand for legalism will . . . now contribute to a renaissance of board power." Personal policies will become more formal, uniform, and centralized. Departmental and school autonomy will probably be reduced. Whereas decisions on faculty appointments, reappointments, promotions, pay increases, and terminations have been initiated at the board level, these decisions are more likely to be administrative decisions, where administrators are agents of the board. He suggested also that the technique and tone of admininstration will be changed. Collective bargaining inevitably places the administration into more of a management role.[163]

E. D. Duryea and Robert Fisk carry the analysis further. They argue, in one way contrary to Boyd, that collective bargaining will improve the opportunities for faculty to become involved in decision-making. During the bargaining procedure it is possible that faculties will be able to deal with a broader range of matters, not only personnel considerations but "decisions on the mission of the university itself." Grievance procedures will also provide opportunities for appeal from administrative decisions. Yet the bargaining process is a two-edged sword. And it may be possible for the state or board to stipulate or insist upon a more "finite and precise kind of accountability from faculty members, including such perquisites as sabbaticals or considerations such as teaching load, time and facilities for research, and student-faculty ratios." Conditions of faculty service in a very broad sense can become subjects for negotiations.[164]

The two writers see some problems. The bargaining process is costly in time and effort. Senior faculty members "may be deeply troubled by their affiliation with what can be called by no other name than 'union.' " They face the tension of seeing themselves as employees and at the same time as professional entrepreneurs—researchers, scholars, consultants.

Duryea and Fisk also see in the conflict between autonomy and accountability the possibility that institutions may regain some of

138

their autonomy. That is to say, in the bargaining process the academic bargaining units may serve as counter forces to the trend toward external control from the state. They suggest that faculty organizations may have to compete effectively with boards for power and authority. Written contracts will replace bylaws.

Myron Lieberman sees the unionization of college and university faculties as "one of the most important developments in higher education in the next decade." He points out that over 65 percent of the nation's schoolteachers are involved in collective bargaining, and he sees a parallel development in higher education. But he sees, and approves, the end of "faculty self-government." He calls this self-government irresponsible and says that the advent of unionization will "inject a measure of management accountability into these matters."[165] He agrees with Boyd in that he finds college and university administrators moving more into management-type roles. However, he predicts that governing boards will lose power, and he sees faculty unions stimulating the organization of student unions.

James Olsen also recognizes the possibility of the growth of student groups. He suggests that "almost invariably, collective bargaining agreements ignore the student interest . . . and abrogate the student voice and role gained in recent years." This will lead to inevitable clashes between student leaders and faculty units. Into this situation the administration will have to move, and Olsen sees the administration becoming more of a management group. What is required is "straight-forward, unadorned management and monitoring—functions which require an administration to plan, control, and coordinate the efficient use of the institution's resources."[166]

It is clear that observers of the same developments come up with rather different conclusions as to the long-range consequences. But we have entered into a new set of conditions, and individual institutions cannot ignore the developments. Matters will not take care of themselves. Philip Semas refers to collective bargaining as being on the threshold of becoming higher education's "issue of the decade."[167] The Education Commission of the States suggests that "no single item seems to portend more controversy than that likely to be generated by the emergence of collective bargaining."[168] Carol Shulman observes, "Faculty collective bargaining, once a radical departure in faculty-administrative relations, is becoming a familiar and permanent feature on many campuses."[169]

Paul Dressel and his colleagues take a fairly dim view of the development of collective bargaining. While they expect an acceleration of the trend toward unionization, they predict that it will lead to a lessened role for the "middle management"—deans and department heads—to greater uniformity in salaries, less flexibility in the academy, and much more centralized decision-making. Collective bargaining will move to state-wide and system-wide levels and destroy much of the autonomy of the separate campuses and will thereby "ultimately promote centralization of decision making." Moreover, collective bargaining "will contravene the individual and departmental autonomy for which many faculty members have battled so long."[170]

But Edward J. Bloustein, president of Rutgers University, speaking out of his experience at Rutgers, is much more favorably disposed.[171] He states that the system of governance will and should be more explicit; that academic quality does not go down; that deterioration of departmental and school autonomy is not necessarily bad; that the management role thrust on administrators should have been assumed long ago; that the functions of university senates are not necessarily curtailed; that collegiality has already broken down, collective bargaining or not; and that bargaining is not devoid of reasoning and consensus-making.

Leon Epstein examines collective bargaining within the general context of the governing process and is much closer to Paul Dressel and his colleagues than to President Bloustein. Epstein writes, "Starkly stated, collective bargaining is a conception of government in which staff members organize as employees to exercise power through bilateral negotiations"; and he sees in this process little chance for professors to continue to act "as quasi-independent practitioners who share managerial authority," even if they continue to want to do so. Under collective bargaining there must be an "identifiable management" as something apart from "employees and their representatives." The negotiations may be limited to matters of salary and work conditions or may extend to broader policy questions, but in either case, argues Epstein, "collective bargaining introduces a measure of bilateral government distinguishable both from unfettered hierarchical authority and from pure professional self-government."[172] Epstein sees collective bargaining thus changing the roles of professors, other staff members, state officials, trustees, administrators, and students. For state institutions he sees more patterns developing in which the negotiations will be between the faculty unions and legislators, governors, and their staff rather than with the administrators and regents—and reaching these authorities is essentially a lobbying process, a new role for faculty members.

It may be noted that in President Bloustein's state of New Jersey the faculty of the state institutions—except those of the community colleges and Rutgers—went on strike in the fall of 1974. This was the first strike to affect an entire multicollege system. The chancellor of the state system, in commenting on the settlement brought about by the governor's back-to-work order, said that the ending of the strike only strengthened the faculty in the opinion that "they can go directly to the governor and get things fixed up."[173] Epstein's prediction seems to have been borne out—faculty unions will bypass administration and regents. The report in the *Chronicle* the following week detailed the steps leading to the governor's intervention.[174]

Kenneth Mortimer and Gregory Lozier have been conducting a long-range research project on collective bargaining with particular reference to developments in Pennsylvania. Among the issues they have been examining is whether collective bargaining has had much of an effect on internal decision-making processes. In reviewing the limited number of contracts available, they found one that provided for faculty input in the selection of college presidents, two that had provisions for selecting academic deans, and three that set procedures for selecting department chairmen. So far the status of faculty senates is unclear, although the authors think the senates may actually be supported in collective bargaining agreements. Some agreements refer to faculty-committee organization, and the structure provisions are "not radically unlike those in existence at many four-year institutions." The general conclusion of the authors, however, is that the whole process is too new to allow any definitive statements on impacts.[175]

In his examination of the impact of collective bargaining on faculty senates, based in large part on an analysis of developments in New Jersey, James Begin finds at this early stage that the collective

141

bargaining process seems to have "enhanced the development of cooperative rather than competitive relationship" between senates and bargaining agents.[176] He notes that a number of patterns are emerging for faculty participation in decision-making in collective bargaining "which do not necessarily lead to the demise of traditional procedures."[177]

In the midst of what seems to be a good bit of conflicting opinion, Philip Semas finds in his review of three recent books on collective bargaining that the "main problem for writers in the field is that even those scholars who know the most about faculty bargaining don't know very much as they themselves will freely admit."[178] He suggests that the rapid growth "and often surprising shifts in the faculty-unionism movement breed humility among those who try to study it." In the meantime the movement continues, and as Semas noted earlier in the year, 1974–75 was destined to see "the most aggressive campaigns so far to organize college professors into unions."[179] The National Education Association was committing $1 million to "basic organizing" of college professors, the American Federation of Teachers was launching a "substantial" effort, and a political activist, James D. Duffey, had been selected to head up the American Association of University Professors as the new general secretary. While organizing efforts were to concentrate in states that have laws giving professors the right to unionize, professors in other states, such as Ohio and Colorado, were working to gain bargaining rights without state legislation.[180]

My own judgment is that the continuing expansion of collective bargaining will change patterns of governance. It will not, however, be so much a question of whether the effect will be beneficial or detrimental as it will be of how faculty will accommodate to new structures and procedures. It is highly unlikely that faculties, once so committed, will abandon collective bargaining; the history of the labor movement indicates the contrary. How, then, will faculty work within the new conditions? Governance of the American university has never been static; the system has been in a state of change from the opening of the Puritans' boarding school on the banks of the Charles to the present day. Some of the ambiguity that Boyd sees as important in the way that faculty have gained power in the past will be lost. Less will be left to the ad hoc approach that has characterized so much of American higher education. But whether the clearer specification of responsibilities and expectations will result in better quality of teaching and other service will, as has always been the case, depend on the individual and private motivation of the faculty members. The new structures will set certain parameters, but faculty will learn to live within them as they have in past structures. There will have to be similar accommodations to new approaches to the question of tenure.

The Students as Participants in Governance

Except in rare instances, students have not shared with the faculty an equal role in the governance of colleges and universities. In medieval Bologna the students held the balance of power for many years, and at those institutions which have been patterned after the Italian model, students still play a large role in directing the university. In northern Europe, however, and in the United States, the move toward including students to a greater degree in governance is a fairly recent phenomenon. Leon Epstein observes that studies of university governance made before 1960 tended to ignore the impact of students on the decision-making process, that "before the late 1960s students did not participate in the university's formal governing structure except in a few marginal areas," and whatever influence they may have exerted as individuals was not considered an aspect of governance.[181] Indeed, in a study published as late as 1967 the authors are quoted as bluntly declaring that they "regard students not as members of universities but as one of several clienteles we choose to put to one side as far as our studies are concerned."[182] And in Canada the Subcommittee on Research and Planning of the Presidents of Universities of Ontario noted that the Duff-Berdahl report on University Government in Canada "devoted two and a half of its one hundred pages to the role of students in the governance of universities." The report was published in 1966. The subcommittee continues, "A year, even six months later, the student role would unquestionably have received ten times as much attention."[183]

By the late 1960s and into the 1970s the topic of the student role in governance in colleges and universities had become a lively one. With few exceptions the reports and analyses of the events on American college and university campuses during this period concluded with calls for greater student involvement in college and university governance. Earl McGrath contends:

143

The evidence indicates that revolutionary changes are occurring in the structure of government in American colleges and universities. Some of the most significant of these alterations in practices which have existed for centuries are related to the role of students in the academic bodies which determine the purposes and practices of higher education. Hardly an institution remains untouched by the activities of students aimed at gaining a voice in majority policy-making decisions.[184]

In the same mood the *Christian Science Monitor* for July 19–21, 1969, carried a full-page report on "Student Power: Can It Help Reform the System?" The opening paragraphs stated that student power is moving in new directions on the campus, that students are "asking for a piece of the action, not to run the university but to input their views into the power structure." Interviews with university officials prompted the reporters to say that there was a "swelling tide of opinion that . . . students have a point when they demand a change in the educational system," and many of the reports dealing with campus problems were calling for involvement of students in institutional governance.[185] The Special Committee on Campus Tensions appointed by the American Council on Education and headed by Sol M. Linowitz recommended that students be given "substantial autonomy in their non-academic activities" and opportunities to "participate in matters of general educational policy, especially in curricular affairs."[186]

Judging from the research of Harold Hodgkinson, students have been gaining more power in the university. On the basis of response from 1,230 presidents to the question of whether student control had increased or decreased between 1958–68, it was reported that in 67 percent of the institutions the amount of student control in establishing regulations governing student conduct had increased, that there had been an increase in 63 percent of the institutions in the amount of student control in institutionwide policy formation, that in 58 percent of the institutions there was more student control in academic decision-making, and that in 55 percent of the institutions there was more student control in enforcing regulations governing student conduct.[187] One of the problems in interpreting these responses, however, is that we have no clear indication what the particular degree of involvement in any one case may have been or may be now. We do have the word of the presidents that there was more involvement or participation in 1968 than there was in 1958, but we do not know whether there was only a bit more or a great deal more, and we only have the presidents' perceptions of what happened, not the students' assessment.

A study conducted by Earl McGrath involved 875 colleges and universities and their responses to questionnaires mailed in September 1969. He found that in 88.3 percent of the colleges students were participating in one or more faculty committees. Most often the student membership was in the faculty curriculum committee. The survey revealed the students were members of faculty curriculum committees in 57.8 percent of the institutions, although they had voting membership in only 46.1 percent. Students were least likely to be found as members of any faculty committee that dealt with selection, promotion, and tenure of faculty members, but McGrath found that 4.7 percent of the institutions reported student participation in such committees, and in 3.3 percent of the colleges responding the students had voting membership in these committees.

Other committees in which students had membership, together with the percentage of institutions reporting that membership, are student life (34.3), library (31.2), public events and lectures (29.1), faculty executive committee (22.7), discipline (18.6), admissions (17.5), planning (9.7), and faculty committee on faculty selection, promotion and tenure (4.7). In addition it was observed that in 20 percent of the institutions students were related in some way to the board of trustees, in 10.6 percent they either had membership in or sat with trustee committees, but in only 2.7 percent did they have voting membership on the board.[188] McGrath observed that the survey, which was undertaken under the auspices of the American Academy of Arts and Sciences, represented the first attempt to secure a comprehensive report on the extent of student involvement in academic government. The main generalization reached by McGrath was that, "although until three or four years ago American colleges and universities severely limited the involvement of students in academic government, now membership in one or another 'faculty' committees is becoming the rule rather than the exception."[189]

An ERIC Clearinghouse on Higher Education review of research on "Student Participation in Academic Governance" included a report of a Gallup Poll in 1971 showing some 81 percent of the student respondents favoring more student participation in making decisions in the colleges. The ERIC review also reported:

> Research surveys on student participation in academic governance have usually tried to determine what current practices and policies are, or have assessed a particular group of attitudes toward the decision-making role of students. . . . Generally, the surveys indicate that student membership on academic committees or other governing bodies is a recent but widespread phenomenon. . . . The kinds of changes that are increasing student control over the university policy are almost as numerous as the institutions reporting them and few regional differences can be found. . . . It is clear, however, that student influence is largely confined to non-academic matters in which students have traditionally had some voice.[190]

The review noted further that researchers seem to be in agreement that students have gained little decision-making responsibility in such areas as curriculum planning, faculty selection, admission, college financing, or general institutional planning.

The *Chronicle of Higher Education,* in an issue dated January 25, 1971, reported on a survey undertaken by the American Civil Liberties Union. The ACLU surveyed 155 college presidents and found that students on most campuses were involved in decision-making in such matters as admissions, student financial aid, planning of buildings and grounds, administrative appointments, and judicial regulations. On the other hand, most of the institutions reported that students were not involved in evaluating the administration or in budget-making. In academic areas traditionally controlled by the faculty, students had been given some role in policy-making but were generally excluded from personnel decisions, and most institutions reported that students were not involved in faculty selection or promotion. In 80 of the institutions students were voting members of the governing boards, and in another 46 students were included as nonvoting members of the boards.[191] Henry Mason reports a survey undertaken by the Office of Institutional Research of East Carolina University involving 85 institutions and undertaken in November-December 1968. It was reported that, of the 59 institutions replying, 45 had included student voting members on at least one committee. In 13 of the institutions students were serving on the university senate.[192]

146

Leonard Hawes and Hugo Trux, in a review of studies of student participation, reported that student involvement was "mild," that most colleges and universities were willing to provide more opportunity than was demanded by the students themselves, and that student concern was primarily with student affairs and the curriculum. Another study, in assessing the impact of student participation, suggested that the student primarily played a protesting role, that complex problems of administration were dealt with in a "very superficial manner" in joint student-faculty groups, that "inordinate amounts of time" were spent trying to brief the student members on the issues, and that students generally felt inadequate to deal with issues and soon lost motivation to participate. Still another study reported limited representation from the students, irregular attendance, "scant orientation" to committee tasks, and inadequate means for discussing committee proposals with fellow students.[193]

Hawes and Trux describe their own study in a large Midwestern land-grant university. Seeking to find out how students actually participated in committee situations, they surveyed 264 non–committee members of the student body and in addition 64 chairpersons. Some 30 interviews involving 14 students, 15 faculty, and one staff member provided more detailed information on various persons' perceptions of the participation of the students in the decision-making process. They found that students were represented on 50 percent of the committees and that among these student representatives 52 percent were graduate students and 33 percent were seniors. In 92 percent of the 593 committees noted, the faculty were found to outnumber the students. The students generally expressed the opinion that they were underrepresented, while most faculty members expressed the opinion that student representation was adequate. The authors concluded that neither faculty nor student committee members had very clearly defined constituencies and that there were no clearly defined ways in which students could learn of the academic community structure. Because of this lack,

> students are largely unaware of existing power integration mechanisms. Consequently, very few clearly defined issue-oriented student groups are formed. . . . Nevertheless, student participation seems to be relatively effective. . . . Although student members influence decisions, this activity does not

result in a better informed, better organized student population, or more satisfactory student-faculty-administration integration.[194]

In a review of the student and faculty participation in policy-making at the University of Minnesota, Ruth Eckert found that the involvement of the students had increased significantly in recent years but that there was still a great distance "to go in awarding junior members of the academic community any substantial voice in its governance."[195] Eckert wrote that one of the major problems in making effective use of students on committees is the short term during which any student can actually serve; it appears that a student has little chance to do more than gain a general orientation to a given committee's role and current problems before his assignment has been completed, because the student's tenure at the university is so short in comparison with faculty tenure. Moreover, students tend to be in the minority in committees and "having only one or two student members on a committee . . . has not encouraged vigorous expression of the students' point of view." One exception at the University of Minnesota has been the Senate Committee on Student Affairs, where the students have held a majority of the membership appointment.[196]

On the other hand, there are some who would suggest that students ought not to become members of faculty committees. James Olsen argues that along with collective bargaining, student participation in governance represents "a departure from the concept that an institution of higher education was a community of scholars," and he doubts that the university can "continue to function and to meet the requirements of the student and of society, while maintaining academic integrity" if this situation develops further.[197]

Robert Wilson and Jerry Gaff reported on a study of faculty attitudes toward student participation in policy-making involving over 1,500 faculty in six different colleges and universities in three states. (Usable responses were received from 70 percent, or 1,069 persons.) The writers found that two-thirds of the faculty replying were in favor of having students involved in formulating social rules and regulations, that 45 percent were prepared to give students an equal vote on committees, and that 21 percent would give students the sole responsibility for their own social regulations. On the other

148

hand, when it came to academic policies, while 60 percent said that students should have some voice, only 36 percent would allow students to vote on academic policy matters and only 9 percent would be willing to grant students "an equal vote with the faculty."[198]

A different perspective on faculty opinion regarding student participation is suggested by Edward Gross and Paul Grambach's study of university goals and academic power among 68 nondenominational universities in the United States. The researchers received responses from 8,828 administrators and 6,756 faculty, 46.4 percent of those asked to participate. Overall, the respondents ranked "run the university democratically" as the twenty-ninth most important goal and "involve students in university government" as forty-fifth. Top ranking went to "protect academic freedom," followed by "increase or maintain prestige."[199] When asked to list goals according to preference, "protect academic freedom" was still at the top, "run the university democratically" advanced to twenty-second, and "involve students in university government" dropped to forty-sixth. One commentator on the Gross and Grambach data suggests that there is evidence that the goals of protecting academic freedom and increasing or maintaining academic prestige may actually conflict with increasing student participation.[200]

Wilson and Gaff found that the faculty sorted themselves out into at least two different groups, one of which would provide considerable room for student involvement and the other of which accepted only a restricted role for students. The positions taken by the faculty in the Wilson-Gaff study reflect what have come to be basic philosophical dispositions. The arguments for student involvement generally include the following: (1) those affected by the educational program should have some larger opportunity to define the nature of the program; (2) the contemporary student is more serious and informed and prepared for participation; (3) if students are to be educated for democratic living, they must participate in democratic decision-making on the campus; (4) students are able to make some judgments about the quality of their education and should help to improve higher education; (5) with the abolition of the doctrine of *in loco parentis* and in keeping with the new styles of student life, students should be treated as adults and admitted to the adult society of the university; (6) students are

149

especially well situated to make judgments about faculty performance and can help in the improvement of instruction.

Against expanding student involvement the following arguments have been advanced: (1) if proportional representation is to be given, students would soon come to dominate the academy, to the long-term detriment of higher education; (2) students are still, in spite of their seeming maturity, students, and by virtue of lack of experience they are unqualified to make long-term decisions for the university; (3) students spend only four years in any one institution, and many spend less; (4) the college or university is constituted by special experience and knowledge, and the students do not have the broad range of experience of a professional; (5) students cannot and will not give the time necessary to carry on the hard work of university governance.

During and immediately after the campus disruptions of the late 1960s and early 1970s, there was an almost universal response that one of the major causes of disruption was that students had not been sufficiently involved in the governance of the university, and recommendation after recommendation followed for increasing that involvement. Among the resolutions of the American Association for Higher Education in March 1969 was one that called for redefinition and clarification of university goals. In the process of redefining and clarifying goals, the universities were asked "significantly to involve all portions of the collegiate community in the re-examination process." It was made clear that students were to be included in the "collegiate community." The American Council on Education's Special Committee on Campus Tensions called for students being given "substantial autonomy in their non-academic activities." The report went on to indicate that students should

> participate in matters of general educational policy, especially in curricular affairs. Since increased participation will contribute to effective institutional decision-making and is also of educational benefit, students should serve in a variety of roles on committees that make decisions or recommendations. In some nonacademic areas students should have effective control; in some general educational policy matters they should have voting participation; in other matters, they should act in an advisory or consultative capacity. Effective student representation will not only improve the quality of decisions; it will also help to insure their acceptability to the student body.[201]

150

In similar ways the President's Commission on Campus Unrest called for "increased participation of student, faculty, and staff in the formulation of university policies."[202] These statements are only samples. Innumerable special reports, monographs, and books have made similar recommendations. Hardly an educational conference of any size failed to include in its consideration the recommendation for more student involvement in decision-making.

Regardless of the position one takes about the degree of student involvement that is desirable, the problem of how most effectively students are to be incorporated into any particular decision-making situation remains. Robert S. Powell, Jr., a graduate student at Princeton, is of the opinion that the particular mechanism for student participation will depend upon the characteristics of an individual campus, that there are not going to be any immediate and spectacular changes, that students will find participation as "boring, tedious, and time-wasting . . . as it is now to the faculty," but that students are capable of being reasonable in their judgments about the university, that students do have the time to spend, that comprehensive university codes embodying the rights and freedoms of all members of the community will be necessary, and that there will be conflict in the process.[203] As Powell has assessed the matter, the key to effective student involvement lies in a clear definition of the rights and freedoms of various groups on the campus.

Another student leader, Jay C. Shaffer, former head of the student government at Ohio State University, argues that one approach that would make existing student governments more attractive to the students would be to provide substantial financial undergirding and to have the university administration "give public evidence of its regard for the student government."[204] He recognizes that there are problems involved in student participation, that students are unsophisticated about the policy process itself, that they are transients, that they do not have access to information essential for effective participation, that student governments usually do not have the facilities normally available to other policy makers, that students are usually students first and policy participants second, and that students are sometimes treated in a condescending manner by those with whom they are working. He argues, however, that these difficulties can be met and that students can become effective policy participants.

151

Shaffer's confidence that student governments, if provided with greatly augmented financial support, would afford the most viable form of student involvement in university decision-making would draw little support from Henry Mason. On the basis of his own reviews of writing and research on the subject, Mason concludes:

> Real student participation in government cannot be accomplished merely by giving real powers rather than trivia to existing "student government." Instead, institutional devices must be found through which "student power" can be incorporated into regular channels of university government.[205]

For his part, he would seem to opt for the position that the basic unit for effective student participation is the department. Students might become voting members of regular departmental committees in which policies are discussed and formulated and nonvoting representatives in departmental faculty meetings where final decisions are made. And, if a separate general student government were to persist, students should be elected from departmental constituencies.

Richard Antes labels the alternatives—the development of a strong and separate student government or the adoption of a community government involving students, faculty, and administration—as extreme positions, and he finds that the more realistic position for university governance will be "to utilize parts of both methods, but to stress the latter method." While leaning to the community government pattern, he goes on to say that "the method will vary with the institution." He also emphasizes that involvement has to be more than simply advising, that students need to have a sense of exercising some impact on the decisions that are made.[206]

In his report prepared for the American Association for Higher Education, Morris Keeton also comes out in favor of employing a flexible approach. Instead of recommending any particular structure of governance, he proposes as a general principle: "Design the student role to obtain contributions available from student competencies and cooperation and to protect the other constituencies and the institution against undue effects of the special interests and limitations that apply on the particular campus."[207] In designing structures Keeton places considerable emphasis upon informal processes "where the intention to share authority is genuine and pervasive," and he urges developing different patterns of participation in response to different types of policy and program decisions required. He calls attention to the existence of various student subgroups on campuses and calls for "flexibility and complexity uncommon to our presently complex society."[208]

The picture that emerges in the mid-1970s is one in which, after the initial waves of almost euphoric advocacy of more direct student involvement in planning university affairs have passed, most institutions have found that simply placing more students on more committees has had very limited impact on the way in which the university as a corporate body decides and plans its future. It seems clear that more students hold more positions on more faculty or general university committees than at any time in the past, and sundry reports continue to call for more such involvement. What is not as equally clear is whether either faculty or students—or administration, for that matter—are any more satisfied with the new state of affairs than with the former. Some faculty argue that with students on "their" committees the committees are no longer faculty committees; they are not sure what kind of committees they have. The students retort that with the majority of the committee being faculty members they, the students, cannot do much anyway, and they manage to absent themselves from more meetings than they attend. Separate, but equal, governance structures do not seem much more effective; student governments have difficulty in maintaining themselves, and they frequently find themselves shut out of the major policy matters anyway.

Various forms of all-university governing units are underway. As we have already observed, by early 1973 there were well over 600 such structures.[209] Earlier, the ERIC Clearinghouse on Higher Education had described such arrangements as the All-College Council at Maryville College in Tennessee, where six students, six faculty members, and six administrative officers constituted a long-range planning group for the college. Three other coordinating councils supplemented the All-College Council, one for academic, one for religious, and a third for social and recreational affairs. Yeshiva had created a College Senate of five administrators, eight faculty members, six students, and one nonvoting alumnus, with jurisdiction over academic standards, admissions policy, curriculum, degree requirements, policy in relation to scholastic performance, grading, and whatever other matters were referred by

153

administration, faculty, or student council. The University of New Hampshire had created a University Senate of 77 members, including 30 undergraduates and 5 graduate students. Syracuse University added 17 graduate and 28 undergraduate students as members of its University Senate.[210]

Some all-university units have already passed from the scene, but the idea is not likely to fade away, nor should it! Some such pattern would seem to hold important prospects for some kind of cooperative effort. But, as Bardwell Smith has so well observed in the discussion of the College Council at Carleton, on which there are seven student members, points of strong contention will emerge, and with all of the positive outcomes—if the group is patient and persistent—those involved must be prepared to strike a balance between the exhaustive discussion and the delegation of responsibility.[211] All-university approaches are important but are not the one best solution. Probably the greatest drawback to most governance schemes based on an all-university structure is that they are too simplistic. Clearly there is no single body that will be able to make all of the decisions in a college or university, especially if the institution is itself large and complex.

It is probably not a good idea to place all decisions before some democratic body equally representative of the public—and few such bodies have yet included any significant member of the "public"—the faculty, and the students. What Robert Helsabeck refers to as a "compound" system is more likely to provide a workable balance of forces. A "compound" system involves several decision-making groups, including an all-university body, if desired. The several groups vary in composition and in procedures followed. The general principle should be that there can be greater participation in resolving matters that have an impact on large numbers of people and less participation in matters that are more specialized and affect fewer people.[212] Clark Kerr, who himself has been on the firing line, comments that the problems of university governance are so complex that no single solution is possible, as situations vary so much from time to time; and no permanent solutions are likely, as institutions change in interests and roles. What is needed is a "practical pragmatic approach. . . . An effort should be made to sort out the general issue of governance into its component parts and then to approach each part in the light of the total problem." He calls for a series of consensuses and the employment of a variety of forms.[213]

We should now turn to suggestions for Dean Neumann, but before we do so we should note, at least in passing, what is happening to another segment of the decision-making process, the administration as represented by the president.

The Changing Role of Administration: The President

Harold W. Dodds, after retiring from the presidency of Princeton University, undertook with support from the Carnegie Corporation, a study of the American college president. The title of his report contained a question, "The Academic President—Educator or Caretaker?" Dodds was convinced that with all of the pressures coming to bear on the president, the answer still had to be that the president must devote 50 percent of his time to educational matters. The president is the educational leader of the institution, and unless he can give sufficient time to this aspect of his leadership, "the outlook for higher education is far more dismal than we are prepared to admit." Dodds could not conceive of the president delegating to others an "overriding responsibility toward the university's primary role."[214] The president's leadership had to be expressed within an academic climate, and according to Dodds the president "must be willing to accept a definition of leadership that brings about change less by the sheer power of his office and more by informal, friendly, and persuasive means."[215] Ralph Prator, writing a year later, apparently agreed, because he referred to the president as "the leader of a specialized team . . . the coordinator, the catalyst, the generalist who draws resource information from people involved in the specialized affairs of the college."[216]

There is a sense of unreality in the comments of Dodds and Prator, especially as we have emerged from the conflicts of the late 1960s and early 1970s. They both seem to be describing a past age, one almost idyllic in comparison to the experiences of academic leaders in more recent years. Speaking out of the tensions of the chancellorship of the University of California, Berkeley, Roger Heynes, later president of the American Council on Education, told the Twenty-third National Conference on Higher Education that the only way in which leadership could operate effectively would be to give more power and effective responsibility to college and university administrators at all levels. He argued that the major

155

decision-making points should be identified and reponsibility and accountability should be centered in specific persons. He went on to say:

I am not suggesting that we should ignore all the data that indicates that organizational effectiveness goes up with broadening the base of leadership. But I think that there is an optimum balance in an organization between corporative and individual decisions and that in the university we are no longer as effective as we could be with a greater centralization of authority in persons.[217]

John Gardner, while still president of the Carnegie Corporation, in his annual report in 1965, came out with a view that is perhaps midway between those of Dodds and Heynes. Observing that in American society the nature of leadership is seldom understood, he said:

Most leaders are hedged around by constraints—traditional, constitutional limitations, the realities of the external situations, rights and privileges of followers, the requirements of team work, and most of all the inexorable demands of large-scale organization, which does not operate on capriciousness. In short, most power is wielded circumspectly.[218]

There are different styles of leadership, depending upon the task and the structure of the organization, but "anyone who accomplishes anything of significance has more confidence than the facts would justify." This quality has been something held in common by outstanding executives, gifted military commanders, brilliant political leaders, and great artists. Too many of the contemporary leaders are not prepared to decide. Instead they seem to prefer to go through a "series of clearances within the organization and let the clearance process settle it." They take polls; they devise statistical systems, cross-accounting systems, and information processing systems. Which is not to suggest that leadership can or should proceed without good information. The leader must know the facts or he is in trouble, but the leader must proceed with a degree of confidence that goes beyond the facts. Gardner refers to the little girl who told her teacher she was going to draw a picture of God. The teacher said, "But, Mary, no one knows what God looks like." To which Mary replied, "They will when I get through."[219]

156

Gardner notes that a good many people ask whether leaders are actually necessary. In the first place, "many scientific and professional people are accustomed to the kinds of problems that can be solved by expert technical advice or action." They see no need for leaders in the traditional sense. And then there are those who argue that leadership may somehow or other be at odds with the ideals of a free society. A good many young people on the contemporary scene argue in this vein. To which Gardner answers that while we may have outgrown certain kinds of leaders, particularly the autocratic, we cannot choose to do without leaders. Leadership is in the nature of social organization, in government, business, labor, politics, education, science, the arts, all fields. Leaders play an important part in creating the state of mind that characterizes society.

> They can serve as symbols of the moral unity of the society. They can make express the values that hold the society together. More important, they can conceive and articulate goals that lift people out of their petty preoccupations, carry them above the conflicts that tear society apart, and unite them in the pursuit of objectives worthy of their best efforts.[220]

These comments, though directed to organizations and leadership generally, would seem appropriately directed to higher education and the role of the president.

David Leslie describes the place of conflict in the contemporary university and suggests that we need to be more honest in seeing that the "modern public university is most emphatically *not* a cloistered retreat for like-minded scholars."[221] Conflict is a way of life in the university and the problem of leadership becomes that of accepting conflict as inevitable and finding how to deal with it in constructive ways. To try to eliminate conflict is unrealistic, short of creating a wholly homogeneous unit—which, by definition, stifles diversity. To overcome conflict by redistributing power may, according to Leslie, result in a cure worse than the disease. Rather than opting for major restructuring of the university, Leslie asks for developing more effective conflict management.

The 1970 Presidents Institute of the American Council on Education stressed the need for a new style of leadership. The report on the institute referred to the new presidents as "crisis managers"

157

and noted that "today's president must know something about new techniques of budgeting scarce resources, labor relations, the legal process, and the mediation of disputes under pressure."[222] David Bergquist's study of presidents in 1972–73 suggested that "increased demands from the faculty, mounting pressures from trustees, and rising student expectations" have all conspired to make the more experienced presidents perceive the job as becoming even more complex:

> The results of this study indicate that a college president can no longer rely on his years of presidential experience to assure the easy completion of defined job tasks. Regardless of the size of the institution or the type of advanced degree held . . . the presidents' job tasks grow increasingly complex, troublesome and difficult to complete.[223]

A report on the college president published in early 1974 was based on intensive interviews with 41 college presidents, 39 chief academic officers, 36 chief business officers, 42 presidents' secretaries, and 28 other officials close to the presidents; 42 institutions were included.[224] Among the generalizations made by the team were that the American college presidency is a relative job in which presidents tend to define their role as a responsive one in which they try to reconcile the conflicting pressures on the college; that the presidency is a parochial job in that institutions choose persons for the presidency who are well known to them; that the office is a conventional one in that the president comes to his job through a "series of filters that are socially conservative"; that the president himself views the job as a very important one, as a reward for his previous career; and that there is much that is myth in the presidency:

> The presidency is an illusion. Important aspects of the role seem to disappear on close examination. In particular, decision-making in the university seems to result extensively from a process that decouples problems and choices and makes the president's role more commonly sporadic and symbolic than significant.[225]

In examining from various sources the normative image of the president, the researchers conclude that there does not seem to be a clear core of objectives that presidents should pursue and "no clear set of attributes that will guarantee success."[226]

Michael Cohen and James March examine and find wanting most reports on "average tenure." They conclude that during most of the twentieth century the median college president has served about ten years.[227] They refer to the president as exercising leadership in "organizing anarchy," and while recommending some steps to combat the prevailing ambiguity, conclude that the fundamental problem of ambiguity will remain.[228]

If we accept the conclusions of Cohen and March, the role of the president as chief administrative officer of an institution of higher education in the mid-1970s is, and will remain, largely ambiguous. There are fewer and fewer instances in which a college or university can claim to be the lengthened shadow of a man. The higher educational enterprise is too complex and the forces working on any institution are too many to enable one person to control the destiny of the institution as might have been the case at the turn of the century. The role of the president, and of any university or college administrator, is not as simple and relatively unencumbered as Dodds found it to be in the late 1950s. Roger Heynes could plead for clearer definition of authority and responsibility in the late 1960s, but as the fourth quarter of the twentieth century begins, strength in flexibility is likely to be the key of effective leadership. Leadership is no less important than it has ever been; there are those who must play a key role in focusing the institution on goals that have been expressed. But it will more likely be an administrative team that will carry on the task. And the team will make use of planning and management skills, will draw upon various kinds of management information systems, as the current jargon has it, and will make use of numbers of planning units.

As Daniel Katz and Robert Kahn perceive it, the leadership is able to have and must have a "system perspective," a view of the total enterprise and its interrelated elements. Leadership calls for a sensitivity to environmental demands and an ability to integrate and harmonize the various subsystems of the institution. The essence of organizational leadership becomes "the influential increment over and above mechanical compliance with routine directives of the organization."[229] And what has happened to the role of the president in the enterprise has also happened to the other administrative officers, whatever their titles.

Building a Compound System

What recommendations can we make to Dean Neumann in his position of leadership in the College of Arts and Sciences in a medium-sized Midwestern university? How should he proceed to develop a governance system that is likely to respond to the goals he perceives developing for his institution? First of all, he must expect to have more involvement on the part of the trustees and the general public. And he should be prepared for the faculty to develop more ways of speaking to institutionwide problems, as reluctant as they may be to devote the time and effort to gaining an overall view. Certainly questions of tenure and collective bargaining will emerge as items of concern with increasing frequency. Students will continue to press for participation; though they may not man the barricades as they did in the 1960s, they will be no less concerned that the institution be responsive to what they see as the immediate and important issues. The president will sense more of the ambiguity of his role, and the other administrative officers, including Dean Neumann, will find themselves more involved in long discussions and team planning than in being the entrepreneurs they may have been in the past—although there will always be a place for *sensitive* entrepreneurship, if such is not a contradiction in terms.

More specifically, Dean Neumann's intuition that he needs a new structure is probably correct. A policy-determining body consisting of a few senior professors will likely prove more and more inadequate for the task of bringing needed reforms to the educational program. Likewise, Assistant Dean Starker's intuition about conflict is likely to prove correct, although putting representatives of the various constituencies in a single room so they can "fight it out" is hardly a solution to the present difficulties. Dean Neumann will need to sit down with his president and help design a "compound system" in which representatives of the public, the faculty and the students are involved in varying proportions on several different bodies dealing, each within its sometimes vague domain, with specific policy matters. The composition and processes of each governing unit will need to be developed in terms of the functions that are assigned to it. Those who are affected by the policies in question should be represented; but the best decisions are likely to come from those who bring a high level of competence and understanding to the problems at hand. Flexibility and firmness, two qualities difficult to combine, will in the long run condition the

160

success of the units. Dean Neumann's own contribution may be greatest in the kind of governance system he helps to devise. Beyond that, he must engage in friendly persuasion and skillful mediation, always keeping in mind that each group will press to have its special interests served. No group alone and no member of a group alone— including Dean Neumann—will be able to serve the best interests of the institution. That requires a complex governance process that Dean Neumann can help to shape, but it will be a process in which he also shares.

Notes

[1]President's Commission on Campus Unrest, *Campus Unrest: The Report of the President's Commission on Campus Unrest* (Washington, D.C.: Government Printing Office, 1970), p. 202.

[2]Carnegie Commission on Higher Education, *Governance of Higher Education: Six Priority Problems* (New York: McGraw-Hill Book Co., 1971), p. 1.

[3]Reginald Edwards, "Emerging National Policies for Higher Education in Canada," in *Higher Education in a Changing World: The World Year Book of Education 1971/72,* ed. Brian Holmes and David G. Scanlon (New York: Harcourt Brace Jovanovich, 1971), pp. 324-325.

[4]Subcommittee on Research and Planning, Committee of Presidents of Universities of Ontario, *Towards 2000: The Future of Post-Secondary Education in Ontario* (Toronto: McClelland and Steward, 1971), p. 39.

[5]Murray Ross, "The Delusion of Academic Power in Canada: The University of Toronto Act," *Minerva,* 10 (April 1972), p. 242.

[6]George Allan, "Twixt Terror and Thermidor: Reflections on Campus Governance," *Journal of Higher Education,* 42 (April 1971), p. 292.

[7]E. D. Duryea, "Reform in University Government," *Journal of Higher Education,* 43 (May 1971), p. 339.

[8]Stanley Ikenberry, "The Organizational Dilemma," *Journal of Higher Education,* 43, (January 1972), p. 23.

[9]Scott Edwards, "An Academic Chairman Looks at Governance," *Change,* 4 (September 1972), p. 24.

[10]T. R. McConnell, "Faculty Government," in *Power and Authority,* ed. Harold L. Hodgkinson and L. Richard Meeth (San Francisco: Jossey-Bass, 1971), pp. 98-99.

[11]Clark Kerr, "Governance and Functions," *The Embattled University,* ed. Stephen R. Graubard and Geno A. Ballotti (New York: George Braziller, 1970), p. 108.

[12]Howard R. Bowen, "Governance and Educational Reform," in *Agony and Promise: Current Issues in Higher Education, 1969,* ed. G. Kerry Smith (San Francisco: Jossey-Bass, 1969), pp. 173-174.

[13]Paul L. Dressel, et al., *Return to Responsibility* (San Francisco: Jossey-Bass, 1972), pp. 178-180.

[14]Duryea, "Reform in University Government," p. 342.

[15]*Ibid.,* p. 13.

[16]Clark Kerr, "Administration in an Era of Change and Conflict," *Educational Record,* 54 (Winter 1973), pp. 38-46.

[17]*Ibid.,* p. 45.

[18]*Ibid.,* pp. 45-46.

[19]Stephen R. Graubard, "Preface," in Graubard and Ballotti, *The Embattled University,* p. xv.

[20]*Ibid.,* p. xvii.

[21]Allan, "Twixt Terror and Thermidor: Reflections on Campus Governance," pp. 292-293.

[22]*Ibid.,* p. 294.

[23]Kenneth P. Mortimer, "The Dilemmas in New Campus Governance Structures," *Journal of Higher Education,* 42 (June 1971), p. 470.

[24]T. R. McConnell, "Accountability and Autonomy," *Journal of Higher Education,* 42 (June 1971), 460.

[25]Earl C. Bolton and Fredric H. Genck, "Universities and Management," *Journal of Higher Education,* 42 (April 1971), pp. 279-291.

[26]Ikenberry, "The Organizational Dilemma," p. 24.

[27]*Ibid.,* p. 34.

[28]Stanley Ikenberry, "Restructuring College and University Organization and Governance: An Introduction," *Journal of Higher Education,* 42 (June 1971), pp. 421-429.

[29]Carnegie Commission on Higher Education, *Governance of Higher Education,* p. vii.

[30]John F. Budd, Jr., "Are College Trustees Obsolete?" *Saturday Review/World,* 1 (March 9, 1974), p. 48.

[31]M. M. Chambers, "Who is the University?" *Journal of Higher Education,* 30 (June 1959), p. 324.

[32]Steven V. Roberts, "Battle Over Academic Freedom at U.C.L.A.," *New York Times,* October 12, 1969, p. 11.

[33]Richard Hofstadter, *Academic Freedom in the Age of the College* (New York: Columbia University Press, 1961), p. 120.

[34]Huburt T. Beck, *Men Who Control Our Universities* (New York: Kings Crown Press, 1948).

[35]Christopher Jencks and David Riesman, *The Academic Revolution* (New York: Doubleday and Co., 1968), p. 269.

[36]Rodney T. Hartnett, *College and University Trustees: Their Backgrounds, Roles and Educational Attitudes* (Princeton, N.J.: Educational Testing Service, 1969), p. 22.

[37]*Ibid.,* p. 49ff.

[38]*Ibid.*

[39]"The Rich, Risky Life of a University Trustee," *Fortune,* 75 (January 1967), p. 124.

[40]James A. Perkins, *The University as an Organization* (New York: McGraw-Hill Book Co., 1973), p. 211.

[41]*Ibid.,* p. 214.

[42]Malcolm G. Scully, "Many Trustees Seek to Assert More Control," *Chronicle of Higher Education,* 8 (May 6, 1974), pp. 1, 2.

[43]Budd, "Are College Trustees Obsolete?" p. 48.

[44]*Ibid.,* p. 49.

[45]Harold C. Martin, "The Board of Trustees and the Making of Academic Policy," *Management Forum,* 3 (May 1974), p. 1.

[46]T. R. McConnell, *The Redistribution of Power in Higher Education: Changing Patterns of Governance* (Berkeley: Center for Research and Development in Higher Education, 1971), pp. 38-40.

[47]Henry L. Mason, *College and University Government, A Handbook of Principle and Practice,* Tulane Studies in Political Science, 14 (New Orleans: Tulane University, 1972), p. 29.

[48]Rodney T. Hartnett, *The New College Trustee: Some Predictions for the Future* (Princeton, N.J.: Educational Testing Service, 1970), p. 41.

[49]Junus A. Davis and Steve A. Batchelor, *The Effective College and University Board: A Report of a National Survey of Trustees and Presidents* (Washington, D.C.: Association of Governing Boards of Universities and Colleges, 1974), p. 24.

[50]Lyman A. Glenny, "State Systems and Plans for Higher Education," in *Emerging Patterns in American Higher Education* ed. Logan Wilson (Washington, D.C.: American Council on Education, 1965), p. 86.

[51]*Ibid.,* p. 87.

[52]Robert O. Berdahl, *Statewide Coordination of Higher Education* (Washington, D.C.: American Council on Education, 1971), p. 4.

[53]*Ibid.,* see pp. 20-21.

[54]Larry Van Dyne, "The Changing Face of Governance in Public Higher Education," *Compact,* 8 (September/October 1974), p. 9.

[55]Academy for Educational Development, *State Planning for Higher Education* (Washington, D.C.: Academy for Educational Development, 1969), p. 5.

[56]Berdahl, *Statewide Coordination of Higher Education,* p. 201.

[57]Allan O. Pfnister and Gary Quehl, *Private Higher Education in the State of Missouri* (Jefferson City: Missouri Commission on Higher Education, 1967).

[58]Allan O. Pfnister, "Developing Relationships Between Public and Private Higher Education," in *New Directions in Statewide Higher Education Planning and Coordination* (Atlanta, Ga.: Southern Regional Education Board, 1970), p. 46.

[59]Lyman A. Glenny et al., *Coordinating Higher Education for the '70s* (Berkeley: Center for Research and Development in Higher Education, 1971), p. 4.

[60]Van Dyne, "The Changing Face of Governance in Public Higher Education," p. 10.

[61]"Education Office Decides to Push '1202' Panels," *Chronicle of Higher Education,* 8 (March 11, 1974), p. 6.

[62]T. Harry McKinney, "Establishment of State Postsecondary Education Commissions," *Higher Education in the States,* 4 (November 7, 1974), p. 186.

[63]T. Harry McKinney, "Section 1202 State Commissions: Patterns of Development and Related Concerns," Robert H. Fenske and Kerry D. Romesburg, eds., in *Current Status, Planning and Prospects of the 1202 State Postsecondary Commissions: Proceedings of a Working Conference at Arizona State University,* Tempe, April 1975, p. 8.

[64]John D. Phillips, "Remarks on Section 1202 of the Higher Education Amendments of 1972," in *Current Status, Planning and Prospects of the 1202 State Postsecondary Commissions,* pp. 1-3.

[65]*Ibid.,* p. 3.

[66]Ben Lawrence, "1202 Commissions Dissolution or Survival," in *Current Status, Planning and Prospects of the 1202 State Postsecondary Commissions,* p. 37.

[67]Cheryl M. Fields, "Affirmative Action: Campus Officers Organize, Assess Their Status," *Chronicle of Higher Education,* 10 (May 5, 1975), p. 8.

[68]Cheryl M. Fields, "29 Universities Warned U.S. May Withhold Contracts," *Chronicle of Higher Education,* 10 (June 23, 1975), pp. 1, 6.

[69]Cheryl M. Fields, "Affirmative Action Reprieve; Universities Agree to Submit Plans in 30 Days," *Chronicle of Higher Education,* 10 (July 7, 1975), p. 5.

[70]Jack Magarrell, "The High Cost of Compliance," *Chronicle of Higher Education,* 10 (July 21, 1975), p. 1.

[71]Cheryl M. Fields, "Affirmative Action: Changes in Offing?" *Chronicle of Higher Education,* 10 (August 18, 1975), p. 3.

[72]M. B. Hackett, *The Original Statutes of Cambridge University* (Cambridge: At the University Press, 1970), p. 65.

[73]*Ibid.,* p. 103.

[74]Hofstadter, *Academic Freedom in the Age of the College,* p. 120.

75Walter Schenkel, "Who Has Been in Power?" in Hodgkinson and Meeth, *Power and Authority,* p. 15.

76*Ibid.,* p. 18.

77T. R. McConnell, "Faculty Government," in Hodgkinson and Meeth, *Power and Authority,* p. 99.

78E. D. Duryea, "Reform in University Government," pp. 347-348.

79Morris Keeton, *Shared Authority on Campus* (Washington, D.C.: American Association for Higher Education, 1971), p. 11.

80*Faculty Participation in Academic Governance,* Report of the AAHE-NEA Task Force on Faculty Representation and Academic Negotiations, Campus Governance Program (Washington, D.C.: American Association for Higher Education, 1967).

81*Ibid.,* p. 18.

82*Ibid.,* p. 24.

83Duryea, "Reform in University Government," p. 348.

84Archie R. Dykes, *Faculty Participation in Academic Decision Making* (Washington, D.C.: American Council on Education, 1968), pp. 41-42.

85*Ibid.,* p. 38.

86*Ibid.,* p. 42.

87Ernest G. Palola et al., "The Reluctant Planner: Faculty in Institutional Planning," *Journal of Higher Education,* 42 (October 1971), pp. 598, 599.

88McConnell, "Faculty Government," in Hodgkinson and Meeth, *Power and Authority,* p. 100.

89*Ibid.,* pp. 102-103. See also Kenneth P. Mortimer and T. R. McConnell, "Faculty Participation in University Governance," in *The State of The University,* ed. Carlos E. Kruytbosch and Sheldon L. Messinger (Beverly Hills, Calif.: Sage Publications, 1970), pp. 111-131.

90Mason, *College and University Government,* pp. 55-70.

91Burton Clark, "Faculty Organization and Authority," in *Academic Governance,* ed. J. Victor Baldridge (Berkeley: McCutchan Publishing Corp., 1971), p. 236.

92*Ibid.,* pp. 237-247.

93*Ibid.,* p. 247.

94Mason, *College and University Government,* p. 77.

95*Ibid.,* p. 81.

96Frederick E. Balderston, *Managing Today's University* (San Francisco: Jossey-Bass, 1974), p. 47.

97*Ibid.,* p. 49.

98James Brann and Thomas A. Emmet, eds. *The Academic Department or Division Chairman: A Complex Role* (Detroit: Balamp Publishing, 1972).

[99]Winston W. Hill and Wendell L. French, "Perceptions of the Power of Department Chairmen by Professors," in Baldridge, *Academic Governance,* pp. 208ff.

[100]Paul L. Dressel and Donald J. Reichard, "The University Department: Retrospect and Prospect," *Journal of Higher Education,* 41 (May 1970), pp. 387ff.

[101]Paul L. Dressel et al., *The Confidence Crisis* (San Francisco: Jossey-Bass, 1970), p. 7.

[102]*Ibid.,* p. 11.

[103]*Ibid.,* 232.

[104]Ikenberry, "The Organizational Dilemma," p. 34.

[105]Dressel et al., *The Confidence Crisis,* pp. 120ff.

[106]JB Lon Hefferlin, *The Dynamics of Academic Reform* (San Francisco: Jossey-Bass, 1969), p. 150.

[107]Philip W. Semas, "U. of New Hampshire Tries Representation Government: Reactions Mixed," *Chronicle of Higher Education,* 4 (July 6, 1970), pp. 1, 6.

[108]Robert S. Morison, *Students and Decision-Making* (Washington, D.C.: Public Affairs Press, 1970). For a report on the development of the Constituent Assembly, see Paul P. Van Riper et al., *Cornell Constituent Assembly: Summer Research Reports* (Ithaca, N.Y.: Cornell University, 1969).

[109]"Joint Student-Faculty-Administration at Lehigh," *School and Society,* 98 (October 1970), pp. 331-332.

[110]ERIC Clearinghouse on Higher Education, *Compendium Series of Current Research, Programs and Proposals,* no. 1: *Governance* (Washington, D.C.: ERIC Clearinghouse on Higher Education, 1970).

[111]William F. Sturner, "University Governance Through the Bicameral Legislature," *Journal of Higher Education,* 42 (March 1971), p. 219, 220.

[112]*Ibid.,* p. 223.

[113]Mortimer, "The Dilemmas in New Campus Governance Structures," p. 471.

[114]*Ibid.,* p. 478.

[115]Kenneth P. Mortimer, "Forms of Campus Governance: Joint Participation, Separate Jurisdiction and Collective Bargaining," paper presented at the Association of American Colleges Annual Meeting," January 16, 1973.

[116]Bardwell L. Smith, "New Governance, Old Problems," *Liberal Education,* 58 (December 1972), pp. 478-487.

[117]*Ibid.,* p. 481.

[118]*Ibid.,* p. 482.

[119]*Ibid.,* p. 484.

[120]*Ibid.,* p. 485.

[121]Florence Moog, "Tenure is Obsolete," in *The Expanded Campus:Cur-Current Issues in Higher Education, 1972,* ed. Dyckman W. Vermilye (San Francisco: Jossey-Bass, 1972), p. 133.

[122]Walter P. Metzger, "Academic Tenure in America: A Historical Essay," in Commission on Academic Tenure in Higher Education, *Faculty Tenure: Report of the Commission on Academic Tenure in Higher Education,* (San Francisco: Jossey-Bass, 1973).

[123]*Ibid.,* p. 122.

[124]*Ibid.,* p. 148.

[125]Elain H. El-Khawas and W. Todd Furniss, *Faculty Tenure and Contract Systems: 1972 and 1974,* Higher Education Panel Reports, no. 22, December 1974 (Washington, D.C.: American Council on Education).

[126]Philip W. Semas, "Tenure: 2 in Every 5 Colleges Are Now Reviewing It," *Chronicle of Higher Education,* 9 (December 2, 1974), pp. 1, 7.

[127]Philip W. Semas, "Bloomfield College Embroiled in a Bitter Fight Over Decisions to Cut Faculty, Abolish Tenure," *Chronicle of Higher Education,* 8 (October 15, 1973), p. 1, 4.

[128]Philip W. Semas, "Southern Illinois Fires 104, Acts to Bar Appeals," *Chronicle of Higher Education,* 8 (January 14, 1974), pp. 1, 8.

[129]Karen J. Winkler, "Bloomfield: A Troubled College is Put In Court Receivership," *Chronicle of Higher Education,* 8 (August 19, 1974), p. 2.

[130]"Southern Illinois to Push Suit Against 19 Teachers," *Chronicle of Higher Education,* 8 (June 24, 1974), p. 2.

[131]Philip W. Semas, "Tenured Professors Have Only Limited Protection Against Emergency Layoffs, Federal Judge Rules," *Chronicle of Higher Education,* 8 (June 24, 1974), pp. 1, 2.

[132]Malcolm G. Scully, "Tenure: An Iowa Court Says Financial Exigency Justifies Firing a Teacher," *Chronicle of Higher Education,* 8 (August 9, 1974), p. 2.

[133]William A. Sievert, "Tenure Dispute Tests 2 Roles of President," *Chronicle of Higher Education,* 8 (May 28, 1974), pp. 1, 2.

[134]*Ibid.*

[135]"Tenure and Retirement: Court Lets University Change Mandatory Age," *Chronicle of Higher Education,* 10, (August 18, 1975), p. 6.

[136]Victor G. Rosenblum, "Legal Dimensions of Tenure," in Commission on Academic Tenure in Higher Education, *Faculty Tenure,* p. 161.

[137]*Ibid.,* p. 193.

[138]See Commission on Academic Tenure in Higher Education, *Faculty Tenure,* p. 13.

[139]*Ibid.,* pp. 1, 215-226.

[140]Commission on Academic Tenure in Higher Education, *Faculty Tenure,* p. 23.

[141]Robert L. Jacobson, "100 Colleges Defer Curbs on Tenure," *Chronicle of Higher Education,* 7 (March 26, 1973), p. 6. See also January 22, 1973, issue of the *Chronicle.*

[142]Commission on Academic Tenure in Higher Education, *Faculty Tenure,* pp. 48-49.

[143]Philip W. Semas, "Tenure Quotas Draw Heavy Fire From Professors' Association," *Chronicle of Higher Education,* 7 (May 7, 1973), pp. 1, 7.

[144]Dabney Park, Jr., "Tenure Shock,"*Chronicle of Higher Education,* 7 (June 4, 1973), p. 16.

[145]Philip W. Semas, "Union Hits AAUP for Its Position on Tenure Quotas," *Chronicle of Higher Education,* 8 (December 10, 1973), pp. 1, 12.

[146]"High Cost in N.J. Upholds State's Tenure Restrictions," *Chronicle of Higher Education,* 8 (April 1, 1974), p. 3.

[147]Philip W. Semas, "Faculty Layoffs: AAUP Revises Its Recommendations," *Chronicle of Higher Education,* 9 (November 11, 1974), p. 2.

[148]"Where College Faculties Have Chosen or Rejected Collective Bargaining Agents," *Chronicle of Higher Education,* 8 (June 10, 1974), p. 24.

[149]Philip W. Semas, "4-Year Colleges to Be Targets of Unionizers," *Chronicle of Higher Education,* 7 (October 2, 1972), pp. 1, 5.

[150]"Collective Bargaining on Campuses," *Chronicle of Higher Education,* 10 (June 9, 1975), p. 5.

[151]"AAUP Revises Policy on Collective Bargaining," *Academe,* (February, 1970), p. 1.

[152]Sanford H. Kadish, "The Theory of the Profession and Its Predicament," *AAUP Bulletin,* 50 (June, 1972).

[153]Robert L. Jacobson, "AAUP Votes Overwhelmingly to Pursue Bargaining," *Chronicle of Higher Education,*6 (May 15, 1972), pp. 1, 2.

[154]Philip W. Semas, "Unions New Chief Sets Sights on Colleges," *Chronicle of Higher Education,* 8 (September 3, 1974), pp. 1, 4.

[155]Philip W. Semas, "Faculty Unionization," *Chronicle of Higher Education,* 8 (July 8, 1974), p. 5.

[156]Philip W. Semas, "Union Balloting; This Will Be a Big Year for It on U.S. Campuses," *Chronicle of Higher Education,* 11 (September 15, 1975), p. 10.

[157]Philip W. Semas, "Where Bargaining Laws Stand in 7 States," *Chronicle of Higher Education,* 10 (September 2, 1975), p. 9. See also Education Commission of the States, *A Legislator's Guide to Collective Bargaining in Education* (Denver, Colo.: Education Commission of the States, 1975), pp. vi-ix.

[158]Philip W. Semas, "Union Balloting," p. 10.

[159]"NLRB's Jurisdiction Upheld," *Chronicle of Higher Education,* 10 (April 21, 1975), pp. 1, 6.

[160]Everett C. Ladd, Jr., and Seymour M. Lipset, *Professors, Unions, and American Higher Education,* (Berkeley: Carnegie Commission on Higher Education, 1973).

[161]See Myron Lieberman, "Professors, Unite!" *Harpers Magazine,* 243 (October, 1971).

[162]Ladd and Lipset, *Professors, Unions, and American Higher Education.*

[163]William D. Boyd, "The Impact of Collective Bargaining on University Governance," *Liberal Education,* 58 (May 1972), pp. 265-271.

[164]E. D. Duryea and Robert S. Fisk, "Higher Education and Collective Bargaining," *Compact,* 6 (June, 1972), p. 41.

[165]Lieberman, "Professors, Unite!" p. 69.

[166]James K. Olsen, "Governance by Confrontation: Adversarialism at the University," *Intellect,* 102 (March 1974), p. 364.

[167]Philip W. Semas, "Faculties at the Bargaining Table; A Special Report," *Chronicle of Higher Education,* 8 (November 26, 1973), pp. 9-10. In the same issue see also other articles, pp. 10-14, and Donald E. Walters, "Collective Bargaining: Helping to Restore Collegiality," p. 24.

[168]See excellent summary in Higher Education Services Division, Education Commission of the States, *Faculty Collective Bargaining in Postsecondary Institutions: The Impact on the Campus and on the State* (Denver, Colo.: Education Commission of the States, May, 1972).

[169]Carol H. Shulman, "Collective Bargaining on Campus: Recent Experiences," in ERIC Higher Education Research Currents, *College and University Bulletin,* 26 (May 1974), pp. 3-6.

[170]Dressel et al., *Return to Responsibility,* pp. 108-109.

[171]Edward J. Bloustein, "Collective Bargaining and University Governance," paper presented at the annual meeting of the Association of American Colleges, January 15, 1973.

[172]Leon D. Epstein, *Governing the University* (San Francisco: Jossey-Bass, 1974), pp. 143-144.

[173]Philip W. Semas, "New Jersey Walkout Ends," *Chronicle of Higher Education,* 9 (December 9, 1974), p. 2.

[174]See Philip W. Semas, "Push Meets Shove in New Jersey," *Chronicle of Higher Education,* 9 (December 16, 1974), p. 3.

[175]Kenneth P. Mortimer and G. Gregory Lozier, "Contracts of Four-Year Institutions," in *Faculty Unions and Collective Bargaining,* ed. E. D. Duryea and Robert S. Fisk (San Francisco: Jossey-Bass, 1973), pp. 123-129.

[176]James P. Begin, "Faculty Governance and Collective Bargaining: An Early Appraisal," *Journal of Higher Education,* 45 (November 1974), p. 589.

[177]*Ibid.,* p. 592.

[178]Philip W. Semas, "Putting Faculty Unions Between Covers," *Chronicle of Higher Education,* 9 (October 7, 1974), p. 10.

[179]Philip W. Semas, "Teacher Unions Girding," *Chronicle of Higher Education,* 9 (September 23, 1974), p. 3.

[180]See Philip W. Semas, "College-Level Bargaining Spurred by State Laws," *Compact,* 8 (July/August 1974), pp. 11-12 (a review of current state legislation on collective bargaining). See also "Strikes and Settlements," *Chronicle of Higher Education,* 9 (September 23, 1971), p. 3; "Unions-Campus Bargaining Elections and Strike Actions," *Chronicle of Higher Education,* 9 (September 30, 1974), p. 2.; "Recent Collective-Bargaining Actions," *Chronicle of Higher Education,* 9 (November 4, 1974), p. 3, and "Require Professors to Pay Union Dues," p. 3, in the same issue; and "Unions Gaining Campus Workers," *Chronicle of Higher Education,* 9 (February 18, 1974), pp. 1, 8.

[181]Epstein, *Governing the University,* p. 162.

[182]Quoted by Epstein from N. J. Demerath, R. W. Stephens, and R. R. Taylor, *Power, Presidents and Professors,* (New York: Basic Books, 1967), p. 4.

[183]Subcommittee on Research and Planning, Committee of Presidents of Universities of Ontario, *Towards 2000: The Future of Post-Secondary Education in Ontario,* p. 39.

[184]Earl J. McGrath, *Should Students Share the Power?* (Philadelphia: Temple University Press, 1970), p. 103.

[185]"Student Power: Can It Help Reform the System?" *Christian Science Monitor,* July 19-21, 1971.

[186]Sol M. Linowitz, *Campus Tensions: Analysis and Recommendations,* (Washington, D.C.: American Council on Education, 1970).

[187]Harold L. Hodgkinson, *Institutions in Transition* (New York: McGraw-Hill Book Co., 1971), pp. 26-29.

[188]McGrath, *Should Students Share the Power?,* pp. 106ff.

[189]*Ibid.,* p. 38.

[190]ERIC Clearinghouse on Higher Education, *ERIC Survey of Current Practices—Student Participation in Academic Governance: Review 1* (Washington, D.C.: The Georgetown University Press, 1970), p. 1.

[191]"Most Students Said to Play Limited Decision Making Role," *Chronicle of Higher Education,* 5 (January 25, 1971), p. 2.

[192]Mason, *College and University Government,* p. 109.

[193]Leonard C. Hawes and Hugo R. Trux IV, "Student Participation in the University Decision-Making Process," *Journal of Higher Education,* 45 (February 1974), pp. 124-125.

[194]*Ibid.,* pp. 133-134.

[195]Ruth E. Eckert, "Participation in University Policy-Making: A Second Look," *AAUP Bulletin,* 56 (Fall 1970), p. 313.

[196]*Ibid.,* pp. 308-314.

[197]Olsen, "Governance by Confrontation: Adversarialism at the University," p. 362.

[198]Robert C. Wilson and Jerry G. Gaff, "Student Voice—Faculty Response," in *The State of the University,* Kruytbosch and Messinger, p. 182.

[199]Edward Gross and Paul V. Grambach, *University Goals and Academic Power* (Washington, D.C.: American Council on Education, 1968), pp. 28-29.

[200]C. Michael Otten, "Ruling Out Paternalism: Student and Administrators at Berkeley," in Kruybosch and Messinger, *The State of the University,* p. 216.

[201]Linowitz, *Campus Tensions: Analysis and Recommendations,* p. 39.

[202]President's Commission on Campus Unrest, *Campus Unrest,* p. 203.

[203]Robert S. Powell, Jr., "Student Power and Educational Goals," in Hodgkinson and Meeth, *Power and Authority,* pp. 65-84.

[204]Jay C. Shaffer, "Students in the Policy Process," *Journal of Higher Education,* 41 (May 1970), p. 344.

[205]Mason, *College and University Government,* p. 86.

[206]Richard Antes, "Involving Students in University Governance," *NASPA Journal,* 9 (July 1971), p. 53.

[207]Keeton, *Shared Authority on Campus,* p. 19.

[208]*Ibid.,* p. 21.

[209]Mortimer, "Forms of Campus Governance."

[210]ERIC Clearinghouse on Higher Education, *Student Participation in Academic Governance.*

[211]Smith, "New Governance, Old Problems," p. 485.

[212]Robert E. Helsabeck, *The Compound System* (Berkeley: Center for Research and Development in Higher Education, 1973), p. 26.

[213]Clark Kerr, "Governance and Functions," in Graubard and Ballotti, *The Embattled University,* pp. 119-121.

[214]Harold W. Dodds, *The Academic President—Educator or Caretaker* (New York: McGraw-Hill Book Co., 1962), p. 2.

[215]*Ibid.,* p. 15.

[216]Ralph Prator, *The College President* (Washington, D.C.: The Center for Applied Research in Education, 1963), p. 102.

[217]Roger W. Heynes, "Stress and Administrative Authority," in *Stress and Campus Response,* ed. G. Kerry Smith (San Francisco: Jossey-Bass, 1968), p. 170.

[218]John W. Gardner, "The Antileadership Vaccine," in *Annual Report of Carnegie Corporation of New York, 1965,* p. 5.

171

[219]*Ibid.,* p. 12.

[220]*Ibid.,* pp. 11-12.

[221]David W. Leslie, "Conflict Management in the Academy: An Exploration of the Issues," *Journal of Higher Education,* 43 (December 1972), p. 709.

[222]Ian E. McNett, "A New Style of Presidential Leadership Is Emerging As 'Crisis Managers' Confront the 1970's," *Chronicle of Higher Education,* 4 (July 6, 1970), pp. 1, 2.

[223]David H. Bergquist, "Performance of College Presidents," *Intellect,* 102 (February 1974), p. 317.

[224]Michael D. Cohen and James G. March, *Leadership and Ambiguity* (New York: McGraw-Hill, 1974), p. xxi.

[225]*Ibid.,* pp. 1-2.

[226]*Ibid.,* p. 57.

[227]*Ibid.,* p. 162.

[228]*Ibid.,* pp. 195-216.

[229]Daniel Katz and Robert L. Kahn, *The Social Psychology of Organizations* (New York: John Wiley and Sons, 1966), p. 302.

Chapter
4
The Curriculum:
Transformation or Tinkering?

John Starker had once suggested, half in jest, I think, that the only way to get anything changed at this university would be to put members of the old guard, some students, some board members, and a few of the young turks together in a room, lock them up, and let them fight it out. I wondered what he thought of that idea now. It was late afternoon, and the sun was slipping into the treetops on the distant horizon as we entered my office in Old Main. We had just left what had become a very lengthy meeting of the general faculty, and we both felt the need to assess what had happened. The session had moved along reasonably well until Professor Dunkelwald presented the first report of the subcommittee on college calendar. Before he quite knew what had happened, the good professor was being alternately attacked and supported with vigorous comments from every part of the room. Starker and I judged that the opposing voices were more insistent than the supporting ones, and at one point we thought we were going to have a shouting match. We had expected some discussion, but hardly what broke out.

As we settled further into the deep chairs, my associate dean broke the silence again, "One thing I could never have predicted was the way Dunkelwald and Crabtree disagreed, in the open and with feeling. Crabtree was so caustic at times that I found myself sympathizing and agreeing with Dunkelwald. I never thought I would agree with that man on anything."

"That's what happens when you put three students, a trustee, and four faculty members on a committee and tell them to take a new look at the college calendar, no limitations. Even Dunkelwald can change his ideas in that kind of a situation."

"I knew the committee was going to come up with a proposal for something different," Starker commented. "I had been talking with Ralph

173

B., one of the students on the committee, just before the faculty meeting. But I didn't think the report would stir up so much comment. Maybe this particular report gave everyone a chance to attack something openly. The faculty has been fairly restrained up to this time."

We had been having progress reports from committees in a series of special faculty meetings this month. We had finally gotten faculty agreement to reexamine the curriculum, and after appointing the committees and giving them some time to get the preliminary work under way, we began the hearings. We did not expect any decisions at this stage, but we wanted the faculty and the other committees to have some idea of what other groups were doing. Besides, if a committee knew it was going to have to report to the faculty, it would have to get down to business. The committee on general education—and we still refer to "general education" here—had provoked a good bit of discussion, but it had been restrained discussion. We thought that the reaction to the calendar committee report would be fairly mild. But that committee, chaired by a known conservative, had come up with a recommendation for terms of varied lengths, ten weeks in the fall, a four-week interterm, and two nine-week terms extended from late January into early June. In itself the proposal was not very startling, but for our university it presented a challenge. We had used the semester as long as anyone present could remember, and the new proposal looked to some to be a disguised quarter system with some incomprehensible extras.

Starker was continuing, "But what got into Crabtree? I've never heard him argue with Dunkelwald before. They've always seen things the same way, and invariably they have come down against any change."

Professor Crabtree had argued that the semester system had been tested for 200 years—he was going a bit beyond our own institutional history— and that we ought to have some compelling reasons before changing anything. He himself had discovered nothing compelling in the committee report. He even argued that there was something "natural" about the semester; during the Christmas break—"breather," he called it—students gain new perspectives and new energy and return in January to do some of the best work of the term. I thought he was going to ask for a special break in May so that the same productivity level could be reached in June.

Several faculty members denounced the proposal as faddish, change for the sake of change. Others contended that short terms could only result in lowered standards, though they failed to identify which standards would be lowered. Still others referred to it as a harebrained idea. On the other hand, the proponents argued for the shortened terms on the basis that students could take fewer courses and concentrate more.

Then I recalled one of the comments made by Professor Dunkelwald. "Do you remember that Dunkelwald suggested that the new calendar

174

might force us to rethink some of our courses, even to redesign them. He seemed enthusiastic at the prospect, as enthusiastic as Dunkelwald can be."

The reaction was even sharper after that remark by the professor. The opponents were now convinced that the dean was trying to put something over on them. Up to this point in time talk of curriculum reform was on a polite level. It was something to talk about, but not to do much about. But now the threat was out in the open. And here was the archconservative, Dunkelwald, trying to sell the idea.

I had appointed Dunkelwald to the committee, and the committee had elected him to chair the deliberations. Starker had opposed the appointment. In spite of his earlier suggesting that the dissidents should all be put together in a room to fight things out, he could not see Dunkelwald on the committee. But I argued that the committee would need some credibility—and what better means than the appointment of one of the older and more respected members of the faculty.

We had wanted to test the wind, and at this time it seemed that we had stirred up a tornado. We wondered how the calendar committee would now react to the faculty opinion.

*There was a knock at the door. My secretary had left long ago. Starker got up and opened the door. Standing there was Professor Crabtree. "I was hoping you would still be here. May I have a word with **you?**" The emphasis on "you" was strong enough to make it clear that Starker was not being invited to stay.*

Curriculum as a System

In his assessment of enrollment prospects after that first unsettling meeting with the president and the other administrative officers, Dean Neumann had become convinced that improving recruitment, as important and critical as that was, could be only one part of the long-range effort his university would need to mount if it were going to do more than just survive the immediate future. Equally important was the greater retention of those who had first elected to attend the university. And perhaps one critical key to better retention would be the development of a curriculum that was both more responsive to the students who were enrolled and distinctive enough to give the university a clearer identity among the two score or so other institutions in the state. In instituting a plan for curriculum development the dean took a conservative approach and one that is typical of most colleges similar to his; he appointed a number of committees and charged each to examine some aspect of curriculum. While he fully expects faculty review will lead to the acceptance of some of the proposals generated by the committees, to the modification of others, and to the rejection of still others, he maintains an implicit faith that whatever results can be combined into some overall pattern. In any event, whatever changes are made will be, he is sure, better than nothing at all.

Joseph Axelrod would not be convinced that whatever results from Dean Neumann's efforts will be better than nothing at all. Axelrod has observed that the lack of long-lasting results of attempts at curriculum innovations,[1] the apparent lack of impact of efforts at change in colleges and universities, may lie in the failure of those involved in designing new curricular elements to have a broad enough conception of all that is involved in changing curricular patterns. In his own studies of curricular reform, he found that while reforms were instituted with enthusiasm, all too often the intended changes did not seem to "take."[2] If anything was evident in the failures, it seemed to him that there had been too little recognition of the curricular-instructional process as a system. One cannot change only one element in the system in any substantial way and expect the change to endure. There is, he contends, "a certain reciprocity between each element in the system and all the other elements . . . and before we can successfully reform one aspect of the process we must understand profoundly the connections between it and the other elements in the system."[3]

By way of illustrating the interrelationships in a curricular system, Axelrod isolates six elements: content, schedule, certification, group/person interaction, student experience, and freedom/control. The first three elements are called structural elements in that they refer to specific elements that are largely determined by the faculty. Faculty establish content in courses, develop the schedule of activities, and determine how the work of the students is to be evaluated or certified; these are elements open to faculty control. The second three elements are implemental in that they are conditions under which the first three elements may operate. The way in which persons interact in the group, the kinds of experience students bring to the learning situation, and the measure of freedom or control that is possible in the learning situation all condition the way in which content, schedule, and certification may be employed. In addition, each element interrelates to some degree with each other element. For example, a liberal arts college undertook to introduce a new kind of freshman composition course, but after a year of effort the plan was not at all working as it should have been. The new plan called for a combination of different class periods such as 30-minute sessions for certain purposes, three-hour sessions for other purposes, and many variations between. The Department of English, responsible for implementing the plan, was accustomed to classes that consisted of three periods of 50 minutes scheduled for three times a week. The new plan also required several different kinds of meeting-places. Without the college having made adequate provision for modifying scheduling in time and place, the content of the proposed course simply could not be adequately developed. However desirable the educational outcomes implied by the content, there was no way for them to be realized.

Changing curriculum involves more than introducing variations in the content of particular courses. The term "curriculum" refers to the sum total of experiences afforded the student in the pursuit of his educational objectives. Content is related to scheduling; both content and scheduling are, in turn, related to certification, the manner in which the work performed is evaluated. The other three elements are likewise related to the first three: the way in which individuals interact within and with the group, the backgrounds students bring to the situation, and the degree of freedom and control that operates within the system. An isolated change will probably have a short life, because the broader setting or system within which the change is instituted may not have been sufficiently taken into account to provide support for the particular change.

College Curriculum Over a Decade, 1965-1975

As one reviews the literature in the mid-1970s about college curriculum, one can hardly fail to be impressed by at least two factors, (1) the great amount of writing that is being published, and (2) the similarity between what in 1965 was reported as new and innovative and that which is reported as new and innovative in 1975.

The Sixties

Early in 1962 the volume *The American College,* with an impressive subtitle, "A Psychological and Social Interpretation of

177

the Higher Learning," and well over a thousand pages of text, appeared. The first printing was exhausted almost at once, and a second printing was issued in April, to be followed by many additional printings and a shorter version entitled *College and Character* two years later. The editor of *The American College,* Nevitt Sanford, expressed surprise at the enthusiasm with which the book had been received; when the writers responsible for developing the book first considered the potential public, they only hoped that the publisher would be able to break even on the enterprise. But *The American College* captured the attention of a wide audience; it was one of the first comprehensive treatments of American higher education in the postwar years.

For one of the chapters in *The American College,* Joseph Katz and Nevitt Sanford collaborated on an essay about curriculm development. They wrote:

> Despite its central place in the program of the college, the curriculum rarely has been made the object of systematic investigation. There is, of course, a vast literature on the curriculum, but most of it has been concerned with descriptions of existing programs and with proposals for reform rather than with the demonstration of effects upon students. . . . It seems to have been almost universally assumed by educators that the college curriculum, as presently constituted, defines the goals of achievement for the student and that the nature of the curriculum is to be largely determined by whatever is the present state of the "body of knowledge." This assumption usually implies (1) an identification of the "body of knowledge" with the curriculum of the graduate school—a very debatable identification—and (2) only very limited attention to the role of such knowledge and the development of the student.[4]

The essay continued with a sometimes eloquent plea for more attention to personality development of students and made a strong case for a much broader conception of the meaning of curriculum.

While Katz and Sanford referred to a "vast literature on the curriculum," the amount of writing by current standards was fairly limited. In the Book Exhibit at the Nineteenth Annual National Conference on Higher Education in 1964, just over a decade ago, less than 100 books were singled out for inclusion as significant volumes under the category of "Undergraduate Curricula." These items carried publication dates from 1958 through 1964, and ranged down to a nine-page circular on "Experimental Colleges Since World War II," published by the Association for Higher Education. Two aspects of curriculum seemed to dominate the writing in this particular collection. At least 25 percent of the volumes dealt in one way or another with questions of general education and liberal education. Another 20 percent could be associated with some phase of teacher education. Various aspects of international education appeared to be the focus of 10 percent of the titles. The remaining 45 percent reflected a wide variety of concerns and included a substantial number of reports on individual institutional programs.

A year later, in 1965, McGraw-Hill published *Higher Education: Some Newer Developments,* in connection with the Twentieth Annual National Conference on Higher Education. The preface to that volume refers to the "crisis of numbers" in higher education and the "flood of students" bearing down on higher educational institutions. The enrollment in 1960 had been 3.6 million students, and a figure of 7 million was projected for 1970 and 8.7 million in 1975. (It may be noted that an enrollment of some 8.5 million had already been reached in 1970, and reports for fall 1975 indicated an enrollment of over 10 million students.) Those who were prepared to assume the role of prophet in 1965 were also anticipating a current expenditure figure of $9.8 billion in 1969-70 (it was actually $21.5 billion). Against this background of a mood of expansion, the editor of the volume, Samuel Baskin, summarized what appeared to be the main trends apparent in 1965. He found the larger institutions seeking to maintain the qualities of smallness while continuing to grow; some among them had created small autonomous colleges, each with its own faculty and student body, within the larger parent body. Independent and honors studies were being adapted to wider audiences, sometimes being introduced as an experience common to all students in an institution. Dormitories were being programmed as centers "for learning as well as living." Considerable attention was being given to applications of television and programmed instruction. Baskin observed considerable experimentation in campus architecture and building design in attempts to provide more effective use of the colleges' teaching and learning spaces. More colleges were moving to year-round operations. Study abroad was becoming possible for greater numbers of students, and more emphasis was being placed on world affairs and international studies. Baskin also found:

An increasing number of colleges are making use of some form of off-campus experience as a part of the student's undergraduate program. The trend here is not so much toward the adoption of alternating programs of work and study, as in colleges operating under the cooperative plan . . . as it is toward the development of flexible calendar plans that require or encourage the student to spend one or more quarters in some kind of off-campus or field experience. . . . Few changes in higher education have come more rapidly than the dramatic increase in programs for the abler or gifted student. . . . Most of the new honors programs make use of a wide variety of procedures in the accomplishment of their objectives. These include seminars, colloquia, independent study, theme groups, senior theses, research projects, waiver of course requirements, advanced placement and credit by examination, use of student honors committees and program development, honors centers . . . and the use of honors students, where feasible, in teaching, research, and counseling roles.[5]

Baskin concluded by indicating that institutions were also giving increased attention to various types of interinstitutional cooperation.

The Current Scene

In the mid-1970s we are experiencing enrollments considerably beyond those projected a decade ago, and, even adjusting dollar amounts for inflation, we find that current expenditures are much beyond those projected in 1964-65. We also find the writing about higher education has increased several-fold. However, as we look to the future, instead of foreseeing a "tidal wave" of students, we are anticipating more gradual growth during the remainder of the current decade and some consider not at all unlikely a leveling off during the 1980s and 1990s. With the "steady state" in enrollment we have also found growing disillusionment on the part of the general public with higher education, and we are experiencing a financial crunch that has been characterized as a "new depression" in higher education. Our mood alternates between deep gloom and hope simply for survival.

We find in current writing about curricular innovation reference to many of the developments reported by Baskin and his colleagues

180

as new in 1965. Perhaps there are fewer suggestions about how to maintain smallness within larger institutions. Independent study has been expanded to include various kinds of "nontraditional" study opportunities. There is somewhat less emphasis placed upon residence halls as centers for learning, as in recent years we have seen a substantial exodus of students from the residence halls (although by the fall of 1974 there appeared to be a reversal in the trend, for financial rather than programming reasons; the move back to the residence halls continued in 1975). We are still writing about the new media and technology. Seminars at the freshman level may be receiving somewhat more attention in 1975 than in 1965. While the primary emphasis may not be upon year-around learning, an incredible variety of calendars has appeared. Study abroad seems to have reached a peak and may be leveling off or declining as costs increase overseas. There continues to be significant development in off-campus experiences, and these are basic ingredients in the expanding nontraditional types of programs for the abler student as greater emphasis is being placed upon the disadvantaged and minority students in the effort to broaden the base of higher education. Interinstitutional cooperation of various types continues, although some of the consortia developed in the 1960s have faced difficulties and some have even gone out of existence.

As we consider the shape and form of the instructional program in the decade ahead, we are told both that the competition engendered by the restriction in funds will lead to more experimentation and that it will eliminate most experimentation altogether. We even have mixed signals regarding the *need* for reform. National conferences and commissions address themselves to innovation and reform, and one state legislature has requested its Council on Higher Education to "submit findings and recommendations . . . concerning ways to encourage the development and implementation of . . . innovative programs."[6] Yet, the Carnegie Commission on Higher Education can report that two-thirds of the students in a national large-scale survey indicated that they were "satisfied" or "very satisfied" with academic life today. Only 12 percent were "dissatisfied" or "very dissatisfied."[7] The report, however, says that in spite of the high level of general satisfaction there are some changes that seem to be desired by both students and faculty members. The changes are of a general sort, such as improvement in teaching effectiveness, achievement of more "relevance" in the curriculum, provision of more creative opportunities for students, and greater attention to the "emotional growth" of the students.[8]

181

Much more forceful in asking for institutional reform is Ernest Boyer, chancellor of the State University of New York. Speaking at the Twenty-Ninth National Conference on Higher Education in 1974, Boyer accused colleges and universities in the United States of failing to recognize and respond to the profound changes in the life pattern of their actual and potential clientele:

> Our people are organizing their lives in strange new ways, yet our colleges have not caught up with this social revolution in our midst. . . . Historically, the span of human life has been chopped into slices. . . . [First] the thin slice of early childhood. . . . [Then] a thicker slice—twelve to twenty years, perhaps—devoted almost exclusively to full-time learning. . . . [Then] the [still] thicker slice of full-time work. And, finally . . . retirement. . . . [And] throughout the years colleges and universities have conformed to this long tradition, serving just one slice of life.[9]

What is needed, Boyer contends, is that higher education construct entirely new arrangements that will respond to the changing social patterns in which life is no longer sliced into discrete periods and in which individuals vary greatly in life style.

While offering a somewhat different set of proposals for the future development of higher education than those discussed by Boyer, Charles Silberman also calls for a reexamination of functions:

> Higher education needs to rediscover its sense of purpose. It will not be easy to do so, for we are just coming out of a twenty-year absence from serious thought about educational goals. . . . there is something irrational in our contemporary neglect of systematic thought about educational goals.[10]

He points up what he considers to be the obvious fact that any curriculum involves judgments about goals and values and the priorities attached to them, and the failure to examine seriously and systematically educational goals results in poor and ineffective curriculum planning.

Not all writers on the subject are sanguine about the outcomes of attempts at reform. Harold Taylor caricatures the typical faculty approach to curricular reform, the appointment of the committee that must represent a cross section of the academic departments, the lack of empirical research or philosophical analysis, and the inevitable compromises, all of which lead to a certain universal sameness in institutional planning:

> The educational plans which result have a sameness about them no matter where they are written, since they tend to accept the same premises and are written by the same kind of people. The curriculum for undergraduates is most often a composite of what each section of the university departments wants to have included in the course material, and the fact of sameness is then interpreted as a kind of universal wisdom among informed scholars as to what constitutes a proper education for all undergraduates. What is actually a consensus of the academic profession as to how its subject matter can be distributed and administered effectively in fairness to themselves is mistaken for a universal educational truth.[11]

In another article, David Bayley of the University of Denver is even more critical of faculty efforts at curriculum change. He observes that so "great is the passion spent in searching for the perfect curriculum" and "so perennially is the search undertaken" that there are "few teachers indeed who are not plunged into despair at the very mention of it." Even more tragic, according to Bayley, is the fact that the only distinctive aspect "of these tiresome, agonizing, and repetitious appraisals is their puniness."[12]

What are we to conclude? We observe that many of the exciting "new" measures advanced in the mid-1970s were discussed in the literature more than a decade ago, that many innovations appear to be old ideas in new dress, but that the demand is no less insistent that higher education adapt to new social conditions; that a complete overhaul of academe is needed, and yet that faculties never really change much of anything. Confusing? Perhaps the confusion and extremes of opinion are indicators of the current wave of concern that all is not right with higher education and, whether innovative or not, programs must be reviewed and either modified or reaffirmed. At least this is the impression that comes as one views the 120 pages of *An Inventory of Academic Innovation and Reform,* another report of the Carnegie Commission. The impression is strong that virtually every college in the country is involved in some kind of "reform" or "innovative" program.[13] This seems to be the case even as we are also reminded that diversity in higher education is declining and that conscious effort will be necessary to maintain what is viewed by some as desirable diversity.[14] In the introduction to *Institutions in Transition,* Clark Kerr finds educational institutions becoming more alike:

> Taken as a whole, the amount of institutional diversity in American higher education is decreasing. This is due partially to the pervasive existence of a single status system in higher education, based on the prestigious university offering many graduate programs and preoccupied with research. There are few alternative models to this system now functioning.[15]

The same theme is expressed in Christopher Jenks and David Riesman's *The Academic Revolution* as they trace the development of the large and influential research universities and the kind of impact those institutions have had upon other institutions, an echo of the position Riesman had earlier taken in *Constraint and Variety in American Education.*[16]

There are some differences of opinion regarding the extent to which innovations, once begun, have been able to persevere. A report in *U.S. News and World Report* states that many of the changes effected during the 1960s are persisting and having an impact upon institutions in the seventies, but it also notes that some of the reforms, including "pass-fail" as a substitute for regular grading, seem to be falling out of favor and that some of the more unstructured "experimental courses" are not as popular as they were initially. The article points out that there is a good bit of experimentation within the context of maintaining academic standards, and that changes in calendar, the adoption of interim programs, efforts at providing more flexible ways of meeting institutional requirements, as well as the reduction of institutional requirements are solid accomplishments.[17]

When Arthur Levine and John Weingart began their study of curriculum change at 26 educational institutions, they assumed that innovative programs such as those which gave students an opportunity to plan their own education would be quite successful, that team-taught and interdisciplinary programs would be enthusiastically received by students, and that various types of innovations would reflect unique strengths and weaknesses. Instead they found:

> Our predictions were a disaster. Contrary to our expectations, we found that students do not participate in programs that permit them to plan their own education. Interdisciplinary and team-taught programs often fail because faculty do not want to teach them. When faculty do teach them, they are unable to integrate their disciplines or to work together. Written evaluations are also unsuccessful because faculty find them too burdensome, students are not interested in them, and graduate schools dislike them. Finally, student and faculty performance—whether in interdisciplinary and team-taught courses, student-centered curriculum, written evaluation grading, or any other structure—proved to be much the same in each program examined.[18]

The writers seem less optimistic than the reporter for *U.S. News and World Report* about the kind of reception innovations have received.

Establishing a Perspective for Reviewing Trends

If Dean Neumann and the university faculty committees are going to respond adequately to the concerns voiced by the general faculty when new curricular proposals are being discussed, they need to be aware of the kinds of programs that have been proposed in other institutions and, whenever possible, how effective such programs have been. A thorough acquaintance with the literature is a basic tool for any group involved in examining and revising curriculum. In the remainder of this chapter we will turn to some of this literature to find out if there are any clear trends. As we begin our examination of the literature, we find that much of it falls within the context of discussions about or reports on "change," "innovation," or "nontraditional" education. One is tempted to conclude, solely on the basis of these categories, that if there is any identifiable trend, it is in some way toward change, innovation, and the nontraditional. As we have already observed, however, the "new" is seldom new in the sense that it has never appeared in the same or similar form before. But, rather than debate whether what is happening is new or

185

different or evidence of change, I propose in the pages that follow simply to report what is being written about curriculum and leave it to the reader to make judgments about degrees or kinds of change. Similarly, when referring to "trends" I am not prepared to debate over how much of a trend, how long a trend, or whether it is a "real" trend. Where possible I try to compare program elements over a span of time. In most cases I can only describe what observers report to be current activities.

Trends as such are difficult to establish. Reports are not equally useful, and data are often not directly comparable. The preparation of the annotated bibliography on nontraditional education by William Mahler illustrates something of the problems involved in locating usable sources.[19] Mahler used the personal files of staff members of the Commission on Non-Traditional Study, materials from persons interviewed for the project, and the files of the Educational Resources Information Center (ERIC). He found more than 10,000 possibly useful references in the ERIC files, reviewed 1,755 abstracts, and reduced the annotations to 173 basic references. There appears to be a good bit of innovation underway, but definitive reports are not always available or accessible. In this review, I make no pretense at being as complete or exhaustive. I am frankly emphasizing sources that are generally accessible. The references at the end of the chapter will identify the sources and provide the reader with specific citations that can be examined in more detail.

To organize a review of curriculum changes, some kind of analytic structure is needed. Recent studies of curriculum innovation and change suggest several possible structures. Ann Heiss's comprehensive review of academic innovation and reform presents findings under five categories: new innovative institutions, institutions within institutions, innovative changes by academic subunits within conventional colleges and universities, procedural innovation, and institutional self-studies. Levine and Weingart report their findings under eight headings: current undergraduate programs, advising, general education, comprehensive examinations and senior year, concentration, alternatives to departments, student-centered curriculum, and grading. The Commission on Non-Traditional Study suggests three categories: broadening opportunities, reshaping institutions, examining alternatives. Axelrod's suggested model for the analysis of curriculum change, as noted earlier, uses six elements: content, schedule, certification, group/person interaction, student experience, freedom/control. There are many other variations.

One of the more comprehensive analyses of curricular change is that of JB Lon Hefferlin. In *The Dynamics of Academic Reform,* Hefferlin reports on a four-year study that draws upon some 16 in-depth case studies of institutions undergoing change and upon a general survey of 110 colleges representing a stratified random sample of American colleges.[20] He isolates three kinds of response that have resulted in new programs. The first is to create new institutions. A second approach is to change or transform existing institutions. The third, and the most frequently found, approach is to change through "accretion" and "attrition." By accretion, an institution adds new programs or emphases, and by attrition, an institution drops programs or emphases.

With some modification, the structure suggested by Hefferlin is employed here; I find that most specific reforms or innovations discussed in reports currently available can be placed in one or another of these three broad categories.

New Institutions

The first type of response noted by Hefferlin is the creation of new institutions. If existing institutions do not accomplish what someone or some group desires, then new institutions are established. In the fall of 1973 the *Chronicle of Higher Education* reported on openings and closings of American higher educational institutions. In spite of the number of institutions that had closed or merged with other institutions, there were more institutions that had either come into existence as new institutions or through the merger with other institutions[21]—there were 85 openings and only 31 closings. With all of the financial and other pressures on higher educational institutions, it is surprising that during the last few years we have continued to experience this net increase in institutions, although not all of the new institutions are responses to pressure for change, and not all of them can by any means be referred to as "innovative" or "experimental."

When Lewis Mayhew described the new colleges for the volume *Higher Education: Some Newer Developments* in 1965, he used

187

as specific examples the University of South Florida, Monteith College of Wayne State University, New College at Hofstra, Oakland University, Florida Presbyterian College, and St. Andrew College, and he referred also to Santa Cruz of the University of California, Chicago Teachers College–North, Grand Valley State College, New College in Sarasota, and Florida Atlantic University. He noted in the introduction to his article that during the period from 1961 through 1964 a total of 146 new colleges and universities had been established in the United States.

Strictly speaking, not all of the institutions reviewed by Mayhew were "new" colleges. Monteith College was created as a special unit within a large university, and New College at Hofstra as a one-year program in an existing institution. St. Andrews College came out of the consolidation of three existing institutions. The others constituted new foundations without antecedent bodies, although Oakland was created as a new unit in a new geographical location of Michigan State University. The College of Basic Studies of the University of South Florida, Monteith College, Florida Presbyterian College, and St. Andrews College took new approaches or new variations to the general education component of undergraduate education.

In characterizing the new institutions in 1965, Mayhew observed that in common they were: (1) seeking "to capture some of the educational potential of small colleges without yielding the undoubted virtue of large size," as, for example, Monteith, New College at Hofstra, Santa Cruz, the University of the Pacific, and Michigan State University in their attempts at a college-within-a-college; (2) developing variations on liberal or general education that established a balance over and against the prevailing trends to early specialization in study; (3) employing, many of them, technological aids such as automated instruction and tapes; (4) avoiding elitism by seeking a fair cross section of good, not just top ability, students; (5) employing to a greater extent than the traditional colleges independent study; and (6) trying, most of them, to create an identifiable intellectual community involving students and faculty together.[22] Mayhew also indicated that most of the new colleges sought to keep the curriculum "within safe and economical bounds"; several were experimenting with large instructional groups and with other than the typical departmental organization. In addition, "in one way or another these colleges are seeking to emphasize internationalism" through area studies, centers for the study of other cultures, research abroad, and language study.

Among the problems Mayhew noted was a major one of recruiting faculty who could adapt to the ideas incorporated into the plans for the new colleges. And although the colleges emphasized in their establishment the primary place of the liberal arts and sciences, pressures for vocational courses soon appeared. Efforts to maintain other than departmental organization faced constant pressure from faculty who were more departmentally oriented than they might have thought at first. Mayhew observed how difficult it was to maintain flexibility in institutions that began with great amounts of flexibility. It was all too easy to transform into difficult-to-change patterns the very aspects that began as innovative or experimental activities. He also found that the programs of the newer institutions appeared to be more the result of an eclectic process rather than the outgrowth of a particular consistent theory or philosophy.

I have reviewed Mayhew's article at some length, because many of the characteristics that identified this group of colleges as "new" and "innovative" are the same characteristics that are attributed to the "new" and "innovative" colleges of 1975. And many of the problems encountered by these colleges in 1965 are being experienced by their latter-day editions in 1975. We seem to have learned little over the decade as we repeat the same experiments and face the same problems.

Since the publication of the article in 1965, New College in Sarasota, Florida, has faced severe financial difficulties and in May 1974 offered to become a branch of the state system.[23] Subsequently, the state agreed to purchase the college and in July 1975 incorporated it into the University of South Florida as an honors college. Florida Presbyterian College has become Eckerd College, and Oakland has grown into a major university in its own rights.

Oakland and Monteith were the subject of a report by David Riesman, Joseph Gusfield, and Zelda Gamson.[24] The three began interviewing faculty and administrators at the two colleges in 1960, when both Monteith and Oakland had been in existence for one year, and their report carries the development through the mid-1960s. As the writers viewed the two institutions, Monteith College appeared to them to represent "a late dedication to the General

189

Education movement"; the dominant group within the social science faculty of Monteith had been influenced by the University of Chicago general education college. The initial Oakland faculty had no particular academic model, but many admired the curricular and academic intensity of such elite liberal arts colleges as Columbia, Oberlin, Swarthmore, Wesleyan—all primarily residential institutions. The researchers found in the aspirations of the two new colleges "an element of revivalism, both in an effort to return to plain living without frills and in a perfectionist hope that a mass of unselected students might somehow be redeemed."[25] Monteith was viewed as an experimental institution, while Oakland was initially planned to become "a full-fledged university in an area previously without any institutions of public higher education. It was intended by its Michigan State University founders to be distinguished rather than distinctive."[26] Monteith, in particular, worked against the traditional departmental organization, and the curriculum was designed to consist of three sequences which would account for about half of the student's program during the first two years, one-quarter in the junior year, and one-half in the senior year.

As one reads the report on Oakland and Monteith, while appreciating the great amount of effort that has gone into developing the two institutions, one comes away with the feeling that significant innovation is hard to come by. The comments of the three interviewers regarding the faculty at the two institutions are particularly noteworthy:

> Again and again in our interviews, faculty said that they were attracted by the opportunity to build a program different from the conventional one. Yet when we drew them out as to the nature of their proposals, they often expressed only marginal differences from prevailing models—differences, in fact, shared by many young specialists in their branch of the discipline. . . . On the whole, [faculty members] saw themselves as engaged in a mopping-up operation against methodological backwardness and fuzzy, unsupported thinking, carrying on the mission of influential mentors from graduate school.[27]

Both colleges were dedicated to developing new approaches to a curriculum for commuter students, but the writers observed:

> The problems of creating a curriculum for commuter students that will neither ignore nor cater to their limitations are hardly

better understood now than they were when Oakland and Monteith began. Moreover, the institutional mechanisms for providing career lines for faculty who want to focus on issues of teaching and learning have yet to be devised.[28]

Differences between the academic atmospheres in the two institutions were observed. The writers found Oakland's atmosphere "like that of a hotel or an apartment house whose guests or tenants are expected to be polite but not particularly neighborly," while on the other hand, they found Monteith "more like a family, where privacy of office and classroom hardly existed." Oakland in the late 1960s had developed a broader clientele, was becoming a university of a cluster-college type, and had moved considerably beyond the general purpose institution it represented at its founding. Monteith was characterized as "an experiment stabilized." It lost its special status in 1964 when the grant for its founding provided by the Ford Foundation was exhausted, but it still operates as a unit within the larger university, and it has secured tenure for several of its faculty members and retains its emphasis on teaching and curricular development, general education, and independent study.

When Ann Heiss almost a decade later describes the "new" institutions, she includes among the group New College in Sarasota, the University of South Florida, Oakland, and Florida Presbyterian College, all referred to by Lewis Mayhew in his earlier article.[29] In addition, she includes Evergreen State College; Federal City College; Hampshire College; the University of Wisconsin at Green Bay; Antioch College in Columbia, Maryland; Thomas Jefferson College in Allendale, Michigan; New York State University College at Old Westbury; Friends World College; Prescott College; and the State University of New York at Purchase. Other examples include the University of California at Santa Cruz and San Diego (the first one is mentioned in Mayhew's article), Nova University, the College of the Potomac, the Learning Community in Portland, Oregon, and Antioch West, San Francisco.

New College in Sarasota, in spite of the change in status in 1975, is described by Heiss on the basis of data for 1972-73 as a thriving institution, with its emphasis upon a curriculum grouped under the three divisions of the natural sciences, social sciences, and nonsciences and with each division focusing upon interdisciplinary courses as well as providing "areas of study" that reflect the more

191

traditional departmental offerings. Students could elect to work for the baccalaureate in three or four years, the basic difference being in how the independent study projects are completed; all students were in residence for nine terms and all students must also undertake a series of independent study projects. Students, in addition, had the option of a contractual or noncontractual program; in the former, the student developed term by term, in consultation with two faculty members, his own sequence of courses, and in the latter the student enrolls in conventional courses.[30] As the honors college of the University of South Florida, New College retains its emphasis on the contract system. For each of the three ten-week terms, students must formulate a contract with a single faculty sponsor. The baccalaureate requires nine successful contracts and four independent study projects as well as a senior research project and an oral baccalaureate examination.[31]

Heiss found the University of South Florida, which has absorbed New College, in 1972-73 placing a heavy emphasis upon general education. Students took one-third of their program in general education studies with a heavy emphasis on interdisciplinary and independent study methods. The emphasis in the original unit of Oakland University on general education is reported to be continuing, with some 48 credit hours extended over a four-year program, but the developments of the other two units of the university are not noted.

Florida Presbyterian College (Eckerd College) in 1971-72 continued to emphasize independent study, and as much as 60 percent of the degree requirements could be taken in the form of independent study. During each of the four years, however, each student also enrolled in an interdisciplinary core course. One of the pioneers in the recent development of the interim term, Eckerd College has initiated a variety of learning opportunities in the winter term under the 4-1-4 calendar.[32]

Evergreen State College presents the student with two options for planning a general education program, a Coordinated Studies Program in which the student selects from a number of interdisciplinary topics, and a Contracted Studies Program that is based on self-paced learning and the student's own individual interest. A report prepared by the Council on Higher Education of the State of Washington emphasizes the "experimental" dimension and directs attention to the career-learning experiences and service-learning experiences; the former are most often arranged as contracted studies and include various types of training internships, while the latter are normally a part of the coordinated studies and involve field placement in service agencies such as Head Start, hospitals, and community action programs. Instead of taking four or five courses, the student is to concentrate on one coherent program at a time.[33]

Hampshire College, founded as an experimental college by the Five-College Consortium in Massachusetts, likewise places heavy emphasis upon individualized programming. Students are to devise their own program, make up their own tests, and pace their own degree progress. The planning for Hampshire was detailed in such early publications as *The Making of a College*.[34] Sponsored by Amherst, Mount Holyoke, Smith, and the University of Massachusetts, the college opened in the fall of 1970. Commenting on the development three months after opening date, John Walsh took note of the 4-1-4 calendar, the three-course student load, and the heavy stress on students "proving themselves able to pursue independent study . . . [since] it is really on the ability of the students to work independently that the concept of controlling the size of the faculty without sacrificing educational quality depends."[35] Visiting the college in 1973, one researcher discovered that faculty found teaching loads heavy, that students were seeking advice and consultation much more than expected, and that faculty in doing many things for the first time—such as developing new courses and interdisciplinary projects—gave much more time to study and preparation than they had anticipated.[36]

Two members of the first class of Hampshire College, Peter Bloch and Nancy Nylen, joined in writing a review of their experiences at Hampshire, in the course of which they pinpoint a number of issues that face every experimental college. First of all, how different can an experimental college be?

> Can it continue to innovate each year? The difficulty in answering these questions is rooted in a lack of clarity regarding the purpose of the school's innovations. Does Hampshire, while being innovative, intend to serve the same intellectual and social objectives as conventional schools? Or is it to explore new goals, new definitions of the educated person, and perhaps even new

193

social values? If the latter purpose is to be served by the college, there is room for constant reevaluation and experimentation. If the college's purpose, however, is to meet the same goals as its neighboring institutions but to do so in a different way, experimentation undoubtedly will be curbed.[37]

Hampshire has apparently, as is suggested in a recent catalog, opted for a middle-of-the-road stance, to be neither radical nor conservative. The students found in this lack of clarity "an inconsistency of educational practice and direction which has been a source of frustration for students and faculty alike."

Hampshire is organized around four multidisciplinary schools, a structure employed to avoid the exclusiveness of the more typical collegiate departmental organization. When students asked for an Educational Studies Program that required resources from several of the schools, the new interschool program was established, but because virtually all of the faculty are assigned to the four schools, interschool programs have a hard time surviving. The student critics found that the schools had quickly become as rigid and protective as traditional departments. Indeed, each school had managed to achieve more political and economic power than a department has had in any other college. Faculty members at Hampshire have apparently used the schools as substitutes rather than as alternatives to departments.[38] The writers also contend that faculty have found it difficult to develop new instructional procedures; faculty are trained in conventional institutions and are "steeped in the conventional processes and rationales of liberal education." And students, by and large, do not come equipped with the skills for dealing with the kind of freedom Hampshire wants to foster.

As an experimental college Hampshire should, suggest Bloch and Nylen, seek to measure progress of students in less conventional ways, but the college finds itself comparing its education to that of other institutions and easily falls into the traditional concern for an adequate transfer policy. To the student critics, however, the notion of transfer equivalency is not only illogical, but it is also counterproductive. Nonetheless, though frustrated with what they view as compromises and fear of risk, the writers end on a complimentary note:

But as the first students at Hampshire College, we have been lucky. We've been able to teach courses, advise other students,

194

design academic programs, and define curricular structures. We've learned how to learn, and we've gained intellectual confidence *and* humility. We hope the forces that push Hampshire into a more conventional mold can be resisted, so that the students who follow us can have experiences as fruitful and rewarding as ours.[39]

One turns from the article with a bittersweet taste—how new and different and innovative can a college be and persist in a context that demands a certain measure of interchangeability?

Federal City College attempts to provide a diversified program for low income groups. Antioch College in Columbia, Maryland, seeks to involve students in wide participation in community action; the academic program is heavily individualized. The University of Wisconsin at Green Bay focuses on ecological relationships. Livingston College of New Jersey State University is an experimental urban-oriented college with an emphasis on education for multiracial students.[40] Thomas Jefferson College in Michigan exposes students to experiences that "demand self-motivation, individual expression, personal and social responsibility, and independence." New York State University College at Old Westbury seeks to work with minority, part-time, and older students. It offers external degree programs, "second chance" programs for older persons, external credit programs, and a variety of professional training programs. Friends World College emphasizes gaining firsthand experience in other cultures. Prescott College is committed to interdisciplinary study and organizes its curriculum around five teaching centers—art and literature, contemporary civilization, man and his environment, the person, and systems and sciences. The State University of New York at Purchase emphasizes the arts, and the freshman program is largely an interdisciplinary study based on broad themes and topics.

If there is any general theme that runs through the four-year colleges that Heiss singles out for profiles, it is the emphasis upon individually developed courses and experiences providing considerable freedom for students. Theme orientations are evident in ecology at the University of Wisconsin at Green Bay, intercultural experiences at Friends World College, and the arts at the State University of New York at Purchase.

195

The inventory developed by Heiss also refers to a number of innovative two-year colleges. As the American Council on Education studies suggest, most of the new institutions established in the 20-year period of time between 1947 and 1967 were two-year institutions. Among those listed by Heiss are Miami Dade Junior College in Florida, Simon's Rock College in Massachusetts, the College for Human Resources in New York, Navajo Community in Arizona, Delta College in Michigan, Nairobi College in California,[41] Loop College in Illinois, the College of San Mateo in California, and the Labor College of Empire State College in New York.

Simon's Rock, although classified as a two-year college in *An Inventory of Academic Innovation and Reform,* characterizes itself as "a four-year residential liberal arts college open to young men and women of all races and creeds who have successfully completed 'college preparatory studies' through the tenth grade of high school."[42] The college grants the associate in arts degree, thus marking it as a four-year upper-secondary and freshman-sophomore collegiate institution. It seeks in the 120 semester-hour program to provide a liberal education that provides "the student with a time for becoming acquainted with the whole range of human inquiry, a time for finding out about himself, the world in which he lives, and his heritage."[43] Only one course is required of all students (beginning in September 1973), and that is English 100. A bachelor of arts degree option is also under examination. The college is organized by divisions, but it lists courses also by departments.

Empire State College is discussed in an article in the *Journal of General Education.*[44] The authors refer to the 1972 Empire State Master Plan which calls for the new institution to be one which

> transcends constraints of space, place and time. . . . It will seek to transcend conventional academic structure which imposes required courses, set periods of time, and residential constraints of place upon the individual student. The College will utilize the variety of State resources available to higher education for students of all ages, according to their desires, interests and capacities. The University will rely on process, rather than structure of education to shape and give it substance as well as purpose.[45]

They point out that Empire State College "has its own president, faculty, and advisory council, but no fixed campus." The college works through Regional Learning Centers, each headed by a dean and responsible for developing programs in one of the eight regions so far established. These regional centers are charged with providing learning centers within commuting distance of those to be served. The learning centers are staffed by one or more full-time mentors or counselors and such part-time faculty as are needed. With the help of a mentor, students develop their programs, based on any or all of the following: independent study, tutorials, cooperative studies, self-study, direct experience, formal courses. The program decided upon is set out in a contract; a full-time contract assumes an investment of 36-40 hours per week, and a part-time contract calls for 18-20 hours a week. The contract arrangements are discussed in more detail in an article by Neal R. Berte in a volume wholly devoted to an exploration of different approaches to individualizing learning.[46]

The emphasis in the literature is, understandably, upon new colleges as innovative and experimental institutions. But not all new colleges are innovative or experimental, nor would all new colleges fit Hefferlin's category of a response to a desire for change. In 1967 the American Council on Education began a systematic inquiry into the development of new colleges in American higher education. The result was the publication in 1972 of a monograph that provides considerable information on 939 colleges founded between 1947 and 1967.[47] In the preface to the report it is noted that more than one-third of the 2,573 colleges and universities existing in 1970 had come into existence after 1947. Two-thirds were founded as two-year community colleges, and the others were four-year colleges and postbaccalaureate institutions. Over half, 55 percent, were under public auspices. It should be noted that 100 of the institutions founded during the survey period no longer existed in 1971.

On an average, over the 20-year period from 1947 to 1967, new institutions of higher education in the United States were founded at the rate of about 45 per year. The greatest growth was during 1965, when 110 new institutions, of which 76 were public two-year colleges, came into existence. Of the 349 private colleges founded during this survey period, 156 were four-year institutions and 50 were postbaccalaureate. During the same 20-year period some 55 private four-year institutions were dropped from the United States

Office of Education directory and presumably went out of existence. Thirty-two of these had been established since 1947. Some 83 percent of the new four-year private institutions had enrollments in the fall of 1967 of less than 1,000 students, and only 17 percent enrolled between 1,000 and 4,999.

From these statistics one gains little insight into the degree to which these new institutions can be considered experimental or innovative. Perhaps one indication that only a small proportion would be viewed as innovative is the response to the question in the ACE survey questionnaire dealing with the use of instructional technology. The presidents of the "new" institutions were the respondents, and it is noted in the report that the high percentage indicating only "moderate" or "little or no" utilization "probably reflect the teaching-as-usual preferences of most faculty members at their institutions."[48] Another indication of the limited degree to which these institutions might be characterized as innovative is the presidents' response to the question regarding the most important considerations in deciding to create a new institution. Only 40 percent of the presidents in the four-year institutions responded that the most important consideration was "demand for educational offering." Some two-thirds responded that the most important consideration was that adequate financing was assured.[49]

Reviewing the status of experimental colleges, Larry A. Van Dyne notes that while differing among themselves these colleges still have much in common in method, philosophy, and even in their jargon. They have their own mimeographed newsletter, their "national resource center," and their own national conferences. And while all claim to be "historic departures from the norm," Van Dyne contends that "many in fact are not," that they have "precedents in other places or other times, and much of what they do is borrowed from A. S. Neill, John Dewey, and even Socrates."[50]

What is significant about the colleges, whether they are in large part newly developed departures or borrowers from the past, is that they attempt to "approach educational reform in a comprehensive way, going far beyond tinkering with grading systems and other piecemeal reforms."[51] Van Dyne summarizes the major "innovations" under three areas: instruction, living arrangements, governance. By and large the experimental colleges seek alternatives to distribution requirements, majors, grades, and lectures, and they

198

provide ways for students to develop their own approaches to learning. Carried to its logical extreme this means in some instances students "negotiate a wholly individualized contract spelling out the scope and content of all, or large parts, of their undergraduate experience." Not all students, however, are able to cope with the lack of structure and new freedom; they drop out or return to conventional programs. When structured, the institution relies mainly on small seminars, independent study, and field work off campus. In living arrangements the experimental colleges seek for some kind of intimacy or "community" that brings students and faculty into "more frequent" and "less formal contact." In governance, efforts are directed toward widening participation in decision-making, "often giving each student and each faculty member one vote on important matters." The effort to extend participation often leads to "long hours in town meetings, discussing and deciding issues both big . . . and small," and the tendency for such meetings to "disintegrate into endless debates of the unsignificant has prompted some experiments to draw back from their early insistence that all issues be decided by everybody."[52]

Not every experiment is successful—if continued existence is a measure of success. Bensalem, an adjunct of Fordham University, was "phased out." Black Mountain College, a much earlier experiment, closed its doors. In December 1974, Prescott College went into bankruptcy and closed.[53] Van Dyne suggests why the experiments are difficult to maintain. Faculty members, cut off from so many of the conventions of higher education—testing, grades, required courses, credit hours, office hours, calendars, classrooms, clocks, and all the rest—experience considerable strain, and they face career risks as well. They can get out of step with the academic reward system, because they become turned off to publish-or-perish, fail to keep up with developments in their erstwhile specialty, and lose status in their departments. The colleges face money problems too, in that many begin on "risk capital," are more costly than the "regular" units, and in time of financial stringency are more and more called upon to prove their worth. They are also concerned as experimental units about how to maintain freshness and remain experimental.

The latter issue was the focus of an investigation undertaken by a doctoral student at the University of Denver. By examining documents covering the development of the institutions and conducting wide-ranging on-site interviews at six experimental colleges—New College in Sarasota, Governors State College in Illinois, Hampshire College, Evergreen State College, Prescott College, and the University of Wisconsin at Green Bay—Randall Kunkel sought to determine how effective these institutions were in maintaining their initial orientation to experimentation in policies and practices.[54] He found a tendency to move to more formal and stable organizational structures, toward clearer definition of roles and functions. While nondepartmental structure and nongraded systems were maintained, both aspects seemed to be under constant threat. Kunkel found the interdisciplinary programming, a major feature in each institution, by and large surviving, but experiencing "considerable difficulty."

> First, there are demanding faculty workloads involved in working out newly formed interdisciplinary offerings. Second, there are the traditional tendencies of many faculty personnel in wanting to devote much of their time to their own disciplines. . . . Third, there is the basic problem of getting diverse egos, both professional and personal, to blend their efforts into a single educational learning bloc—no easy task in itself. Then there is the added problem of monitoring this group through the use of poorly organized, administratively chaotic centers or divisions.[55]

He also found the independent study features, while maintained, were "threatened constantly by both faculty and student factors." And his general observation is that the most influential general factor that works against the development of innovative educational environments is the "traditionalism of the attitudes and beliefs of the constituents of the innovative institutions." In short, the internal parties—faculty, students, administration—generally prove to be their own worst enemies.

Van Dyne's review noted the pressures being put on experimental colleges to provide evidence of their uniqueness, to show why they should be maintained. Robert Brown suggests that the key questions in any evaluation of experimental colleges are: "Should experimental colleges be evaluated? What form should evaluation take? How does selectivity affect evaluative efforts? What are some of the technical problems facing evaluators of experimental colleges?"[56] The answer to the first question, he states, is a clear affirmative. Evaluation is needed "to facilitate decision-making about a program by providing data-based conclusions about the worth of various dimensions of the program and to stimulate hypotheses and suggestions about productive changes in it."[57] Any evaluation must be of a comprehensive nature and Brown proposes a four- and five-year period involving a planned series of mini-evaluations as a useful model. The selectivity problem—students in such programs are largely self-selected—poses some serious problems for evaluation. Experimental colleges need experimental and innovative evaluation procedures; a simplistic input-output model will be ineffective.

I have attempted to present here an overview of the new colleges. The overview is just that; it is not a complete treatment, but the intent has been to be illustrative rather than exhaustive. Articles, reviews, and studies relating to the new colleges appear with some regularity. Much of the literature takes the form of impressionistic reports on one or a small group of programs; definitive studies are yet to be undertaken. One gains the impression of much activity and of the hope for some "breakthrough" in collegiate education. This reviewer is sobered, however, by the observations of Bloch and Nylen on the first years of Hampshire College.[58] Paul Dressel is even less sanguine about the potential for significant change:

> Innovation in education has too frequently been a leap from one rigidity to another and ultimately equally rigid pattern, for any attempt to achieve complete flexibility leads to chaos and to the imposition of some type of structure. Unless that structure is provided by a statement of objectives so that flexibility in the program is always examined and adjusted in relation to its effectiveness in achieving those goals the inevitable result is a retreat toward traditional patterns and practices. This, as I read it, is the history of innovation in American higher education.[59]

In his well-documented review of the development of *The Upper Division College,* Robert Altman reaches a not dissimilar conclusion, but he does so from a different perspective. Reflecting on the experience of the College of the Pacific which had launched one of the earlier attempts at a junior-senior college, Altman comments:

> The College of the Pacific had eventually discovered what many other experimental programs involving the structure of education had discovered: that a single institution, regardless of the

degree to which it is internally satisfied with an organizational structure different from that of those institutions with which it interacts, cannot continue to operate under those conditions if the other institutions (or accrediting bodies or athletic conferences) do not make certain necessary adjustments.[60]

One is tempted to incorporate this statement into a form of "Altman's Law," so universal does its application seem to be. Even the College Program of the University of Chicago with its demonstrated success in areas important to the faculty of the college succumbed.

A group of institutions to which no reference has been made in the preceding review of new colleges is that small collection of what Altman, in his excellent volume, calls the "upper division college." One will find that, as with other "innovations," the upper division college is rooted in the past, in proposals of such nineteenth century leaders as Wayland at Brown and Tappan at Michigan. The University of Georgia even launched a short-lived upper division program prior to the Civil War. The more recent efforts of the College of the Pacific, the University of Chicago, the New School Senior College in New York, Concordia Senior College, Flint and Dearborn Colleges, Florida Atlantic, the University of West Florida, Pratt Senior College, and the Capitol Campus of Pennsylvania State are fully examined by Altman, and the problems and failures as well as the successes are well documented. To these should be added Governors State University and Sangamon State University in Illinois.

There are a number of directories describing in more or less detail the new colleges as well as other innovative and experimental programs. John Coyne and Tom Hebert have compiled what they subtitle *A Guide to Alternatives to Traditional College Education in the United States, Europe and the Third World.*[61] While it begins with a chatty orientation to college-going with advice on buying everything from typewriters to used VW's, the guide also contains descriptions of well-known and not-so-well-known experimental colleges. A number of the entries are based on impressions gained during the authors' visits to campuses. In all, 100 colleges in the United States are described, and the listing contains institutions that do not appear in many other references. Another section of the volume contains information about foreign study opportunties.

A team of four have produced a *Guide to Alternative Colleges and Universities*.[62] This volume lists over 250 "innovative programs," and provides a brief write-up of each. A number of the institutions were visited by one or more of the authors, although much of the information was secured by phone. Most of the colleges listed are not new colleges, but they are institutions in which, in the perspective of the authors, some innovative program is underway. The entries range from the University of Alabama to Western Washington State College with its College of Ethnic Studies and cover campus-based B.A. programs, two-year A.A. programs, external degree programs, special programs, and a small sample (four) of the free universities.

Transformation of Existing Institutions

Under this heading we include reorganized colleges, "colleges-within-colleges," and cluster colleges. The latter two types of programs are included, because the presence of programs extensive enough to constitute a "college-within-a-college" or another cluster college is likely to have significant impact on the parent college, an impact sufficient perhaps to transform aspects of the parent college. In grouping these three program structures together, however, we recognize that we are faced with the classification problem that plagues so much of the writing about innovation in instructional programs and changes in curriculum. There are few standards or accepted conventions for listing and describing institutional programs. Strictly speaking, Monteith College, mentioned earlier in this chapter as a "new" college, should be viewed as a college-within-a-college as should the New College at Hofstra and Raymond, Elbert Covell, and Callison Colleges of the University of the Pacific, all three of the latter institutions discussed in the 1965 report by Lewis Mayhew as "new" colleges. Two institutions listed in Heiss's study as new institutions, Kalamazoo College and Alice Lloyd College, are not new colleges, but they are institutions that have in significant ways transformed or extended their programs. Until we have developed some more widely accepted nomenclature—and that seems at this point in time a remote possibility, given the recent state of the art of curriculum study—we are often going to find the same program described under quite different categories by different writers.

203

Accepting the present confusion in nomenclature, I shall with minimal apology proceed with this description of programs, sometimes discussing a particular program under more than one category and, in so doing, merely reflecting the literature from which the illustrations are drawn.

As examples of the transformation of institutions, Hefferlin draws from history the references to the change in Brown University in 1850, Antioch in 1921, and St. John's in 1937, as well as Parsons in 1955. In each of these instances, an existing program was set aside and a new model was instituted. Francis Wayland was able to bring about significant changes in Brown. In 1919 Antioch College had almost reached the stage of closing, graduating fewer than a dozen students a year, and the trustees tried to give it away to the YMCA, but the YMCA rejected the offer. Arthur Morgan, one of the trustees, then became president and introduced his idea of cooperative education. St. John's College was at the point of bankruptcy in 1937 but Stringfellow Barr and Scott Buchanan quite literally created a new institution based upon a set of 120 classics as the new curriculum. Millard Roberts took small, denominational Parsons College and catapulted it to the front page with his new funding and instructional theories. For a period of time Parsons was one of the most talked-about colleges in the country, but some of Roberts's ways of manipulating the funds and the institution ultimately led to the destruction of the college; Parsons closed in 1974.

More recently, by adapting certain new elements, Beloit, Kalamazoo, Goshen and Colorado College show how changing one element may influence the whole institution. Beloit College adopted a new calendar, a combination of on- and off-campus work, and in so doing virtually created a new institution. Kalamazoo took the calendar revision a step further and built in a significant component of study abroad. Goshen College in Indiana, a small Mennonite college, introduced in the late 1960s a Study-Service Term that has had profound implications for the entire structure of the institution. Colorado College was "transformed" when it moved into its modular programming. Courses had to be reconstituted, teaching methods had to be changed, and the pattern of life for students and faculty was altered significantly.

Are Beloit, Kalamazoo, Goshen, and Colorado College "transformed" colleges? While in each case the changes were primarily in

204

calendar, at this stage in their developments both Beloit and Kalamazoo would seem to be fully as "transformed" as Antioch was at an earlier time with the introduction of the cooperative study program. In similar manner, Goshen College, although it would probably not refer to itself as a "transformed" college, has taken on significant new characteristics with the introduction of the Study-Service Term, which calls for each student, during the sophomore year, to be involved in a trimester away from the campus and in a developing country. Goshen units have gone to Central America, the Caribbean, and South America. In recent graduating classes, over 95 percent of the students have participated in such programs. The college is attempting in a conscious way to incorporate the experiences of the trimester abroad into the life of the campus. With so many students having participated in a particular kind of off-campus experience, the campus itself over a period of time becomes transformed. More recently Goshen has also reexamined its total curriculum, with special attention to the general education or liberal studies aspect.[63]

The dean of Colorado College, in a brief report during the third year of that College's new program, refers to the structural change as having "enormous impact on the academic life of the College." Courses are offered one at a time, in nine blocks, each three-and-a-half weeks in length. Each block is separated by four-and-a-half days beginning on Wednesday noon and ending the following Monday. The essential feature of the program is the block course of three-and-a-half weeks. Faculty and students normally are involved in only one course at a time. Scheduling of class meetings is variable; on some days the class may meet for two to three hours, or the class may not meet at all, or small groups may meet in tutorials or conferences. Each course has its own room available for classes and study. An evaluation during the second year revealed that 90 percent of the students and 73 percent of the faculty preferred the new structure. Class attendance has risen, suspensions for academic failure have dropped, and the number of interdisciplinary courses has increased.

The format for teaching, grading, and class interaction at Colorado College has changed in significant ways in many of the units. The dean concludes that the new structure has encouraged "more varied and effective pedagogy." There are gains and losses. It appears that the single-course system "makes it somewhat more difficult to impart comprehensive factual knowledge," but the dean is of the opinion that there have been gains in developing the desire to learn, developing critical tools of thinking. He finds that "students are more eager to learn and their intellectual sophistication is greater." A longer-term evaluation remains to be undertaken, but there seems little question that Colorado College, even with its select student body and long-time academic reputation, is a "transformed" college.[64]

While Ann Heiss refers to Alice Lloyd College in Pippa Passes, Kentucky, as a new college, perhaps it would be more appropriate to speak of a transformed college. Established for service to the young people of Appalachia, it has effectively extended its outreach to incorporate an extensive community-service program in which one-sixth of the students spend their summers plus two weekends a month during the school year living and working in remote regions of Appalachia. It is this outreach program that brings to an institution that already had a unique purpose a new ingredient that would probably qualify Alice Lloyd College to be called a "transformed" college.

There are colleges other than Kalamazoo, Beloit, Goshen, Colorado College, and Alice Lloyd that have been "transformed." From an earlier period of time, and still continuing, are such institutions as St. John's College and Antioch College.[65] These two colleges are established in their transformations.

What all of these transformed colleges have in common is that an existing institution, more or less traditional, has through the introduction of a significant change in calendar, or instructional technique, or program experienced more than a simple addition in programming. The college as a whole has been influenced by the introduction of the new element, and the environment of the college has been sufficiently changed to make it a new kind of enterprise.

That not all transformations "take" and not all those that do take are viewed as unqualified successes is suggested by Harvey Shapiro in his review of a series of essays on Antioch-Putney, Bensalem College of Fordham, Fairhaven College of Western Washington State, Old Westbury, and Franconia. Less than enthusiastic about the outcomes of the experimental institutions and programs discussed, Shapiro concludes:

If some of the essays reflect the fuzziness, romanticism, and half-digested psychology that motivated educational reform in the sixties, the book's last chapter, inevitably called "meditation," echoes another common theme: like the reformers they depict, many of the authors have gone on to other interests. . . . Having set out for utopia and been washed ashore, many of the experimenters have given up, masking their retreat in a dust cloud of rhetoric about getting in touch with their bodies and getting their heads together. D. W. Brogan once noted that Americans are notoriously short-term crusaders, and nowhere does that seem more accurate than on the nation's university campuses, where the population is transient and the attention span even more so.[66]

Variation on the Theme: The College-within-a-College. Because the introduction of a new element can lead to the transformation of the college as a whole, we include in this section a brief review of units that have come to be labeled as a "college-within-a-college." Few of the listings available manage to include all such institutions, and the list that follows, although it appears to be more extensive than others that we have yet discovered, undoubtedly fails to include all of the programs underway. When we refer to a "college-within-a-college" we are referring to a discrete program with an identifiable faculty and an identifiable student body. While faculty and students may also participate in other work in the parent college, they can be clearly identified with the college-within-a-college, and faculty usually devote most of their teaching effort to that special unit. In most cases, also, the college-within-a-college has budgetary and administrative support.

Some of the programs listed below are just underway, while others have "matured" to the extent that they have become accepted administrative units within an institution. Some are experimental in the sense that they may be phased out or are in the process of being phased out as some of the lessons learned are either incorporated into the parent college or discarded as nonproductive—or if the efforts have not been characterized as nonproductive, at least they have failed to capture the interest and enthusiasm of the faculty as a whole. For example, the Experimental College at the University of Wisconsin in the early 1920s, although by its own measures a success and one that excited the enthusiasm and support of both faculty and students, went out of existence because of lack of support among the

207

faculty of the parent college of arts. Similarly, the four-year unified College of the University of Chicago, although it enjoyed a long history, went out of existence in 1957-58 as a separate unit because of active opposition on the part of the faculty within the divisions. While elements of the College remain as part of the undergraduate experience of students at the University of Chicago, the administrative degree-granting unit no longer exists.

The list that follows includes colleges within colleges that are either in existence at the present time or have only recently gone out of existence. Bensalem, included in the list, is an example of the latter.

Monteith College
University of South Florida Basic College
New College at Hofstra
New College, University of Hawaii
New College, Nasson College
New College, University of Alabama
New College, San Jose State University
The Experimental College at Berkeley (the so-called Tussman College)
The Residential Colleges at Michigan State University (Lyman Briggs, James Madison, Justin Morrill)
The Residential College at the University of Michigan
Johnston College at Redlands
Tufts Experimental or "College Within"
Hutchins School of Liberal Studies at California State College, Sonoma
The Experimental College at Dartmouth
The Experimental College at California State, San Francisco
Fairhaven and Huxley Colleges, Western Washington State University at Bellingham
Centennial College at the University of Kansas, Lawrence
Christ College at Valparaiso University
Paracollege at Saint Olaf College
College III, University of Massachusetts, Boston
Project Ten, University of Massachusetts, Amherst
The College of Creative Studies, University of California, Santa Barbara
The Small College, California State College, Dominguez Hills
Bensalem College at Fordham

The last-named college, Bensalem, lasted for six years. The first class of 30 students was carefully selected on the basis of intellectual and personal standards. The college was designed to be self-directive, liberal, self-evaluative; it was to operate on the basis of group consensus. Among the problems was that consensus was never easily arrived at and the self-selective nature of the college tended to isolate it from the rest of the university. Finally it was terminated.

On the other hand, one of the more recently established units, Paracollege at Saint Olaf, an undergraduate church-related college in Northfield, Minnesota, recently concluded its experimental period by being incorporated into the college as a separate unit. In 1968 the faculty of Saint Olaf College, in response to many of the same kinds of concerns that were surfacing on many campuses, authorized the establishment of what came to be called Paracollege. Paracollege was to provide opportunities for those who found the more conventional patterns of course requirements and course structure restrictive, or as some were wont to say, irrelevant. The new unit was established to be a part of the campus community in which any idea could be considered and could be put to the test. Implicit in the agreement to establish Paracollege was the intention to incorporate into the main or regular college such procedures and practices as might prove desirable after trial in the Paracollege. In this way, Paracollege was to be the initiating and innovating unit.

In the course of a special review during 1973-74 (the program had been under the continuing review of an office of evaluation established at the time that Paracollege was launched), the All-College Committee concluded that the college should be given the status of a continuing unit, on par with any other department or unit in the parent college. The "experiment" was judged a success and worthy of incorporation into the ongoing structure of Saint Olaf. Thus, instead of remaining the experimenting unit feeding new ideas into the regular college, Paracollege gained a life of its own as an alternate route for students admitted to Saint Olaf. What remains to be seen is what happens as Paracollege, created as an experimental college, continues as an accepted part of the parent institution. Will it continue to be as inventive, as experimental, as innovative? Or will the innovations become sufficiently accepted to give Paracollege so much stability that it simply becomes another department or unit with the college? And, with the formal acceptance of Paracollege into the parent college, where will the inventive and creative urge that helped create the institution find a place in the parent institution? How does an institution maintain this growing edge?

Project Ten at the University of Massachusetts, Amherst, is another type of "college-within-a-college." It is a residential, living-learning experimental unit that almost closed down after the first two years of operation. In 1972 it was given a director and a new lease on life in the form of an additional five-year trial. During the first two years, "doing your own thing" apparently meant "turning on," and experimentation meant trying new drugs; Karen Winkler, in reviewing the program, observed that, "as in other innovative programs trying to give students freedom to pursue their own educational goals, many of Project Ten's members drifted into confusion."[67] With Charles Adams as director, however, the project apparently has developed sufficient structure to gain faculty support for the extended trial period. Project Ten allows students to design their own programs for the first two years at the university. Half of their courses are usually from the regular university offerings and the other half may be selected from over 40 seminars given in the dormitory. The major stress is on the humanities, and the laboratory sciences have been virtually excluded. The project seeks applications from highly motivated students.

Another "college-within" experiment that got off to a shaky start and is now apparently well on the way to winning an established place in the parent institution is Johnston College at Redlands University. Founded in 1969 as "a totally autonomous nontraditional college" with 20 faculty and 182 students, Johnston soon found itself in conflict with Redlands's rather more limited view of its autonomy; after a year and a half the first chancellor of the new college was fired. Four-and-a-half years later, while the basic design of the college remains unchanged, both Redlands and Johnston people seem convinced that the two educational approaches can coexist in peace.[68] Johnston works with a flexible curriculum, a contract system, no grades, and written evaluations of all courses. The college is governed by nine committees of faculty and students, and decisions are by consensus. The college has its own admissions officer and registrar, as well as chief executive officer. Recently it added its own development program.

Another Variation: Cluster Colleges. Ann Heiss offers a definition of the cluster college concept that makes a useful distinction not always observed in other references to cluster colleges. She writes, "Broadly defined, the cluster college concept is realized when a number of semi-autonomous colleges—either on the campus of a larger institution or in close proximity to each other—share, to a significant extent, faculties, and services."[69] This definition enables one to distinguish between the cluster colleges and the colleges-within-colleges, the former consisting of several more or less autonomous units, co-equal, but parts of an interrelated complex, and the latter designating a special unit, also more or less autonomous, but part of a larger institution. Jerry Gaff's otherwise very useful volume tends to combine the two concepts, although the term "subcollege" is usually applied to the college-within-a-college and the term "federated colleges" appears to be reserved for what Heiss describes as the cluster college concept.[70]

In terms of Heiss's definition, the following institutions would seem to qualify as cluster colleges:

Claremont Colleges
    Pomona College
    Claremont Graduate School and University Center
    Scripps College
    Claremont Men's College
    Harvey Mudd College
    Pitzer College

Atlanta University Center of Higher Education
    Atlanta University
    Morehouse College
    Spelman College
    Morris Brown College
    Clark College
    Interdenominational Theological Center

University of the Pacific
    Raymond College
    Elbert Covell College
    Callison College

University of California, Santa Cruz
    Cowell College
    Stevenson College

211

Crown College
Merrill College
College Number Five

Oakland University
Charter College
New College
Allport College

Grand Valley State Colleges
College of Arts and Sciences
William James College
Thomas Jefferson College
College IV
F. E. Seidman Graduate College of Business

Such units as Justin Morrill, Lyman Briggs, and James Madison at Michigan State University are more on the order of several colleges within a college as would be Revelle, Muir, and Third College of the University of California at San Diego and Hutchins, the School of Expressive Arts, and the School of Environmental Studies at California State College, Sonoma. But the lines are never altogether clear, and as Gaff reminds us, the cluster college concept is as old as Oxford and Cambridge. In the United States, however, the cluster college concept probably can be traced to the beginnings of the Claremont Colleges in 1925. The Claremont Colleges have developed as a federation of institutions; each unit maintains its independence, but all share in certain educational resources. The Atlanta University Center of Higher Education began in 1929, and there was no further development of the cluster college concept until the University of the Pacific established Raymond College. The cluster college is thus a late-comer to the higher educational scene in the United States, and it still represents a very small segment of this scene. It is possible, however, that some expansion of colleges within a college in a particular location could develop into a cluster college. Gaff finds the existing cluster colleges "tend to be quite traditional, perhaps even reactionary," and "committed to the traditional values."[71] I think this judgment is perhaps too sweeping, particularly when one reviews such programs as the free-wheeling contract system at College IV of the Grand Valley State Colleges and the inter-disciplinary and independent work in Raymond College in the University of the Pacific.

The cluster college concept would seem to provide an effective way of restoring collegiality to the complex universities and a way of renewal and perhaps survival for many small colleges. In the latter instances, however, because geographical proximity is a prerequisite and few institutions are able to or prepared to change locations, few additional clusters of this type are likely to be developed. Large and complex universities may develop more subunits, but we do not see the cluster concept as the wave of the future.

Change by Accretion and Attrition

This section deserves a major heading because it encompasses so many variations and because change by accretion and/or attrition is by far the most often found change. While it is not difficult to identify a number of new institutions that appear to have been instituted as innovative or experimental institutions, or to identify as many, or more, of the "college within a college" type, or even to identify a limited number of "transformed" colleges, the major developments in instructional programs have been more of the piecemeal type. While the outworn jest is frequently repeated that it is easier to move a cemetery than to change the curriculum, it will be seen that relatively few institutions have been untouched by some kind of change, be it limited or extensive, in the instructional program during the last decade. What is deceptive is that the basic stance of an institution, the established program, may not appear to have changed in significant ways, but departmental or program changes have been going on from year to year.

As Hefferlin observes, under normal circumstances the major process of academic change is that of accretion and attrition, "the slow addition and subtraction of functions to existing structures." For, as Hefferlin points out, accretion and attrition are the most common means of change "primarily because they are the most simple."

Unlike radical reform, they are small-scale, undramatic, and often unpublicized. By accretion an institution merely encompasses a new program along with the old—a new occupational course, a research project, a new undergraduate tradition. And through attrition, other programs and functions are abandoned, either because they become outdated—like compulsory chapel—or because they come to be performed by other institutions.[72]

It probably will be impossible ever to compile an adequate inventory of these kinds of changes, simply because they are going on most of the time and are seldom reported outside the institution or outside of a small circle of persons acquainted with the institution, but let us examine some illustrations.

General Education

In the first volume of the *Report of the President's Commission on Higher Education* issued late in 1947 the statement was made, "The crucial task of higher education today . . . is to provide a unified general education for American youth. Colleges must find the right relationship between specialized training on the one hand, aiming at a thousand different careers, and the transmission of a common cultural heritage toward a common citizenship on the other."[73] The report was addressed to the general theme of "Education for Free Men," and the authors had made the broad criticism that current college programs were not "contributing adequately to the quality of students' adult lives either as workers or as citizens." It contends that since the turn of the century the curriculum of the liberal arts colleges had been both expanding and disintegrating "to an astonishing degree" and as a consequence there was little sense of unity or direction within the curriculum. It observed that the trend was toward specialization and away from any sense of order or direction and contended that "the failure to provide any core of unity in the essential diversity of higher education is a cause for grave concern."

Some 60 years before, reacting to the elective system which had been developed under the leadership of Charles W. Eliot at Harvard, A. Lawrence Lowell, to become the president of Harvard at Eliot's retirement, was criticizing the lack of unity in the college curriculum. He observed that "for a score of years the college has been surrendering the selection of the studies to be pursued by undergraduates more and more into the hands of the students themselves" and suggested the result was not unlike that of "a sick man in an apothecary's shop . . . moved to choose the medicine he required from the appearance of the bottle on the shelf."[74] He went on then to argue for some kind of compromise between specialization and what he referred to as "general education." Later, as president, in his annual report for 1908-09, he noted that "the most significant movement during the year was that looking toward a modification of the elective system, and this resulted from an effort of much wider scope to improve the condition of scholarship among undergraduates." The move was toward providing the opportunity for the undergraduate to concentrate in one subject while distributing the rest of his program widely, "to require every student to make a choice of electives that will secure a systematic education, based on the principles of knowing a little of everything and something well."[75] Distribution was structured according to four general groups of subjects, and every student was required to take something in each group. The four groups were the arts of expression—language, literature, fine arts, and music; the natural and inductive sciences; the inductive social sciences—history, politics, and economics; and the abstract or deductive studies—mathematics and philosophy, including law and diverse kinds of social theories.

The Cooperative Study in General Education, which continued between January 1939 and September 1944 with support from the General Education Board and sponsorship by the American Council on Education, involved some 25 colleges in an effort to bring about changes in general education programs, to develop a "broader and more realistic perspective of the problems of general education," and to provide opportunity for exchange of information on experimentation.[76] The final report of the study was issued the same year as that of the President's Commission on Higher Education and stated that the development of adequate programs of general education represented the crucial need in American higher education.

Two years before the President's Commission issued its report and the Cooperative Study published its findings, Harvard had issued *General Education in a Free Society,* a volume that became one of the more, if not most, often quoted sources for statements on general education during the last half of the 1940s. That report stated that education has two functions. On the one hand it was to "help young persons fulfill the unique, particular functions in life which it is in them to fulfill," and on the other hand to "fit them so

215

far as it can for those common spheres which, as citizens and heirs of a joint culture, they will share with others."[77] After some 50 pages of analysis of the place of education in American society, the volume reiterated the position: "Our conclusion, then, is that the aim of education should be to prepare an individual to become an expert both in some particular vocation or art and in the general art of the free man and the citizen."[78]

It would not be too much of a generalization to say that the concern with general education in its various manifestations—and the term came to include an incredible variety of approaches—dominated curricular concerns in American higher educational institutions from the late 1930s through the 1950s. Russell Thomas, in surveying curricular development from 1800 through 1960, began his review with the statement, "For more than a quarter of a century *general education* has been a major concern of higher education in America. In its name curriculums have been reorganized, administrative structures of colleges have been altered, and countless workshops, conferences and self-study projects have been undertaken to the end that higher education might be improved. A forbidding volume of literature has been published on the subject."[79]

In June 1972, as it issued another in its volumes of reports and recommendations, the Carnegie Commission on Higher Education suggested that one of the significant problem areas facing contemporary American higher education was "the collapse of general education into a potential or even actual disaster area." Elaborating upon the point made earlier in the volume, the commission report stated:

> We regret the new tendency to relinquish concern for general education. It amounts to faculty abandonment of a sense of engagement in undergraduate educational policy. Some students protested the "breadth" requirements, and some faculties that removed them have put nothing in their place. This does not demonstrate attention to student dissatisfactions, but, instead, a lack of interest in the general education of undergraduate students or lack of conviction about what should be done. Thus, at some colleges like Antioch, when the students were given an "open" freshman year, many asked for more guidance—they felt bewildered and neglected.[80]

216

The report goes on to state that it is not advocating the return to some standard "breadth" requirement or a reinstatement of "survey" courses, but there is concern lest the intentions of general education be lost. It is even suggested that the terms "general education" and "liberal education" be dropped, and it is proposed that the concept of "broad learning experience" be used instead. Education should be for breadth, to provide a person with

> a chance to comprehend some major aspect of world cultures
> and human thought; the chance to get a wider perspective than
> the discipline or the individual elective provides; the chance to
> learn outside familiar paths, to absorb new points of view, to
> approach big problems and absorb data about them and to
> analyze them; a chance to expand the competence to think about
> new areas and to understand broad new situations; a chance,
> even, to discover some new interest that may lead to a new field
> of major concentration.[81]

And the way to provide such opportunities is to develop several options from among which students may choose: the report specifies as one of the recommendations, "consideration should be given to establishing campus by campus a series of coherent options for broad learning experience among which students may choose."[82] The concern for general education is reiterated in subsequent volumes of the commission. The report on purposes and performance lists as first among the ways in which the campus can aid in the development of the students, assisting the student in "acquiring a general understanding of society and the place of the individual within it—this is the role of 'general' education and it includes contact with history and with the nature of other cultures." Later, in the same report, the commission calls for making available to students "more broad learning experiences" and subsequently argues that higher education has "a fundamental obligation to preserve, transmit, and illuminate the wisdom of the past, to find, preserve and analyze the records of the past."[83] The final report of commission calls for a "renovation of general education" and the provision of optional programs directed toward "broad learning experiences."[84]

And yet Joseph Axelrod and his colleagues, in discussing the failure of old models of curriculum, suggest that much of the confusion in the discussions of college curriculum "has risen out of the terms *breadth* and depth." In making this criticism, they observe that the trends in curriculum since 1960 are toward stressing more the structural than the substantive aspects of knowledge. That is to say, the emphasis is less upon "covering" the content of a particular discipline and more on the process by which one comprehends within the discipline. They see as one of the signs of a trend a "return to the interdisciplinary course and the recommendation on many campuses that means be discovered for supporting such courses." They argue for a unity and suggest that "liberation from the conceptual trap of the breadth-depth framework can take place only as progress is made toward the discovery of a workable principle of unity for baccalaureate programs."[85] The distinction between general and specialized studies, between liberal arts and professional education, between occupational and transfer curricula, they say are "false distinctions for today and certainly for tomorrow, however useful they might have been in some other world of the past." They find that new curriculum models involve breaking the wall down between the curriculum and the world outside, however slowly this is happening. Community involvement has moved from being a part of the extracurriculum into the "very fabric of course assignments." The city itself becomes a laboratory. In the ideal curriculum, according to the authors, the focus would be on the great issues, would emphasize the human problems that exist in the community, and students would be encouraged to go off-campus to look into such problems or "even to engage in actions affecting them."[86] But the ideal program is far from being achieved. Referring to an extensive survey of baccalaureate requirements carried out by the U.S. Office of Education, the writers observe that the survey shows the dominant curriculum pattern is to have one-fourth of the requirements for the baccalaureate in major-field courses, about half in general education, and the remaining one-fourth in elective courses. Courses leading to a bachelor of science degree rather than a bachelor of arts degree tend to have somewhat larger requirements in the major subject and a reduction in the elective courses.

Earlier, Paul Dressel and Frances DeLisle examined the course offerings of 322 institutions over a period of ten years. They found that the prevailing pattern for general education was to designate between 31 and 40 percent of the total requirements for graduation as general education courses. Nearly 90 percent of the colleges were found within the group designating from 21 to 50 percent of all courses as required. This was slightly higher than ten years before, in

1957, when 82 percent of the colleges fell within this group. Within the general education requirements they found some slight variations over previous distributions, but the median percentage requirement for both periods was 37 percent. This 37 percent could be broken down into 17 percent of the courses in the humanities, including English composition and speech, 10 percent in the natural sciences and mathematics, and 10 percent in the social sciences.

Within the humanities almost 40 percent of the institutions were found to have specific requirements in English composition, literature, foreign languages, philosophy, and religion. The authors conclude that "there appears to be a reduction in the requirement of specific courses balanced by an increase in general distribution requirements so that the total requirement has remained unchanged." With regard to the natural sciences, the observation is that

> most colleges and universities specify an undergraduate requirement in the natural sciences. The colleges not doing so are those which do not prescribe courses or credits in any area. . . . The prevailing pattern is to require from five to ten percent of the total credits to be selected from the natural sciences. Usually about one-half of the work is to be taken in a laboratory science, but some colleges provide nonlaboratory courses and apparently accept these as fulfilling the requirement.[87]

In the social sciences over 90 percent of the colleges specify an undergraduate requirement. Within the requirement there seems to be a continuation of the traditional emphasis on the historical study of Western civilization. The writers found that "there has been essentially no change in the total requirements over the 10-year period among the institutions in the sample."[88]

Dwight R. Ladd reviewed changes in educational policy that took place during the 1960s at 11 institutions—the University of California at Berkeley, the University of New Hampshire, the University of Toronto, Swarthmore College, Wesleyan University, Michigan State University, Duke University, Brown University, Stanford University, Columbia College, and the University of California at Los Angeles. Ladd includes in his report information about developments in some other institutions as well. With regard to general education, he observes that programs in general

219

education have traditionally emphasized either a structured program, "made up of specially designed core courses not defined to a single discipline," or "a distribution or breadth requirement built largely on regular departmental course offerings."[89] Among the institutions he surveyed, he found that only Columbia and Michigan State had continued with specially designed general education courses. Michigan State maintained a sequence of courses in the University College, the successor to the Basic College. The other institutions in the sample that Ladd examined maintained some form of distribution requirements. For example, New Hampshire and Stanford required one course, "Introduction to Contemporary Civilization," and specified the other requirements under a distribution plan. As Ladd describes it:

> Under the typical distribution requirement, the student took a certain number of courses in the traditional divisions of the curriculum—the humanities, the social sciences, and the natural sciences—plus a course in English composition and a foreign language. The makeup of the divisions, the number of courses required, and other details vary, but the foregoing are characteristic of virtually all the requirements.[90]

In discussing the implications of this move away from prescribed courses or sequences, Ladd notes that Daniel Bell of Columbia seems to be alone in proposing an *increase* in the general education requirements. In the reports from the institutions that Ladd surveyed, in all of the other cases except one, generally a reduction is proposed in the number and range of courses required.[91] Michigan State University proposed neither a reduction nor an increase.

But even though Bell advocated increasing general education requirements, when Columbia undertook a revision of its general education program during 1973-74, characterizing it as the "first reform of its general-education curriculum since 1919," the new structure has fewer specific requirements and a wider range of options. It consists of a weekly seminar open to everyone in the university, the intent of which is "to evaluate past humanities courses and to discuss new interdisciplinary ones that would mix . . . undergraduate and graduate students," together with a series of smaller seminars within the professional schools and 13 new interdisciplinary courses involving such topics as "The Use and Abuse of Science and Technology."[92]

220

Within the structure of distribution requirements the changes were so varied that Ladd found it difficult to summarize them. He found that Wesleyan had eliminated all specific requirements and now left it up to the student to design his own general education program. He also noted that, in "several cases where the distribution requirements previously had to be met from lists of prescribed courses in the natural sciences, the social sciences and the humanities, it was [now] generally proposed that any course in those areas be permitted to satisfy the requirement, and . . . advanced courses in a field would be permitted to serve the purpose."[93] Ladd interpreted the data from the studies of the 11 institutions as an indication of a loss of confidence in general education; the reports "indicated considerable lack of confidence that the general education programs were very well related to the needs and backgrounds of many contemporary students, and they generally proposed arrangements that would give the students more opportunity to seek out courses that would more newly meet his perceived requirements."[94]

In their survey of 26 institutions, including 3 that were also reviewed in Ladd's study (Brown, Stanford, and Columbia), Levine and Weingart concluded that general education had failed. While it would seem that with the increasing need of a technological society for greater specialization, general education would be increasingly important to provide a basis for common humanity among people, they found that no program they examined, with the possible exception of St. John's, succeeded in providing this type of general education.[95] They expressed lack of sympathy with the general distribution approach, because they found the bridges that presumably were to be built between the divisions of knowledge were not being constructed:

> There are few general educationists left. Scholarship forces scholars so far apart that they can no longer understand each other. These people are clearly unable to help their students perceive the breadth of their endeavors. . . . Universities have reached the point where professors in the same department do not have to associate with one another, as noted by the proliferation of journals of different topics in the same field.[96]

They examined the core courses, or as they characterize them, "the common, broad, interdisciplinary survey required of all students," at Columbia, Eckerd, Reed, and at Stevenson and Cowell Colleges of Santa Cruz. Their observation was that the team-taught lecture generally suffered from a lack of cohesion, and that the larger the group of participating faculty, the greater the difficulty in integrating the lectures. They found that Justin Morrill College abandoned a common lecture in its "Inquiry and Expression Program," a team-taught program, after one year.

At least in the colleges they reviewed, they found that student reaction to the distribution type of program was in the main one of indifference. "Few students at any school felt that the distribution forced them to take courses they ordinarily would not have taken."[97] Among the distribution requirements in the 26 colleges studied, they found that the requirements in foreign languages had undergone the least change.

Among different approaches to general education where some specific general education program was desired, Levine and Weingart found the freshman seminar to be "the most popular, fastest-growing structure in freshman education." And they also found that faculty and student opinion of the freshman seminars was generally positive.[98] Nevertheless, four significant problems were mentioned in all, or most, of the programs: "The courses are above the freshman level; the instructor is not conducting the seminar but only a lecture course; the courses lack content; and freshmen are often too shy to participate fully." They also found the persistent problem of "the faculty's lack of interest, specially in rigidly departmentalized colleges and graduate-oriented universities."[99]

Among the programs that still attempt to provide a coherent form of general education, Levine and Weingart reviewed and reported on the Yale Directed Studies, the Berkeley Experimental College Program, and St. John's Four-Year Program. In common, these programs are intended for a self-selected group of students working through a core format which absorbs all or part of the participant's time. The Yale program was judged to be "unashamedly elitist," one that aimed to accept only those students who have shown the highest academic promise. Slightly less than 20 percent of the freshman class, or approximately 220 students, apply each year, and between 70 and 95 are admitted. Students with College Board scores below 750 are rarely accepted. The courses in the program are specifically designed for the program and are open only to the Directed Studies students. In a student critique of the courses, Yale found that the students in their work receive greater faculty attention, a sense of community results from the structure, and the survey courses are viewed as being better than those in the regular curriculum. Yet, some participants still found a lack of any integrated approach.

The Experimental College Program at Berkeley began in September 1965 and after the end of the academic year 1969 was discontinued. For each of the two cycles of the program, applications were received from 325 of the 4,800 entering freshmen, and 150 students were randomly selected. Students were required to take one course per semester outside of the program, with two-thirds to three-quarters of the academic load taken within the Experimental College. The curriculum was divided into four periods: Greece, Seventeenth Century England, The American Constitutional Founding, and The Contemporary Scene. Theme oriented, the program explored such ideas as freedom and authority, the individual and society, war and peace, conscience and the law, and acceptance and rebellion. The program included lectures, seminars, and conferences. Attrition in the program seemed to be fairly high; about 40 percent of the students left the program, but some observed that this was the same as the percentage of students initially enrolled in the regular program who left the university. Those who completed the program expressed some difficulty, however, in making the transition from the college to the upper division of the university.[100]

Although the Berkeley experiment died after a few short years, it may have a reincarnation of sorts in Strawberry Creek College. Charles Muscatine, together with colleagues Sellers, Scott, and Hubert and Stuart Dreyfus have inaugurated a two-year program, the New Collegiate Seminar Program, as Strawberry Creek College, named for a stream that makes its way through the Berkeley campus. As Fred Hechinger reports the development, "Unobtrusively housed in a primitive, two-story wooden barracks of World War II vintage, the program is billed as an attempt to 'open a new path to undergraduates aiming for high-quality liberal education with a contemporary flavor.' "[101] Initially, 72 freshmen and sophomores are participating in six seminars averaging 12 students each as the basic activity. The seminars continue for one or more quarters and are led by a full professor who is assisted by a graduate student from a different field "in order to stress the relevance of more than one discipline to the particular topic."[102] The results of each seminar are to be presented for review by all members of the college. Students also enroll in some courses in regular departments. Throughout the two years of the program, students and teachers are to evaluate each other.

The St. John's program, one of the longer-lived reforms in general education, is maintaining its basic structure of seminars and tutorials and wholly prescribed curriculum. Preceptorials were added in 1962 and provide a nine-week period in which juniors and seniors, with a tutor, can study one book or theme at a time and in depth. The weekly lecture also continues as a part of the original program. The program has been in operation since 1937.[103]

Heiss appears to be more optimistic about the status of general education, and in addition to the colleges already mentioned by Ladd and Levine and Weingart, she refers to the University of Michigan; the University of California at Los Angeles, Santa Barbara, Davis, and Riverside; Shimer College, which in 1974 was fighting for its life; Ottawa College; Vassar; the University of Hawaii; Whittier; Hobart and William Smith Colleges; Saint Olaf College; Goshen College and Beloit College, both of which have been mentioned as "transformed" colleges; Oklahoma College of Liberal Arts in Chickasha, the program of which by 1974 had already reverted to a more traditional structure; Manhattanville; Hiram College; and Barat College.[104]

It is difficult to generalize from the profiles presented by Heiss, because the range of activities included under changes in general education varies so much. For example, the reference to changes in general education at the University of Michigan is to one small unit, the Residential College, "in which diverse offerings replace the liberal arts core of the traditional curriculum and students share responsibility for the character and quality of their academic program." The Michigan program includes "seminars, independent study on individual projects, work-study integrated with course work in the student's major, and a 'furlough semester' during which a student may work on anything he chooses." At Santa Barbara, the Heiss profile calls attention to the creation of the new unit, the College of Creative Studies, which involves a total curriculum structure, not simply that which might be referred to as "general education." On the other hand, at Berkeley the "change" in general education is limited to the modification of the art survey courses which have been reorganized into small units taught by senior professors. We expect that what is "new" in the program is that senior professors are willing to take the undergraduate teaching assignments.

The revisions at Vassar involve providing three approaches to a baccalaureate: an independent study program, a concentration in a discipline, and a multidisciplinary concentration. The specific changes in general education relate primarily to the second approach, the concentration in a discipline leading to the more traditional collegiate degree program, where several variations are possible in the general requirements. Whittier has gone to a contract basis for all of its courses, but the changes in general education appear to be limited to the first year of exploratory course work. Beloit has introduced a "Great Books" course that focuses on great issues and ideas of man, and at the upper division the college has provided a seminar on "Contemporary Issues." Hobart and Smith Colleges combine several introductory courses, one or two bidisciplinary courses, and a freshman tutorial. Manhattanville dropped distribution requirements and has moved to a student-designed program of study. Hiram College in 1969 introduced an interdisciplinary studies program, combined with a ten-day Freshman Institute prior to the opening of the school year. Barat's efforts are in freshman studies programs, although it is also developing a senior-year integrative sequence.

What is one to infer from these reports? Perhaps general education is not quite as moribund as Levine and Weingart suggest, but if there is any perceptible trend it seems to be one of moving away from prescribed courses to general distribution requirements and from distribution requirements to individually designed or contracted sequences. While there continue to be developed new integrated and new freshman and lower division sequences, the prevailing mood seems to be that of allowing the student "to do his own thing" and to build his own program—albeit with some guidance within broad areas resembling a former approach to distribution requirements.

The total programs of general education earlier developed by the University of Chicago and recommended for Harvard and

Columbia seem in the mid-1970s to be less the norm and more the exception. The University of Chicago, providing one of the most extensive efforts at developing a total sequence in general education (four years, including the equivalent of the last two years of high school and the first two years of college), continued for approximately a quarter of a century but underwent reorganization in 1957-58 when the major system and a more typical four-year baccalaureate program was introduced. While maintaining a "lower college" consisting of two years of more or less required common-core subjects, the university went on to develop an "upper" college that included one year specialization in any one of the four divisions and a year of electives. The first two years of the old college were dropped. The program underwent further revision in the mid-1960s, and while many of the earlier interdisciplinary courses remained, presently the structure at Chicago has become more of a restricted distribution sequence. The program recommended by the Harvard Committee was never fully introduced, and by the mid-1960s an introduction of an optional feature left very little of the recommendations of the Harvard Committee intact.

What is the status of general education in the mid-1970s? The *Chronicle of Higher Education* in November 1973 carried the headline, "Student Demands for 'Practical' Education Are Forcing Major Changes in Curricula."[105] The report called attention to the apparently growing preference of students for "practical education that can be put to use immediately" and student demand for "short career-occupational education, a credential, and a job." Not only is student demand causing institutions, according to the report, to offer more career-oriented courses, but it is encouraging the development of various types of less than baccalaureate sequences. Students may return later for the B.A., but "a growing number are not inclined to complete four years of traditional college." And the force of such a development is to "downgrade interest in general-education type courses or sequences."

A subsequent article in the *Chronicle* pointed up the impact of the "new practicality" on the humanities, a basic element of any general education sequence.[106] According to Malcolm Scully, students are "reportedly abandoning theoretical, abstract, and purely academic fields for those that relate directly to jobs." Enrollments are down in English and history and the foreign languages. Some faculties are turning to "applied humanities," to the application of the skills of people in the humanities to interdisciplinary problems wherein the humanist teams up with faculty in the more applied fields to deal with immediate issues from a humanistic viewpoint. Whether the combinations will gain support among the general run of academicians remains to be seen.

But the signs are far from clear. While the evidence seems to be mounting that student orientation to the practical and the applied is forcing a retreat from some of the more traditional modes of general education, Scully finds in some places a resurgence of interest in those same modes. Among the examples he uses is Stanford University, where

> a number of students have become frustrated by the lack of requirements and long for the discipline of the program of general education. The university has reinstated an elective program called "structured liberal education."[107]

He goes on to quote Charles Frankel of Columbia University, Robert Nisbet of the University of Arizona, and others to document the proposition that there is emerging a conservative academic counterrevolution.

Nathan Glaser refers to the "crisis of general education,"[108] which he sees in relation to one broad area of study, the social sciences, and the difficulty of incorporating the social sciences into general education. The problem Glaser poses is not related to student disinterest but to the disinclination (or inability) of certain disciplines to address themselves to the traditional concerns of general education. Over the years, even in the survey or interdisciplinary approach to general education, the social sciences have found the greatest difficulty in accommodating to the general education emphasis on general understanding and cultural heritage.

An evaluation of student reactions to the Integrated Liberal Studies Program of the College of Letters and Science of the University of Wisconsin, Madison, suggests that reasons students give for dropping out of this two-year sequence of prescribed courses reflect much of the same mood described in two of the *Chronicle* articles above.[109] Samuel Kellams found a significant decrease in the persistence rate in the program which was established in 1948. During the first 15 years of its existence, an average of 55 percent of the freshmen enrolling in Integrated Liberal Studies completed four semesters of the program, while in 1967 only about 20 percent continued through the four semesters.[110] In questioning those who dropped out, he found that 53 percent complained about "intensity of focus," some 35 percent found the courses not appealing to their interests, and 23 percent found the course material (content and teaching) unexciting. Others called into question the lack of flexibility and the lack of contact with other students in the university. (Since students could give more than one reason, the percentages add to more than 100).

In his review of general education, Stanley Ikenberry finds the broader movements in higher education as a whole having a decided impact on the form and future of general education: "In very large part, the difficulties of general education have come from its sometimes valiant attempts to swim upstream against the major currents of society and against the dominant forces in American colleges and universities."[111] The expansion in enrollments, the move to "universal" postsecondary education, the diversity among students, the growth of professionalism and specialization, and the diversity in views about the functions of higher education, these and other developments work against the traditional conceptions of general education. And if general education is to survive, says Ikenberry, there must be a complete reformulation that "must recognize the substantial changes that have taken place in American higher education during recent decades." He calls for a sweeping reexamination of the assumptions on which general education programs have been built.

As James G. Rice of Stephens College (Missouri) observes the great variety of activities currently labeled "general education," he asks, "Is general education going in all directions at once?"[112] Indeed, with so much variation in application, one may well ask whether the term "general education" is useful any longer. But Rice argues that in spite of the apparent chaos there is some rhyme and meaning to it all. The many experiments in general education can be grouped under five broad categories: mixing real-life experiences with academic and campus experiences; developing interdisciplinary and problem-centered courses and programs; providing "primary experience"; emphasizing independent work; and providing ways for expanding and heightening the student's awareness of other persons, of the world, and himself. The common theme in most of these approaches, says Rice, is that they "relate themselves to personality-based learning theory and . . . they are searches for a pedagogy consonant with it."[113] He goes on to argue that general education is quite alive and that

> the common core of undergraduate experience which we call general education is now on many campuses being sought not in a common content, subject matter, body of knowledge, but in common experiences, common problems, common exposures to reality and the larger society.[114]

Rice strongly affirms that general education's time has come again.

We have examined in greater length the developments in general education, because concern for general education seemed to dominate so much of the thinking during the 1940s and through much of the 1950s. While there were certainly other aspects of the curriculum that were under study and that were changed during that period, how to develop more effective general programs was a recurring theme—and it seems to remain, in various forms, as a concern in the 1970s. But we now turn to some of the other developments. While they are not dealt with in the same depth as general education has been, and while an exhaustive listing is not provided, attention is given here to some of the more frequently noted among the developments.

Concentration or Major

Along with the examination of general education and the common aspects of curriculum, there has been a continuing concern about the nature and extent of the specialized area, the concentration or major. While Lowell was out of sympathy with the free-elective system fostered by his predecessor, Charles W. Eliot, he did not during his own administration attempt to go back to a wholly prescribed curriculum. As we have already noted, he announced that Harvard was combining the general education and concentrated studies in a fairly well defined undergraduate sequence. At the same time David Starr Jordan in California was encouraging the development of the major-minor system at Stanford. During the twentieth century most undergraduate colleges have adopted a combination of breadth and depth, variations on the general education and major or concentration systems.

In their review of developments between 1957 and 1967 in a random sample of 322 institutions, Paul Dressel and Frances DeLisle found that the way in which undergraduate colleges organized the "depth experience" varied considerably. Approximately 85 percent of the institutions reviewed called for some type of concentration for "pursuing a discipline or program of special interest to insure understanding in depth in at least one area of man's knowledge."[115] The most frequent pattern was that of the departmental major. Approximately one-fourth of the institutions in the sample specified a departmental major without any reference to a minor or secondary emphasis, and over half indicated the departmental major with a minor or secondary emphasis. Barely over 2 percent specified an interdepartmental, divisional, area, or theme type of concentration. Between 1957 and 1967 the emphasis upon the departmental major without minor or secondary emphasis increased from 18.9 percent to 24.8 percent of the institutions. The specification of a departmental major with a minor or secondary emphasis decreased during this period of time from 62.4 percent of the institutions to 56.2 percent. During the same period of time the number of institutions indicating no specific requirements for a major concentration increased from 15.5 percent to 16.8 percent.[116]

Within the arts and humanities the number of credit-hours specified for the major or concentration increased slightly. Both in 1957 and 1967 the modal requirement was 24 to 32 credits, or eight courses, but 45.3 percent of the institutions specified that type of concentration in 1957 and only 39.1 percent specified it in 1967. Moreover, in 1957 nearly two-thirds of the institutions required 24 to 32 credits or less, while in 1967 only 53.7 percent specified 24 to 32 hours or less. That means that a higher proportion of the institutions required beyond 24 to 32 credits in 1967 than was the case in 1957.

In the natural sciences there was a similar change, but perhaps not as striking. The sciences in both periods specified more hours for a major or concentration than was the case for the arts. In both periods the modal pattern was 24 to 32 credits; in 1957 some 38.5 percent of the institutions made this specification, but by 1967 the

230

percentage had decreased to 33.9 percent. Likewise, in 1957 just over one-half of the institutions specified between 24 and 32 credits or less, for a major in the sciences; in 1967 this proportion had gone down to 46.9 percent. In other words, more than half of the institutions required more than 24 to 32 credits for a major in the sciences in 1967. Dressel and DeLisle note that, "though prevailing practices can be identified, the course and credit requirements for a major concentration vary widely and are difficult to interpret or compare because of different concepts of what constitutes a major." Thus, while the broad outlines can be drawn, it is difficult to generalize beyond what we have noted above.

In the 26 institutions examined by Levine and Weingart, it was found that the emphasis continues to be upon the departmental major or concentration. They noted, however, that departments in the social sciences, humanities, and arts have lessened the requirements somewhat, "so that only one-fourth to one-third of a student's courses must be in his major, and have reduced the number of specific requirements to as few as one or two common courses."[117] They found that the departments in the natural sciences, however, have maintained a large number of required courses in the major sequence. It is somewhat difficult to interpret these findings, since in the review by Dressel and DeLisle it appears that the humanities and arts had actually increased their requirements for a major during 1957-67, while Levine and Weingart suggest a decrease in the requirements. The samples of institutions may be sufficiently different in the two studies to account for the apparent discrepancy.

Levine and Weingart make note of several variations of the departmental major. At Bard College freshmen may select a "trial major" to provide some degree of concentration early in the student's career. The "success" of the program seems, however, to be questionable. The writers also found a few schools that have provided double or joint majors; Santa Cruz and Haverford are singled out, but in both institutions considerably less than 10 percent of the students undertake joint or double majors. Another variation was the interdepartmental major, but the writers found this option employed in a limited number of cases. In 9 of the 26 institutions there were "student-created" majors in which students were allowed to write a proposal for a concentration, describing the courses and independent study combinations planned. Approval of the major "usually involves consultation with a number of people—

231

advisers, department chairmen, and prospective teachers," and in spite of the fact that most of the plans submitted by the students were accepted, relatively few students made use of the option. Three of the 26 schools—St. John's, Sarah Lawrence, and New College at Sarasota—did not specify a concentration or major.

Among the institutions Ladd studied, he found that all of the institutions required a major or concentration, and relatively little had been done in the way of reviewing this area of the curriculum in the self-studies undertaken by the colleges. Ladd suggests that "this appears to be forbidden territory for college or university committees, and vigilantly guarded turf of the departments."[118] He suggests that students and faculties generally were able to influence very little the content of the typical departmental major. Only Michigan State University and Brown examined in their self-studies the content and scope of majors. The Michigan State study suggested a reduction in the total number of majors and Brown proposed more opportunity for student-designed majors. Ladd's generalization is: "In sum, then, the major or concentration remains a focal point in undergraduate education. Since few of these reports really discuss the matter, there was apparently never any question but that it should so remain. A few reports did delve into the basic nature of the major, but none included any serious analysis of what an undergraduate program might be without a major."[119]

The review by Heiss does not attempt to summarize the current status of departmental majors or concentrations but rather points up those cases in which some variations have been introduced. She notes:

> Within the past several years many colleges and universities have introduced structural changes to try to make academic institutions more functional and relevant to the social context in which they operate. These changes include the formulation of interdisciplinary centers, intradepartmental units, planning or coordinating committees or commissions, and information and referral offices that make the resources of the institution available to industry and government service agencies, or act as ombudsman for the campus community.[120]

Reference is made to the introduction of human resources, community service, and public affairs types of curricula. Among the institutions noted are: the college of Human Resources and Education at the University of West Virginia; the Wallace School of Community Service and Public Affairs at the University of Oregon; the College of Environmental Design at the University of California at Berkeley; the College of Human Development at the Pennsylvania State University; the College of Human Ecology at Cornell University; the Institute for Human Services at Boston College; the Division of General and Interdisciplinary Studies at the University of Washington; and the Division for Experimental and Multidisciplinary Programs at the University of New York at Buffalo, which is a series of small living-learning units and special workshops designed to undertake programs that single departments had not been able to sustain.

In their discussion of "Alternatives to Departments," Levine and Weingart found a number of examples of what they called "extradepartmental programs and broader faculty organization." Bard has used divisions as the major structural units. Eckerd and New College at Sarasota also started with an emphasis on divisions, and Reed uses divisions for administering course offerings. In addition, the University of California at Santa Cruz, the University of Wisconsin at Green Bay, and Prescott College had developed interdisciplinary structures "to avoid departmental domination." At Bard, Eckerd, New College, and Reed, the divisions, however, apparently had little impact upon the development of interdepartmental concentrations. Santa Cruz was satisfied with the divisional arrangement, although it found the interdisciplinary structure something of a barrier in seeking new faculty. The Prescott structure at that time seemed to remain viable, although some students complained that programs and offerings were "either too diverse or too broad." Green Bay appears to have been successful in maintaining its structure, although Levine and Weingart suggest that even Prescott, Santa Cruz, and Green Bay have not been "completely successful in establishing an interdisciplinary structure."[121]

While there have been shifts in credit-hour requirements for majors—mostly minor in character—and while there have been some attempts to develop alternatives to the departmental structure—still on a limited scale in comparison to the prevailing structure—the mid-1970s have been characterized in perhaps greater measure with shifts in enrollments and emphases among academic departments. Issues of the *Chronicle of Higher Education* for the last few years provide partial documentation for these shifts. Undergraduate enrollments in history courses have dropped by 12.6 percent between 1970-71 and 1973-74. Faint comfort was derived by some observers in that decreases in New England and the South were of a smaller order than elsewhere.[122] Yet while enrollments in history generally were declining, medieval studies were experiencing a boom of sorts. In 1960 there were 2 centers of medieval studies at universities in North America, but by early 1974 there were more than 40, and many colleges—from Yale to Swarthmore to Central Missouri State—were reporting steady increases in both graduate and undergraduate enrollments.[123]

Foreign language departments have experienced even more rapid declines. One recent survey reported a 10 percent decline between 1970 and 1972.[124] The basic reason for the decline appears to be the move on the part of many institutions to drop foreign languages as a graduation requirement—down from 92 percent of the institutions in 1966 to 77 percent in 1970, and continuing to decline somewhat. On the other hand, "exotic" languages such as Chinese, Hebrew, Japanese, and Swahili have had increased enrollments. Language departments are in some institutions seeking to recover enrollments by developing courses that emphasize the uses of foreign language in employment and travel.[125]

Psychology faces the opposite situation. Enrollments have been increasing dramatically, and it is estimated that from 5 to 10 percent of college students in the United States are majoring in psychology.[126] Within the field of psychology, students apparently favor clinical over experimental concentrations. With the high enrollments in the field, some observers are questioning whether this is all to the good. It is noted that all too many persons with an undergraduate degree in psychology "wind up taking jobs that have nothing whatever to do with the subject."[127]

Sociology departments, also experiencing increased enrollments, are reexamining the functions of their degree programs, particularly at the graduate level. One sociologist, Paul Lazarsfeld, advocates more programs in applied sociology, because sociologists have had trouble in bridging the gap between finding data and knowing what to do about them.[128] Some political scientists have also been calling for more "relevance" in their course work:

234

Peace studies have proliferated. The study of political establishments is now balanced by courses on less traditional topics. Students no longer learn all their political science in classrooms, but often earn credit by working in government offices.[129]

The social sciences generally seem to be experiencing growth in enrollments even as they are reassessing programs and sequences.

Enrollments in physics are reported to be declining. Chemistry faces both boom and shortages. Enrollment has been growing at the undergraduate level—probably aided by the dramatic increases in premedicine and other health-science programs—while enrollments in graduate programs have declined sharply.[130] For the natural sciences generally, some observers foresee new programs and increased enrollments as the impact of the energy crisis is felt; "energy studies" will become one of the new glamour fields.[131]

The last few paragraphs have touched only lightly and nonselectively on shifts in enrollments and emphases among academic departments. The resulting picture is far from clear if one seeks some firm basis for projecting developments in the next five to ten years, but what does emerge is an apparent responsiveness by most departments to new developments in the academic market. Perhaps it is in the adjustments (or lack of adjustments) among academic departments that some of the most significant curricular changes will take place in the next decade.

New Fields for Concentration

In addition to various interdepartmental and interdisciplinary concentrations, a number of new types of studies have emerged. Heiss notes the following: ethnic studies, black studies, environmental studies, non-Western studies, women's studies, futuristics, computer science, policy science, arms control and foreign policy, peace studies, the management of change, forensic science, drug and alcohol addiction, and ethics in medicine. She notes that approximately two-thirds of the colleges and universities in the country have introduced programs in ethnic studies. Black studies are found in over 400 institutions. Urban and environmental studies are apparently growing rapidly. More than 100 colleges and universities offer courses in the field of futuristics, concerned with planning and forecasting.

John Creager, in a study undertaken by the American Council on Education and based on responses from 669 institutions in the spring of 1973, found 57.1 percent of the institutions reporting interdepartmental or interdisciplinary courses with 94 percent of the private universities reporting this type of program. He also found that 44.7 percent reported ethnic studies, 14.6 percent reported women's studies, and 18.4 percent reported off-campus studies in special American subcultures.[132]

The literature on ethnic studies has become voluminous; I do not attempt to assess the impact of such studies on the American college campus, but simply note in passing comments that have appeared in educational publications. The *Chronicle of Higher Education* devoted an issue in May 1972 to "Higher Education and the Black American." John Crowl's article in that issue summarized developments to that date. Ann Heiss's *Inventory* noted that some 400 institutions included black studies in the curriculum. Crowl reports that 200 institutions had some sort of black studies program and another 400 offered courses in black history or culture.[133] He listed among the difficulties encountered by the programs: many of the more politically oriented black students criticize the programs for being too academic; some black educators consider the programs poorly conceived and planned; many programs have received only grudging acceptance in white academic circles; some administrators say there is a lack of qualified faculty members; the programs may constitute the only black presence on white campuses; some programs, especially those established with outside funds, face cutbacks in funds. Yet, with all of the problems, black studies programs seem to have gained enough acceptance to be able to anticipate continuance at most major institutions. Indeed, a new subfield called "black politics" appears to be developing within political science.[134] A study conducted in 1972 and involving interviews with 209 sociologists from a representative group of 70 colleges and universities in the United States explored patterns of response to the black studies movement.[135] Four basic patterns are described—embracement, antagonism, accommodation, and withdrawal or dropout. Among the 209, some 28 percent were characterized as embracers, 22 percent as antagonists, 30 percent as accommodators, and 20 percent as dropouts. As the author notes, "The finding that young sociologists, blacks, and perhaps women were more favorably disposed toward black studies might have been expected."[136]

236

The emergence of white ethnic studies has been observed as the latest addition to the list of special-interest-group studies that began with black studies in the late 1960s.[137] The new programs are variously labeled "Euro-American," "immigrant," or "white ethnic" studies, and they deal with the experiences in America of European immigrants. In New York several Italian-American projects are in evidence. The University of Minnesota has established an Immigration Studies Collection. Sonoma State College in California has courses in Euro-American studies. There is a growing number of courses under the title of "Jewish Studies." Not all observers are predicting significant growth in these areas. Norman Lederer, director of the University of Wisconsin system's Ethnic and Minority Studies Center, sees a "relatively drab" future for white ethnic studies.

Women's studies seem to be growing in number and variety. One reporter notes a growth from a "handful" of courses in the late 1960s to an estimated 2,000 such courses offered in 1973-74, studies that examine the "roles, contributions, and treatment of women."[138] Courses range from those based in a single discipline, such as the history or psychology of women, to broad, interdisciplinary courses examining women's status. Some 75 programs, as distinct from the offering of one or more discrete courses, have been established in the last three years, and four universities were reported during 1973-74 to be offering master's degrees in women's studies.

Calendar Variations

While over the years there had been some shifting between the quarter and semester calendars, the semester structure (two semesters of 15 to 17 weeks per academic year) provided the typical college calendar during the first half of the twentieth century. Then in the early 1960s, with the introduction, or perhaps it was reintroduction, of the intersession, a variety of new types of college calendars emerged. In her review of the current status, Heiss gives examples of the intersession with the 4-1-4 format (two terms of semester length, during which students enroll in four courses, and an intersession of approximately one month with enrollment in one course), the 3-3 structure (students enroll in three courses during each of three quarter-length terms of 10 to 12 weeks), the modular course plan (students enroll in one course in 3- to 4-week blocks of

237

time), the varied semester-length calendar, movable calendars (students may begin at almost any time during the year), presessions, and postsessions.[139] While the semester plan apparently continues to predominate, it does so by far less of a margin than was the case before the new plans were adopted.

Among the newer calendars, one of the more popular is the 4-1-4 with the intersession. Over 500 colleges and universities have introduced some kind of January intersession, although not all of the colleges have adopted the four-course pattern for each of the longer sessions. The University of Denver, for example, is maintaining a quarter calendar but has introduced a three-week period in December as an intersession. Other institutions have maintained the semester structure with courses of varying credit-hour designations, while still employing the intersession. While Bennington and Sarah Lawrence Colleges had incorporated an interim and off-campus unit in their calendars in the 1920s, the great interest in the 4-1-4 developed in the early 1960s with the efforts of Florida Presbyterian College, now Eckerd College. Indeed, the program is popular enough to have generated a professional association known as the Four-One-Four Conference, which publishes an *Interim Digest* and an annual catalog listing the interim courses of member institutions. Florida Presbyterian College has reported from its studies that the interim encourages a more relaxed approach to learning and that students apparently perform better— at least they earn higher grades and fewer of them fail courses. Jack Rossmann of Macalester College reports on some of the research undertaken at that institution.[140] At Macalester the grading is on a satisfactory-unsatisfactory basis only, courses offered during the interim are different from those offered during the regular term, and students may undertake independent and off-campus study projects. Over the years, Macalester has noticed a significant decrease in the percentage of students enrolling in on-campus faculty-directed group courses, and an increase in the off-campus independent study and off-campus faculty-directed group courses. On-campus independent study has remained fairly stable. Approximately 40 percent of the students took courses outside of their major area, although students majoring in the fine arts enrolled predominately in fine arts courses during the interim. Over the years approximately three-quarters of the students have rated the interim term as "extremely rewarding" or "more than usually rewarding." Rossman finds that the interim course has also influenced some of the general university

238

policies, including the expansion of the satisfactory-unsatisfactory grading system, the reduction of general institutional requirements, and the introduction of new procedures in regular-term courses.

James Davis reviews some of the reasons for calendar changes.[141] He suggests that the major focus in the 4-1-4 calendar is upon the single term and it is probably the interim that accounts for its popularity; the one-month period and one-course unit provide opportunities for experimentation not found in the regular term. The trimester, three semester-length terms, has been identified with the University of Pittsburgh, the University of Michigan, and Harper College, although a number of other institutions have adopted this variation. In many of the institutions the summer trimester becomes in effect two or three shorter term units. Colorado College has been identified with the modular course plan, although its program is a variation of the calendar of Hiram and Eureka Colleges. Colorado College uses the basic unit of three-and-a-half weeks of study followed by a four-and-a-half day break.

Another way of looking at the college academic calendar is to place it within the broader context of the organization of instruction. Eileen Kuhns and S. V. Martorana refer to four organizational modes: (1) concurrent courses, (2) time modules, (3) academic modules, and (4) competency.[142] The advantage of employing their perspective is that it enables one to examine calendar variations in terms of the broader and more fundamental issues residing in the instructional process, and as the writers suggest, such an analysis "may offer the possibility of an educational synthesis which is more holistic for the individual student than the current discipline-based organization of knowledge."[143]

Procedural Changes

One may include in this category a wide variety of programming elements including new grading systems, variations on advising, development of contract and performance-based courses, various types of off-campus programs, honor programs, and the like.

In their review of 26 colleges, Levine and Weingart found that one of the major problems in any variation in grading systems was the reaction of graduate schools. Nontraditional grading patterns generally met with problems; traditional grades were readily accepted by the graduate schools:

> At the twenty sample schools, with four explainable exceptions, a clear pattern was observed: traditional grades accompanied by no graduate school difficulties, or non-traditional grades accompanied by graduate school difficulties. . . . The problems created by graduate schools offer little promise of prompt resolution. Even at those universities with non-traditional grading systems at the undergraduate level, many administrators and faculty refuse to change admissions policies at their own graduate and professional schools. The University of Michigan Medical School, for example, will not accept written evaluations from the Residential College; the Law School, in contrast, will accept the evaluations but will not promise to read them. Similarly, many graduate departments at Brown will not consider pass/fail-graded Brown students.[144]

The writers found that letter and numerical grades, presumably more objective, were in fact not so; they commented that their "study does not substantiate the objectivity usually attributed to letter and numerical grades." Ten of the 26 schools in their review used written evaluations, but problems involved in these included length of time required for writing "good" evaluations, poorly designed evaluation forms, and lack of commitment on the part of the faculty to produce adequate descriptions. Oral examinations were used in a limited number of cases. Some colleges used covert grading, letter-graded systems employed only for external use, and variations of the pass/fail and credit/no credit systems. No one of the systems was without difficulty, although the writers leaned toward some type of written evaluation.

In the review undertaken by Ladd, all of the colleges and universities employed a more or less standard letter-grade system. While there was agreement that grading creates fears and anxiety and that any system appeared to be "deceptively refined" and "inadequate in the dimensions of work that it measures and the amount of information about progress that it provides," all of the studies Ladd reviewed accepted the necessity for some kind of evaluation and with few exceptions retained the traditional system. Swarthmore and Brown proposed written comments, and Brown and Stanford introduced a total "pass-erase system."[145]

Heiss found that approximately two-thirds of the nation's colleges and universities had introduced some variation of a pass-fail system. Some 8 percent of the colleges were reported as not recording failing grades, and approximately 70 percent of the institutions restricted the number of pass-fail courses open to a student to one-fifth of the program or to one course per term. Others limited the option to courses outside of the student's major. Other variations in grading included the "cumulative portfolio," in which written comments by instructors, statements by students, and samples of work were combined in a comprehensive review of student progress. A number of colleges had also introduced outside examiners, particularly in situations involving off-campus and external-degree programs.

A survey of the acceptance of grades at 350 undergraduate institutions, 200 graduate schools, 50 law schools, and 50 medical schools revealed that the traditional A-to-F grading system is favored by most undergraduate institutions as well as by graduate and professional schools.[146] It appears that the more nontraditional grades that a student has on his record, the more problems he faces in transferring to other colleges or gaining admission to professional study. Undergraduate institutions are more open to nontraditional grading systems than are graduate and professional schools. Yet, as Harold Hodgkinson has observed, the pass-fail option seems to be on the increase.[147]

Barbara von Wittich gathered data on 1,331 Iowa State University students enrolled in elementary foreign-language courses during the spring quarter, 1970, in order to determine if there were any differences in performance between students enrolled under a pass-fail system and those enrolled for conventional grades. Since instructors were not aware which students were enrolled under pass-fail, they provided letter grades for all students, and it was possible, using the letter grade as the criterion, to compare performance of the two groups. Just over one-third of the students enrolled under pass-fail. When compared with other students in the language classes, when compared with their performance in other subjects taken under the letter-grade system, and when compared in other pass-fail versus letter-grade course enrollments, students enrolled for pass-fail generally performed at lower levels in those pass-fail courses. The writer concluded that any subjects involving cumulative learning should not be offered under pass-fail "if good results and adequate progress are expected."[148]

Another area in which considerable attention is being focused is that of advising. Here too the wholly adequate system is yet to be found. Levine and Weingart discovered in their sample of institutions that there continues to be a fairly clear division between "the affective and cognitive components of learning," and most university counseling programs separate academic and personal advising. Most faculty, students, and administrators interviewed by the two writers judged the advising to be poor. Indeed, they judged that as many as three-fifths of the students in the schools "chose not to see their advisor, and a significant number of students indicated instead a preference for obtaining advice from administrators, faculty, and student friends."[149] Generally little incentive was offered to faculty members for advising; the role of the adviser was ill-defined. The writers concluded that, with the exception of one institution, the advising systems were "grossly inadequate." Perhaps the key to the inadequate advising, according to Levine and Weingart, is that "faculty are rewarded largely for research and teaching in their specialty, so that their interests necessarily exclude advising."[150]

Variations in advising noted by Levine and Weingart were the use of student advisers at Brown and Justin Morrill Colleges. At three institutions the freshman-seminar instructors served as freshman advisers. One college had introduced a group advising session called "Freshman Inquiry." The session took place toward the end of the freshman year and the freshmen were required to prepare a 1,500-word essay for the inquiry regarding their current intellectual position and their plans for a future course of study. Most of the faculty and students involved in the program found it helpful.

In his review, Ladd contended that the core of the academic-advising problem lay in the "large size and the routinization and superficiality of relationships which seem to accompany it" in the typical American university. All of the systems he reviewed had in common the intent "to provide students with information about courses and programs available and requirements to be met." He also found a type of "policing" involved in that the advisers were to make sure that the student completed the kinds of requirements the institution had established. These systems were also to "insure that

242

each student had a faculty member to whom he could go for advice about courses, program selection, or career choices and (at least as students generally see it) to whom he could talk in an informal fashion."[151] All of the institutions studied noted that advising was a major problem and that by-and-large faculty members simply did not accept or like the advising job:

> Few faculty members care to see themselves as a cog in the bureaucratic machinery—as mere initialers of student course schedules and as policemen. Most faculty members also have a real and undoubtedly healthy reluctance toward becoming involved with students' emotional problems. . . . A second problem concerns the amount of time that advising can consume. . . . A further problem has, in a sense, been created by changes recommended in the studies . . . moves toward greater freedom for students involve a responsibility to ensure that students who wish it have ready access to sound advice. . . . Faculty advisers frequently do not know enough about courses and programs available or about requirements to give students good advice even if they wanted to take the necessary time. . . . Thus the advising system tends to fail both as a channel of information and as a basis for significant contact between students and faculty members.[152]

Ladd was of the opinion that the information functions could probably be better met by more timely, clear, and informative descriptions of courses, programs, and requirements. He also suggested the need for developing an advising core, but he immediately recognized the difficulty of securing faculty commitment even at this level.

In the material she reviewed, Heiss found evidence of some movement toward making advising "as important for faculty as is the classroom teaching role."[153] Examples singled out were the University of California at Irvine, Ottawa University, Evergreen State College, and California State University at San Jose. Chatham College in Pittsburgh has developed a broad range advising system in which each student is assigned to an adviser who is to assist in defining goals, in selecting the context within which the goals may be realized, and in interpreting students' test results to the individual. Advising for freshmen begins a week before classes, and at the end of the second semester one week is designated as advising

243

week. As another variation, a number of institutions have established the office of ombudsman, and "as a disinterested intermediary, the ombudsman can take a student's complaint or concerns to the appropriate office without implicating him"[154] Heiss suggests that the role of the ombudsman can be very important on a campus, especially in the early stages of policy decisions.

Seeing the Larger Issues

The particular issues confronting Dean Neumann in the faculty forum had to do with whether the university should consider adopting a new academic calendar. The dean was surprised at the amount of discussion provoked by the report of the subcommittee. Yet, Professor Dunkelwald himself provided the clue to the reaction his committee's report aroused when he suggested that adopting a new academic calendar might require faculty members to reexamine their courses, both in content and method of teaching. At least to some of the faculty the interrelatedness of curricular elements described by Joseph Axelrod became all too obvious. Changing time spans allotted to classes could easily affect much more than the number of hours a class met. Professor Dunkelwald's committee will have to examine more carefully the consequences of their proposal, and Dean Neumann will have to make sure that the work of the subcommittee on academic calendars is taken into account by the other curriculum subcommittees. The review of literature in the preceding pages should be of help to the dean and the faculty committees in that it suggests the range of concerns that have surfaced in recent years and also something of how other institutions have responded to those concerns.

As I have already noted, I have not intended that this review reflect all, or even a majority, of the current developments in curriculum among colleges and universities in North America. Rather, I have pointed to those developments which would seem most to relate to undergraduate and particularly smaller undergraduate colleges. For those who wish to explore some of the developments in greater depths, the references in the "Notes" should be helpful, in particular Ann Heiss's *Inventory of Academic Innovation* and Patricia Cross's *Planning Non-Traditional Programs*.[155] The annotated bibliography by William Mahler in the latter volume is especially helpful.

244

Other specific variations found in colleges and universities in the United States deserve more attention, were this chapter to attempt to be more comprehensive. Cooperative education, hardly new, is apparently experiencing a resurgence of interest. Established in 1906 at the University of Cincinnati, and the factor that transformed Antioch College in 1921, cooperative education grew slowly until the mid-1960s. In 1960 there were about 60 institutions with cooperative education programs, and now there are over 400.[156] Courses by newspaper are in their second year and are available in some 200 dailies and weeklies.[157] External degree programs are growing;[158] the Twenty-Ninth National Conference on Higher Education devoted considerable attention to these programs and to learning contracts.[159] Endorsed by the Commission on Non-Traditional Study,[160] the external degree was greeted with some words of caution earlier in a paper by Stephen Bailey.[161] The three-year baccalaureate at first seemed to be gaining a following, but institutons are apparently having second thoughts.[162]

These and numerous other variations are being discussed in the current literature on instructional programs in higher education. One may take the position that little that is radically new has appeared in the last decade, but it is difficult to escape the conclusion that more colleges and universities are engaged in some form of curricular study and/or revision than ever before. By far, most of the attempts fall within Hefferlin's third category, accretion or attrition, and the long-range success of such efforts will probably be directly related to the extent to which consciously or unconsciously those responsible for changes are able to take into account Axelrod's observations regarding the systemic nature of curricular reform. Some institutions find themselves transformed, and new institutions continue to surface—to note Hefferlin's two other categories. The major challenge to new institutions is to maintain the uniqueness that justified their founding—and to survive. The challenge to all institutions, including Dean Neumann's university, is to assess at regular intervals the effectiveness of the curriculum, to be sensitive to student concerns while maintaining a clear sense of identity, and to be prepared to change emphases to meet new needs. The university is an open system that must interact with its environment without being overcome by that environment.

Notes

[1]See also Arthur Levine and John Weingart, *Reform of Undergraduate Education* (San Francisco: Jossey Bass, 1973).

[2]Joseph Axelrod, "Curricular Change: A Model for Analysis," *Research Reporter,* Center for Research and Development in Higher Education, University of California, Berkeley, 3 (no. 3, 1968), p. 1.

[3]*Ibid.*

[4]Joseph Katz and Nevitt Sanford, "The Curriculum in the Perspective of the Theory of Personality Development," in *The American College,* ed. Nevitt Sanford (New York: John Wiley and Sons, 1962), pp. 418-419.

[5]Samuel Baskin, ed., *Higher Education: Some Newer Developments* (New York: McGraw-Hill Co., 1965), pp. 318-332.

[6]Council on Higher Education, *Innovative and Non-Traditional Study Programs* (Olympia, Wash.: Council on Higher Education, State of Washington, 1972), p. 1.

[7]Carnegie Commission on Higher Education, *Reform on Campus: Changing Students, Changing Academic Programs* (New York: McGraw-Hill Book Co., 1972), p. 10.

[8]*Ibid.,* p. 2.

[9]Ernest L. Boyer, "Breaking the Youth Ghetto," in *Lifelong Learners—A New Clientele for Higher Education,* ed. Dyckman W. Vermilye (San Francisco: Jossey-Bass, 1974), pp. 5-6.

[10]Charles E. Silberman, "The Remaking of American Education," in *New Teaching, New Learning,* ed. G. Kerry Smith (San Francisco: Jossey-Bass, 1971), p. 229.

[11]Harold Taylor, *Students Without Teachers* (New York: Avon Books, 1969), p. 153.

[12]David H. Bayley, "The Emptiness of Curriculum Reform," *Journal of Higher Education,* 43 (November 1972), pp. 591-592.

[13]Ann Heiss, *An Inventory of Academic Innovation and Reform* (Berkeley: Carnegie Commission on Higher Education, 1973).

[14]Carnegie Commission on Higher Education, *Priorities for Action: Final Report of the Carnegie Commission on Higher Education* (New York: McGraw-Hill Book Co., 1973), p. 48.

[15]Harold L. Hodgkinson, *Institutions in Transition: A Profile of Change in Higher Education* (New York: McGraw-Hill Book Co., 1971), p. xv.

[16]See Christopher Jencks and David Riesman, *The Academic Revolution* (Garden City, N.Y.: Doubleday and Co., 1968), and David Riesman, *Constraint and Variety in American Education* (Garden City, N.Y.: Doubleday and Co., 1956).

[17] "A Report Card on All Those Campus Reforms of the 60s," *U.S. News and World Report,* 76 (May 6, 1974), pp. 29-30.

[18] Levine and Weingart, *Reform of Undergraduate Education,* p. 8.

[19] See William A. Mahler, "An Annotated Bibliography with Overviews," in *Planning Non-Traditional Programs,* ed. K. Patricia Cross et al. (San Francisco: Jossey-Bass, 1974), pp. 175-218.

[20] JB Lon Hefferlin, *The Dynamics of Academic Reform* (San Francisco: Jossey-Bass, 1969).

[21] "College Openings and Closings," *Chronicle of Higher Education,* 8 (September 24, 1973), p. 2.

[22] Lewis B. Mayhew, "The New Colleges," in Baskin, *Higher Education: Some Newer Developments,* pp. 19-20.

[23] "New College Offers to Join University of South Florida," *Chronicle of Higher Education,* 8 (May 20, 1974), p. 5.

[24] David Riesman, Joseph Gusfield, and Zelda Gamson, *Academic Values and Mass Education: The Early Years of Oakland and Monteith* (New York: Doubleday and Co., 1971).

[25] *Ibid.,* p. 15.

[26] *Ibid.,* pp. 16-17.

[27] *Ibid.,* pp. 68-69.

[28] *Ibid.,* p. 78.

[29] See Heiss, *An Inventory of Academic Innovation and Reform,* pp. 1-17.

[30] See *Bulletin of New College,* 6 (September, 1970).

[31] James Feeney and Gresham Riley, "Learning Contracts at New College, Sarasota," in *Individualizing Education by Learning Contracts,* ed. Neal R. Berte (San Francisco: Jossey-Bass, 1975), p. 11.

[32] See *Bulletin of Florida Presbyterian College,* 1971-72.

[33] Council on Higher Education, *Innovative and Non-Traditional Study Programs,* pp. 54-57.

[34] Franklin Patterson and Charles R. Longworth, *The Making of a College,* Hampshire College Working Paper no. 1 (Cambridge, Mass.: The M.I.T. Press, 1966).

[35] John Walsh, "Hampshire College: A Quest for Quality, a Balanced Budget," *Science,* 170 (November 27, 1970), p. 955.

[36] Randall P. Kunkel, "A Study of the Maintenance and Alteration of Policies and Practices in Selected Innovative Institutions of Higher Education," Ph.D. dissertation, University of Denver, 1973, pp. 107-108.

[37] Peter Bloch and Nancy Nylen, "Hampshire College: New Intents and Old Realities," *Change,* 6 (October 1974), p. 39.

[38] *Ibid.,* p. 41.

[39] *Ibid.,* p. 42.

[40] See Diane Ravitch, "The Dreams of Livingston College," *Change,* 1 (May/June 1969), pp. 36-39.

⁴¹See Orde Coombs, "The Necessity of Excellence: Nairobi College," *Change,* 5 (April 1973), pp. 38-44.

⁴²*Announcements of Simon's Rock College,* 1973-74, p. 6.

⁴³*Ibid.,* p. 8.

⁴⁴L. Drewe Keller and Victor P. Meskill, "Empire College—Fad or Innovation?" *Journal of General Education,* 25 (October 1973), pp. 187-198.

⁴⁵*Ibid.,* p. 187.

⁴⁶Neal R. Berte, "Individualizing and Contracting," in Berte, *Individualizing Education by Learning Contracts, op. cit.,* pp. 1-8.

⁴⁷American Council on Education, *New Academic Institutions: A Survey* (Washington, D.C.: American Council on Education, 1972).

⁴⁸*Ibid.,* p. 87.

⁴⁹*Ibid.,* p. 29.

⁵⁰Larry A. Van Dyne, "Experimental Colleges: Uneasy Freedom, Mind-Bending Strains—and Hope," *Chronicle of Higher Education,* 6 (May 15, 1972), p. 4.

⁵¹*Ibid.*

⁵²*Ibid.*

⁵³Malcolm G. Scully, "Struggle in Prescott," *Chronicle of Higher Education* 10 (August 18, 1975), p. 7.

⁵⁴Kunkel, "A Study of Maintenance and Alteration of Policies and Practices," pp. 198ff.

⁵⁵*Ibid.,* pp. 211-213.

⁵⁶Robert D. Brown, "Evaluation of Experimental Colleges," *Journal of Higher Education,* 43 (February 1972), pp. 133-134.

⁵⁷*Ibid.,* p. 134.

⁵⁸See Bloch and Nylen, "Hampshire College: New Intents and Old Realities."

⁵⁹Paul L. Dressel, ed., *The New Colleges: Toward An Appraisal* (Iowa City: American College Testing Program, 1971), preface.

⁶⁰Robert A. Altman, *The Upper Division College* (San Francisco: Jossey-Bass, 1970), p. 76.

⁶¹John Coyne and Tom Hebert, *This Way Out: A Guide to Alternatives to Traditional College Education in the United States, Europe and the Third World* (New York: E. P. Dutton and Co., 1972).

⁶²Wayne Blaze et al., *Guide to Alternative Colleges and Universities* (Boston: Beacon Press, 1974).

⁶³See Allan O. Pfnister, "Everyone Overseas! Goshen College Pioneers," *International and Educational Cultural Exchange,* 8 (fall 1972), pp. 1-12. Also see *The Humane Studies Program: Perspectives on Meaning and Destiny,* A Prospectus on General Education Developed by the Goshen Faculty, September 1973.

248

64George A. Drake, "An Analysis of the Colorado College Plan," *Critique: A Quarterly Memorandum of the University of Toledo Center for the Study of Higher Education* (March 1973). See also Jack Magarrell, "One-Course-at-a-Time Plan Is a Success at Colorado College," *Chronicle of Higher Education,* 8 (December 17, 1973), p. 3.

65For recent reviews of St. John's College, see Philip W. Semas, "Keeping Quiet Is Hardest Part of Job for a Tutor at St. John's College," *Journal of Higher Education,* 43 (February 28, 1972), pp. 1, 4; also Gerald Grant and David Riesman, "St. John's and the Great Books," *Change,* 6 (May 1974), pp. 28-36, 62-63. Antioch College is discussed in Gerald Grant, "Let a Hundred Antioch's Bloom," *Change,* 4 (September 1972), pp. 47-58.

66Harvey D. Shapiro, "Lights That Failed" (review of *Five Experimental Colleges,* ed. Gary B. MacDonald), *Change,* 6 (July/August 1974), pp. 57-58.

67Karen J. Winkler, "Innovative, Exciting, or Freaky, Project Ten Gets 5-Year Trial," *Chronicle of Higher Education,* 7 (November 20, 1972), p. 1.

68Beverly T. Watkins, "Johnston College Confounds Skeptics," *Chronicle of Higher Education,* 11 (September 15, 1975), p. 6.

69Heiss, *An Inventory of Academic Innovation and Reform,* p. 19.

70Jerry G. Gaff et al., *The Cluster College* (San Francisco: Jossey-Bass, 1970). See especially the listing on pages 16-17 in which federated and subcolleges are grouped under the general heading of "subcollege."

71*Ibid.,* p. 35.

72Hefferlin, *Dynamics of Academic Reform,* p. 25.

73The President's Commission on Higher Education, *Higher Education for American Democracy,* vol. 1, *Establishing the Goals* (Washington, D.C.: Government Printing Office, 1947), p. 49.

74A. Lawrence Lowell, "The Choice of Electives," in *At War with Academic Traditions in America* (Cambridge: Harvard University Press, 1934), p. 3. The article originally appeared in the *Harvard Monthly,* 1887.

75A. Lawrence Lowell, "Annual Report for 1908-1909," in *At War with Academic Traditions,* pp. 238-239.

76Executive Committee of the Cooperative Study in General Education, *Cooperative in General Education* (Washington, D.C.: American Council on Education, 1947), p. vii.

77The Committee on the Objectives of General Education in a Free Society, *General Education in a Free Society* (Cambridge, Mass.: Harvard University Press, 1955), p. 4.

78*Ibid.,* p. 54.

79Russell Thomas, *The Search for a Common Learning: General Education 1800-1900* (New York: McGraw-Hill Book Co., 1962), p. 1.

[30]Carnegie Commission on Higher Education, *Reform on Campus: Changing Students, Changing Academic Programs*, p. 42.

[81]*Ibid.,* p. 43.

[82]*Ibid.,* p. 45.

[83]Carnegie Commission on Higher Education, *The Purposes and the Performance of Higher Education in the United States: Approaching the Year 2000* (New York: McGraw-Hill Book Co., 1973), p. 41.

[84]Carnegie Commission on Higher Education, *Priorities for Action,* p. 28.

[85]Joseph Axelrod et al., *Search for Relevance* (San Francisco: Jossey-Bass, 1969), pp. 64-65.

[86]*Ibid.,* pp. 68-69.

[87]Paul L. Dressel and Frances H. DeLisle, *Undergraduate Curriculum Trends* (Washington, D.C.: American Council on Education, 1969), p. 23.

[88]*Ibid.,* p. 25.

[89]Dwight R. Ladd, *Change in Educational Policy: Self-Studies in Selected Colleges and Universities* (New York: McGraw-Hill Book Co., 1970), p. 170.

[90]*Ibid.,* p. 171.

[91]See Daniel Bell, *The Reforming of General Education: The Columbia Experience in Its National Setting* (New York: Columbia University Press, 1966).

[92]Karen J. Winkler, "By Reforming General-Education Program, Columbia Hopes to Remotivate Students," *Chronicle of Higher Education,* 8 (December 3, 1973), p. 2.

[93]Ladd, *Change in Educational Policy,* p. 172.

[94]*Ibid.,* p. 176.

[95]Levine and Weingart, *Reform of Undergraduate Education,* p. 50.

[96]*Ibid.,* p. 51.

[97]*Ibid.,* p. 27.

[98]*Ibid.,* p. 29.

[99]*Ibid.,* pp. 30, 35.

[100]*Ibid.,* pp. 40-44.

[101]Fred M. Hechinger, "An Academic Counter-Revolution," *Saturday Review/World,* 2 (November 16, 1974), p. 64.

[102]*Ibid.*

[103]Levine and Weingart, *Reform of Undergraduate Education,* pp. 44-50.

[104]Heiss, *An Inventory of Academic Innovation,* p. 60.

[105]Beverly T. Watkins, "Student Demands for 'Practical' Education Are Forcing Major Changes in Curricula," *Chronicle of Higher Education,* 8 (November 26, 1973), p. 2.

[106]Malcolm G. Scully, "Student Focus on Practicality Hits Humanities," *Chronicle of Higher Education,* 8 (February 4, 1974), pp. 1, 3.

[107] Malcolm G. Scully, "Signs of a 'Counter-Reformation' Hearten Academic Conservatives," *Chronicle of Higher Education*, 8 (March 18, 1974), pp. 1, 6.

[108] Nathan Glaser, "Social Sciences and the Crisis of General Education," *Chronicle of Higher Education*, 8 (November 5, 1973), p. 16.

[109] See Watkins, "Student Demands for 'Practical' Education," and Scully, "Student Focus on Practicality."

[110] Samuel E. Kellams, "Students and the Decline of General Education," *Journal of General Education*, 24 (January 1973), p. 218.

[111] Stanley O. Ikenberry, "The Academy and General Education," *Journal of General Education*, 23 (October 1971), p. 177.

[112] James G. Rice, "General Education: Has Its Time Come Again?" *Journal of Higher Education*, 43 (October 1972), p. 533.

[113] *Ibid.*, p. 536.

[114] *Ibid.*, p. 538.

[115] Dressel and DeLisle, *Undergraduate Curriculum Trends*, p. 27.

[116] *Ibid.*

[117] Levine and Weingart, *Reform of Undergraduate Education*, p. 64.

[118] Ladd, *Change in Educational Policy*, p. 181.

[119] *Ibid.*, p. 184.

[120] Heiss, *An Inventory of Academic Innovation*, p. 73.

[121] Levine and Weingart, *Reform of Undergraduate Education*, p. 80.

[122] "History Courses Losing Students: Survey Shows 12-pct. Enrollment Decline," *Chronicle of Higher Education*, 9 (September 23, 1974), p. 7.

[123] Malcolm G. Scully, "Boom in Medieval Studies Is Seen As More Than a Passing Fad," *Chronicle of Higher Education*, 8 (May 13, 1974), pp. 1, 10.

[124] Malcolm G. Scully, "Unprecedented Enrollment Drop Hits Languages," *Chronicle of Higher Education*, 7 (June 18, 1973), pp. 1, 3.

[125] Malcolm G. Scully, "Language Departments Fight Dip in Enrollments," *Chronicle of Higher Education*, 8 (November 12, 1973), p. 3.

[126] Philip W. Semas, "Student Interest in Psychology Is Booming," *Chronicle of Higher Education*, 6 (September 27, 1971), pp. 1, 6.

[127] Cheryl M. Fields, "5-10 Pct. of Students Major in Psychology, But After Graduation, What Do They Do?" *Chronicle of Higher Education*, 8 (May 20, 1974), p. 9.

[128] Karen J. Winkler, "Sociologists Still In Demand, But Job Outlook Is Clouded," *Chronicle of Higher Education*, 7 (September 10, 1973), pp. 1, 6.

[129] Edward R. Weidlein, " 'Relevance' Is Pressed in Poli Sci," *Chronicle of Higher Education*, 7 (October 16, 1972), p. 5.

[130] "Mixup in Chemistry: Simultaneous Booms and Shortages Upset Old Staffing Formulas," *Chronicle of Higher Education*, 8 (August 5, 1974), p. 7.

[131]Philip M. Boffey, "Energy Studies Seen Becoming 'A Glamour Field,' " *Chronicle of Higher Education,* 8 (December 24, 1973), pp. 1, 4.

[132]John A. Creager, *Selected Policies and Practices in Higher Education,* American Council on Education Research Reports, vol. 8, no. 4, 1973 (Washington, D.C.: American Council on Education, 1973).

[133]John A. Crowl, "Black Studies: The Bitterness and Hostility Lessen, but Criticism Persists," *Chronicle of Higher Education,* 6 (May 30, 1972), pp. 6-7.

[134]"Poli-Sci's New Field: 'Black Politics,' " *Chronicle of Higher Education,* 9 (November 4, 1974), p. 8.

[135]Wilson Record, "Response of Sociologists to Black Studies," *Journal of Higher Education,* 45 (May 1974), pp. 364-391.

[136]*Ibid.,* p. 391.

[137]Cheryl M. Fields, "White Ethnic Studies Are Spreading; They Focus on European Groups' Experiences in America," *Chronicle of Higher Education,* 7 (April 16, 1973), pp. 1, 6.

[138]Cheryl M. Fields, "Women's Studies Gain: 2,000 Courses Offered This Year," *Chronicle of Higher Education,* 8 (December 17, 1973), p. 6.

[139]See Heiss, *An Inventory of Academic Innovation,* p. 47ff.

[140]Jack Rossman, "The Interim Term After Seven Years," *Journal of Higher Education,* 42 (October 1971), p. 603.

[141]James Davis, "The Changing College Calendar," *Journal of Higher Education,* 43 (February 1972), pp. 142ff.

[142]Eileen Kuhns and S. V. Martorana, "Of Time and Modules: The Organization of Instruction," *Journal of Higher Education,* 45 (June 1974), p. 431. For a listing of some of the colleges with short winter interterms "or other academic calendars that vary from the traditional ones," see "149 Colleges with Innovative Calendars," *Chronicle of Higher Education,*8 (January 21, 1974), pp. 9-10.

[143]*Ibid.,* p. 437.

[144]Levine and Weingart, *Reform and Undergraduate Education,* pp. 125ff.

[145]Ladd, *Change in Educational Policy,* p. 190.

[146]Beverly T. Watkins, "A-to-F Grading System Heavily Favored by Undergraduate, Graduate Institutions," *Chronicle of Higher Education,* 8 (November 12, 1973), p. 2.

[147]Harold L. Hodgkinson, "Pass-Fail and the Protestant Ethic," *Chronicle of Higher Education,* 7 (December 11, 1972), p. 8.

[148]Barbara von Wittich, "The Impact of the Pass-Fail System upon Achievement of College Students," *Journal of Higher Education,* 43 (June 1972), pp. 499-508.

[149]Levine and Weingart, *Reform of Undergraduate Education,* p. 12.

[150]*Ibid.,* p. 18.

[151]Ladd, *Change in Educational Policy,* p. 163ff.

[152]*Ibid.,* pp. 164-165.

[153]Heiss, *An Inventory of Academic Innovation,* p. 56.

[154]*Ibid.,* p. 59.

[155]See Heiss, *An Inventory of Academic Innovation and Reform,* and Cross et al., *Planning Non-Traditional Programs.*

[156]Malcolm G. Scully, "Co-Op Education, Alternative Work and Study, Gains Fans," *Chronicle of Higher Education,* 8 (October 23, 1973), p. 7.

[157]Beverly T. Watkins, "Paper Campus," *Chronicle of Higher Education,* 9 (September 30, 1974), p. 4.

[158]Larry A. Van Dyne, "External-Degree Programs Give New Life to University 'Extension,' " *Chronicle of Higher Education,* 6 (May 22, 1972), pp. 1, 2.

[159]Dyckman W. Vermilye, *Lifelong Learners—A New Clientele for Higher Education,* Current Issues in Higher Education, 1974 (San Francisco: Jossey-Bass, 1974). See also Council on Higher Education State of Washington, *Exploring the External Degree,* Conference Report, May 24, 1973, University of Washington, Seattle, and *Journal of Higher Education,* 44 (June 1973).

[160]Commission on Non-Traditional Study, *Diversity by Design* (San Francisco: Jossey-Bass, 1973), pp. 41, 42.

[161]Stephen K. Bailey, "Flexible Time-Space Programs: A Plea for Caution," in *The Expanded Campus,* Current Issues in Higher Education, 1972, ed. Dyckman W. Vermilye (San Francisco: Jossey-Bass, 1972), pp. 172-176.

[162]See Philip W. Semas, "Bachelor's Degree in Three Years Gaining Favor," *Chronicle of Higher Education,* 6 (January 31, 1972), p. 1, 5; and subsequent report, Philip W. Semas, "3-Year Degree Not Catching On As Anticipated," *Chronicle of Higher Education,* 7 (May 14, 1973), p. 1, 5. Also, for a good overview, see Edward L. Allen, "The Three-Year Baccalaureate," *Journal of General Education,* 25 (April 1973), pp. 61-73.

Chapter
5
Financing the Program: Clearing Ahead or Continuing Storms?

"Professor Ernst would like to see you at your earliest convenience." It was my secretary on the intercom. She continued, "You have some time tomorrow afternoon. What about 3:30?"

I looked over at my desk calendar and tomorrow's schedule. For a moment I nourished the hope that she had made a mistake and that the afternoon was taken up. But, as usual, she was right. I did have some time after 3:00. With what must have been obvious lack of enthusiasm and after all too long a pause, I said, "Looks okay. Let's make it from 3:30 to 4:00. I'll see him then." I was about to add that I was not sure what we might accomplish, but I said no more.

Ernst chaired the faculty advisory committee on budget for the college and was also the head of the Department of Chemistry. I knew what he wanted to talk about. It was the announcement the president had made at the faculty meeting earlier in the week. It had been the first regular meeting of the faculty in Arts and Sciences for the year, although the fall term had already been under way for some time. After pointing out how much better off we were than many neighboring institutions, the president went on to say that to maintain our healthy position we would have to do some belt-tightening. Enrollment had held up, but the hoped-for increase had not materialized, and he hoped that we would be able to pare our spending for the year by 5 to 8 percent. He was reluctant to make such an announcement, but we had always maintained a strong fiscal position, and the trustees, after reviewing the conditions in September, requested that we be more conservative in our spending for the year. While it might be possible to restore some of the funds later, it would be better to be conservative now and avoid spending money we might not have.

"But, sir!" It was Professor Ernst asking for the floor. "When we met as an advisory committee with the dean last April, we were assured that the budget then being prepared for the trustees would be firm for the year. We worked hard on that budget, and we think it was an honest request."

"Yes, it was a good budget, and we appreciate the work you and others did. But we also expected some increase in enrollment. That has not materialized. Costs are up more than we could have anticipated. We just think it's wise to be on the conservative side now. We can begin watching expenditures early in the year. And that's better than finding ourselves facing a big deficit in June."

"But, can't the advisory committee discuss this? Is the decision final?" persisted Ernst.

"I'm sure that Dean Neumann will be meeting with you. I was pleased when he requested that the advisory committee be appointed. I know that you will be able to work things out and meet the request of the trustees."

There were other questions about whether the reductions had to be across the board, whether this meant we would have to curtail the study abroad program recently—and, to my way of thinking, belatedly— introduced, whether this would have implications for decisions about tenure and promotion. The president assured the questioners that the dean and advisory committee would be discussing these matters. He then thanked the faculty for their splendid cooperation, said that the strength of the university was in its very capable faculty, and asked to be excused to meet another appointment.

I had gone into the first fall meeting of the university administrative staff a few weeks before with much more confidence than had been the case a year ago. While I could not report any spectacular gains in enrollment, I could say that we had managed to hold our own. On the basis of my review of the enrollment situation in colleges and universities generally, I knew that we were still benefiting from the slightly increasing college-age population and that our experience this year was only a temporary reprieve. But, at least we had not lost ground. We had time to continue to work on our recruitment program. The curriculum committees were also taking hold, and even the academic calendar subcommittee had recovered from its first encounter with the general faculty. All in all, I had been reasonably pleased with my first year. Then the president said that the trustees were insisting on a balanced budget, that costs had gone up—fuel was out of sight—and that we would have to economize. He reminded us that we had managed a faculty salary increase, a modest one, but still an increase when some neighboring institutions had been forced to place a freeze on salaries. And we had also avoided a tuition increase, although we would probably have to do something for next year. All of this meant that unless we found ways to cut back expenditures by nearly 10 percent this year and another 5 percent next year, we faced serious deficits. He later agreed to a reduction of 5 to 8 percent for this year. As the dean of the largest unit in the university, with the most faculty and some of the more expensive research programs, I knew where the pressure to economize was going to be. My temporary pleasure at being able to report a stabilized enrollment disappeared.

The budget for the current year had been put together carefully last spring. I had asked for an advisory committee on budget from the faculty, and I was convinced that, because we had opened the college accounts to that group and had discussed in some detail our income and expenditures, the departments had worked to stay within the limits we had set. In April we had worked on the assumption of an 8 to 10 percent increase over the year just ending. We knew that with inflation we were actually only maintaining the same level as for the current year. But we agreed to work under those limitations. Now, a cutback of any amount meant that our buying power for the new year would actually be less than for last year.

I had delayed calling together the advisory committee. I was still convinced that it had been a wise move to appoint the committee last spring, but I was not quite sure how to proceed with this unexpected request for further reductions in the budget. Associate Dean Starker was studying the expenditures of the previous year to find what might be done to achieve further economies. But such an analysis takes time, and I would have preferred to put off the meeting with Professor Ernst until we were better prepared to speak to the issues. But I also knew that Ernst's department was one that was particularly under pressure. Costs of equipment and supplies had skyrocketed. And it was a good department, with a fine national reputation. Ernst understandably did not want to see something he had worked hard to build now being curtailed.

How had we managed to get into this situation? When I reviewed the financial statements of the university in the spring before accepting the appointment as dean, I knew there were problems. But this university had a good record over the years, and its financial condition was certainly superior to that of the institution where I was then serving as a department chairman. Now we were in the same position, or we might be even worse off. What had happened in these 18 months—18 months that now seemed like a lifetime.

I phoned Starker's office. "He's not in right now. He left for the computer center a half hour ago. Said something about another set of print-outs."

"Tell him to come to Dean Neumann's office as soon as he gets back."

The Emergence of the Crisis

Dean Neumann's university somewhat belatedly arrived at a point that other colleges had reached much earlier in the 1970s. While Neumann had been aware of a "financial crisis" and had even heard reference to a "new depression," he had not until now been faced with the threat of cutbacks in what seemed to be an already lean budget. What was happening? This was the same question asked by many administrators and faculty when Earl Cheit's report was issued in the latter part of 1970. Cheit had studied the financial condition of 41 colleges and universities, and he estimated that over 60 percent of the colleges and universities in the United States were headed for financial trouble or were already in financial difficulty. The title of his report was *The New Depression in Higher Education,* and it soon became a new password. Just emerging from half a decade of disruption that had culminated in Kent State in May 1970, higher educational institutions seemed to be moving from one time of crisis into another. The new crisis was a financial one.

Many observers were convinced that higher educational institutions were already well into the new depression before Cheit's report appeared. Clark Kerr, chairman of the Carnegie Commission on Higher Education, stated in the foreword to the Cheit study:

> The decade of the 1960s was characterized by the most rapid growth and development of institutions of higher education in American history. . . . But toward the end of the 1960s, signs of financial stress began to be apparent in the world of higher education and by 1970 increasing numbers of institutions were facing financial difficulties as the flow of funds from various sources ceased to rise at the rapid rate that had been experienced from the late 1950s to about 1967.[1]

He suggested that there was a "clear connection between the extraordinary growth of the first seven years of the decade and the financial stringency that began to emerge toward the end of the decade." With the increase in enrollments, institutions had also increased the quality and variety of course offerings, had expanded special programs, and had increased the proportion of graduate students. All of these developments added cost and, together with growing rates of inflation, contributed to sharp increases in the cost per student.

258

Cheit's study included 41 institutions, but by using a weighting formula and taking the 41 as representative of higher educational institutions nationally, he projected that 19 percent of all colleges and universities were in financial difficulty and that an additional 42 percent were on the way to financial trouble. That left only 39 percent that appeared not to be in financial difficulty. Generalizing from his sample, Cheit said that private institutions were more likely to be in financial difficulty in the spring of 1970 than were public institutions, and that universities, when compared to other types of institutions, were even more likely to be facing financial pressures. Comprehensive public colleges and two-year colleges seemed least likely to be in financial straits.

Earlier in 1970, *Business Week* magazine anticipated Cheit's findings in a three-page report on the financial crisis on the campus. Referring to the efforts of two small colleges to avoid fiscal disaster, the report said that such incidents, "obscured by the daily barrage of headlines about campus unrest, signal a financial crisis in higher education that is taking on alarming dimensions." An executive associate of the Association of American Colleges had observed that one-half of all private liberal arts colleges were drawing on their endowments in one way or another to meet operating expenses and that the number of such institutions that were operating in the red had increased 50-fold in the past five years. The president of Oberlin College, where the accumulated deficit over the past four years had reached $400,000, said that "the future looks grave indeed." Not only had a number of smaller schools closed, but larger institutions such as Case Western Reserve, Yale, Columbia, Georgetown, New York University, and the University of Pennsylvania were feeling the pressure. Inflation accounted for much of the difficulty, but the decline in federal support appeared to be a significant element as well. [2]

Even before Cheit and *Business Week* called attention to the fiscal problems of higher institutions, *Fortune* magazine had in October 1967 reported the financial forecasts from 20 private institutions and had estimated that the deficits of these institutions would be $3 million by the spring of 1968 and a decade later could climb to $110 million. In commenting on the *Fortune* article, Virginia Smith suggested that one of the reasons for the appointing of the Carnegie Commission on Higher Education in 1967 was a growing concern over college and university financing. [3] She observed that the period from 1957 to 1967 had been higher education's "golden decade" fiscally. It was a time when expenditures rose from $5 billion to $15 billion and enrollment rose from 2.5 million to 5.5 million. But the growth in income had not kept pace with the rising costs, and the late 1960s made it increasingly clear that higher education "was in a state of financial distress far more drastic than the usual institutional problem of making ends meet."[4] By the end of 1970 it was clear that public as well as private institutions were facing financial pressures; many institutions were delaying new programs, cutting back existing ones, postponing salary increases, and simply not filling vacant positions.

William Bowen, in one of the first reports issued by the Carnegie Commission, documented the way in which productivity in universities had not kept up with the increases in instructional costs, which were increasing at an average rate of 7.5 percent per year. In one part of his report, Bowen was able to show that the direct instructional cost per student over the period from 1955-56 to 1965-66 had reached 8.3 percent per year for the private universities he examined. He attributed the rising unit costs to the increased responsibilities taken on by universities and to the rising costs of educational technology. He referred to some significant operating deficits reported in the last academic year for which he had data, and he suggested that many other universities had avoided deficits only by declining to undertake financial commitments for which there was actually serious need; in this sense there were "educational deficits" far in excess of the reported financial deficits. While no major university had been forced to close down, and while it was unlikely that such would be the case, Bowen observed that mere survival was hardly the test for well-being and that the danger was not that the major private universities would disappear, but that "they will be unable to continue to meet their current responsibilities, let alone to develop in step with national needs."[5]

And the problem was not exclusively that of the private institutions. In a report of the National Association of State Universities and Land-Grant Colleges prepared in July 1971, it was noted that 12 public universities had finished the 1970-71 academic year in the red. The report stated that

> five years ago there was not a single public university in the country with an operating funds' deficit. Last year there were 12

that ended the academic year in the red, and 11 universities were already predicting that they will finish this year with more expenses than they have funds to meet.[6]

The situation first became apparent during the 1966-67 academic year when the University of Nebraska joined Cornell University in reporting an operating deficit for the year. Cornell, one of the private members of the National Association of State Universities and Land-Grant Colleges, had experienced deficits since 1965-66, but Nebraska was the first public member to report a deficit. In 1967-68 the University of Rhode Island also reported a deficit. The significant decline began in 1968-69, and the article predicted a continuing growth in the number of institutions facing difficulties. As institutions withdrew monies from general funds and savings to cover the deficits—since some public universities are prohibited by state law to run deficits—most of their working capital was depleted. The result was the demand for more funds from the states and the introduction of sharp economy measures on the campus. Economy measures already reported, in the order of frequency employed, were deferred maintenance, elimination of new programs, and freezes and cutbacks on faculty positions. Increasing enrollments and rising inflation appeared to be the two main factors in creating the problem; legislative grants simply were not keeping up with the needs.

In October 1969, M. M. Chambers observed that while state appropriations of tax funds for higher education had increased by more than 337 percent over the decade ending with 1969-70, there were "increasing signs of and causes for disquiet and apprehension about the future support of public higher education." While state support had continued to rise in actual dollars appropriated, it "continues to decline as a percentage of total income at most universities."[7] Among the state universities and land-grant colleges, tuition and fees had increased by an average of 16.5 percent during the year to compensate for lack of funds from the state legislatures.

The Crisis Develops. By January 1970 the picture appeared even darker. A lead story in the *Chronicle of Higher Education* referred to a large private university being forced to phase out six Ph.D. programs, to a private college running deficits totalling $959,000 over four years, to another institution in which 91 students had to drop out because there was not enough money to give them financial aid, to an institution approving the largest tuition increase in its history because of rising costs and shrinking support, and to still another suspending a project to help 200 high school students from deprived backgrounds to get ready for college because federal funds were not available. Many of the difficulties were attributed to significant reductions in federal support. The article stated:

> Some federal programs have been severely curtailed or eliminated in this era of "tight budgets." Other sources of support have not been adequate to pick up the slack in academic budgets. . . . college and university officials are perhaps most concerned about erosion of their endowments. Continuing deficits force them to use up their endowment capital for current operating expenses.[8]

It was further noted that while there was no overall statistical picture showing the erosion of the financial position of private universities, there seemed little doubt that such an erosion was underway. The public colleges were also curtailing programs because of cutbacks, and reference was made to "huge tuition hikes" made at the University of Wisconsin, the three land-grant institutions in Florida, Indiana University, Purdue, Iowa State University, the University of Iowa, and the University of Maryland.

Testifying before the House Special Subcommittee on Education in March 1970, Clark Kerr said that the financial squeeze on higher education was probably having its greatest impact on the large research universities and the small liberal arts colleges.[9] During the year, Congress and the White House continued to battle over the amount and kind of support that the federal government would provide for higher education.

While federal funding had taken a downturn, it at first seemed as though private giving was on the increase. Reporting on private gifts to U.S. colleges and universities during 1968-69, the Council for Financial Aid to Education and the American Alumni Council noted that U.S. colleges and universities received a record $1.8 billion in private gifts during the year and that this represented the largest gain since 1964-65. Two years earlier, during 1966, there had been a decline of 1.2 percent in giving. However, 1968-69 seemed to indicate that increases were again to be expected. The 1968-69 increase was largely for capital purposes, and unrestricted gifts had

262

actually declined. Support from religious denominations also showed a sharp decline.[10] Then, the next report of the Council for Financial Aid to Education showed that for 1969-70 there was an actual dollar decrease in giving for the first time in more than a decade. Colleges and universities realized $20 million less in 1969-70 than 1968-69.[11]

Situation Worsens in 1970-71. At the beginning of the academic year 1970-71 the financial crisis appeared to be deepening. John A Crowl wrote, "The financial crisis that people in higher education have been talking about for years may finally have arrived."[12] He reported that several small colleges had closed their doors and that others were reporting severe problems. Among the larger institutions, Princeton University's deficit for the most recent fiscal year had reached $600,000, and the university was projecting a deficit of more than $2 million for the fiscal year then in progress. A small college in Missouri was offering to rename itself after anyone who would give it $5 million. Columbia University was predicting a $15 million deficit, and St. Louis University was closing its school of dentistry and phasing out its engineering program. The land-grant colleges were continuing to increase their charges. Crowl summarizes, "Put in its simplest terms, the problem facing most colleges today is this: At a time when the costs of operating a college are rising dramatically and rapidly, traditional sources of income, although increasing, are climbing rather slowly."[13] Inflation was one of the chief causes of the problem, but along with "normal" inflation there wre significant increases in building costs and prices for equipment and supplies. It was reported that 21 institutions had closed in the course of the year.

As the year wore on, M. M. Chambers reported that in spite of an increase of nearly $1 billion in funds to state institutions in 1970-71, it appeared that a growing number of public colleges and universities would be forced to curtail programs and services. Even though the gains in appropriations were impressive they were not able to keep up with increased demands, costs, and inflation. The National Association of State Universities and Land-Grant Colleges said that "austerity operations are becoming a fact of life for a growing number of institutions."[14]

The beginning of 1971 was greeted with more gloomy reports. At the meeting of the Association of American Colleges, a report of a study of 500 colleges and universities indicated that the average private institution went from a small operating surplus in 1967-68 to a small deficit in 1968-69, but that the deficit multiplied by a factor of five by 1969-70 and that it was expected to be even larger by 1970-71. The researcher, William W. Jellema, estimated that the total deficit experienced by the private higher educational institutions over the four-year period was nearly $370 million. Jellema reported that "most colleges in the red are staying in the red and many are getting redder, while colleges in the black are generally growing grayer."[15] About one-fourth of the 554 institutions surveyed indicated that they were spending unrestricted endowment principle. Other actions to meet the deficits included raising tuition, increasing fund-raising activities, deferring maintenance, retrenching expenditures, transferring funds from other reserves, reducing depreciation loans, and spending appreciation on endowment funds. One of the significant factors contributing to the poor financial condition of the private colleges was the increasing amount of money the institutions were spending on student aid. As tuition went up, more students needed more aid.

In response to the tightening financial situation, colleges began cutting budgets and effecting economies wherever possible. As the budget-making began for 1971-72, colleges were cutting expenditures in the current year and allowing smaller increases in spending for the coming year. John Crowl reported in the *Chronicle of Higher Education* in February 1971 that expenditures at some institutions would be smaller in 1971-72 than during the 1970-71 year, in spite of continuing inflation. He quoted the president of Bowdoin College, who contended that the financial situation was "growing worse rather than better" and that colleges were being forced "to reexamine their entire program."[16] New aid from federal and state governments, hoped for by many, was not forthcoming. The task became that of "trying to pare expenditures as much as possible without sacrificing academic quality or institutional morale."[17] Crowl noted that virtually all of the colleges had announced budget cuts. Princeton University, for example, was recommending expenditures of nearly $1 million less for 1971-72 than for 1970-71 and was also calling for a tuition increase. The University of Maryland announced that no faculty or staff vacancies would be filled for the remainder of the current year. Michigan State University had asked its administrative units to cut budgets 1.5 percent in the current year. Stanford University, which earlier had planned to cut $2.5 million over a four-year period had revised its goal to cut $6 million over a five-year period.

A week after the *Chronicle* summary appeared, at the meeting of the American Association of State Colleges and Universities, the president of the association suggested that concern with "fiscal bankruptcy" had replaced student unrest as the top worry of the state college presidents. He said that the group was predicting "a financial crisis that is rapidly worsening for public as well as private colleges and universities."[18]

The news continued to worsen, and in assessing the trends among the legislatures holding regular sessions in 1971, Crowl noted that legislators intended to keep a close watch on how money would be appropriated. In a survey of 33 state boards, all but 4 indicated that financing would be the most serious problem facing the legislatures that year.[19] Signs of the times included a bill introduced in the Illinois legislature to require public institutions to report to the state government all income other than state funds, consideration in the Iowa legislature of a measure that would forbid the Board of Regents to grant paid sabbatical leaves to faculty members, and the move in Indiana, one of the few states at that time without a state coordinating agency, to establish one. It was also reported that 11 states were considering some form of reorganization of the state system of public higher education. The chancellor of the community college system in California said that those institutions were facing their worst financial crisis since the Depression.

In the latter part of February 1971, in the annual report of the Carnegie Corporation, Alan Pifer said that the financial problems of private institutions could well be the first stage in a progressively worsening situation ending in their demise.[20]

As the year continued there were differences of opinion about the nature and extent of the financial crisis. In testifying before a Congressional committee, Alice M. Rivlin, a Senior Fellow at the Brookings Institution and former assistant secretary for planning and evaluation in the Department of Health, Education, and Welfare, argued that there was no *general* crisis of higher education finance. Rather, she said, there are "several sets of factors affecting various kinds of institutions in various ways at the same time, some permanent and some temporary."[21] At about the same time, the

Association of Governing Boards of Universities and Colleges was meeting in Cincinnati, Ohio. That group seemed to have no doubt but that there was a financial crisis, and speakers at the meeting called for sweeping academic reforms. It was even suggested by one speaker that the financial pressures might lead to reforms and efficiencies that would be to the ultimate good of education.[22]

By July 1971 the National Association of State Universities and Land-Grant Colleges reported from its March-April survey that 41 of 76 public institutions responding to the survey had failed to increase their budgets by 10 percent.[23] That same week the 39 new presidents participating in the Annual Presidents' Institute of the American Council on Education reported that they were more worried about money and less worried about student unrest than had been the case among previous participants in the annual conference.

The one bright spot for 1970-71 was not known until a year later, when the Council for Financial Aid to Education reported that in 1970-71 private gifts to U.S. colleges and universities, after experiencing the decline in the previous year, had again increased and had reached a record high. Major cause for the increase was the giving of alumni and "non-alumni individuals." Income from these groups compensated for the decrease that year in contributions by corporations, foundations, religious denominations, and miscellaneous donors.[24]

More Gloom in 1971-72. The academic year 1971-72 began with the cheerless news that more than 100 private colleges and universities were facing fiscal disaster. William J. Jellema, in a follow-up of his 1970 survey, found that for 1970-71, the average private college had underestimated its 1969 deficit by nearly 25 percent. Moreover, the average deficit for 1970-71 was nearly eight times larger than two years earlier. If such deficits were to continue, nearly half of the nation's private colleges and universities would be bankrupt within ten years.[25]Jellema had asked the colleges during the summer of 1971 to provide him with actual 1969-70 figures and to update the 1970-71 projections. He found that the average private institution, which at an earlier date had estimated that its 1969-70 deficit would be $104,000, actually incurred a $131,000 loss. And, whereas earlier the colleges had projected a deficit of $120,000 for 1970-71, they were now projecting an average deficit of $158,000.

Jellema estimated that 122 of the 507 colleges surveyed had exhausted their liquid assets and had no usable reserve funds to draw upon to cover future deficits.

As the year continued, there were reports that dismissals of tenured faculty members were becoming more common in budget-cutting. A report by the Association of American Colleges found 7 of 54 liberal arts colleges replying to a survey indicating that they had already been forced to terminate at least one tenured faculty member in an effort to save money. Several other institutions were anticipating similar action.[26] The Council for Financial Aid to Education, however, was able to look back on 1971-72 as another record year for giving. Whereas in the previous year it was the increase in alumni and other individual gifts that accounted for the growth in contributions, it was a major increase in contributions by foundations that made the difference in 1971-72. Also, there were significant increases from business corporations as well as continuing increases from alumni and other individuals.[27]

Possible Turnaround in 1972-73. As the 1972-73 academic year got underway, the annual survey of state spending on higher education reported by M. M. Chambers indicated that the *rate* in growth of state support had decreased with the appropriations for 1972-73. While appropriations overall increased, the rate of increase was considerably less than for a previous two-year span.[28]

By December 1972 one writer, however, was suggesting that the financial crisis was easing. Robert L. Jacobson reported that, "for the first time since higher education's financial problems reached the 'crisis' stage several years ago, a sizeable number of private colleges and universities have begun to report signs of recovery."[29] He wrote that in a number of cases operating deficits had declined or disappeared, that alumni contributions were up, and that the institutions, according to their own estimates, had become more skillful in managing their financial affairs. A number of those interviewed suggested that the main factor was that institutions were beginning to apply more effective management procedures. An example given was Syracuse University which had a deficit of over $500,000 the previous year and deficits of $1 million each year during two prior to that. The university imposed a moratorium on salary increases, froze budgets in some departments, and cut budgets in others. Now Syracuse reported that it expected to raise salaries by about 5 percent in January and to finish the academic year without a deficit. In addition to claiming better management, the college said that enrollments were up and that tuition had been increased. In the meantime, the National Commission on the Financing of Postsecondary Education, appointed in 1972, was underway.

In April 1973 Earl Cheit, who had coined the term "the new depresson in higher education," made a second report. This report was based on a detailed follow-up of the same 41 institutions on which he had reported in 1971. He found that by increasing their use of cost-control measures, the majority of the 41 had managed to escape or avoid serious financial trouble in the intervening period. As a matter of fact, 26 of the 41 institutions regarded the current financial situation to be the same or better than it was two years earlier. However, 18 of the 41 institutions expected the situation to deteriorate if the present trends continued over the next three years.[30]

Once again, private giving to the support of higher education increased. In reporting 1972-73, the Council for Financial Aid to Education found another record year. This time the major course of the increase was gifts by individuals and parents of students. The increase overall from the previous year, 1971-72, was 8.7 percent.[31]

Increasing Optimism in 1973-74. With the beginning of academic year 1973-74, optimism seemed to be increasing. Reporting in September 1973 Beverly T. Watkins found a "cautious optimism and cautious pessimism" characterizing "the financial mood of the nation's colleges and universities as academic year 1973-74 gets underway."[32] She found that many of the private colleges were showing signs of recovery, although some were hesitant in saying that the long-term picture was as bright. On the other hand, the number of public colleges confronting serious financial problems appeared to be on the rise. The American Association of State Colleges and Universities was reporting that the proportion of institutions in its membership experiencing critical and severe financial problems was on the rise.

By October 1973 Bloomfield College, a private college that sought to restore stability by cutting faculty and abolishing tenure, was in the midst of a battle which subsequently led to the closing of the institution and placing of it in a receivership for bankruptcy. Southern Illinois University gained natural attention when in January 1974 it terminated the employment of 104 faculty and staff members in order to reduce budgets. With the advent of the energy crisis, colleges and universities in the early months of 1974 were faced with sharp increases in heating costs. The financial crisis was far from over.

In February 1974 the American Council on Education was arguing that, in spite of serious and wide-spread financial difficulties among colleges and universities, the future was much more positive. The council analysis contended that tuition revenues would continue to grow, that state support was increasing, that corporate profits were up, that foundation support was beginning to increase again, and that federal support was increasing at a rate faster than any other time in the last five years.[33]

But earlier in the year, a study by the University of Michigan's Center for the Study of Higher Education suggested that inflation may have been obscuring the true condition of financially troubled colleges. The study was of 48 private colleges over a period between 1964 and 1973. It was found that the spending per student increased from $1,849 per student in 1964 to $3,282 in 1973, a rise of 77 percent in nine years. Applying a correction factor for inflation, however, it was found that the actual spending per student had increased only 10 percent over the nine-year period and that during the past two years it had actually declined slightly, from $2,075 to $2,036. The study suggested an even greater decline in spending in terms of uninflated dollars per student. On the other hand, the number of colleges operating at a deficit within the study had decreased between 1972 and 1973.[34]

In May 1974 the president of Georgetown University was cautioning that Phase II of the financial crunch for private higher education was just around the corner. He was convinced that in Phase II more private institutions would disappear. The problem, as he saw it, was that during the first phase of the financial crisis budgets had been reduced drastically and tuitions had gone up. In the next round, neither possibility may be open to private institutions.[35]

In June 1974 we began to read announcements about the way in which funds were again shrinking. A report from the National

Center for Educational Statistics suggested that endowment funds of the nation's colleges and universities had shrunk by 1.1 percent during fiscal year 1973.[36] And gifts from private sources were apparently leveling off. The annual report of the Council for Financial Aid to Education revealed that the total income for 1973-74 was the same as for 1972-73, some $2.24 billion. Taking into account inflation, the 1973-74 funds represented a decrease. Gifts from individuals had dropped sharply, but support from corporations, foundations, and religious denominations increased sufficiently to balance off the losses from that source. Gifts from alumni were down by 5 percent and from nonalumni by 7.3 percent. Gifts from religious denominations were up by 17.7 percent. Overall, however, the largest single source of income was still the alumni; they provided 22.7 percent of the $2.24 billion in gifts for 1973-74.[37]

Crisis Continues in 1974-75. As we entered academic year 1974-75, we were presented with a very mixed picture, and some of the optimism generated in the previous year began to dissipate. For some private colleges, a combination of increased tuition and wide-ranging economies seemed to have restored a measure of fiscal stability to the enterprise. Others were still accumulating debts at a frightening rate, and the sound of closing doors continued. Some observers were convinced that the combination of increased tuition and cost-cutting budgeting had reached something of a logical limit; there were few places left to cut without impairing quality, and tuitions may have reached the upper limits. Others were convinced that neither was the case, and that there were still untapped sources of income.

Among tax-supported institutions the picture was also mixed. In some, enrollment pressures continued, and appropriations, according to the institutions, did not keep up with the costs. Heavily dependent upon the appropriations, these institutions found that for every student not covered with increased funds to meet the increased cost of education, other cutbacks were required. Other institutions experienced drastic declines in enrollment. Four-year public colleges were the hardest hit by the recent shift in enrollment patterns and many of these colleges were being forced to reduce staffs and services.

In November 1974 Sidney P. Marland, now president of the College Entrance Examination Board, predicted that student financial funds for higher education from federal, state, and private resources would probably be $2 billion less than those needed for the 1975-76 academic year.[38] During the fall of 1974 foundations were reporting cutbacks in their funding, and it was noted that more and more U.S. universities were making contacts overseas in their search for funds.[39] In the meantime, states were reported raising their contributions to higher education. Karen Winkler in November 1974 reported an increase in state student aid of 25 percent, the largest increase in history. It was noted that a decade ago only 12 states provided student assistance programs but that now 22 have such programs underway.[40] But, according to Marland, even these increases would not meet the vastly increased needs.

Signs of the times in early 1975 included the announcement by Duke University that the School of Forestry and the primate research center would be phased out because of financial problems. A student protest may have delayed the decision on the School of Forestry, at least temporarily.[41] In Florida the community college system threatened to cut back enrollments to meet budget reductions of 3.3 percent when, contended the colleges, they were already unable to meet commitments.[42] And the National Center for Educational Statistics revealed that for the previous year, 1973-74, expenditures in colleges and universities grew much less than the consumer price index. The 1973-74 expenditures were up 6.8 percent over the previous year, but the consumer price index had increased by 11 percent in the same period. The colleges were not even keeping even with inflation.[43] In April the Ford Foundation announced it would reduce staff and expenditures by one-half in four years. In 1973-74 the foundation spent $220 million, and it planned to cut back to $100 million per year.[44]

Confidence in the recovery of higher education was hardly assisted by the report in the *Chronicle of Higher Education* in late April that the University of Wisconsin system had developed a handbook, produced by a System Advisory Planning Task Force and requested by the governor of the state, on how to close down parts of the university.[45] The handbook detailed the criteria for deciding which universities should be shut and which programs should be eliminated. Estimates were made of the savings, and the costs, of closing various elements of the system. A companion article in the *Chronicle* noted that in budget-making in the spring of 1975 the Wisconsin system was to reduce the present budget by $10.5

271

million, that inflation had already effectively removed $23.1 million, and that denial of state support for 6,000 additional students enrolled was tantamount to another $9.6 million reduction.[46] By September 1975 the state legislature rejected the governor's proposals for phasing out portions of the university, and the phase-down plan itself was phased out.[47]

The Common Fund for Short-Term Investments, an agency created to help colleges improve earnings on funds available only for brief periods of time, reported in the spring of 1975 that its investment earnings had fallen below the guaranteed minimum return and it had to dip into its own reserves.[48] And the academic year ended with reports that because of inflation the real spending on basic scientific research in 1975 was expected to decline by 8 percent from the 1974 level, with far-reaching impact on the nation's colleges and universities where 61 percent of the basic scientific work was being performed.[49] A state college president, resisting requests of the State Department of Education in Pennsylvania for a list of employees to be laid off, was told to conform or be fired himself. He furnished the list. The Pennsylvania state colleges were faced with the possibility of cutting more than 1,300 employees from the payroll.[50]

No Relief in Sight in 1975-76. After almost a decade of battling the threat of fiscal disaster, American colleges and universities found little genuine reason to relax as they moved into the second half of the 1970s. In August the presidents of the city colleges of New York proposed that the City University be shut down temporarily. Faced with the possibility of a third wave of major budget cuts, they contended that under such conditions they could not maintain standards or general academic quality.[51] A month later New York's state commissioner of education asked the City University of New York to institute tuition charges of $600 to $800 per year, a proposal often rejected in the past by the commission.[52] And in October Chancellor Robert Kibbee proposed that the university reduce enrollment by 20 percent over the next three years by setting numerical limits on freshman admissions; the open-admissions policy would apply only to new high school graduates. Kibbee contended that reductions in enrollment could result in faculty and staff cutbacks of as much as 20 percent.[53] It was clear that the problems of CUNY were far from solved.

President Gerald Ford vetoed the $7.9 billion appropriations bill for the fiscal year that began July 1, 1975. The bill contained $2.4 billion for higher education, from which Ford had requested legislators to cut $434 million. Early in September both houses of Congress voted by quite comfortable margins to override the veto. In the meantime, educational agencies had been operating by legislative resolution at the 1975 funding level. The appropriations bill provided a 4 percent increase over the previous year's level, wholly insufficient to keep up with inflation.[54] The victory for education, such as it was, has to be considered against some efforts in Congress at tax-law changes that could alter incentives for making contributions to educational and charitable institutions.[55]

Enrollments were up in the fall of 1975, but the financial problems were greater too. Legislatures of Florida, Georgia, and Rhode Island imposed salary freezes on employees of public colleges.[56] Statewide governing and coordinating boards were entering more directly into the determination of courses and curricula. Robert Berdahl found that nearly half of the state boards were undertaking reviews that could lead to elimination or consolidation of courses or programs.[57] Notices went out to 188 employees of the Pennsylvania state colleges system that their jobs will be eliminated at the end of the academic year.[58] Western Michigan University announced that between 150 and 175 faculty members would be released, effective April 30, 1976, because of financial exigencies.[59] And the Danforth Foundation announced it would no longer solicit new grant proposals in the field of higher education.[60] There was even a proposal that a national commission whose membership would include no educators should be appointed by the President of the United States to determine how and where American higher education should retrench in the face of the economic crisis.[61]

In 1975-76 words such as cutback, layoff, retrenchment, and budget-cutting had become commonplace. It was perhaps becoming evident to some observers that the optimism of 1973-74 was premature. In the ensuing two years, it was clear that American higher educational institutions would be living with the financial crisis through most of the 1970s and perhaps beyond. But when a "crisis" becomes part of the day-to-day existence, is it any longer a "crisis"? Higher education had moved well into a different mode of existence, and the institutions that would cope successfully would learn to live with new patterns of funding and with much more

273

planning and public pressure than ever before. Dean Neumann is not likely to arrive at some lasting solution in his meeting with Professor Ernst and the budget committee. Rather, he must be prepared for long-term planning that will take into account the shifting pressures and demands of year to year developments. The overview of the developments from 1967-68 should provide Dean Neumann and others with a perspective that will better prepare them for the pressures ahead. Anyone expecting a simple and all-embracing solution, however, is doomed to disappointment.

In the pages that follow are reports of what some writers and some institutions have discovered about the situation and how they are dealing with it. First is a review of sources of income, considering whether there is any way of increasing these sources; then a discussion of categories of expenditures and what institutions have attempted to do in becoming more "efficient" through instituting economies; and finally we turn to general issues of policy as these relate to both income and expenditures, noting what several national commissions have suggested as possible approaches to dealing with the situation.

Patterns of Income

The broad categories for displaying sources of income are fairly well accepted—tuition and fees, support by state and local government, income from the federal government, gifts from private philanthropy, and endowment earnings. These constitute the basic categories of Educational and General income. Refinements of the categories are possible and are used by institutions in reporting income for various purposes.

To the Educational and General income are generally added income from Auxiliary Enterprises and Student Aid. This use of categories is fairly well established and accepted. What is difficult to secure are comparable figures from one report or study to another. The annual reports—always issued two to four years after the actual year of experience—of the Department of Health, Education, and Welfare are not always comparable from year to year. For example, in 1968-69, these reports inserted a new category, Other Current, which included major public-service programs previously reported under government research, related activities, and in other portions

274

of the Educational and General revenue. Yet, the data collected by HEW remains the most comprehensive available to reviewers. In the summaries that follow the basic source will be the data of HEW, but we shall also be drawing heavily from the report of the National Commission on the Financing of Postsecondary Education[62] and several of the publications of the Carnegie Commission on Higher Education, particularly the report by June A. O'Neill.[63]

Overall Distribution of Income

Total income for current operations for institutions of higher education in 1971-72, the most recent year for which fairly complete data are available, could be $26.4 billion, $29.5 billion, or $30 billion, depending upon the source of information used. All of the figures are ultimately derived from data provided by the Department of Health, Education, and Welfare through the National Center for Educational Statistics. The first figure is that reported in June 1974 and derived from data made available by the National Center for Educational Statistics.[64] This was the same figure, or one very close to it, that was used in a January 1972 report of *College Management* in which the estimated income for 1971-72 was $26.5 billion.[65] The second figure is taken from the report of the Commission on the Financing of Postsecondary Education and refers to total support provided American colleges and universities in 1971-72.[66] The last figure is one used by the Committee for Economic Development in a report on financing of higher education issued in October 1973.[67]

Some of the differences in the above figures are due to rounding, and others are due to different ways of calculating what constitutes actual income. For example, in many of its calculations, the Carnegie Commission suggests that leaving student-aid income in the educational income account is probably to double count it as institutional income, and the commission subtracts this amount in many of its calculations.[68] But whatever source one uses, the increase over the past few decades is impressive. Using figures directly from HEW publications, we find that total income for 1939-40 was in the vicinity of $720 million. By 1949-50 it had climbed to $2.4 billion, in 1959-60 it was $5.8 billion, and in 1969-70 it was $21.6 billion—and in 1971-72 it totaled $26.4 billion.

275

For the analyses that follow we are more concerned about the way in which the income is distributed according to source than with the gross dollars involved. The Commission on the Financing of Postsecondary Education observes that one must have a frame of reference with which to assess data for planning. One way of establishing this frame of reference is to identify level of financing by source and recipients. Using the data for 1971-72, the last year for which "reasonably complete" data are available, and following the calculations of the commission, we find that tuition and fees constituted over a third (34.9 percent) of the total income for current operating purposes. However, as the commission observes, of the estimated $10.3 billion in tuition and fees, only $5.9 billion can be said to come directly from students and their parents. The commission attributes most of the remaining $4.4 billion to federal grants and to a limited degree to state and local government and private philanthropy. On this basis, tuition and fees are seen to constitute 20 percent of the total current operating expenditures. The distribution, according to the Commission on Financing Postsecondary Education, is shown in table 4. State and local government provide the next largest portion of the income, just over 30 percent. However, when one allocates a portion of the student-fee income to the state and local government, the proportion becomes 31.6 percent.

On the face of it, the federal government contributes only 14.2 percent to the total current operating expenses (4.2 $\div$ 29.5). When, however, that portion of the student fee derived from federal support is included, the federal government provides 27.4 percent of the current operating expenses.

Private philanthropy and endowment provide approximately 8.5 percent of the total income (2.5 $\div$ 29.5). Again, if we assume that a part of the student payment for tuition and fees is provided by private philanthropy, this proportion of the income increases to 9.1 percent.

Auxiliary enterprises and other activities provide 11.9 percent of current operating revenue.

The changing composition of American higher education is reflected in the changes in the proportion that gross tuition and fees has constituted in current operating income. O'Neill begins her

Table 4
Major Sources of Income for Postsecondary Education, 1971-72 (in billions)

Source of Income	Institutional Support	Aid to Students	Total Support	Percentage of Total
Student payments for tuition and other fees	$5.9*	—	$5.9	20.0%
State and local government	9.0	0.3	9.3	31.6
Federal government	4.2	3.9	8.1	27.4
Private philanthropy and endowment income	2.5	0.2	2.7	9.1
Auxiliary enterprises and other activities	3.5	—	3.5	11.9
Total	$25.1	$4.4	$29.5	100.0%

*Net of aid received by students from public and private sources and paid to institutions for tuition and fees.
Source: National Commission on the Financing of Postsecondary Education, *Financing Postsecondary Education in the United States* (Washington, D.C.: U.S. Government Printing Office, 1973), p. 69.

analysis of sources of income with the year 1939-40. At that time private higher educational institutions claimed the larger portion of student enrollments, and when the income for all institutions was lumped together, tuition income provided, according to O'Neill, 38.1 percent of Educational and General income. As enrollments in public institutions surpassed those in private institutions, any ratios of tuition to income (Educational and General or total) showed tuition as a steadily declining portion until the late 1960s, when tuition again began to provide an increasing portion of current income. The Commission on Postsecondary Education found that gross tuition constituted 17.2 percent of total (Educational and General plus Auxiliary and Student Aid income) current income in 1961-62 and by 1971-72 had reached 21.9 percent.[69] (The difference between the 20 percent used by the commission in the earlier reference above and the 21.9 percent used in this context is due to the employment of different base figures.) Table 5 is based on data provided in annual and periodic reports of the U.S. Office of Education. The percentages will differ slightly from those reported by O'Neill and the Commission on Financing Postsecondary Education, because I have not attempted to make some of the adjustments applied by O'Neill and the commission; the general trends apparent in the table are, however, the same that are found in the two other reports.

Table 5
Tuition and Fees as a Percentage of Educational and General Income

Year	Percentage	Year	Percentage
1909–10	26.5	1949–50	21.4
1919–20	24.3	1959–60	24.6
1929–30	30.0	1967–68	24.3
1939–40	35.0	1969–70	26.8

Source: Based on data reported in annual issues of *Financing Statistics of Institutions of Higher Education: Current Fund Revenues and Expenditures,* issued by the Department of Health, Education, and Welfare, and *Higher Education Finances: Selected Trend and Summary Data,* periodically issued by the same agency.

The overall generalization is that apart from the upswing in the 1930s and, with the spectacular increase in public higher education, the downswing in the 1940s, tuition and fees have constituted a remarkably stable 25 percent of Educational and General income.

The Commission on Postsecondary Education does not attempt to provide an overview of the long-range trends in state and local or federal financing, but it analyzes in considerable detail recent developments in these areas. O'Neill shows a fairly stable proportion of income from state and local governments from 1939-40 to 1967-68, and notes the significant increase in federal funding in the late 1940s. Using gross figures from reports from the U.S. Office of Education, table 6 shows the proportion that federal and state and local governments have contributed to Educational and General income. Even these approximations must be interpreted

Table 6

Government Funds as a Percentage of Educational and General Income

Year	Federal Percentage	State and Local Percentage
1909-10	6.6	29.0
1919-20	7.3	35.6
1929-30	4.2	31.5
1939-40	6.8	30.8
1949-50	28.5	30.0
1959-60	22.1	32.5
1963-64	27.6	30.4
1967-68	24.3	34.0
1969-70	16.3	39.8

Source: Based on data reported in annual issues of *Financing Statistics of Institutions of Higher Education: Current Fund Revenues and Expenditures,* issued by the Department of Health, Education, and Welfare, and *Higher Education Finances: Selected Trend and Summary Data,* periodically issued by the same agency.

with caution, because the proportions are probably, particularly in recent years, underestimates. As the Commission on the Financing of Postsecondary Education has pointed out, substantial income from federal sources is hidden in the gross tuition payments.

Nevertheless, one can see the significant increase in federal funding that began in the 1940s.

The sharp decrease in federal funding for 1969-70 may be somewhat distorted, since it was that year that the Office of Education separated income for research and development centers and hospitals and placed it under a new category. If one takes a portion of that income and places it back into Educational and General and considers it as federal support, the percentage goes up somewhat. A fair estimate would be somewhere between 22 and 23 percent. Yet, the policy of the federal government to cut back support for research and certain other programs beginning in 1967-68 is still fairly clearly indicated.

The pattern for private gifts and grants shown by O'Neill indicates an increased proportion between 1939-40 and 1959-60 and a decrease in 1967-68.[70] Based on the data provided by the U.S. Office of Education, table 7 shows that private gifts and grants constituted

Table 7

Private Gifts and Grants as a Percentage of Educational and General Income

Year	Percentage	Year	Percentage
1909–10	4.85	1959–60	8.05
1919–20	4.35	1963–64	7.05
1929–30	5.35	1967–68	6.15
1939–40	7.05	1969–70	6.07
1949–50	6.40		

Source: Based on data reported in annual issues of *Financial Statistics of Institutions of Higher Education: Current Fund Revenues and Expenditures,* issued by the Department of Health, Education, and Welfare, and *Higher Education Finances: Selected Trend and Summary Data,* periodically issued by the same agency.

just under 5 percent of Educational and General income in 1909-10, that this source provided 8.05 percent in 1959-60, and then began to decline to 6.07 percent in 1969-70. O'Neill does not show as sharp a decline in the period for which she provides data, but the same general trend seems apparent.

Endowment earnings have become less and less a source of income. As O'Neill shows, in 1939-40 endowment earnings produced 13.5 percent of Educational and General income, while in 1967-68 this source provided only 2.8 percent of current income. A similar pattern is revealed over a longer period of time in table 8. In 1909-10, endowment income provided 17.4 percent of the Educational and General income, declining slowly until the 1940s, when increased federal income changed the pattern of financing significantly. From the 1940s to the present date, endowment income has constituted a small proportion of Educational and General income.

Table 8

Endowment Income as a Percentage of Educational and General Income

Year	Percentage	Year	Percentage
1909-10	17.4	1959-60	4.4
1919-20	15.2	1963-64	3.4
1929-30	14.05	1967-68	2.6
1939-40	12.4	1969-70	2.7
1949-50	5.2		

Source: Based on data reported in annual issues of *Financial Statistics of Institutions of Higher Education: Current Fund Revenues and Expenditures,* issued by the Department of Health, Education, and Welfare, and *Higher Education Finances: Selected Trend and Summary Data,* periodically issued by the same agency.

The preceding description has made no distinction between public and private institutions, nor has it made distinctions between types of institutions within the categories of public or private. The Commission on Postsecondary Education shows that in 1971-72 tuition provided somewhat over one-third of *total income* for private institutions, while it constituted only approximately 15 percent of the income for public institutions.[71] Using Educational and General income as the base, O'Neill shows that in 1967-68 tuition and fees constituted 43.8 percent of the income for private institutions and only 14.7 percent of the income for public institutions. But even this does not provide the full story, since by the late 1960s some private institutions were deriving 75 to 80 percent of Educational and General income from tuition. Indeed, some were approaching 90 percent dependence on tuition and fees.

Income from state governments, exclusive of that channeled through tuition, constituted less than 2 percent of the income for private institutions and over 56 percent of the income for public institutions. Federal income provided over 30 percent of the income for private institutions in 1967-68 and just over 22 percent of the income for public institutions in that year.[72]

Philanthropy provided comparatively more income for private than for public higher educational institutions. O'Neill shows 12.7 percent of the income for 1967-68 in private institutions being derived from private gifts and grants, as compared to only 2.6 percent in public institutions. My own calculations show that in 1969-70 approximately 13.3 percent of the Educational and General income of private institutions was derived from private gifts and grants. Both my figures and those of O'Neill show considerable fluctuation between 1939-40 and 1967-68.

Likewise, private colleges receive comparatively more from endowment than do public institutions. According to O'Neill's figures, in 1967-68 endowment earnings constituted 6.6 percent of Educational and General income for private institutions and only 0.4 percent for public institutions.

As was suggested at the beginning of this summary, while individual institutions will and do vary from any average distributions, we need some frame of reference from which to assess data. These distributions, historical and contemporary, provide such a frame of reference. We now turn to a consideration of some of the issues relating to each of the sources of income.

Tuition and Fees as a Source of Income

Few matters were being as roundly debated in the literature in the mid-1970s as those relating to tuition charges. It is not difficult to understand why this is the case, because one's position with regard to tuition can reflect many basic attitudes toward higher education. While the immediate reaction to proposals either to increase or to decrease tuition may be based on costs and the need for more or less revenue, the question of whether tuition should constitute a larger or smaller proportion of costs is essentially, to use the title of the Carnegie report, the question of *Higher Education: Who Pays? Who Benefits? Who Should Pay?*[73] In an earlier treatment of the same theme, M. M. Chambers asked the question *Higher Education: Who Pays? Who Gains?*[74] As a nation, the people of the United States have accepted the principle that common schooling should extend through the secondary level. While attending such schools is not totally without cost, by public policy we are committed to providing an essentially free and tax-supported system of schools through the elementary and secondary levels. Such is not the case in higher education. Or, at least, there is no uniformity of opinion regarding the extent to which higher education should reflect the same principle as that found in secondary education.

The issue becomes one of assigning benefits. We seem generally to be convinced that free schooling through the secondary level is important because society as a whole benefits from having an educated citizenry. However, in its report of June 1973 the Carnegie Commission suggested that at the postsecondary level it may be the individual who primarily benefits. Observing that there is presently no wholly satisfactory way of assessing individual as against societal benefits, the commission concluded that that proportion then borne privately (about two-thirds) in relation to the proportion of cost borne publicly (about one-third) is "generally reasonable":

> We note that for one item—additional earned income by college graduates—about two-thirds is kept privately and about one-third is taken publicly in the form of taxes. We also note that this two-thirds to one-third distribution of total economic costs has been a relatively stable relationship for a substantial period of time.[75]

In basic disagreement with such a position, M. M. Chambers has earlier stated, in keeping with a long-held conviction, that

283

higher education "benefits" every citizen, of whatever age, sex, or educational status; hence its cost should be equitably apportioned to all by means of a tax system adjusted to economic conditions. In short, "higher education is essentially a public function and a public obligation—not a private privilege or a private caprice."[76] Chambers refers with approval to a statement made by the Iowa State Board of Regents adopted in 1967 that the state university is an instrument of the open democratic society with the basic function of opening opportunity to young men and women of all classes and thus providing educated people to serve the economy and society. He continues:

> One of the most significant American innovations and one of the most cherished American institutions has been free public education. The idea is well established that education at the elementary and secondary levels should be free to all regardless of socio-economic class. Since the founding of our public universities and especially since the land-grant movement starting in 1862, under Abraham Lincoln, it has been equally accepted that public higher education should be open to all at low cost.[77]

Or, to put the matter in other terms, education may be viewed either as investment or consumption. As John Vaizey observes:

> Goods and services can broadly be divided into two classes: those from which consumers derive immediate benefit, which are called consumption, and those which are used in production to produce over a long-term, called investment. Education must be one or the other, or both.[78]

He goes on to say that education is a consumer good in that people value it for itself, and spend their money for it; they decide to spend money for education instead of for other things. It is also an investment in that it produces long-term results, not only for the people who themselves are educated but for the larger society. The issue becomes then, at the risk of oversimplification, that there are some who emphasize education as consumption, for the immediate benefit accruing to those who participate in it, while others view it as investment, with the benefits accruing to a larger portion of society and over a longer period of time.

The differing points of view regarding higher education are not new ones. The positions are expressed more sharply, however, in times of social stress and of financial pressure. Such was the situation in late 1973 when two reports, both appearing to lean toward the concept of education as private consumption, proposed increasing tuition charges within the public sector. Reaction was fast in coming. The Carnegie Commission, the issuer of one of the reports, subsequently issued a supplemental statement to explain and defend its position.[79]

The basic report of the Carnegie Commission appeared in June 1973 and observed, as already noted, that about two-thirds of the cost of higher education was being borne in various ways privately; it argued that this proportion was probably correct. While the original Carnegie report contained a number of recommendations regarding funding patterns—a temporary increase in public funding, a redistribution of governmental costs from the states to the federal government, a redistribution of student subsidies in favor of those from low income families, an increase in subsidies to institutions in the private sector—the recommendation most vigorously attacked had to do with increasing tuition in public colleges and universities until it reached a level of about one-third of the educational costs of those institutions. This was to be compared with what then seemed to be the current level, at which in public institutions tuitions covered one-sixth of such costs. The report was not advocating full public costing, but it suggested that students could directly bear one-third of the cost.[80] The report freely acknowledged that such an increase on the part of public institutions would have a favorable effect upon private institutions.

The report of the Committee for Economic Development appeared in October 1973.[81] This report indicated that the two major financial issues which had emerged were that many private institutions were unable to raise tuition levels high enough to cover the cost because of competition from public institutions and that public institutions, on the other hand, were finding it difficult to secure expanded or even constant-level appropriations from the state legislatures. Both public and private institutions faced difficulties, and the proposal of the committee, in addition to urging institutions to be more effective managers of resources, was that there be increased grants and loans made to students through the federal government and that tuition and fees be increased until they "approximate 50 percent of instructional costs (defined to include a reasonable allowance for replacement of facilities) within the next five years."[82]

285

Even before the official release of the CED report, the American Association of State Colleges and Universities on September 25, 1973, contended that the report leaned too heavily toward the private universities and middle and upper-middle income groups. The executive director of the association argued that the proposal was a direct attack on middle and lower income American families. Very early in the debate Representative James G. O'Hara, chairman of the House subcommittee responsible for writing education legislation, stated that as long as he was chairman of the House subcommittee he would be very "inhospitable to proposals that the state universities and community colleges raise their tuition—or that federal funds be made any harder for the real middle-income student to get."[83] And he went on to say that in his opinion there should be a return "to the policy on which our land-grant and community colleges were founded—free higher education for all who can profit from it, without any financial barriers at all."[84]

Subsequently, O'Hara wrote an extended article for *Change* in which he said, "I am becoming more and more concerned that a concerted effort to raise tuitions at public institutions—to make private institutions more attractive to prospective customers by making public ones less attractive—is underway. I think it is a very wrong-headed effort."[85] He argued with the basic assumption that education benefits only the student. While recognizing that a college education substantially increases a student's likely income, he contended that the concept of education as investment rather than expenditure "is an old as this nation—older, in point of outright statutory recognition, than the Constitution itself,"[86] and he referred to the Northwest Ordinance of 1787 as a case in point. He stated:

> I think we must try to create the opportunity for every American—whatever his background, his economic class, his age, or the point he has reached in his career—to have access to a full range of postsecondary education opportunities to the full extent he can benefit from them. The student just coming out of high school; the mature person who wants to change a career or who finds that his career is threatened by technology; the person approaching retirement who wants to live a richer life—to each of these the doors of postsecondary education must be open, and kept open.[87]

In November 1973 at a meeting of the American Association of State Colleges and Universities, and subsequently at a meeting of the National Association of State Universities and Land-Grant Colleges, similar statements were adopted referring to the need to maintain the century-long concept of no or low tuition in public higher education and of providing maximum educational opportunity through the maintenance of the low-tuition principle.[88] The two groups endorsed a position paper issued jointly urging the continuation of no or low tuition. Arguing against student-aid programs, they contended that such programs are "subject to the annually shifting political and economic priorities of governments and private lenders and are undependable means to aid low- and middle-income students."[89]

In February 1974 the American Council on Education issued a statement on tuition policy. Beginning with the proposition that all of those seeking postsecondary education should have access to a broad range of opportunities and that high quality postsecondary education be maintained "through the healthy coexistence of public and private institutions," the council disagreed with the proposal for accelerating the rate of increase in tuition among public institutions. Asking for strong support of private institutions, the council suggested that "a judicious mixture of student loans, scholarships and fellowships, and cost-of-instruction grants—the cost shared by our state and the national government—can assist our private institutions without increasing the cost to students in the nation's public colleges and universities."[90]

Later in the year, in September 1974, a group charged with developing papers on key isues for the Democratic National Committee appeared to be coming out strongly against tuition increases. Joseph D. Duffey, general secretary of the American Association of University Professors, in a paper prepared for and delivered to the group, argued that advocating increased tuition in public institutions "leans heavily upon the argument that the main benefits of higher education accrue to the individual rather than to the society itself, and therefore the individual should pay the major costs of such education." Differing with this position, Duffey proposed that the basic federal thrust should be toward student support, that a minimum of two years of post–high school education should be considered due to every American, that federal funding policy should encourage an access to education for all ages, and that, "as a first step," federal support for postsecondary education should increase from approximately $1.5 billion to $2.5 billion.[91]

In the meantime, tuition and fees continued to increase for both public and private institutions. Overall costs for attending college had risen 40 percent in four years, according to a report by the College Scholarship Service of the College Entrance Examination Board. Reporting on comparison of costs between 1970-71 and 1974-75, the College Scholarship Service indicated that the average yearly cost for commuting students at public four-year colleges had increased over this period of time by 17.5 percent, to a total of $2,085 per year. For private four-year institutions, the increase had been on the order of 16.5 percent, to a total of $3,683. For residential students, the increases over the same period of time had been 7 percent for public four-year institutions, to a total of $2,400, and 9.4 percent for private four-year institutions, to a total of $4,039. These costs included tuition and fees, room and board, and expenses for travel and personal needs.[92]

Among public institutions tuition and fees alone had increased over this period of time from $395 to an average of $541 in 1974-75. In private four-year institutions the increases in tuition and fees were from $1,517 to $2,080 in 1974-75. Perhaps the sign of the times is a note in the December 16, 1974, *Chronicle of Higher Education* to the effect that Stanford was proposing the largest tuition increase in its history, an increase of 12.9 percent—from $3,375 to $3,810, effective in the fall of 1975.[93]

On the other hand, at least one state university system has taken an opposite approach. In the fall of 1973 the University of Wisconsin Center at Fond du Lac slashed its two-semester tuition charge from $476 to $150. Subsequently, the center reported an enrollment increase of 47 percent for the year. The director of special projects for the University of Wisconsin system was of the opinion that the enrollment increase was largely a response to the tuition cut. A second center, one at Rice Lake reported a 23 percent increased enrollment following a reduction in its two-semester tuition of $515 to $180. For the other university centers, the average enrollment increase was on the order of 7 percent.[94]

These developments prompted the president of the University of Wisconsin system to propose cutting tuition in half for undergraduate students who were residents of the state.[95] (The tuition during 1974-75 for the system ranged from $500 to $628 for resident students.) The proposal went to the university's regents, who subsequently approved it, but it immediately met opposition in the statehouse. The move on the part of the regents was to stem what seemed to be a general enrollment drop among many of the institutions in the system. For those expressing concerns that the decrease in tuition for the public institutions would have a detrimental effect upon private institutions, one official suggested that the plan would be accompanied by increases in current state tuition grants for private colleges.[96]

The Community College of Vermont has approached the matter in a wholly open-ended way. The Board of the Vermont State Colleges decided in 1973 that the Community College of Vermont would start charging tuition—in a fashion. At registration time the students were told that to meet the needs of the college $30 per course would be required, but that it was up to the individual to decide how much might be paid. The board approved a one-year trial of the approach and will make some assessment at the end of the year.[97] The situation of the Community College of Vermont is, it should be noted, atypical. It has no campus, no buildings, no permanent faculty, and 1,500 students scattered throughout the state. Two-year degrees are awarded on the basis of individually contracted learning programs and demonstrated competence.

For private institutions, increasing tuition without providing for additional student-aid funds is likely to restrict an already tightening "market." One of the first reports of the Carnegie Commission demonstrated quite clearly that the net return from tuition increases is likely to be less than anticipated. William G. Bowen's study of the income-expenditure patterns in major private universities was issued in 1968. In that study Bowen singled out for special analysis three institutions, Chicago, Princeton, and Vanderbilt. He noted that between 1958 and 1966 the tuition at these institutions had increased at an average rate of slightly over 8 percent per year. He then deducted expenditures on student aid from the gross fee and calculated an index of the net fee income per student which could be compared with the index of gross fee income per student. During the period of time under study he found a widening gap between the gross fee income per student and net fee income per student. Indeed, when he compared changes over a shorter period of time, between 1962 and 1966, he found that while the gross fee income per student had increased more than $400, the net fee income per student had increased less than $90.[98] Simply increasing tuition does not necessarily lead to significant increases in usable income for the institution!

Considerable attention has been given to the "tuition gap" between public and private institutions, the difference between tuition charged by private colleges and universities and that charged by public institutions. The Commission on the Financing of Postsecondary Education has provided an analysis of the differential and contends that, while such a gap is real, its significance is probably greatest for the upper-middle-class students, those who, because of family income, are not eligible for grants or scholarships. The commission suggests that the tuition gap does not actually exist for students in the lowest income group, because this group receives a large share of the grants and other aid for tuition cost. The problem is, however, that in providing assistance for lower income students many private institutions may be offering larger aid packages than they can actually continue to afford. Table 9, based on data reported by the commission, shows that the greatest tuition gap is among research universities, where in 1971-72 private institutions were charging, on an average, tuition 4.8 times greater than that of public institutions. When, however, tuition assistance is taken into account, and net tuition costs are considered, the ratio goes down to approximately 3.9.[99] While the ratio declines somewhat when net tuition is considered, the difference is still, it seems, significant.

As a further piece of information, the commission points out that in 1972 private institutions were reporting student grants 41 percent in excess of funds provided for or designated as income for student aid. As long as enrollments were going up, the colleges could avoid the consequences of student-aid deficits and price discounts. Next year's enrollments would cover the losses. Besides, the price discounts could be used to attract a student body with a desired social, economic, and cultural mix. With stable or decreasing enrollments, however, institutions can no longer be sure of attracting enough students to cover the cost-price gap.

Given the present competition among collegiate institutions for students, institutions may continue to use student aid funds and

290

other unrestricted funds to discount the advertised tuition (price) in order to attract students to their institutions. This discounting continues to be a potential cause of financial distress. To the extent that institutions attempt to cover the cost of this discounting by increasing the advertised tuition to all students, the tuition charges for students who are not grant recipients will become inflated.[100]

Table 9

Average Ratio of Private to Public Tuition According to Reported Tuition Charges, by Selected Carnegie Classifications in 1969-72

Institutional Type	1969-70	1970-71	1971-72
Large Research Universities	4.2*	4.4	4.6
Other Research Universities	4.9	4.8	4.8
Large Ph.D. Granting Institutions	3.1	3.5	3.4
Small Ph.D. Granting Institutions	5.0	4.4	4.2
Comprehensive Colleges	4.8	3.4	3.3
Comprehensive Colleges, limited	4.5	3.6	3.2
Selective Liberal Arts Colleges	4.4	3.4	3.2
Other Liberal Arts Colleges	4.7	3.4	3.1
Two-year Colleges	1.6	3.0	3.5

Source: National Commission on the Financing of Postsecondary Education in the United States, *Financing Postsecondary Education in the United States* (Washington, D.C.: U.S. Government Printing Office, 1973), p. 203.

*The figures in each column have been determined by dividing the average tuition for private institutions of each type by the average tuition for public institutions of that type. Thus, in 1971-72, tuition in private research universities was 4.6 times that in public research universities.

The problem becomes even more sharply defined as we note the manner in which the College Scholarship Service has revised its estimates of how much money parents should be expected to contribute to the cost of their children's education. The new schedule, going into effect for 1975-76, shows a sharply reduced figure in all of the categories. The reduction was made in September 1974 because of a projected 18 percent increase in the Consumer Price Index between February 1973 and December 1974. The scholarship service, in calculating parental contributions, deducts items such as taxes, medical expenses, retirement allowances, and other special costs from a family's total income to calculate an "adjusted income." It is on the basis of the adjusted income that the service indicates expected contributions. For example, a family with an adjusted income of $8,000 was expected to contribute $900 for one child in college in 1974-75. This is reduced to $290 in 1975-76. At the upper levels of income, a family with an adjusted income of $20,000 was expected to contribute $6,270 to the support of one child in college in 1974-75; in 1975-76 this is reduced to $4,910. These adjustments have the effect of having students eligible for more financial aid from outside sources. The only problem is that comparable increases in available funds from outside sources are not in sight.[101]

If parents are faced with the necessity of reducing the amount they can contribute to the student's support, where do they go for support? One source has been the federally insured low-interest student loans (FISLs). But defaults on loans have been cutting into the amount of money that can be made available to students. In the President's budget message in early 1974, a major goal stated was an expansion of the guaranteed student-loan program. And, in the request presented in January 1975, there was a $31 million increase over the previous year's budget request. However, of the $31 million increase, some $26 million was directed to cover defaults, while only $5 million would cover interest subsidies which the government pays for needy students. Moreover, in the request for a $30.8 million supplemental appropriation for fiscal 1974 it was noted that all of this money would be needed to pay increased 1973 and 1974 defaults. It was estimated that the cost of defaults had risen over the past three years from $46 million in fiscal 1973 to $88 million in fiscal 1974 and to $115 million to cover fiscal 1975. Default figures were actually higher than these estimates, because the interest payments, collected defaults, and other deposits to the program, in addition to the actual appropriations requested, helped cover the debts. It appeared that the growing defaults were due to the increased amount of loans that had reached repayment status.[102]

A report in the fall of 1974 indicated that the federal government could be faced with a loss of over a half-billion dollars in defaults. It was estimated that 25.3 percent of the loans outstanding as of January 1, 1974, would never be repaid by the borrowers. In fiscal 1974 alone, an estimated 14.5 percent of the students who owed repayments to lenders defaulted on them, constituting a loss of $138 million since the program began in 1966. By the end of 1974 it was anticipated that the default rate would rise to 18.5 percent and result in a cumulative loss of $274 million and that the total loss could subsequently go over one-half billion dollars.[103]

Faced with the serious defaults, the U.S. Office of Education proposed in October 1974 new criteria for removing colleges and universities from the guaranteed student-loan program. Among the proposed requirements was one that the institution would have to establish "a fair and equitable refund policy." The school would have to refund tuition and fees to a student holding guaranteed loans within 30 days of the date it is notified the student is withdrawing. In addition, no more than 10 percent of the student loans in repayment status at the institution could be in default, no more than 20 percent of the students receiving loans at the campus could withdraw during a given academic term, and no more than 6 percent of the institution's revenue from tuition and fees could come from loans. It was also proposed that new rules cover the educational and commercial lenders who make the guaranteed loans.[104]

It was becoming clear also that there was some relation between the level of defaults and the type of school in which the defaulters were registered. It was noted that students in proprietary schools made up nearly 58 percent of the defaults, that those at public institutions constituted 33 percent of the defaults, and those at private colleges 9 percent. Originally the loans were intended mainly to assist middle income students meet the increasing costs of a college education, but in 1968 Congress opened the federally insured loan program to proprietary schools, and in 1974 these schools claimed about 45 percent of all loan money out under the program. There have been claims that some of the larger proprietary schools have profiteered through the manipulation of student-aid grants. In the fall of 1975 the Department of Health, Education, and Welfare initiated a special investigation of the entire student-loan program.[105]

293

In spite of the problems attending the FISL program, it appeared that as academic year 1974-75 got under way, government-insured loans were apparently more available in 1974-75 than during the previous year. However, the dollar amount had not reached the peak lending rate of the 1971-72 academic year, and for some students the situation was still tight. It was noted that "for freshmen, as for other new borrowers, for poorer students, for city dwellers, for students at high-priced institutions, at graduate schools, and at community colleges, much of the picture is still gloomy."[106] The student-aid picture brightened considerably by fall 1975. More students were applying for more financial aid than ever before, but more money was also apparently available. One of the major factors in the improved situation was the basic-opportunity-grants program. One commentator observed that the program, then in its third year, had "apparently begun to fulfill its intended role—to act as the cornerstone around which all other aid can be built."[107] There were also increased funds for the college work-study program, and more funds were available under the federally insured student-loan program in 1975 than in 1974.

As federally insured loans and federal loans and grants emerged as major sources of student aid, another federal program was experiencing difficulty in late 1974. The National Direct Student Loan Program, established in 1959 as the National Defense Student Loan Program, was facing serious defaults. Under this program institutions could make loans directly to students rather than requiring students to seek loans on their own from banks as is the case for the guaranteed program. It was developing that defaults were high in the direct-loan program as well as in FISL. Potential defaults on loans at least 120 days past due in fiscal 1973 were running at 14.2 percent, or $261 million, on about 1.84 billion dollars in matured loans. No estimate had been made for fiscal 1974 or 1975. It was contended that collection of loans had low priorities among student-aid officers at institutions; individual campuses had not followed through on delinquent accounts. Apparently an increasing number of institutions were turning to outside collection agencies.[108]

Another factor entered the loan picture when in 1974 the Internal Revenue Service began to enforce a 1973 ruling that "forgiven" loans would be considered income and that taxes would have to be paid in the year that the loans were cancelled. It was argued by the

IRS that the loans were made primarily for the benefit of the grantor and could not be considered tax-exempt scholarships. It was noted that many state and federal programs, as well as privately sponsored programs, provided for a cancellation of all or part of loans to persons in selected occupations in return for the agreement to serve in low income or poorly staffed areas or to instruct the handicapped. The particular loans affected were those under the National Direct Student Loan Program, the Nurse Training Act of 1971, the Comprehensive Health Manpower Act of 1971, and certain state programs. The reaction of students and state officials was that there had been no notification that the funds would be taxed when the loan was made.[109]

As long as tuition remains a substantial source of income for higher educational institutions—and in 1975 it seemed to be on the way to becoming more of a factor in even public institutions—and as long as public policy calls for increased accessibility to higher education, irrespective of family income, student-aid programs are critical elements in the financing of higher educational institutions, and federal funds constitute a significant portion of student aid. Federal funding, however, seems to have developed by accretion rather than by any systematic analysis and formulation of overall policy. A National Task Force on Student Aid Problems, with former U.S. Commissioner of Education Francis Heppel as head, issued a draft report in April 1975 referring to the federal involvement as a "luxuriant tangle of programs, policies and procedures that has become all but impenetrable, even to professional aid administrators, let alone the students, the system's intended beneficiaries." The report endorsed the current diversity of student-aid programs, however, while asking for more standardized application forms and methods of computing awards and better coordination of application and award schedules.[110]

Early in 1974, nine private colleges participating in a two-year study sponsored by the Alfred P. Sloan Foundation concluded that, in spite of the complexity of the federal funding, more dollars would have to be made available from federal sources. All private colleges needed significantly expanded loan programs if they were to help their students meet rising expenses. It seemed clear to this group that the only thing ahead was "periodic, probably annual, increases in tuition."[111] The nine colleges involved in the study—Amherst, Brown, Dartmouth, Harvard, Massachusetts Institute of

Technology, Mount Holyoke, Princeton, Wellesley, and Wesleyan—said that they were asking students more and more often to rely on financial aid. Unable to enlarge their own scholarship funds at this time, the only other possibility was to rely increasingly on loan funds. While some thought had been given to having the colleges set up their own private loan programs, this was rejected in favor of more participation in the federally subsidized guaranteed student loan program. The report referred to the Student Loan Marketing Association which was sponsored by the government to buy and sell loans under the guaranteed student loan program. Under this association, colleges become lenders by being able themselves to borrow money on a short-term basis from SLMA.

Another approach to assisting students to meet expenses emerged early in 1971, the so-called deferred tuition plan. The Ford Foundation announced that it would support for a limited trial run a plan that would enable students to meet college costs through long-term loans that could be repaid at a fixed percentage of their future annual earnings. Some 25 institutions had indicated interest in participating in such a plan, which was to permit students, regardless of need, to borrow up to the full cost of their higher education from a single agency and pay it back over some 30 years with the repayments based on yearly income. This would mean that some students could eventually pay back more than they had borrowed, while others might repay less. A Presidential advisory panel in 1967 had proposed a similar plan under the title of Educational Opportunity Bank.[112]

A month later Yale University announced that it was going to initiate its own version of the plan by allowing students to defer their tuition for up to 35 years in return for a fixed percentage of their future annual income. Yale planned to finance its program with the aid of a few wealthy alumni and through its own borrowing power. According to the Yale plan, the student would make a contract with the university to postpone as much as $800 a year, and for each $1,000 deferred, the student would pay back a percentage of his yearly income over a maximum of 35 years. The contract could be canceled up to six months before the student was due to graduate, in which case the debt would be converted to a more common type of loan. In addition, a participant could end his repayments at any time by giving the university enough to bring his total payments to one-and-one-half times the amount of tuition originally postponed, plus administrative costs.[113]

In March 1971 Duke University indicated that it might attempt such a plan in the fall of 1971. It was suggested that initially the plan might involve 100 to 150 upperclassmen and graduate students.[114] In the meantime, some public college groups had indicated definite opposition to such a plan. And the year after it had indicated interest in backing such a program, the Ford Foundation decided not to finance the experiment. It was reported that, after a year-long study, the foundation concluded that it had insufficient additional private capital to make the investment in such a program worthwhile and that it also was of the opinion that the risk in financing what was then coming to be called income-contingent loans was too great for most academic institutions to undertake by themselves.[115] The story also suggested that Ford might later propose a modified plan. In October 1972 a Ford Foundation task force proposed a plan called "pay-as-you-earn," or PAYE. Under the task force proposal, the repayment schedule would be fixed in advance and the amounts to be paid back annually would increase according to a predetermined scale of the borrower's anticipated earnings. Those whose income would not meet the schedule could defer payments a year. At the end of the loan period, the college would absorb the amounts still outstanding. The plan would also be tied to the federal government's existing guaranteed-loan program. The task force suggested that only the government in the long run is capable of bearing the capital risk involved in such types of programs. The Ford Foundation was not itself entering into the program but was suggesting it as an alternative to the type of program adopted by Yale.[116]

In the meantime, Yale indicated in the fall of 1971 that 22 percent of the undergraduates had asked to participate in the first year of the university's deferred tuition plan. It was reported that more than 80 percent of those who asked for deferments asked for the maximum amount, $800 per year. And at Duke University, 40 undergraduates and 33 professional school students signed up for deferred payments.[117]

Picking up on the earlier suggestion of the Ford Foundation, federal student-aid officials examined proposals to modify the guaranteed-loan program to take on some aspects of the income-contingent plan. In March the government announced that it had rejected the proposed variation. Initially, some officials favored the idea, but the announcement indicated that budgetary considerations made a graduated repayment schedule unfeasible. There was fear that graduated repayments would increase the government's liability to pay defaults, already severe enough with the insured-loan program.[118] At Harvard, where such a modified program was under way, some revisions were already being considered. Northwestern University was reported to expect to try some form of income-contingent loans in the fall of 1973. The rejection of the plan, however, by the government, apparently caused revisions in some of the planning of the nine colleges that had earlier participated in the Sloan study and that were planning a cooperative pay-as-you-earn program for 1974.

Three years before, in March 1971, Governor John J. Gilligan had suggested an income-contingent loan plan for the state of Ohio. Under the proposal, every student in Ohio would be obligated to repay the state the full amount of the direct state subsidy the student had received while in school, and the repayment would be on the basis of future income. No student would be obligated to repay more than the state subsidy, and if the student did not receive sufficient income, then the subsidy would not be repaid or would be repaid only in part. A variation of the plan was proposed by the Ohio Board of Regents in the summer of 1972. Neither of the plans was adopted by the legislature.

Clifford W. Wharton, Jr., in an article in December 1971, attacked income-contingency plans as a threat to a great national commitment to free public higher education. Turning to the argument of who pays and who benefits, he contended that the income-contingency plans emphasized returns to the individual, while historically the United States had emphasized free access to education and the returns to society. He stated that "the income-contingency loan idea constitutes a definite shift away from public decisions and responsibility for the support and control of higher education toward a philosophy of private responsibility and private enterprise, with major consequences."[119] And with Wharton's comment we find ourselves back in the earlier debate over "who benefits" and "who should pay."

As we enter the last half of the decade of the 1970s the debate over the proper role of tuition as a source of income for higher educational institutions continues. Nowhere is higher education wholly without charge to the individual student and nowhere does tuition wholly cover the cost a student's education. There is every indication that tuition is becoming a larger factor in financing even public institutions, but it is also clear that more kinds of student-aid funds are being made available. Whether the funds available will be enough to meet the needs continues to be debated. In the foreseeable future tuition is going to remain a significant item of income for higher educational institutions, public as well as private. And there is little indication that the student-aid tangle is going to become any less complex. It would take combinations of federal, state, and private grants and loans to help large numbers of students to make up the difference between available personal funds and the fees assessed by institutions. As a 1974 publication of the American College Testing Program observed, neither the no-tuition schemes nor the full-cost-tuition scheme has the slightest chance of wide acceptance, because each "in its own way represents a position out of step with current economic conditions and political reality."[120] It is highly unlikely that either educators or taxpayers would seriously argue that the state should provide postsecondary education in its public institutions free of all charges—although there is some sentiment for making junior or community college education virtually free of direct cost to the student. And it is just as unlikely that taxpayers would endorse any plan to assess students the full cost of instruction. Some combination of funding will continue to be the norm. We turn now from the direct charges to the individual to the participation of state governments in funding.

The State Government as a Source of Income. While tuition is and will continue to be a significant source of income for higher education, when all higher institutions are considered together, it is apparent that the single largest source of current operating income for higher educational institutions is state and local government; and in this combination most of the funds are derived from state rather than local sources. According to the Commission on the Financing of Postsecondary Education, state and local governments provide 31.6 percent of the total current income (Educational and General, Auxiliary Enterprises, and Other, combined). As a percentage of Educational and General income alone, based on data supplied by the commission, state and local governments account for 35.8 percent of this income.

Most of the income derived from state governments is directed to tax-supported institutions within the territorial limits of the state granting the funds. In recent years, however, state-funded scholarship and grant programs have come to provide significant funds for some private higher educational institutions. The Commission on the Financing of Postsecondary Education reported that in 1972-73 some $348.2 million had been awarded to 748,700 students, to make an average award per recipient of $465. The amount awarded by states almost doubled over the four-year period between 1969-70 and 1972-73. In 1969-70 the states awarded $191.5 million to 487,000 individuals, for an average grant per person of $393.[121]

June O'Neill shows a continuing growth in income from state and local sources over four decades, from 1930 to 1968. The growth rate between 1930 and 1968 was 9.5 percent; between 1960 and 1968, however, income from state and local governments increased by 15 percent.[122] The most significant growth, of course, has been among the public institutions. In another calculation, O'Neill shows the percentage of income from state and local funding to private institutions decreasing (to constituting 1.8 percent in 1967-68 in comparison to 3.1 percent of the income for private institutions some 26 years before, 1939-40.)[123] As suggested above, however, the state scholarship and grant funds, which are reflected only in tuition payments, have become significant only since 1968, and state support in toto, even if indirect, has increased to private institutions.

Based on my own calculations, employing data from the U.S. Office of Education reports, table 10 shows the trend in the proportion that state and local funds provide within Educational and General income for all (public and private) institutions combined. The data are for 1909-10 through 1969-70. Note that there has been some fluctuation but that the proportion of income derived by all higher educational institutions from state and local funds reached its highest point in 1969-70 (39.8 percent).

For a number of years M. M. Chambers has monitored the state funding of higher education. His calculations show that for the two-year period from 1967-68 to 1969-70 state appropriations to higher educational institutions, when all states are combined, increased by 38.5 percent. During the next biennium, from 1969-70 through 1971-72, appropriations continued to increase, but by only 24 percent. For the next biennium, from 1971-72 through 1973-74, there was again an increase, this time by 25 percent.[124]

The most recent data on state support involve some overlap with a previous biennium and show that for 1972-73 through 1974-75,

Table 10

State and Local Government Funds as a Percentage of Educational and General Income

Year	State and Local Percentage of Educational and General Income
1909–10	29.0
1919–20	35.6
1929–30	31.5
1939–40	30.8
1949–50	30.0
1959–60	32.5
1963–64	30.4
1967–68	34.0
1969–70	39.8

Source: Based on data reported in annual issues of *Financing Statistics of Institutions of Higher Education: Current Fund Revenues and Expenditures,* issued by the Department of Health, Education, and Welfare, and *Higher Education Finances: Selected Trend and Summary Data,* periodically issued by the same agency.

appropriations increased 29 percent. It may be noted, however, that an estimated two-thirds of the increase has already been used up by inflation, and that the actual increase is actually less.[125] And when the figures are adjusted to the loss of buying power, it appears that six states have actually lost ground in the last two years: Hawaii, down 22 percent; Texas, down 6 percent; Minnesota, down 5 percent; Maryland and West Virginia, down 2 percent; and North Dakota, down 1 percent. It may also be noted that over the past ten years the increase in state appropriations for higher education has been 349 percent; however, when this increase is adjusted for inflation, the effective increase is probably only 152 percent. South Carolina, Pennsylvania, Massachusetts, Connecticut, and Alaska led the other states during the last decade in the amount of increase appropriated for higher education.

The Center for Research and Development in Higher Education at the University of California at Berkeley calculated for each of the states the percentage of total revenues devoted to higher education

301

for the decade from 1963 through 1973. The largest proportion was given by the state of Wyoming, 37.6 percent of total revenue. This proportion has remained fairly stable since 1963. Oregon represented the next largest, granting 28 percent of its total revenues to higher education in 1973; this is to be compared with 20 percent in 1963.

Among those states with very extensive systems of higher education, the proportion of state revenue granted to higher education is somewhat less than in Oregon, but the total amounts are considerable. California, with almost $6 billion in state revenue, appropriated 16.9 percent to higher education in 1973, an increase over the 15.6 percent of less than $2 billion in revenue appropriated in 1963. New York, with state revenues of almost $7.7 billion in 1973, appropriated 9.6 percent to higher education; this is also an increase over the 6.8 percent of $2.3 billion in revenues in 1963. Pennsylvania has perhaps shown the most significant increase. In 1973 it appropriated 10.7 percent of $3.7 billion in revenues, while in 1963 it appropriated 5.4 percent of $1 billion in revenues. In 1973 Michigan appropriated 13.9 percent of its revenues; Illinois, 8.8 percent; Ohio, 18 percent; and New Jersey, 10.6 percent, to mention only a few others. In each of these last four states, with the exception of Illinois, the proportion of state revenue appropriated to higher education has increased since 1963.[126]

It is clear that state governments are heavily involved in financing higher education. The total funds granted to colleges and universities has increased significantly in recent years, although inflation has dampened some of the impact. Yet the tax-supported institutions have contended that appropriations have not kept pace with increases in costs.

Even as state governments have experienced increased demands from tax-supported institutions, they have moved in recent years to provide assistance, often indirect, to private institutions. The main form of assistance has been through state scholarship and grant funds. By late 1974 there were student-assistance programs in 41 states and trust territories.

As the Commission on the Financing of Postsecondary Education has observed, state and local support for private colleges and universities goes back to the colonial period, the first instance of which was the public financing for the support of Harvard College in 1636. Harvard received public funds through the early decades of the nineteenth century. The same pattern was followed among the eastern states in several other institutions.[127] Public support of private higher education changed dramatically after the Morrill Act of 1862, and in time the aid became limited to indirect forms such as allowing institutions to be exempt from state and local property taxes. More recently, however, there has been a resurgence of effort on the part of the states to assist private institutions, particularly in states where private institutions are numerous and serve substantial proportions of state residents. The commission observes:

> In the states that have acted to provide direct or indirect aid to private colleges and universities, the primary justification has been that, without such aid, private institutions would no longer be able to compete for students against heavily subsidized public institutions. Private institutions would thereby lose their ability to provide a diversity of educational experience and to serve students who would otherwise attend tax-supported public institutions.[128]

The commission refers to the Heald Committee which urged that aid be given to private institutions in New York because such institutions would "give American education a diversity and scope not possible in tax-supported institutions alone," since the private institutions "have an opportunity to emphasize, if they wish, individualistic patterns of thought, courses of social action, or political or religious activity."[129]

While a number of state constitutions bar the use of public funds for private institutions, the majority of the state courts "have not tended to interpret the state constitutions narrowly and have generally followed the lead of the United States Supreme Court."[130] The general principle has been that when the state funds are used for a "public purpose" the question is less a matter of who handles the money than the purpose for which it is used.

> The greater portion of measurable state and local aid to private collegiate institutions is provided in the form of student financial assistance, either to all students, regardless of whether they attend a public or private institution, or only to those who attend private institutions. But many states also provide direct

303

or indirect aid to private institutions. In 1951-52, the 50 states and the District of Columbia provided an estimated 185 million in measurable aid, direct and indirect, to private colleges and universities.[131]

The Commission on the Financing of Postsecondary Education refers to 19 states in 1972 providing *direct* aid to private colleges.

Much of state aid to private institutions, however, is indirect, and the growth in state scholarship and grant programs, the primary mode in which state aid is provided to private colleges, has been in large part a development of the past decade, and within this decade, the greatest activity has been within the five years of the 1970s. In October 1971 the *Chronicle of Higher Education* reported that 13 state legislatures enacted new measures during the year to provide financial aid to private colleges or students in private institutions, and that several other states had broadened existing private-college aid programs or had increased their appropriations. The report indicated that 35 states were providing, some of them indirectly, aid to private colleges and universities.

There has been some interest in having the state provide direct forms of aid to private institutions. Minnesota and Oregon adopted in 1971 a provision whereby the state could "contract" with private colleges for the education of state residents. That same year Illinois, Maryland, and Washington adopted programs of direct grants to private institutions.[132] In 1971, 12 states also permitted private institutions to use the state's borrowing authority for bonds or loans to construct buildings, and for several years Indiana and Michigan have allowed residents tax credits against state income tax for contributions to private colleges.

While a total of 35 states provided some form of aid in 1971 directly or indirectly to private colleges and universities, and while some among them had programs that had not yet been funded, by February 1972 at least 22 states were operating state-funded scholarship programs and providing in 1971-72 a total of $279.4 million to private institutions. Only eight states had provided scholarship programs as recently as a decade before. Larry Van Dyne stated that "the dramatic increase marks the emergence of the programs both as a significant source of student financial aid and as an important means of indirect public aid to private colleges and universities."[133] Among the 22 states with comprehensive programs, the largest were in New York ($76.2 million in scholarships), Pennsylvania ($55.5 million), Illinois ($39.4 million), New Jersey ($22 million), and California ($18.8 million). Generally students could apply their grants at either private or public colleges. All but seven of the states (Connecticut, Massachusetts, New Jersey, Pennsylvania, Rhode Island, Vermont, and Wisconsin) limited the use of the scholarships to colleges within their own boundaries.

By late 1974 the number of state student-assistance programs had increased from 22 to 41 states and trust territories. Nine others had programs pending in the state legislatures, and only four states— Alabama, Arizona, Hawaii, and Louisiana, did not have, or were not proposing, financial-aid programs. (Alaska was not included in the study.) The aid programs increased grants from $364.2 million in 1973-74 to an estimated $456.9 million for 1974-75. The funds went to 797,153 students as compared with 734,818 the year before.[134] The trend continued toward allowing students to take their awards to either public or private institutions. Only about 4 percent of the $456.9 million was restricted to use in public colleges and in only two states, Colorado and Virginia, were grants entirely excluded from private institutions, but in most states the grants had to be used in institutions within the state. Three states accounted for over 50 percent of the student-aid dollars, New York, Pennsylvania, and Illinois. The new federal program of state student-incentive grants, which provides matching funds to states to establish or expand scholarship programs, apparently had an influence in the expansion of the state-sponsored student aid.

The most authoritative source of information on the development of the state programs is provided in the annual reports of the National Association of State Scholarship Programs prepared by Joseph D. Boyd, executive director of the Illinois State Scholarship Commission. Boyd began issuing his reports in 1970. He notes that the first comprehensive state program for residents to attend public or nonpublic programs was probably developed by Maryland around 1825. New York established its program in 1913, Oregon in 1935, and then there were no further developments until California began its program in 1956.[135]

One of the more comprehensive overviews of the development of state aid to private education has been prepared by Richard Millard

305

of the Education Commission of the States.[136] He refers to 39 states that have authorized programs to make funds available to private institutions directly or indirectly. (The 41 noted in the previous paragraph included trust territories.) The 11 states which did not at the time of the report have specific programs included Wyoming with no private institutions, and with the exceptions of New Hampshire and Delaware, were states in which private higher education has not had a very large role. Student aid was the predominant method of providing funds, and 35 states were reported to have authorized programs in this area, although in Colorado, Nebraska, and Oklahoma the programs had not been funded. Some of the states, such as California, Connecticut, New Jersey, New York, and Wisconsin, had developed fairly complex programs. In 15 states, tuition equalization grants had been provided specifically for students in private institutions.

Some 18 states provided direct institutional assistance, and some of these also had student-aid programs. There are a number of variations in the way in which the direct aid was made available. New York, Illinois, Maryland, and New Jersey utilized formulas based on the number of students or number of degrees; Connecticut and North Carolina related the funds to the grant or scholarship holders in the institutions; while the remaining 12 states made grants to specific institutions or parts of institutions. Another approach has been through contracts, whereby states contract with private institutions for certain services. Some 16 states have developed contracts, usually, but not always, with specific institutions for specific programs. Eleven states also have provided bonding authorities which enable institutions to borrow funds for construction on the basis of tax-free bonds.

Millard notes that in addition to the major categories of student aid, direct institutional aid, contracts, and facilities and education for health professions, there were other provisions. Indiana and Michigan offered state income tax credits to individuals or corporations donating to private higher educational institutions. Illinois provided funds to encourage consortia among private or private and public institutions. New York provided endowed chairs for scholars at private as well as public institutions. South Carolina has made it possible for private institutions to utilize the state purchasing office, and Virginia has exempted private institutions from the state sales tax, while Michigan has exempted them from the gasoline tax. Minnesota has developed an interinstitutional television and library program that includes private institutions.

In sum, by 1974 there were 41 states and territories providing some kind of student-assistance program. The Commission on the Financing of Postsecondary Education observes that approximately 60 percent of the state tuition monies in 1972-73 went to students at private colleges and universities.[137] Larry Leslie and Jonathan Fife examined responses from samples of scholarship winners in New Jersey, New York, Illinois, California, and Pennsylvania for one year in each state but variously among the states from 1971 through 1973. They concluded that in general the private sector appeared to gain more than did the public sector. In particular, the California and New Jersey programs, both designed to help the private sector, were successful in raising the demand for private higher education. In the other three states, private institutions still benefited, but with a smaller percentage of the aid recipients.[138]

The Commission on the Financing of Postsecondary Education is of the opinion that continued growth in student-aid programs is likely to occur for the next few years, especially "in the form of non-competitive grants for students attending public and private institutions."[139] The commission also reports an interest in many states to increase aid to private institutions, both because representatives of private colleges and universities have become more effective in presenting their cause and because many private institutions have unused instructional capacity.

We would observe, however, that in states where both public and private institutions have stopped growing, the friction between public and private institutions has begun to increase significantly. Even at an earlier point in time the question of whether public funds can be used for private institutions has been the subject of several court tests. In September 1963 the Horace Mann League, a nonprofit organization, and nine individuals, suing as taxpayers, challenged the constitutionality of four statutes enacted by the Maryland state legislature which appropriated money for matching grants to four religiously-affiliated private colleges for the construction of facilities. These were Hood, a liberal arts college for women affiliated with the United Church of Christ, Western Maryland College, a coeducational institution affiliated with the Methodist

307

Church, and Notre Dame College and St. Joseph College, each controlled by a Catholic religious order. The case was brought to the Maryland Circuit Court of Anne Arundel County. The court held that the four grants did not constitute an unconstitutional aid to religion, that the Horace Mann League did not have standing as a plaintiff, and that the individual taxpayer plaintiffs did have standing. The case then went to the Maryland Court of Appeals, and the higher court upheld the decision of the lower court with respect to Hood College, but ruled that Western Maryland College, Notre Dame College and St. Joseph College were sectarian educational institutions and that their grant of state funds violated the First Amendment and the Fourteenth Amendment of the United States Constitution. The case then went to the U.S. Supreme Court which on November 14, 1966, refused to review the decision and in effect left the earlier decision of the Maryland Court of Appeals stand. The effect of the decision was to prohibit state grants to institutions that were clearly of a sectarian nature.[140]

Two of the colleges were in the news again in late 1974. Maryland had in 1971 passed a state law designed to aid 17 financially ailing private institutions in the state. The law granted aid according to the number of degrees each college conferred each year, but it banned the use of state funds for sectarian purposes. In October 1974 the U.S. District Court, by upholding the law, made it possible for $1.8 million in state funds to be given to the four church-related colleges. In making the decision, two members of the three-judge federal panel said that "the religious programs at each school are separable from the secular programs, and the latter are the only beneficiaries of state aid." The lawyer for the colleges commented that the suit represented the first challenge of a general-purpose aid program for private and church-related colleges.[141] Subsequently the case went to the Supreme Court, and in a five-to-three vote the court refused to block an order of the U.S. District Court that upheld a state law aiding the four colleges.[142]

The district court had relied on the 1971 Supreme Court decision, Tilton v. Richardson, that held that federal funds could be used to help church-related colleges as long as the purpose of the grant was specifically secular, its primary effect was not to advance or inhibit religion, and the aid avoided "excessive government entanglement with religion." That decision had been made in July 1971 when by a five-to-four margin the U.S. Supreme Court upheld the constitutionality of federal construction grants to church-related colleges as long as the buildings financed with government funds were not used for sectarian purposes. That case originated out of a protest over grants made to four Catholic colleges in Connecticut under the Higher Education Facilities Act of 1963. The crucial point was whether the primary or principal effect of the aid advanced religion. The court did at that time, incidentally, overrule one portion of the 1963 law, a provision that after 20 years the buildings financed by the government could be used for any purpose, including a religious one.[143]

In another test, the U.S. Supreme Court in 1973 had upheld the constitutionality of limited state assistance for construction of physical facilities at church-related colleges. At issue was the South Carolina facilities act which allowed revenue bonds to be issued for both public and private colleges. A revenue bond had been planned for the Baptist College of Charleston, South Carolina. The state law allowed such bonds as long as the facilities were not used for sectarian instruction or as places of worship. Relying on arguments similar to those in the Tilton v. Richardson case, the court held that there was no basis to conclude that the college's "operations are oriented significantly towards sectarian rather than secular education," even if it were a church-related college.[144]

We have already referred to the comments of the Commission on the Financing of Postsecondary Education regarding state assistance to private institutions. As the commission sees it, the primary argument that has been given is that support helps to maintain private institutions and private institutions give a diversity in scope that would be less likely if there were only tax-supported institutions.[145] The same general position is taken by the Carnegie Commission in its report on the state's responsibility for postsecondary education. That report comes out in favor of "some state support of private colleges and universities." The statement argues that graduates of private and public institutions benefit society equally and at the same time private institutions can provide "diversity, innovative opportunities, models of interest in the individual students, and standards of autonomy useful to all higher education."[146] The statement further comes out in favor of state subsidy of tuition costs for students without financial resources to meet the costs of private institutions and in favor of federal assistance to meet subsistence costs. Tuition should generally rise to a point of narrowing the gap between private and public tuition.

309

We also favor state contractual support for special endeavors, such as medical schools, and greater state use for construction grants or establishment of state-created bond-issuing agencies for loans for the benefit of private as well as public institutions. When this aid is not sufficient, we favor subsidies, on a per-student basis, of up to one-third of the subsidy given students in state institutions. A full effort should be made to preserve the private sector in a condition of health and vigor.[147]

The report also states that in many states private colleges and universities, although representing a small portion of the enrollment, "have served as buffers against excessive political control of state universities and colleges." Independent institutions provide "a yardstick against which degrees of governmental control can be measured" and can serve "as a basis for effectively resisting excessive control."[148]

In a later report dealing with general issues in financing, the commission contends that "states should increasingly support private institutions in ways that best preserve institutional independence, and that also make possible, in particular, the attendance of more students from low-income families."[149] This particular report urged that assistance be made in proportion to ability to pay. That is, there should be greater assistance to low income students than to others. It was pointed out, however, that private institutions should be prepared "to consider methods of accountability along with methods of public funding."[150] And it was at this point that the Carnegie Commission also urged an increase in tuition costs at public institutions, together with availability of student aid for lower income students.

William H. McFarlane has written a number of pieces dealing with state assistance to private institutions. Among other things, he notes "competitive excellence is uniquely characteristic of America's pluralistic structures for higher education. The variety of educational styles espoused by private colleges is especially needed today."[151] In a publication for the Southern Regional Education Board, McFarlane stated that inclusion of the private sector in state-sponsored systems "can also make available an extensive accumulation of educational facilities, programs, personnel and services, which have been established and maintained with little or no

310

involvement of state funds."[152] In a subsequent monograph he explored the legal and political issues for state aid to private higher education and suggested that the controversy over state support to private institutions may involve "political attitudes more than legal uncertainties."[153] This latter volume provides a good overview of some of the issues that have been raised as well as an analysis of court decisions up to the date of the report.

One writer, however, warns private colleges against overdependence on state support. In her summary of the present condition and future prospects of private colleges, Carol Shulman calls attention to an observation by William Jellema that "private colleges that receive aid may be in difficulty if the aid does not continue, since they are still morally responsible for the education of their students if state aid lapses."[154] Jellema suggests that an institution will be tempted to adjust its program on the basis of state aid and may find itself in an awkward position if aid declines. In addition, state aid may be tied to state-resident status, which forces a college to concentrate on state students rather than on a more national student representation. It is also pointed out that state private institutions and universities accepting state aid must also accept a greater degree of state involvement in their educational management.

At the 1973 meeting of the American Association for Higher Education, Ernest L. Boyer, chancellor of the State University of New York, spoke favorably of state aid to private colleges. He, too, however, pointed out that the aid could not be given without restriction, and he indicated that the funds should be given for "selected programs." He said that public aid to private institutions would be forthcoming "provided those colleges helped the state meet clearly defined, explicitly stated public needs and provided they operate such programs on the basis of standards equally comparable to those imposed upon the public institutions. This is the price that public institutions should be willing to pay for public support."[155]

In the mid-1970s state governments were deeply involved in financing higher education. Continuing what had become by the early twentieth century direct support of state-maintained and state-controlled higher educational institutions, the states were also, in a variety of ways, supporting private institutions as well. Higher education, however, had become one of several competing agencies for state funds as social welfare, highways, and other services demanded ever increasing subsidies. As we were able to see in the overview of the developing financial crisis in the early pages of this chapter, state-supported colleges and universities have faced severe pressures as budgets have been reduced, cutbacks ordered, and staff reductions imposed. Yet, for the greater part of American higher education, the 50 states remain the primary source of income and will continue to be so in the foreseeable future. The shape and form of state-supported higher education will probably change in response to growing legislative and state board involvement, but the states are not likely to abandon what has become one of the most significant educational developments in the Western world, the establishment and growth of the American state universities. Private institutions in the mid-1970s were seeking to work out means of maintaining their identity as separate and independent institutions while still seeking, largely through indirect means, increasing state assistance in funding. We can only predict increasing tension at this point and concessions on both sides—if private higher education is to remain a vital force in the higher educational pattern of the 50 states. Private higher education will also continue to press for more federal support, and it is to that source of funding that we now turn.

The Federal Government as a Source of Funds

In an essay published in the late 1960s, Roger Freeman recalled that in the early years of the decade there was among administrators in higher educational institutions a "basic and instinctive objective to the general proposition of federal support to higher education." He was referring in this comment to a statement made in 1962 by the vice president and controller of Tulane University. As late as 1964 a Committee on Financing Higher Education, sponsored by the American Association of Universities, strongly objected to the expansion of federal activities in higher education. And in 1967, Freeman himself was referring to the "American tradition of education as a state-local and private responsibility" being "more deeply rooted than it appears on the surface."[156] Ironically, at the same time that the committee of the American Association of Universities was objecting to the expansion of federal activities into education, the Education Facilities Act was passed, and few institutions subsequently neglected the opportunity to tap this new source of funds for capital expansion.

A decade later, the objection to federal involvement seems to have dissipated. Indeed, the change of attitude required less than a decade. At a meeting of the Association of American Colleges (AAC) in January 1971, the leaders of the nation's private colleges organized to launch a campaign for increasing financial aid from the federal government. Meeting at the same time as the AAC, the Council of Independent Colleges and Universities declared that it was going to work for new governmental aid to students and institutions. The president of the AAC commended the council on its position and said that such an organization would help to put together "a grass-roots support not previously available in like degree through any of our existing Washington association."[157] By 1974 eight higher education associations were asking for substantial increases in funds from the federal government, including a program of direct grants.[158] It is obvious that the climate of opinion had shifted drastically. In the light of the worsening financial situation of higher educational institutions, both public and private, it is not difficult to understand why the shift in opinion had occurred.

For 1971-72, the Commission on the Financing of Postsecondary Education reported that the federal government provided $4.2 billion in institutional support. Adding to that figure the aid to students through various federal plans, an additional $3.9 billion, brings the total federal involvement to $8.1 billion, or 27.4 percent of total current operating income for the year.[159] A report for 1973-74 (fiscal 1974) shows a federal commitment of over $9.4 billion. Of this amount, almost one-fourth was expended in veteran's education and training.[160] There could be little doubt that the federal government was heavily involved in financing postsecondary education.

The earliest federal assistance to postsecondary education began with the land policy developed under the Articles of Confederation. A resolution adopted in 1780 provided that lands ceded to the Confederation would be settled and developed in an orderly manner to form new states for the Federal Union. The Territorial Ordinance of 1784 provided that such lands would be divided into rectangular territories, each of which would have a territorial government as soon as 20,000 inhabitants were reported. The Northwest Ordinance of 1785 provided that prior to the sale of these federal lands—Virginia, Massachusetts, and Connecticut in the meantime had ceded vast territories—they would be surveyed into townships six miles square and that section 16 of each township should be reserved for the maintenance of a public school. Subsequently, the Ordinance of 1787, with the oft-quoted words, "Religion, Morality and Knowledge being necessary to good government and the happiness of mankind, schools and the means of education shall be forever encouraged," authorized land grants for the establishment of educational institutions, and the sale of lands to the Ohio and Scioto companies established the principle of granting lands for the support of higher education.

As one report observes, these grants provided the first instance of federal financial assistance for education, and "with this enactment, the National Government embarked upon a program of educational support unique among national governments in its commitments to State and local autonomy and in the responsibility it assumed for a public function of national interest."[161] The federal government has subsequently developed a variety of programs and procedures to support a broad range of educational undertakings. The procedures include "grants of land, financial grants and loans, allocations of surplus commodities and federally-owned property, operation of special educational programs and institutions, and the cost of services or contracts."[162]

After the Ordinance of 1787, the next significant federal move was in the first Morrill Act of 1862, in which grants of public land were made for the establishment and maintenance in the states of agricultural and mechanical colleges. A series of additional acts, including the second Morrill Act in 1890, provided needed additional support.

It was in the 1940s, however, that federal policy took an even more distinct turn in support of higher educational institutions. During World War II colleges and universities were called upon to provide military training programs and to undertake research and study in support of the war effort. With the Servicemen's Readjustment Act of 1944 (GI Bill) the federal government initiated the largest scholarship program in history. This act, followed by subsequent legislation on behalf of disabled veterans, veterans of the

Korean War, orphans of veterans, and others, have resulted in nearly one-quarter of the current federal funds for postsecondary education being devoted to education and training for veterans.

Writing in the late 1950s, Robert Calkins assessed the development of federal assistance to postsecondary education at that point in history. He observed that nearly 36 percent of the Educational and General income of higher educational institutions was derived from the federal government in 1943-44, a slightly larger share than came from federal sources during the peak of the GI enrollment in 1947-48, and he contended that the government involvement was "important in preserving the fiscal solvency and the operating effectiveness of higher education during the war."[163] The new development for the late 1950s, Calkins stated, was the "phenomenal growth of federal grants and contracts for research." He could find no reliable estimate of the total amount of the funds employed at that time, but he suggested that it had risen to well over $400 million in 1959,[164] and he noted the growing reliance of both public and private institutions on public funds. Richard Schrader estimated that while in 1963 less than half of the country's higher educational institutions had received federal support, by 1967 well over 80 percent of these institutions had received some form of federal support.[165]

In tracing the development of the pattern of federal support, we note that from 1959-60 to 1966-67 total support increased from $1.1 billion to more than $3.3 billion. Within these sums, Ernst Becker estimates that the proportion provided for research declined from 75.2 percent in 1959-60 to 66.2 percent in 1966-67. Support for construction of facilities had increased during this period, although by 1966-67 it had begun to decline.[166] Using these same figures, Schrader attributes only one-third of the federal expenditure to research and development. However, when one takes into account the funds spent on facilities and equipment, training grants, and institutional grants, all related to research in some way, his figures closely approximate those of Becker.[167] Schrader further generalizes that prior to the 1960s the federal funds were almost exclusively on a "quid pro quo basis, with the government awarding funds to institutions to achieve some goal deemed important by Congress and the federal agencies." He notes, however, that a shift occurred during the sixties to federal support of higher education "as a national goal in its own right."[168]

As the Commission on the Financing of Postsecondary Education has sketched the development of federal support, it notes the expansion of interest from predominately research in the early 1960s into the concern for the preparation of teachers and college faculty, the improvement of instruction, and the development of instructional facilities. Spending for research began to reach its peak in 1965, and much of the federal support of students and institutions was at least partially consolidated in the Higher Education Act of that year. In the same year, the Health Professions Education Assistance Amendments provided aid for students in the medical professions and increased institutional aid for improving the quality of teaching in those fields. The federal role has continued to broaden, "with increasing emphasis on student aid and on vocational training at the postsecondary level to promote access and choice for low-income students." The commission has suggested that while each new federal program carried its own specific rationale or objective, the overall growth of federal support was justified on two grounds, either (1) as an extension of existing federal policy, or (2) a conviction that state and local governments would not be willing to provide adequate support for postsecondary education.[169]

It is difficult to form an overview of the various agencies that are involved and the types of programs that are funded through federal agencies. The Commission on the Financing of Postsecondary Education identified in 1972 approximately 380 separate programs of support administered by more than 20 federal agencies, and this excluded a number of programs and authorizations administered by the Departments of Defense, State, the Interior, and the Treasury and several other agencies.[170] Schrader refers to more than 40 federal agencies as sources of funds to higher education. He notes, however, that 95 percent of all federal support comes from only 8 agencies, and 99 percent of all federal support from only 13.[171]

Between 1952 and 1967, the dates used by Schrader to examine the pattern of federal support, there were some significant shifts among the several agencies in the proportion to which they were represented in the overall research grants. In 1952 the Department of Defense accounted for 70 percent of the research grants, while in 1967 this department accounted for only 20 percent of the grants. In 1952 the National Institutes of Health accounted for 10 percent of the grants and in 1967 for 33 percent of the grants. The National Science Foundation had increased from 1 percent of the grants in 1952—it was established in 1950—to 15 percent of the grants in 1967.

316

When considering all of the funds granted, the agency showing the most rapid growth in federal funds expended for higher education has been the Office of Education. The Commission on the Financing of Postsecondary Education shows that in 1972 the Department of Health, Education, and Welfare accounted for almost 45 percent of the total grants to higher educational institutions. *The commission includes in its total figures the amount of student aid* and shows federal expenditures of over $8 billion for 1971-72, considerably above the figures used in some of the other reports on federal funding. Table 11 is taken from the report of the commission.

Table 11

Selected Postsecondary Education Outlays, by Major Participating Agencies, Fiscal 1972 (in Millions)

Agency	Amount	Percentage of Total
Department of Health, Education and Welfare	$4,090.4	44.3%
Veterans Administration	2,006.5	21.7
Department of Defense	1,082,6	11.7
Department of Labor	898.2	9.7
National Science Foundation	390.2	4.2
Subtotal	$8,467.9	91.7%
All Other Agencies	769.0	8.3
TOTAL	$9,236.9*	100.0%

*Includes an estimated $1.1 billion in student aid that helps students meet their normal living costs. This amount is excluded from the figure of $8.1 billion reported in other sections of the commission document.

Source: Commission on the Financing of Postsecondary Education, *Financing Postsecondary Education in the United States* (Washington, D.C.: U.S. Government Printing Office, 1973), p. 107.

The most recent report of federal expenditures for American higher educational institutions is for the year 1973-74. That report shows that the expenditures have continued to increase. For fiscal 1974 the federal government expended nearly $9.4 billion, the distribution of which is shown in table 12.

Table 12

Distribution of Federal Expenditures for Higher Education, Fiscal 1974, by Percentage of Total Expenditure

Agency	Percentage of Total Federal Expenditures for Higher Education
Office of Education	22.9
Student Assistance	(17.8)
Construction	(0.8)
Developing Institutions	(1.1)
Education Professions Development	(0.8)
Other	(2.4)
Other HEW Programs	37.3
National Institutes of Health	(18.5)
Health Resources Administration	(7.7)
Social Security Survivors, Educational Benefits	(6.6)
Other	(4.4)
Other Agencies	39.8
Action: Peace Corps, Vista, University Year for Action	(1.1)
Agricultural Research and Extension	(4.4)
Veterans' Education and Training	(24.7)
National Science Foundation	(6.1)
Other	(3.5)

Source: "Higher Education's Share of U.S. Budgets," *Chronicle of Higher Education,* 9 (February 10, 1975), p. 6. Total funds = $9,356,371,000.

It will be noted that the largest single expenditure item is veterans' education and training, which constituted 24.7 percent of the federal outlay in 1973-74. Note also that among the Office of Education funding items, the largest was for student assistance, 17.8 percent of the total.

318

Thus, we have the general picture of federal funding through fiscal 1974. While it would be possible to refer to many other analyses of federal funding, it would seem more appropriate for our concerns in this chapter to turn to the issues that currently have surfaced regarding federal funding.

Schrader points out that, among the problems that have arisen in the increasing federal support of higher education, one of the greater difficulties has been created by a system that centers on support of individual research projects. In effect, the federal government has been buying scientific ideas on a piecemeal basis rather than investing in the educational process, so that "(1) it has encouraged the brilliant minds in the scientific laboratories to concentrate on research and to dissociate themselves from the students; and (2) it has allowed the military to extend its dominance over large areas of university thinking through mission-oriented research projects." While Schrader's judgment might be debated on both points, it is worthwhile noting some of the other effects that he sees in increased federal financing of higher education. These include instability, where cutbacks and shifts in funds affect individuals and institutions; confusion over accountability, where researchers get caught between the institution and the funding agency; loss of control on the part of the institutions; unevenness of support; mismatch between the traditional departmental structure of the institution and the social objectives of the federal agencies; instability of income for the institution; lack of focus, since there is no single federal focus of concern; and loss of integrity, where colleges and universities are pressured into goal-oriented research that could threaten the integrity of the basic institutional character.[172] Yet, even if these are the disadvantages, and there are many who would agree with Schrader, the fact of federal support, as political and uneven as it may be, seems to be with us.

In one of the first of the Carnegie Commission reports, Ronald Wolk discussed five alternative methods of federal funding: categorical aid, aid to students, grants to institutions, tax relief, and revenue sharing.[173] Most of the federal support in the past has been in the form of categorical aid, through grants, contracts, or loans in support of a specific project or goal. Wolk contended that virtually all of the aid in 1967 could be described as categorical aid, in the sense that the federal government had designated the funds to be spent in certain areas which were deemed to be of national concern;

319

there was no "completely unrestricted or undesignated support to colleges and universities." As we have already noted, the major portion of the categorical aid was in the form of research grants. (Wolk also listed funds for facilities as a form of categorical aid.)

The second form of support, aid to students, had really begun with the GI Bill in 1944, and by 1967 additional student-aid programs had been developed. In 1958 the National Defense Education Act provided for undergraduate student loans and graduate fellowships and loans. The federal government provided 90 cents for every dollar loaned, and the institution contributed 10 cents. The loans included a forgiveness feature if students became teachers. The Higher Education Act of 1965, Title IV, provided the first federal scholarships for undergraduates through the Economic Opportunity Grants, under which needy qualified students could receive $200 to $800 in the freshman year and $200 to $1,000 each succeeding year, if the student remained in the upper half of his class. This same act also provided grants to institutions to assist in college work-study programs for students who needed part-time work in order to continue their education. The legislation provided that the government would pay 90 percent of the wages and the institution would pay 10 percent initially, with the federal share decreasing to 75 percent in 1967-68, but this provision was subsequently delayed. The act also introduced the guaranteed loans for college students, under which the federal government would pay 6 percent interest on the loan during the time the student was in college and 3 percent during the repayment period.

Wolk observed that in one sense institutions were already receiving aid in the form of institutional grants. The National Defense Graduate Fellowships and funds awarded by other federal agencies generally carried with them an institutional supplement to offset tuition and educational costs. Also, the National Science Foundation awarded grants under several different programs. Title III of the Higher Education Act of 1965 authorized grants to developing institutions. Since the late 1960s there have been a number of proposals for additional direct assistance to institutions. Among them, the Miller Bill sought to provide funds for advancing science by providing institutional grants based on a formula related to an institution's participation in basic research, the number of high school graduates in the state, and the number of advanced

320

degrees awarded by the institution. In general, however, little momentum has been developed in favor of institutional grants.

In the fourth area, tax relief, Wolk notes that colleges and universities have benefitted from tax laws over the years. As nonprofit educational institutions, they generally do not pay property taxes, income taxes, or capital gains on their investments. Institutions have also benefitted from tax allowances for philanthropic contributions that permit individuals to make deductible gifts. There have been a number of proposals to expand tax benefits by granting relief directly to parents, allowing them to claim extra person exemptions or increased standard exemptions or to claim tax credits for educational expenses up to a certain maximum.

Under revenue sharing Wolk notes that pressure had been building for returning to the states significant portions of the national revenue to enable them to meet their governmental responsibilities. Some action has been taken in this direction, but revenue sharing as a significant element in aiding higher education is yet to be developed.

Wolk's volume was issued as a discussion piece, to raise some of the issues relating to federal funding of higher education. The first in the series of Carnegie reports on the subject was issued shortly after. In that report and a supplement issued two years later, the commission advocated massive increases in federal support, from $3.5 billion in 1967-68 to $13 billion in 1976-77.[174] There were some differences in the items included between the original report and the 1970 supplement, but both placed heavy emphasis upon directing federal funds through student-aid programs. In the original proposal it was recommended that slightly under one-third of the federal aid be in student-aid programs; almost as much in research; approximately one-fourth in cost-of-education supplements; and the remainder in construction, a foundation for the development of higher education, and special programs. The 1970 supplement recommended an increased proportion going to student-aid funds, nearly 40 percent; somewhat of a reduction in research; and approximately the same in cost-of-education supplements.[175]

It was through the cost-of-education supplements that the Carnegie Commission recommended direct grants, based on the number of federal grant holders enrolled. The commission also advocated construction grants and special purpose grants—increased funding of aid to developing institutions, library support, and international studies.

The Carnegie Commission took the position that "first priority should be given in achieving equality of educational opportunity" and that such a goal was best to be achieved by eliminating barriers to equal access to higher education and to progress within higher educational institutions. One of the proposals for student aid included a recommendation for a federal contingent-loan program whereby students would repay federal loans through a fixed percentage of their incomes. Earlier, a panel headed by Professor J. Zacharias of M.I.T. had proposed the development of an Educational Opportunity Bank.[176] The so-called Zacharias Plan was not well received, but a report from the Secretary's Office of the Department of Health, Education, and Welfare proposed a National Student Loan Bank, in which the repayment for long-term loans would be at a fixed schedule rather than dependent upon the individual's income.[177]

In 1972 the Carnegie Commission developed a special set of proposals dealing with general institutional support. In advancing the arguments for such support, the commission reiterated its earlier stand that basic support and responsibility for higher education should remain with the states and private initiative, that students should be given maximum freedom in choosing institutions to attend, that federal aid should not encourage states and private sources to reduce their support, and that the autonomy of institutions should be preserved.

The 1972 Carnegie report suggested six approaches to institutional support, all related in some way to the Equal Opportunity Grants that had been established under the Higher Education Act of 1965. The commission had already advocated increased funding of the Educational Opportunity Grants. Among the arguments advanced for institutional grants were the following: (1) additional operating funds based on those received from state and private sources were necessary to improve and/or maintain the quality of instruction; (2) under the categorical aid programs, many colleges were bypassed, and institutional grants would provide broader assistance to institutions worthy of support; (3) certain levels and types of educational programs essential nationally could be assisted in direct grants; (4) direct grants would encourage educational innovation.[178]

In its next report, issued in 1973 as a comprehensive review of financing policies, the Carnegie Commission came out even more clearly for what it called a "redistribution in total governmental costs from the states and localities to the Federal Government." It took the position that the federal government has a larger and more expansible income, that it has a special interest in and responsibility for providing equality of opportunity, and that the federal government has special responsibilities for basic research.[179] Estimating that the federal share of total governmental costs (federal, state, and local) in 1973 was just under 43 percent, the commission urged that by 1983 the federal share be at the 50 percent level. The Higher Education Act of 1972 provided for Basic Opportunity Grants, and the commission, while recognizing the new program as "a major step in the direction of removing financial obstacles to access to college," asked for full funding of the program and raising of the ceiling (then $1,400) on the grants. The Carnegie Council on Policy Studies in Higher Education, a successor to the commission, in one of its first reports reiterated the position that the federal government should provide 50 percent of all public funds for higher education.[180]

The report from the Office of the Secretary of HEW that proposed the National Student Loan Bank pointed up that the major issue in federal aid to higher education revolved around the relative emphasis that should be given to student aid versus institutional aid. Both types of aid are needed and it is unlikely that the federal government would limit itself to one or the other. However, the particular emphasis given to student aid or institutional aid would depend on the objectives set for higher education. If the emphasis is on improving accessibility to higher learning, then student aid becomes a primary medium. Institutional aid reflects more concern with the quality of higher education per se.[181] The report emphasized two major commitments for federal policy, the promotion of equality of opportunity and the strengthening of graduate education and research. In both instances, the report called for aid to students rather than to institutions, although it also suggested a flexible program of institutional-development grants, administered by the National Science Foundation, the National Institutes of Health, the Office of Education, and the

National Foundation on the Arts and the Humanities. In addition, it recommended that the cost-of-education allowances for federal graduate fellowships should be increased.

The Committee for Economic Development in late 1973 also emphasized that the federal government should make grants to students and recommended a decrease in categorical institutional aid from the federal government and a significant increase in aid to students.[182] The committee called for more efficiency in the management of institutions and an increase in the tuition paid by students in public institutions.

The National Commission on the Financing of Postsecondary Education, also reporting in late 1973, did not make a specific recommendation on funding patterns, but analyzed the implications of eight different financing plans, ranging from shifting the responsibility of financing postsecondary education from public and private sources to students and parents to increasing in significant ways public aid through providing greater assistance to students.[183]

Perhaps the most comprehensive review of the positions in current debate over federal financing was made by Howard R. Bowen at the annual meeting of the Association of American Colleges in January 1974. Bowen noted that in the late sixties considerable attention was given to the possibility of direct institutional grants from the federal government. In 1967 and 1968 virtually all of the major institutional associations went on record favoring institutional grants, and the "common plea was to retain all the then existing forms of federal aid and add institutional grants—the new money to be distributed according to formulas yet to be devised." Bowen observed:

> The proposal for federal institutional grants was based on three tacit assumptions. One was that expenditures would continue to rise rapidly because of growing enrollments and rising costs. Another was that, though federal categorical aid was desirable, it did little to meet the basic operating costs of institutions and unrestricted funds were needed as well. The third assumption was that the steady rise of tuitions would be on principle socially harmful.[184]

Within this framework, the search then began for suitable formulas to be used for distributing federal aid.

Within the next few years, however, according to Bowen, the focus began to shift from general institutional aid to establishing as the major goal for new federal programs the encouragement of needy and lower-middle-income students to attend college. The principle was clearly expressed in the Higher Education Amendments of 1972. During the early 1970s, according to Bowen, three proposals emerged: (1) higher education could and should be more efficient, and the continuing increase in cost should be slowed down; (2) the tuition differential between public and private institutions should be decreased and support of public colleges and universities should come relatively more from tuition and relatively less from taxes; (3) long-term loans of substantial amounts should be employed for financing students.[185]

Most recently, according to Bowen, the new focus has been sharpened by six reports, the report of the Committee on Economic Development, the report of the National Commission on the Financing of Postsecondary Education, two Carnegie Commission reports, the report of the National Board on Graduate Education, and the second Newman report. In summarizing the six reports, he found the following emphases: (1) the efficiency of higher education should be improved; (2) tuition in public institutions should be raised to perhaps a third or even half of instructional costs; (3) access should be available to all qualified students, and student aid should be extended in the form of grants to low income students and loans to low and middle income students; (4) loans should become a more prominent part of the student-aid program and practical long-term loan programs should be invented and adequate capital to fund them should be raised; (5) student aid should be portable; (6) private institutions should be assisted by any of several types of tuition offsets, which would have the effect of narrowing the tuition gap, and possibly by institutional grants; (7) tax incentives for charitable giving should be strengthened; (8) federal fellowships and traineeships for graduate students should be restored at least in part, and basic research should be supported at rising levels; (9) ways of financing life-long and recurring education should be developed.[186]

In 1971 the American College Testing Program published the results of an invitational seminar held the previous year in

325

Washington, D.C. In reflecting on the various papers, one commentator at the seminar argued that at that time the strongest political pressure on behalf of aiding higher education in Washington favored increased funding of existing programs, and that while there was some support for general aid, it probably did not have the adequate political support to establish any programs.[187] Another commentator noted that, although most persons seemed to favor a continuation of federal aid to students with a sizable grant program, "the major obstacle to the development of a federal strategy for aiding higher education was found to be the division that exists in the relative emphasis to be given to direct institutional aid and loans to students."[188] And while direct institutional aid might enable institutions to hold the line on tuition and provide a larger measure of autonomy, it was also viewed as a relatively expensive method of providing federal assistance in that it aided those who could pay as well as those who were unable to do so.

While Bowen's summary at the meeting of the AAC included references to the report of the Newman task force, it is worth singling out some of the specific recommendations of the task force report on "National Policy and Higher Education." The task force held that the principal role of the federal government in postsecondary education lies in: (1) preserving an open society and the conditions necessary for a free competition of ideas; (2) overcoming inequities facing specific individuals and groups; and (3) supporting research, development, and other "strategic interventions" of the type that no other level of government can afford. For assisting in preserving an open society and free competition, the Newman panel called for matching federal funds for state scholarship and fellowship programs and partial support for a state fund for project grants to support innovative educational programs in public and private institutions. In support of equalizing educational opportunities, the group called for support of new approaches to education in combination with continued student aid. The report also called for the federal government to serve as a catalyst and source of leadership for reform and innovation.[189]

While, as the previous references have indicated, the mood in Washington seems to have shifted from advocating general institutional support to favoring student support, a series of actions in Washington during mid- and late 1974 presents an interesting picture. In May, eight higher educational associations urged

Congress to appropriate at least $200 million in general aid during 1974-75. The request was included in a $2.7 billion "counter budget" presented to the House of Representatives subcommittee handling appropriations for the Department of Health, Education, and Welfare. The eight associations involved were: American Council on Education, American Association of Community and Junior Colleges, American Association of State Colleges and Universities, Association of American Colleges, Association of American Universities, National Association of State Universities and Land-Grant Colleges, National Catholic Educational Association, and National Council of Independent Colleges and Universities.[190] By June, however, the possibilities for enacting legislation for direct aid to colleges and universities seemed fairly remote.

The Higher Education Amendments of 1972 had adopted the principle of giving funds to institutions on the basis of the number of students receiving federal aid enrolled in those institutions, but no funds had been appropriated for the program. When, in June, college administrators pressed for providing funds for direct aid to colleges, they were greeted with "a cool reception," and Representative James G. O'Hara, chairman of the House Special Subcommittee on Education, told the educators that there "seems to be rather a remote possibility of funding that program in the near future" and went on to say that he was dubious about institutional aid.[191]

In August, however, two members of the Senate Appropriations Committee, Senator Robert C. Byrd and Senator Warren G. Magnuson, proposed that $50 million be added to the appropriations bill for the Department of Health, Education, and Welfare for the current fiscal year. Senator Byrd pointed out that the funds would provide some measure of relief to both public and private institutions, based on the amount of federal support to students enrolled in the institutions.[192] Subsequently, although the Senate subcommittee recommended $50 million more for the Department of Health, Education, and Welfare than had been recommended by the House, the recommendation for institutional-aid grants was rejected by the Senate Appropriations Subcommittee.[193] Yet, apparently, the idea of institutional aid was still alive, and the Higher Education Amendments of 1972 provided at least some basis for future consideration.

327

Later in 1974 Senator Lloyd Bentsen of Texas announced that he would sponsor a proposal to give taxpayers a tax credit on money they saved for their children's or their own post-high-school education. His proposal would relate tax credits to money placed in special "educational savings plans." According to his proposal, a taxpayer could contribute up to $250 annually to such savings plans for every dependent and subtract 20 percent of that contribution from his federal income tax.[194]

Voucher systems have also been proposed both at the state and federal levels. In an article in *Change* magazine in October 1973, Henry Levin contended that the pattern of public funding of higher education was moving toward a drastic revision, that the greatest share of public support for colleges and universities had been in the past granted directly from federal and state governments to the institutions themselves but that in the future the major share of such funds would be given to students to use at the college or university of their choice. We have already noted the apparent swing of the federal government to various types of student-aid programs, but Levin refers to the voucher system as a possible means of increasing student aid. To him, the Higher Education Amendments of 1972, with a provision for the Basic Educational Opportunity Grants of up to $1,400 per year, were not unlike the movement in the state of Ohio for using a loan program to replace much of the present public support of higher education and the Wisconsin plan for the combination grant-loan program.[195]

Referring also to the National Commission on Postsecondary Education and the 1973 report of the Committee on Economic Development, Levin found reflected in the various plans of the commission a substantial shift from institutional support to student funding. The several plans emphasized providing students with grants or loans which could be applied to tuition and other costs of attending either public or private institutions. Levin contended that such an approach bore similarities to the much discussed educational voucher system that had been suggested for elementary and secondary schools. The rest of his article was given to weighing the impact of a voucher system, which he apparently sees in one form or another as a distinct possibility in the future.[196]

In September 1973 a panel of the President's Science Advisory Committee recommended that young people at the age of 16 be given educational vouchers equivalent to the average cost of four years of college. The vouchers would be usable for vocational training as well as higher education and could be used at any time of life following the completion of compulsory education at age 16. The committee argued that an educational voucher system would "equalize the subsidy to all youth that now goes only to those who attend college" and would provide a variety of options for young people not presently available.[197] While the Office of Economic Opportunity in 1971-72 provided preplanning grants to three school systems for a preliminary design of an educational voucher system at the elementary and secondary levels, the voucher system has not gained great headway either at the elementary and secondary level or in postsecondary education.

Many different proposals continue to emerge, but the basic orientation as we enter the last half of the decade of the 1970s seems to lie in finding the most effective way of providing student aid. Representative James G. O'Hara of Michigan, who took over the House of Representatives' Higher Education Subcommittee in 1973, has emerged as one of the leading spokesmen for maintaining low tuition and providing student aid. A report in the *Chronicle of Higher Education* in January 1974 indicated that O'Hara was giving top priority to student aid,[198] and in late 1974 *Change* magazine referred to his continuing efforts to emphasize low tuition and student aid. In his address to the American Council on Education in October 1974 O'Hara said that he would "seek to construct a student aid system that recognizes that low tuition has done more for improved popular access to postsecondary education than all the student aid programs put together. I will certainly give no aid and comfort to a system which tacitly encourages the raising of tuitions as a means of maximizing an institution's piece of the federal pie."[199]

Other Sources of Income

Endowment income has provided a decreasing proportion of the Educational and General income over the years, decreasing from 17.4 percent in 1909-10 to less than 3 percent in 1969-70. William Bowen's review of the financing of major private universities indicated that for Chicago, Princeton, and Vanderbilt, whereas endowment income constituted 43.5 percent of their Educational and General income in 1924-25, it had fallen to 13.4 percent of their

329

income in 1965-66; and for all private universities the shift was from 13 percent in 1955-56 to 8.8 percent in 1963-64.[200]

June O'Neill's analysis shows the decrease in the proportion that endowment earnings constitute of Educational and General funds to be even more striking. On the basis of her analysis, endowment earnings constituted 13.5 percent of the income for all institutions in 1939-40, but this had dropped to 2.8 percent in 1967-68. For private institutions, the decrease was from 25.2 percent in 1939-40 to 6.6 percent in 1967-68.[201]

In June 1974 a preliminary report from the National Center for Educational Statistics indicated that total dollar amount in endowment funds of the nation's colleges and universities had decreased slightly, by 1.1 percent, during 1972-73. While the bulk of the endowment funds is still with private colleges and universities, $12.6 billion in 1973 in comparison with $2.5 billion for public institutions, the funds for private colleges and universities had decreased by 1.6 percent while those for public institutions had increased by 2 percent, giving an overall decrease of 1.1 percent.[202]

Jack Magarrell reported in late 1974 on another facet of the shrinking endowment fund problem. Beginning in the late 1960s a growing number of higher educational institutions adopted a "total return" approach to investment and spending of endowment funds. Under the total-return concept, increases in stock value were viewed as spendable income, and such "new" funds provided a financial boost for hard-pressed institutions. With declining stock prices rather than increasing stock values, however, the idea of total return is being reexamined. The Ford Foundation had earlier (in 1969) sparked interest in the total-return approach through two reports on college investment policies.[203]

While endowment funds will continue to be significant for some institutions, it is highly unlikely that such funds will provide significant additional income for institutions in general. This by no means suggests that endowment funds are inconsequential, but it does suggest building of endowment as such is not likely to provide a large measure of increased funding for current needs of higher educational institutions. Endowment perhaps becomes a reserve or a basis for funding special projects that could not be carried by other current income.

Gifts and grants from private sources constituted approximately 6 percent of the Educational and General income in the early 1970s. Using the gross data reported in the periodic studies issued by the U.S. Office of Education, one can see an increase in that proportion through the 1950s and a slight decrease in the 1960s. Table 13 shows the way in which the gifts and grants from private sources have changed as a percentage of Educational and General income.

Table 13

Gifts and Grants from Private Sources as Percentage of Educational and General Income

Year	Gifts and Grants as Percentage of E. and G. Income
1909-10	4.85
1919-20	4.35
1929-30	5.35
1939-40	7.05
1949-50	6.40
1959-60	8.05
1963-64	7.05
1967-68	6.15
1969-70	6.07

Source: Based on data reported in annual issues of *Financial Statistics of Institutions of Higher Education: Current Fund Revenues and Expenditures,* issued by the Department of Health, Education, and Welfare, and *Higher Education Finances: Selected Trend and Summary Data,* periodically issued by the same agency.

The more refined calculations of O'Neill, although for a shorter period of time, indicate the same general trend. In 1939-40, gifts and grants from private sources constituted 7.7 percent of Educational and General income for all institutions, increased to 8.8 percent in 1953-54, began to decrease slightly during the late 1950s, and had dropped to 6.4 percent in 1967-68. For private institutions, the change was from 13.8 percent in 1939-40, up to 16.6 percent in 1953-54, decreasing during the rest of the 1950's and dropping to 12.7 percent in 1967-68.[204]

It should be noted that while the data above show a decrease in the *proportion* that gifts from private sources constitute of the Educational and General income, the dollar amounts contributed each year had been increasing more or less regularly until 1969-70. In 1969-70 there was a decrease not only in the proportion that private gifts constituted of Educational and General income, but there was also a dollar decrease. The Council for Financial Aid to Education reported that the income from gifts and grants for 1969-70 was $20 million less than for the previous year. This was contrasted with an estimated 15 percent gain the previous year. The picture was a mixed one, since support for private four-year institutions dropped the greatest amount, while support for public four-year institutions rose by almost 17 percent.[205]

The following year, however, the situation changed, and gifts from private sources reached a new high of $1.86 billion for 1970-71. The major source for the growth was the increase in giving by alumni and by "non-alumni individuals." Yet, within this overall increase, giving from business corporations declined, the first time that this segment had contributed less than in a preceding year over a period of some 12 years. Between 1956-68, corporate contributions to education had increased on an average of 10.8 percent a year.[206] The sources of giving have shifted from year to year. In 1972, based on a review of the experience of 1970-71, the prediction was for substantial increases in coming years from foundations and bequests.[207] The following year the total from bequests was down, while foundations, as a matter of fact, did raise grants by 25 percent.[208]

For 1972-73 private giving to public four-year colleges was also up significantly, 20 percent over the previous year; the largest sources of gifts were individual friends of the institutions and parents of students.

In the fall of 1974, the situation among the foundations, earlier expected to provide a major source of increased giving, was far from optimistic. In September 1974 Jack Magarrell wrote that foundation funds "have been caught in the stock-market dive, just when higher education's needs for foundation support are increasing rapidly."[209] Carnegie assets had dropped to $222 million, down from $342 million a year ago. The assets of the Rockefeller Foundation valued at $840 million at the end of 1973, had fallen in nine months to less than $600 million, and the Ford Foundation assets had dropped from $3 billion to $2 billion. Magarrell reported that the situation was viewed in such a serious light that McGeorge Bundy, president of the Ford Foundation, had asked the foundation's trustees to consider the possibility of dissolving the foundation and distributing the assets.

While the assets were down, the earnings of the foundations had remained fairly stable, but since many foundations during the years of rising stock market prices used some of their capital gains for grants, they found themselves in a position of needing to sell stocks to raise the same amount of money, which further reduced their shrinking assets. The Ford Foundation indicated that it would be cutting back on its grants, from a current fiscal year's budget of $208 million to a goal of $100 million for the fiscal year ending September 30, 1978.[210] Most of the foundations, however, were holding firm, and the Carnegie Corporation even suggested that it would try to be a little more generous, in spite of the stock market situation.

Balancing the cutbacks or a steady state in foundation giving may be a predicted increase in corporate support during 1973-74. At least that was the tentative conclusion of the Council for Financial Aid to Education in late 1974. The optimism was based on an informal survey among a sample of leading companies in which it appeared that, in spite of the stock market situation, profits had been increasing. On the basis of past experience in relating profits to contributions, the council estimated that gifts from business could reach more than $500 million in 1973-74, $75 million above the contributions for 1972-73.[211] The president of the American Council on Education, Roger Heyns, was less than convinced by the projections of the Council for Financial Aid to Education, as he observed that, in the presence of rapid inflation, "corporations may not continue to maintain their traditional relationships between profits and charitable giving." When the reports were in, private gifts for 1973-74 remained at the same level as for 1972-73; there was no spectacular increase.[212]

And at least one businessman, David Packard, chairman of the board of Hewlett-Packard Company and former deputy secretary of defense, was arguing that corporations should no longer make unrestricted gifts to private colleges and universities. Maintaining that universities harbor faculty members and students hostile to corporate interests, he asked corporations to focus money and energy on schools and departments that are strong and that "contribute in some specific way to our individual companies or to the general welfare of our free enterprise system."[213] He did not gain a large following, and Allen Pifer, president of the Carnegie Corporation, and McGeorge Bundy, president of the Ford Foundation, in particular criticized Packard's position.

Toward the close of 1974, another report in the *Chronicle of Higher Education* pointed out that American universities are apparently entering the business of seeking funds abroad. It was reported that American institutions were making contacts in Tokyo and Teheran, and an official of the Council for Financial Aid to Education indicated that the organization was trying to find a way to make clear to the oil-rich countries of the Middle East and other countries that send students to the United States that paying tuition is not enough, that the governments and businesses have a responsibility to support the institutions that supply or educate personnel. The story reports in particular on the activities of the University of Michigan, Stanford University, and Yale.[214]

An early 1975 issue of the *Wall Street Journal* reported how a number of smaller colleges offering predominately liberal arts programs have branched out into career education. Lambuth College in Tennessee has introduced a project in cooperation with Holiday Inns. Cazenovia College was almost ready to close in the spring of 1974, but has now increased enrollment by branching out into courses for investment managers, horse breeders, and is even renting the college playhouse to a commercial movie-theater owner. Marymount Manhattan College teaches technical writing, English composition, and other topics on the premises of Pfizer, Inc., the New York pharmaceutical firm. LaVerne College in California operates dozens of continuing education centers from Hawaii to Florida. Most of the colleges indicate that a move into career education represents a permanent change in the orientation of the school.[215]

Not only are colleges taking other approaches to the curriculum in order to compete in the market place, but some institutions have moved into a broad range of business operations. *U.S. News and World Report,* in commenting on the development, says:

Colleges and universities, adjusting to an unprecedented financial bind, are coming up with new ways to produce more income from land, buildings and other campus facilities.

Many institutions have developed programs that pay off not only in money but in improved community relations.

Some are opening their libraries, restaurants, bookstores and recreational rooms to the public for a modest fee.

Others are transforming campuses into low-cost summer resorts between school terms.[216]

Universities are sharing stadiums with other groups. A number of colleges are forming subsidiary corporations to invest college funds in revenue-generating property. For example, Florida Institute of Technology in Melbourne has established a firm called University Enterprises, Inc., to market spin-offs from research and development at the institute. Knox College in Illinois in 1969 established several corporations to administer an investment program in commercial property, a resort complex in Utah, and a racetrack, the latter of which has been sold. Hood College was reported to be studying the feasibility of a $7 million facility that would combine housing for students and commercial offices and apartments for rental to the general public. Mankato State College in Minnesota and the University of Alabama, Tuscaloosa, have leased entire dormitories to organizations engaged in mental rehabilitation. These are just a sample of the programs underway. From another source, we learn that Purdue University has turned used computer cards into a source of income.[217]

Reducing Expenditures

As we have already noted, any apparent turnaround in financing of higher education observed by Cheit and others appeared to be less a matter of securing new sources of income and more a matter of reducing expenditures. Howard Bowen's assessment of the current state of the debate over financing higher education, referred to earlier, noted that during 1973 one of the top concerns was that the efficiency of higher education be improved. It is worth noting,

335

however, that in his summary eight of the concerns related to increasing income and only one to improving efficiency.[218]

There are some who have suggested that maximum economies have already been achieved and that very little in the way of reduction can be accomplished. The Reverend Robert J. Henley, president of Georgetown University, speaking to the Association for Institution Research in May 1974, contended that another financial crunch for private education was on the way—in the first phase of the financial crisis most institutions had already put their instructional budgets through the wringer, and there simply was very little more in the way of economy that could be achieved.[219]

The answer is probably at some point between, namely that economies are still possible, but there are limits to the economies that can be effected. As the Carnegie Commission report on more effective use of resources indicates, "higher education must work on both sides of the equation—more money and more effective use of it. It should both obtain the money it really needs and maximize its output from this money."[220] That particular report documents the way in which the unit cost, cost per student, has considerably increased in higher education. Referring to data compiled by June O'Neill, the report shows that educational cost per credit-hour has consistently increased more rapidly than the consumer price index from 1953-54 to 1966-67. For this period of time as a whole, educational cost rose at an annual average rate of 3.5 percent, as compared with the rate of 1.6 percent for the consumer price index, a difference of 1.9 percentage points. And among private higher educational institutions the rate was 4.8 percent, or 3.2 percentage points more than the consumer price index. The difference in behavior of cost between public and private institutions was particularly pronounced for the universities.[221] The commission report goes on to show differences between upper division and lower division work and between graduate and undergraduate work, with the highest average cost per student being considerably higher at the graduate level.

An earlier report issued under the auspices of the Carnegie Commission had documented the same phenomenon. Bowen's study of *The Economics of the Major Private Universities* had shown that direct cost per student had increased more rapidly than the economy-wide cost index, except during the wartime inflation years of 1915-20 and 1940-48. In the "normal," peacetime periods, Bowen observed that

> the cost per student rose substantially more than the economy-wide cost index. Indeed, the remarkable thing about our results from these three peace-time periods is that the numerical values of the compound growth rate for both our economy-wide cost index and our index of cost per student are so similar—the former ranging from 1.5 to 2.2 percent per annum, and the latter ranging from 7.5 to 8.1 percent per annum.[222]

Other economists had provided similar documentation, and although the different reports vary somewhat in describing the percentage increases in student cost, all show that student costs have grown more rapidly than the consumer price index. Some have argued that the increase in cost is endemic to the educational process. Whereas in industry the output per man hour during the twentieth century has gone up, in education the output, if anything, has decreased. Higher educational institutions have benefited from some of the technological innovations, but the trend has been toward lowering teaching loads, enriching programs, multiplying activities. Education participates in the general category of industry in which increases in productivity come more slowly than in the economy as a whole and in which the cost per unit may be expected to increase more than costs in general.

While this line of reasoning may have been acceptable in the past, it is being challenged currently, and the Carnegie Commission, among others, has not only called for more efficiency but has contended that more efficiency is possible. The commission argues that two general procedures are open: (1) reducing the total number of years of student training and (2) reducing the cost per student hour. It has contended that by 1980 it would be possible to reduce expenditures by 10 percent by decreasing the length of students' time in college and by another 10 percent in a variety of other ways.[223]

In detailing its argument in favor of cost reduction, the commission contends that the principal sources of savings include the following: (1) reducing the number of students by accelerating programs and reducing the number of reluctant attenders; and (2) making more effective use of resources in relation to students in

337

attendance by halting the creation of new Ph.D. programs, achieving minimum effective size for campuses now below that size, moving toward year-round operation, cautiously raising the student-faculty ratio, reexamining the faculty teaching load, improving management by better selection and training of middle management, creating more alternative programs off-campus, and establishing consortia among institutions.[224] It argues against what it considers unwise though tempting short-run economies such as reducing necessary maintenance, reducing library expenditures for new books and journals, and failing to increase student aid as tuition and fees increase. The Carnegie Commission also calls for improving the budget-making process by more effective analysis and programming.[225]

The themes in the Carnegie Commission report have been expressed in various ways and with different emphases in virtually all of the other approaches to cost-cutting. Sidney Tickton, who more than a decade earlier had popularized long-term budget projections in the Ashford College case, continues to emphasize the necessity for more effective planning.[226] In an article in *Compact,* the journal of the Education Commission of the States, Tickton points out that there are basically only two approaches to improving the financial conditions, to increase income and to hold down costs. To cut or hold down cost can be done primarily through higher student-faculty ratios and more efficient use of space, but neither of these approaches have had much impact, Tickton notes, because

> faculties have wanted lower faculty-student ratios. [They claim] lower ratios means better quality education, though this certainly is a matter for debate. . . . No one anywhere really has wanted better use of space. Presidents, fund raisers, donors, government officials have all wanted buildings for every purpose at every location—and without any real regard for the future cost or amortization of plant.[227]

He argues, however, that regardless of past attitudes, current pressures are forcing institutions to deal with both student-faculty ratios and more efficient use of space.

The plea for more effective planning may be found in a score of reports. James Harvey summarizes a number of the reports on institutional planning available through March 1971.[228] The Ohio

338

Board of Regents under its Management Improvement Program during the 1971-73 biennium developed a very detailed planning manual,[229] distributed widely by the Management Division of the Academy for Educational Development. The Management Division of AED has since 1971 distributed a number of publications relating to planning procedures, beginning with one that listed 148 ways for colleges and universities to meet the financial pinch.[230] In 1972 it distributed an adaption of Paul C. Reinert's essay on survival for private higher education, *To Turn the Tide*. Rienert's essay called for efforts to begin within the institution and called upon the president to take initiative.[231]

Planning is emphasized heavily in the report of the National Commission on the Financing of Postsecondary Education. One of the concluding chapters of that report is directed toward developing better procedures for institutional costing and data reporting. The commission noted improved institutional accountability as one of its objectives: "institutions of postsecondary education should use financial and other resources efficiently and effectively and employ procedures that enable those who provide the resources to determine whether those resources are being used to achieve desired outcomes."[232]

Howard Bowen and Gordon Douglass have taken the planning procedure another step by making a detailed analysis of cost and outputs of instruction at a hypothetical small liberal arts college.[233] Charles Benson and Harold Hodgkinson have also developed a series of proposals for improving efficiency in colleges and universities. Subtitling their volume "New Strategies for Financing Social Objectives," they have analyzed the need for skilled manpower and ways of allocating resources—including a reference to Planning Programming Budgeting Systems and a review of financing patterns. One chapter deals more particularly with ways of achieving efficiencies and summarizes the variety of approaches that have been used to achieve more efficient planning and programming.[234]

Earl Cheit's second look at the new depression in higher education contains summaries of reports from the 41 institutions included in his original study. Cheit observed that, with the growing awareness of the cost-income squeeze, institutions began to develop new managerial practices and organizational relationships. The

339

short-term consequence of this development was a sharp reduction in the rate of growth of the institutions' expenditures. But he suggested that this development led to a longer-term consequence:

> Questions of money eventually lead to questions of purpose, and these new management practices and organizational relationships form the evolving system by which schools are making the transition from money questions to purpose questions. The additional consequence of these new practices and relationships, therefore, is the development of new administrative and faculty standards of judgment about educational quality and purpose.[235]

He observed that although the new financial stability was fragile and might prove to be short run, it nevertheless was a significant achievement. He found that during the intervening two years between the original study and the review, virtually all of the institutions had come to an increased campus-wide awareness of rising costs and their implications; all but five of the institutions reported that faculty, students, and staff members had become more aware of costs. Faculty and staff had become more alert to the realities of the cash flow within the organization. And while there was some reduction in expectation regarding future developments, even some concern that innovation might be restricted, there was more of a climate open to future change. There was also more of an acceptance of the idea of a "managed institution."[236]

Some 30 of the 41 institutions had begun to develop overall strategies for better management. More attention was being given to the reduction of costs. Indeed, Cheit found that "the reduction of expenditure growth is now as central, or more central, to administrative outlook than increasing income."[237] With regard to cost-cutting, it was found that appeals for voluntary efforts by operating units were not particularly effective, that administrative decision was needed. In the process of cutting cost, however, it was found that administration cannot appear to act arbitrarily, that across-the-board cuts were generally ineffective and that better approaches were deferring, freezing, cutting, pooling various activities, better purchasing, more efficient scheduling, and improved food handling and dormitory management.

Cheit also found some change in the role of the administration. He suggests that in the recent past a new program was the product of

340

faculty initiative for the most part, but that, as administrators have taken on more of the managerial role, their task has been to provide in advance the conditions that make operations and new programs possible. The administrator is now becoming a key element in deciding whether, when, and on what terms change is possible.[238] This also leads to concern on the part of the faculty concerning their role, and Cheit observed the establishment in many institutions of faculty-staff committees designed to assure participation in planning and budgeting.

The Committee for Economic Development, in its statement on the management of financing colleges issued in late 1973, called for colleges and universities to employ more effective management procedures and suggested that colleges might move toward using management principles and techniques that have proved effective in business and government.[239] A series of articles in the *Journal of Higher Education* in January 1974 explored some of these management procedures, and individual authors argued both for and against some of the applications generally being advocated.[240] Harold Howe II, however, the Ford Foundation's vice president for education and research in speaking to the Association for Institutional Research in May 1974, warned that the problem-solving power of new management techniques had been oversold, and one of the most limiting aspects had been in the area of values.[241] And at a meeting sponsored by the Educational Testing Service, another foundation executive warned that it was not "unreasonable to fear that higher education will buy the productivity of instructional technology by selling part of its soul" and urged against ignoring human qualities in higher education in the search for greater efficiency.[242]

There is a host of manuals on new approaches to budgeting and management. It is abundantly clear that techniques are readily available for achieving more efficient use of resources and space. Most of the handbooks, however, will not be very helpful to institutions if the staff attempts to apply the bewildering array of suggestions directly. As much as anything, it seems, there is need for the development of a climate that accepts an institution as a managed enterprise and that provides the machinery whereby those affected can participate in some critical decisions relating to expenditures. In this context, the development of a series of three- to five-year projections becomes critical to maintaining a sense of having some control of, rather than being controlled by, circumstances.

The Dean's Next Moves

To Dean Neumann one must say that the decision to establish an advisory committee on budget, whatever his original motives might have been, was sound. The committee can now be of considerable importance in communicating to the faculty as a whole the best judgment as to what the conditions facing the university are. The committee can also examine ways of working within the new budget limitations. What Dean Neumann and the committee need at this point is a clearer understanding of what the general conditions in financing higher education are and how the university relates to those conditions. In large part this chapter has attempted to provide the kind of overview Dean Neumann and countless other deans and committees need. They need to know something of how American colleges and universities found themselves facing the financial crisis, what forces were operating, and what the prospects for the future seem to be. They need also to know what has been the past experience with various sources of income and how the general funding picture has been developing. While Dean Neumann's university has its own patterns of income, it can hardly escape the impact of moves in federal and state financing of higher education. Nor can it be unaffected by what is happening in giving from private sources. The committee also needs to know more about the experiences of other institutions in the search for more efficiency and better management. But, ultimately, Dean Neumann and his committee need to develop their own planning, the kind of planning that takes into account the special circumstances of that university. The quality of that planning will be improved if the committee can approach its work with the kind of perspective the data in this chapter should provide.

Notes

[1]Earl F. Cheit, *The New Depression in Higher Education* (New York: McGraw-Hill Book Co., 1971), p. 1.

342

[2]"The Financial Crisis on the Campus," *Business Week*, May 30, 1970, p. 56.

[3]Virginia B. Smith, "College Finances: Ills and Remedies," *Research Report No. 4*, American Association for Higher Education, February 15, 1971, p. 3.

[4]*Ibid.*

[5]William G. Bowen, *The Economics of the Major Private Universities* (Berkeley: Carnegie Commission on Higher Education, 1968), pp. 3-4.

[6]"People's Colleges in Trouble," *Compact*, 5 (October 1971), p. 8.

[7]"States Vote $6.1-Billion in Tax Funds for Higher Education for 1969-70," *Chronicle of Higher Education*, 4 (October 27, 1969), p. 1.

[8]"Reductions in Federal Support Force Colleges to Retrench; Programs Cut, Students Dropped," *Chronicle of Higher Education*, 4 (January 19, 1970), p. 1.

[9]Cheryl M. Fields, "Research Universities Hardest Hit: Kerr," *Chronicle of Higher Education*, 4 (March 16, 1970), p. 7.

[10]John A. Crowl, "Colleges and Universities Get Record $1.8-Billion in Private Gifts During 1968-69," *Chronicle of Higher Education*, 4 (April 27, 1970), pp. 6-7.

[11]Robert J. Jacobson, "Gifts to Colleges Dip, First Time in Ten Years," *Chronicle of Higher Education*, 5 (April 5, 1971), p. 1.

[12]John A. Crowl, "Financial Crisis Worsens for Colleges; Some Close, Many Show Deficits," *Chronicle of Higher Education*, 4 (August 31, 1970), pp. 1, 2.

[13]*Ibid.*, p. 2.

[14]John A. Crowl, "Some Public Colleges Face 'Austerity Operations' Despite $7-Billion in State Funds for 1970-71," *Chronicle of Higher Education*, 5 (October 12, 1970), pp. 1, 4.

[15]"Average College Deficit Increases Five-Fold in Year," *Chronicle of Higher Education*, 5 (January 11, 1971), pp. 1, 8.

[16]John A. Crowl, "Colleges Cutting Their Budgets in Cost Squeeze," *Chronicle of Higher Education*, 5 (February 8, 1971), pp. 1, 6.

[17]*Ibid.*

[18]" 'Fiscal Bankruptcy' Replaces Student Unrest As Top Worry of State College Presidents," *Chronicle of Higher Education*, 5 (February 15, 1971), p. 5.

[19]John A. Crowl, "State Colleges Face Austerity, Accountability," *Chronicle of Higher Education*, 5 (March 1, 1971), pp. 1, 5.

[20]See Alan Pifer, "The Responsibility for Reform in Higher Education," in *The Report of the President, Annual Report of Carnegie Corporation of New York, 1971* (New York: Carnegie Corporation of New York, 1971), pp. 3ff.

[21]Cheryl M. Fields, "No General Crisis, No Need for General Aid, Panel Told," *Chronicle of Higher Education,* 5 (May 3, 1971), p. 2.

[22]John A. Crowl, "Fiscal Crisis, Need for Academic Reform Called Inseparable," *Chronicle of Higher Education,* 5 (May 3, 1971), p. 3.

[23]Robert L. Jacobson, "41 State Institutions Said to Be in Financial Straits: 10 Expect to Finish Current Fiscal Year in Red," *Chronicle of Higher Education,* 5 (July 5, 1971), pp. 1, 5.

[24]"Private Giving to Universities Breaks Record," *Chronicle of Higher Education,* 6 (April 10, 1972), pp. 1, 5.

[25]John A. Crowl, "100 Institutions Reported Facing Fiscal Disaster," *Chronicle of Higher Education,* 6 (September 27, 1971), pp. 1, 5.

[26]Larry A. Van Dyne, "Some Budget-Cutting Colleges Firing Tenured Professors," *Chronicle of Higher Education,* 6 (November 15, 1971), p. 6.

[27]"Foundations Raise Grants by 25 Percent," *Chronicle of Higher Education,* 7 (April 30, 1973), pp. 8, 9.

[28]Larry A. Van Dyne, "Rate of Growth in State Support Down Sharply," *Chronicle of Higher Education,* 7 (November 13, 1972), p. 1.

[29]Robert L. Jacobson, "Financial Crisis Easing, Number of Colleges Say," *Chronicle of Higher Education,* 7 (December 4, 1972), p. 1.

[30]Robert L. Jacobson, "Control of Cost Found Saving Many Colleges," *Chronicle of Higher Education,* 7 (April 16, 1973), p. 1.

[31]"Private Giving to Colleges Hits Record High," *Chronicle of Higher Education,* 8 (April 8, 1974), pp. 1, 6.

[32]Beverly T. Watkins, "Some Private Colleges Say Worst Is Over, Fiscally: Others Gloomy; Many State Campuses Feel Pinch," *Chronicle of Higher Education,* 7 (September 24, 1973), pp. 1, 7.

[33]Jack Magarrell, "Brighter Signs Seen in Funding of Universities," *Chronicle of Higher Education,* 8 (February 25, 1974), pp. 1, 2.

[34]"Inflation Held Masking Some Colleges' Troubles," *Chronicle of Higher Education,* 8 (April 15, 1974), p. 3.

[35]Jack Magarrell, "Another Crunch Coming, Private Institutions Warned," *Chronicle of Higher Education,* 8 (May 20, 1974), p. 5.

[36]"College Endowment Funds Shrink 1.1 Pct. in Year," *Chronicle of Higher Education,* 8 (June 10, 1974), p. 8.

[37]"Again: $2.24-Billion in Gifts," *Chronicle of Higher Education,* 10 (March 24, 1975), p. 6.

[38]"A $2-Billion Aid Gap," *Chronicle of Higher Education,* 9 (November 4, 1974), p. 5.

[39]"Fund Raisers Look Overseas," *Chronicle of Higher Education,* 9 (November 11, 1974), p. 6.

[40]Karen J. Winkler, "States Raise Aid to Students 25 Pct.," *Chronicle of Higher Education,* 9 (November 10, 1974), pp. 1, 6.

41"Proposed Cuts at Duke Spark Student Protest," *Chronicle of Higher Education,* 10 (March 10, 1975), p. 2.

42"Open Door May Close," *Chronicle of Higher Education,* 10 (March 10, 1975), p. 7.

43"Campus Spending vs. Inflation," *Chronicle of Higher Education,* 10 (March 10, 1975), p. 4.

44Jack Magarrell, "Ford Foundation: A Drastic Cutback," *Chronicle of Higher Education,* 10 (April 7, 1975), pp. 1, 3.

45Jack Magarrell, "How to Fold a Campus," *Chronicle of Higher Education,* 10 (April 14, 1975), p. 6.

46"The Ways of Retrenchment," *Chronicle of Higher Education,* 10 (April 14, 1975), pp. 6-7.

47"Phase-Down Plan Phased Out in Wisconsin," *Chronicle of Higher Education,* 11 (September 29, 1975), p. 11.

48"Fund's Earnings Off," *Chronicle of Higher Education,* 10 (March 12, 1975), p. 8.

49Philip M. Boffey, "Government Plays Down News of Cutback in Research Aid," *Chronicle of Higher Education,* 10 (July 21, 1975), p. 1.

50"Slowdown in Shippensburg," *Chronicle of Higher Education,* 10 (July 21, 1975), p. 3.

51Jack Magarrell, "Shut Down CUNY?" *Chronicle of Higher Education,* 10 (August 4, 1975), pp. 1, 7.

52"C.U.N.Y. Asked to Charge Tuition," *Chronicle of Higher Education,* 11 (September 15, 1975), p. 2.

53"Enrollment Cut Proposed at City U of New York," *Chronicle of Higher Education,* 11 (October 20, 1975), p. 2.

54"Congress Overrides Veto of Education Funds," *Chronicle of Higher Education,* 11 (September 15, 1975), p. 3.

55"Fund-Raisers' Aim: Save Tax Incentives," *Chronicle of Higher Education,* 11 (September 22, 1975), p. 3.

56"Campus Salary Freezes Voted by 3 Legislatures," *Chronicle of Higher Education,* 10 (August 15, 1975), p. 6.

57Jack Magarrell, "Politics, Not Formulas, Now Cutting Budgets," *Chronicle of Higher Education,* 11 (September 22, 1975), p. 11.

58"Statewide Layoffs: Notices Go Out to 188 in Pennsylvania," *Chronicle of Higher Education,* 11 (September 29, 1975), p. 11.

59"Western Michigan to Lay Off More Than 150 Professors," *Chronicle of Higher Education,* 11 (October 14, 1975), p. 2.

60"Danforth Retrenches," *Chronicle of Higher Education,* 11 (September 22, 1975), p. 5.

61Malcolm G. Scully, "Who Should Plan Cuts?" *Chronicle of Higher Education,* 11 (October 20, 1975), p. 9.

[62]National Commission on the Financing of Postsecondary Education, *Financing Postsecondary Education in the United States* (Washington, D.C.: U.S. Government Printing Office, 1973).

[63]June A. O'Neill, *Sources of Funds to Colleges and Universities* (Berkeley: Carnegie Commission on Higher Education, 1973).

[64]"Income and Outgo of American Colleges and Universities, 1970-73," *Chronicle of Higher Education,* 8 (June 24, 1974), p. 1.

[65]Velma A. Adams, "The Cost of Higher Education, 1971-72," *College Management,* January 1972, pp. 10-15.

[66]National Commission on the Financing of Postsecondary Education, *Financing Postsecondary Education,* p. 69.

[67]Committee for Economic Development, *The Management and Financing of Colleges* (New York: Committee for Economic Development, 1973), pp. 12-13.

[68]Carnegie Commission on Higher Education, *Higher Education: Who Pays? Who Benefits? Who Should Pay?* (New York: McGraw-Hill Book Co., 1973), p. 25.

[69]National Commission on the Financing of Postsecondary Education, *Financing Postsecondary Education,* p. 72.

[70]O'Neill, *Sources of Funds to Colleges and Universities,* p. 17.

[71]National Commission on the Financing of Postsecondary Education, *Financing Postsecondary Education,* p. 72.

[72]O'Neill, *Sources of Funds to Colleges and Universities,* pp. 16-17.

[73]Carnegie Commission on Higher Education, *Higher Education: Who Pays? Who Benefits? Who Should Pay?*

[74]M. M. Chambers, *Higher Education: Who Pays? Who Gains?* (Danville, Ill.: Interstate Printers and Publishers, 1968).

[75]Carnegie Commission on Higher Education, *Higher Education: Who Pays? Who Benefits? Who Should Pay?,* p. 3.

[76]M. M. Chambers, *Higher Education: Who Pays? Who Gains?,* p. 91.

[77]*Ibid.,* pp. 98-99.

[78]John Vaizey, *The Economics of Education* (New York: Free Press of Glencoe, 1962), p. 26.

[79]Carnegie Commission on Higher Education, *Tuition: A Supplement Statement to the Report of the Carnegie Commission on Higher Education on "Who Pays? Who Benefits? Who Should Pay?"* (Berkeley: Carnegie Commission on Higher Education, 1974).

[80]*Ibid.,* pp. 9-10.

[81]Committee for Economic Development, *The Management and Financing of Colleges.*

[82]*Ibid.,* p. 6.

[83]Karen J. Winkler, "Proposals to Hike Public-College Tuition Hit in House," *Chronicle of Higher Education,* 8 (October 9, 1973), p. 1.

[84]*Ibid.,* p. 6.

[85]James G. O'Hara, "The Social Necessity for Low Tuition," *Change,* 5 (Winter 1973-74), p. 10.

[86]*Ibid.,* p. 76.

[87]*Ibid.*

[88]William A. Sievert, "Colleges Begin Drive to Save Low Tuition," *Chronicle of Higher Education,* 8 (November 19, 1973), p. 1.

[89]*Ibid.,* p. 10.

[90]Jack Magarrell, "Brighter Signs Seen in Funding of Universities," *Chronicle of Higher Education,* 8 (February 25, 1974), p. 8. See also "Text of Council's Statement on Tuition," following the lead story by Magarrell.

[91]Philip M. Boffey, "Support for Low Tuition: Democratic Party Policy-Makers Appear to Be Ready to Oppose Increases at Public Institutions," *Chronicle of Higher Education,* 9 (September 23, 1974), p. 4.

[92]"Cost of College Rises 40 Pct. in Four Years," *Chronicle of Higher Education,* 8 (March 25, 1974), p. 1.

[93]"Stanford Increases Tuition by 12.9 Percent," *Chronicle of Higher Education,* 9 (December 16, 1974), p. 1.

[94]"Campus Slashes Tuition: Enrollment Jumps 47 Pct.," *Chronicle of Higher Education,* 8 (June 24, 1974), p. 6.

[95]"U of Wisconsin Proposes Cutting Tuition in Half," *Chronicle of Higher Education,* 9 (September 30, 1974), p. 2.

[96]Cheryl M. Fields, "Cutting Tuition in Half; Wisconsin Plan Under Political Attack," *Chronicle of Higher Education,* 9 (October 29, 1974), p. 7.

[97]Jack Magarrell, "College Leaves It Up to the Students: How Much Will You Pay?" *Chronicle of Higher Education,* 8 (May 20, 1974), p. 3.

[98]Bowen, *The Economics of the Major Private Universities,* pp. 36-39.

[99]National Commission on the Financing of Postsecondary Education, *Financing Postsecondary Education,* pp. 203-205.

[100]*Ibid.,* p. 208.

[101]Malcolm G. Scully, "How Much Can Parents Pay?" *Chronicle of Higher Education,* 9 (September 23, 1974), p. 2.

[102]Karen J. Winkler, "Student Defaults on Loans Prove Costly to U.S.," *Chronicle of Higher Education,* 8 (February 11, 1974), pp. 1, 5.

[103]Karen J. Winkler, "Defaults Up: Failure of Students to Repay Guaranteed Loans May Cost the Government $508-Million," *Chronicle of Higher Education,* 9 (September 30, 1974), p. 7.

[104]Karen J. Winkler, "Tough Rules on Student Loans: Colleges Could Be Removed from Program," *Chronicle of Higher Education,* 9 (October 21, 1974), p. 6.

[105]Larry Van Dyne, "The FISL Factories," *Chronicle of Higher Education,* 10 (August 4, 1975), pp. 4-5.

[106]Karen J. Winkler, "Student Loan Outlook: Partly Sunny," *Chronicle of Higher Education,* 9 (October 29, 1974), p. 3.

[107]Karen J. Winkler, "Narrowing the Student-Aid Gap," *Chronicle of Higher Education,* 11 (September 29, 1975), pp. 1, 6.

[108]Cheryl M. Fields, "Loans: Another Program Suffers Defaults," *Chronicle of Higher Education,* 9 (November 4, 1974), p. 4.

[109]Karen J. Winkler, "Are Cancelled Loans Taxable?" *Chronicle of Higher Education,* 8 (July 8, 1974), p. 6.

[110]Karen J. Winkler, "The Student-Aid Tangle," *Chronicle of Higher Education,* 10 (April 14, 1975), pp. 1, 12.

[111]Karen J. Winkler, "9 Private Institutions Press for Expanded Student Loans," *Chronicle of Higher Education,* 8 (February 19, 1974), p. 1.

[112]"Ford Foundation May Back Trial of Student Loan Plan," *Chronicle of Higher Education,* 5 (January 11, 1971), p. 5.

[113]"Deferred Tuition Planned at Yale: Ford Studying It," *Chronicle of Higher Education,* 5 (February 8, 1971), p. 1.

[114]"Duke May Try Deferred Tuition," *Chronicle of Higher Education,* 5 (March 15, 1971), p. 3.

[115]"Ford Decides Not to Finance 'Pay-As-You-Earn,' " *Chronicle of Higher Education,* 6 (February 22, 1972), pp. 1, 4.

[116]Robert L. Jacobson, "Ford Group Would Alter 'Pay-Earn,' " *Chronicle of Higher Education,* 7 (October 16, 1972), p. 4.

[117]"22 Pct. at Yale Defer Tuition in New Plan," *Chronicle of Higher Education,* 6 (October 10, 1971), p. 4.

[118]Robert L. Jacobson, "U.S. Turns Down Pay-As-You-Earn Loan Approach," *Chronicle of Higher Education,* 8 (March 5, 1973), pp. 1, 5.

[119]Clifford R. Wharton, Jr., "Study Now–Pay Later: Threat to a Great Commitment," *Chronicle of Higher Education,* 6 (December 6, 1971), p. 8.

[120]Robert F. Carbone, *Alternative Tuition Schemes* (Iowa City: American College Testing Program, 1974), p. x.

[121]National Commission on the Financing of Postsecondary Education, *Financing Postsecondary Education,* p. 96.

[122]O'Neill, *Sources of Funds to Colleges and Universities,* p. 25.

[123]*Ibid.,* pp. 16-17.

[124]Larry Van Dyne, "State Spending on Universities Is Up 25 Pct.," *Chronicle of Higher Education,* 8 (November 5, 1973), p. 1.

[125]Jack Magarrell, "State Support: Up 29 Pct. in 2 Years," *Chronicle of Higher Education,* 9 (October 2, 1974), p. 1.

[126]"Higher Education's Share of State Appropriations," *Chronicle of Higher Education,* 8 (May 6, 1974), p. 9.

[127]National Commission on the Financing of Postsecondary Education, *Financing Postsecondary Education,* pp. 85-86.

[128]*Ibid.,* p. 86.

[129]*Ibid.*

[130]*Ibid.,* pp. 87-88.

[131]*Ibid.,* p. 88.

[132]John A. Crowl, "13 More States Move to Help Private Colleges," *Chronicle of Higher Education,* 6 (October 18, 1971), p. 1.

[133]Larry A. Van Dyne, "States Double Scholarship Aid Over 2 Years," *Chronicle of Higher Education,* 6 (February 7, 1972), p. 1.

[134]Karen J. Winkler, "States Raise Aid to Students 25 Pct.," p. 1.

[135]Joseph D. Boyd, "An Examination of State Efforts to Remove Financial Barriers to Postsecondary Education," in *Trends in Postsecondary Education* (Washington, D.C.: U.S. Department of Health, Education, and Welfare, 1950), p. 59.

[136]Richard M. Millard, "State Aid to Non-Public Higher Education," *Higher Education in the States,* 4 (no. 5, 1974), pp. 149-151.

[137]National Commission on the Financing of Postsecondary Education, *Financing Postsecondary Education,* p. 97.

[138]Larry L. Leslie and Jonathan D. Fife, "The College Student Grant Study: The Enrollment and Attendance Impacts of Student Grant and Scholarship Programs," *Journal of Higher Education,* 45 (December 1974), p. 669. The reader should also read the comments of George B. Weathersby on the Leslie and Fife study as well as the authors' rejoinder; see George B. Weathersby, " 'The College Student Grant Study': A Comment," *Journal of Higher Education,* 46 (September/October 1975), pp. 601ff.

[139]National Commission on the Financing of Postsecondary Education, *Financing Postsecondary Education,* p. 101.

[140]Allan O. Pfnister and Gary H. Quehl, *Private Higher Education in the State of Missouri* (Jefferson City: Commission on Higher Education, 1967), pp. 57ff.

[141]"State Funds for Church Colleges O.K., Says Court, If Purpose Is Secular," *Chronicle of Higher Education,* 9 (October 29, 1974), p. 2.

[142]"Supreme Court Refuses to Halt State Aid to 4 Church Colleges," *Chronicle of Higher Education,* 9 (December 2, 1974), p. 6.

[143]John A. Crowl, "High Court Upholds Grants for U.S. for Construction on Catholic Campuses," *Chronicle of Higher Education,* 5 (July 5, 1971), pp. 1, 8.

[144]Cheryl M. Fields, "Supreme Court Upholds State Aid for Facilities at Church Colleges," *Chronicle of Higher Education,* 7 (July 2, 1973), pp. 1, 5.

[145]National Commission on the Financing of Postsecondary Education, *Financing Postsecondary Education,* p. 86.

146Carnegie Commission on Higher Education, *The Capital and the Campus: State Responsibility for Postsecondary Education* (New York: McGraw-Hill Book Co., 1971), p. 4.

147*Ibid.*

148*Ibid.,* p. 65.

149Carnegie Commission on Higher Education, *Higher Education: Who Pays? Who Benefits? Who Should Pay?,* pp. 8-9.

150*Ibid.,* p. 9.

151W. H. McFarlane and J. L. Chronister, *Virginia's Private Colleges and the Public Interest: The Case for a Pluralistic System* (Durham, N.C.: National Laboratory for Higher Education, 1971), p. 5.

152William H. McFarlane, *State Support for Private Higher Education* (Atlanta, Ga.: Southern Regional Education Board, 1969), p. 7.

153William H. McFarlane and Charles L. Wheeler, *Legal and Political Issues of State Aid for Private Higher Education* (Atlanta, Ga.: Southern Regional Education Board, 1971), p.5.

154Carol H. Shulman, *Private Colleges: Present Conditions and Future Prospects,* ERIC/Higher Education Research Report, no. 9 (Washington, D.C.: American Association for Higher Education, 1974), p. 30.

155"Give State Aid to Private Colleges That Meet Public Needs: Boyer," *Chronicle of Higher Education,* 7 (March 19, 1973) p. 1.

156Roger Freeman, "Needed: Another Seven to Eleven Billion Dollars," in *Higher Education in the Revolutionary Decades,* ed. Lewis B. Mayhew (Berkeley: McCutchen Publishing Corp., 1967), p. 282.

157John A. Crowl, "Private Colleges Mapping Drive for More Funds," *Chronicle of Higher Education,* 5 (January 18, 1971), pp. 1, 3.

158Cheryl M. Fields, "8 College Associations Urge Congress to Give Institutions General Support," *Chronicle of Higher Education,* 8 (May 20, 1974), p. 5.

159Commission on the Financing of Postsecondary Education, *Financing Postsecondary Education,* p. 69.

160"Higher Education's Share of U.S. Budgets," *Chronicle of Higher Education,* 9 (February 10, 1975), p. 6.

161"Federal Programs for Education and Related Activities," *Digest of Educational Statistics,* 1971 (Washington, D.C.: Government Printing Office, 1972), p. 107.

162*Ibid.*

163Robert D. Calkins, "Government Support of Higher Education," in *Financing Higher Education: 1960-70,* ed. Dexter M. Keezer (McGraw-Hill Book Co., 1959), p. 188.

164*Ibid.,* p. 189.

350

165Richard M. Schrader, "The Growth and Pitfalls in Federal Support of Higher Education," *Journal of Higher Education,* 40 (December 1969), p. 705.

166Ernst Becker, "The Financing of Higher Education: A Review of Historical Trends and Projections for 1975-76," in *Trends in Post-Secondary Education,* pp. 101-102.

167Richard M. Schrader, "The Growth and Pitfalls in Federal Support of Higher Education," p. 708.

168*Ibid.*

169Commission on the Financing of Postsecondary Education, *Financing Postsecondary Education,* pp. 104-105.

170*Ibid.,* p. 106.

171Richard M. Schrader, "The Growth and Pitfalls in Federal Support of Higher Education," pp. 709-710.

172*Ibid.,* p. 714.

173Ronald A. Wolk, *Alternative Methods of Federal Funding for Higher Education* (Berkeley: Carnegie Commission on the Future of Higher Education, 1968), pp. 9ff.

174Carnegie Commission on Higher Education, *Quality and Equality: New Levels of Federal Responsibility for Higher Education* (New York: McGraw-Hill Book Co., 1968), p. 8.

175Carnegie Commission on Higher Education, *Quality and Equality: Revised Recommendations* (New York: McGraw-Hill Book Co., 1970), pp. 32-33.

176Panel on Educational Innovation, *Educational Opportunity Bank: A Report of the Panel on Educational Innovation to the U.S. Commissioner of Education* (Washington, D.C.: Government Printing Office, 1967).

177Office of the Assistant Secretary for Planning and Development, U.S. Department of Health, Education, and Welfare, *Toward a Long-Range Plan for Federal Financial Support for Higher Education: A Report to the President* (Washington, D.C.: Government Printing Office, 1969), pp. 68-73.

178Carnegie Commission on Higher Education, *Institutional Aid: Federal Support to Colleges and Universities* (New York: McGraw-Hill Book Co., 1972), pp. 13-15.

179Carnegie Commission on Higher Education, *Higher Education: Who Pays? Who Benefits? Who Should Pay?,* p. 5.

180See Karen J. Winkler, "Carnegie Council Bids U.S. Raise Support," *Chronicle of Higher Education,* 10 (March 10, 1975), p. 9.

181Office of the Assistant Secretary for Planning and Development, HEW, *Toward a Long-Range Plan for Federal Financial Support for Higher Education,* pp. 20-21.

[182]Committee for Economic Development, *The Management and Financing of Colleges,* p. 83.

[183]Commission on the Financing of Postsecondary Education, *Financing Postsecondary Education,* pp. 270-292.

[184]Howard R. Bowen, "Financing Higher Education: The Current State of the Debate," in *Higher Education, Human Resources and the National Economy: Addresses and Discussion Papers from the Sixtieth Annual Meeting of the Association of American Colleges* (Washington, D.C.: Association of American Colleges, 1974), pp. 25ff.

[185]*Ibid.,* pp. 27-28.

[186]*Ibid.,* p. 36.

[187]John P. Mallan, "Current Proposals for Federal Aid to Higher Education: Some Political Implications," in *Financing Higher Education: Alternatives for the Federal Government,* ed. M. D. Orwig (Iowa City: American College Testing Program, 1971), p. 321.

[188]M. D. Orwig, "The Federal Government and the Finance of Higher Education," in *Financing Higher Education: Alternatives for the Federal Government,* ed. M. D. Orwig (Iowa City, American College Testing Program, 1971), p. 352.

[189]"Newman Panel on the Federal Role in Higher Education," *Chronicle of Higher Education,* 8 (October 29, 1973), p. 6.

[190]Cheryl M. Fields, "8 College Associations Urge Congress to Give Institutions General Support," p. 7.

[191]Karen J. Winkler, "Outlook Dim for Direct Aid to Colleges, Universities," *Chronicle of Higher Education,* 8 (June 24, 1974), p. 5.

[192]"Institutional Aid: Still Alive," *Chronicle of Higher Education,* 8 (August 5, 1974), p. 6.

[193]Karen J. Winkler, "U.S. Funds for Colleges," *Chronicle of Higher Education,* 8 (September 3, 1974), p. 5.

[194]"A New Tax-Credit Plan" *Chronicle of Higher Education,* 9 (November 18, 1974), p. 4.

[195]See "New Higher Education Financing Proposed in Wisconsin," *Compact,* 5 (February 1971), pp. 28-30.

[196]Henry M. Levin, "Vouchers and Social Security," *Change,* 5 (October 1973), pp. 29ff.

[197]"Panel Backs Voucher Plan for Education," *Chronicle of Higher Education,* 7 (September 10, 1973), p. 2.

[198]Cheryl M. Fields, "House Subcommittee Head Gives Top Priority to Student Aid," *Chronicle of Higher Education,* 8 (January 28, 1974), p. 7.

[199]William McNamara, "The O'Hara Curriculum," *Change,* 6 (December/January 1974-75), p. 48.

[200]Bowen, *The Economics of the Major Private Universities,* pp. 41-42.

[201]O'Neill, *Sources of Funds to Colleges and Universities,* pp. 16-17.

[202]"College Endowment Funds Shrink 1.1 Pct. in Year," p. 8.

[203]Jack Magarrell, "Re-thinking the Endowment," *Chronicle of Higher Education,* 9 (November 18, 1974), p. 7.

[204]O'Neill, *Sources of Funds to Colleges.*

[205]Jacobson, "Gifts to Colleges Dip, First Time in Ten Years," p. 1.

[206]"Private Giving to Universities Breaks Record," *Chronicle of Higher Education,* 6 (April 10, 1972), p. 1. See also John A. Crowl, "Business Support of Education Drops 9 Pct.", *Chronicle of Higher Education,* 6 (November 22, 1971).

[207]"Report Sees New Trends In Giving," *Chronicle of Higher Education,* 6 (May 22, 1972), p. 3.

[208]"Foundations Raise Grants by 25 Pct.," *Chronicle of Higher Education,* 8 (April 30, 1973), p. 9. See also "Gifts, Grants to Colleges Up, Bequests Down in 1971-72," *Chronicle of Higher Education,* 7 (July 2, 1973), p. 1.

[209]Jack Magarrell, "How Firm the Foundations?" *Chronicle of Higher Education,* 9 (September 30, 1974), p. 1.

[210]"Ford Fund to Cut Grants," *Chronicle of Higher Education,* 9 (December 23, 1974), p. 1.

[211]Jack Magarrell, "Corporate Gifts," *Chronicle of Higher Education,* 9 (October 7, 1974), p. 9.

[212]"Again: $2.24-Billion in Gifts."

[213]Malcolm G. Scully, "Corporations' Unrestricted Gifts to Universities Stir New Debate," *Chronicle of Higher Education,* 8 (November 12, 1973), p. 1.

[214]Jack Magarrell, "Fund-Raisers Look Overseas," *Chronicle of Higher Education,* 9 (November 11, 1974), p. 6.

[215]Roger Ricklefs, "Squeezed for Money, A Number of Colleges Revamp Curriculum," *Wall Street Journal,* 92 (February 18, 1975), pp. 1, 24.

[216]"Colleges Go Into Business to Make Ends Meet," *U.S. News and World Report,* January 27, 1975, p. 33.

[217]"Purdue's Used-Card Salesmen Gain $14,000 for University," *Chronicle of Higher Education,* 8 (May 20, 1974), p. 5.

[218]Bowen, "Financing Higher Education: The Current State of the Debate," p. 36.

[219]Jack Magarrell, "Another 'Crunch' Coming, Private Institutions Warned."

[220]Carnegie Commission on Higher Education, *The More Effective Use of Resources* (New York: McGraw-Hill Book Co., 1972), p. 15.

[221]*Ibid.,* pp. 34-35.

[222]Bowen, *The Economics of the Major Private Universities,* p. 20.

[223]Carnegie Commission on Higher Education, *The More Effective Use of*

Resources, p. 9.

224*Ibid.,* pp. 16-18.

225*Ibid.,* p. 23.

226See Sidney G. Tickton, "The Long-Term Budget Projection: A New Management Tool for Colleges and Universities," in Keezer, *Financing Higher Education, 1960-70,* pp. 138-161.

227Sidney G. Tickton, "Meeting the Financial Pinch," *Compact,* 5 (October 1971), p. 31.

228James Harvey, "College and University Planning," *Financing Higher Education: College and University Planning,* ERIC Research Reports (Washington, D.C.: American College Public Relation Association, 1971), pp. 22-33.

229Ohio Board of Regents, *Planning—Universities* (Columbus: Ohio Board of Regents, 1974).

230Management Division, Academy for Educational Development, "148 Ways Colleges and Universities Are Meeting the Financial Pinch," pamphlet, (New York: Academy for Educational Development, n.d.).

231Paul C. Reinert, S. J., *Rescue Begins at Home* (New York: Management Division, Academy for Educational Development, 1972). See also other publications of the AED.

232Commission on the Financing of Postsecondary Education, *Financing Postsecondary Education,* p. 321.

233See Howard R. Bowen and Gordon K. Douglass, *Efficiency in Liberal Education* (New York: McGraw-Hill Book Co., 1971).

234See Charles S. Benson and Harold L. Hodgkinson, *Implementing the Learning Society* (San Francisco: Jossey-Bass, 1974).

235Earl F. Cheit, *The New Depression in Higher Education—Two Years Later* (New York: McGraw-Hill Book Co., 1973), p. 15.

236*Ibid.,* p. 64

237*Ibid.,* p. 66.

238*Ibid.,* p. 67.

239Committee for Economic Development, *The Management and Financing of Colleges,* pp. 22-23.

240Stephen A. Hoenack and Alfred L. Norman, "Incentives and Resource Allocation in Universities," *Journal of Higher Education,* 45 (January 1974), pp. 21ff. See also in the same issue articles by Leslie and Johnson; Minohan; and Wilkowski.

241"Ford Aide Warns Colleges on Management Panaceas," *Chronicle of Higher Education,* 8 (May 13, 1974), p. 5.

242"High Quality Seen Lifting Education's Productivity," *Chronicle of Higher Education,* 8 (May 13, 1974), p. 5.